Ayrshire

A Historical Guide

Dae ye speir me gin I be a Christian, and dae ye no ken that I am an Ayrshireman?

David Craufurd of Kerse

Well said, old mole! Canst work i' th' earth so fast? A worthy pioneer!

Hamlet

Ayrshire

A Historical Guide

Thorbjørn Campbell

Birlinn

First published in 2003 by
Birlinn Limited
West Newington House
10 Newington Road
Edinburgh EH9 1QS

www.birlinn.co.uk

ISBN 1 84158 267 0

British Library Cataloguing in Publication Data
A catalogue record for this book is available from the British Library

Typesetting and origination by Brinnoven, Livingston
Printed and bound by Creative Print and Design, Wales

For Mary Seaward

CONTENTS

FOREWORD

My father was a local government official in Ayrshire and his job, winter and summer, took him far and wide over the highways and byways of the old county. For thirty-seven years he was never happier than when cruising along some leafy unfrequented road in Carrick or entering the portals of some great industrial undertaking in Cuninghame. He was not a desk man, and in later years when he was promoted and relatively office-bound, his sunny nature suffered something of an eclipse. Many were the stories he brought home to us, and I would occasionally suggest that he should write a book entitled *Old Ayrshire* by One Who Knows. He would decline the challenge, saying, in his mild way, that he had a fancy to end his days out of jail. The book remained unwritten. Here is one of the more printable tales.

During the Second World War, when Hermann Göring's Luftwaffe were doing their best to eradicate British war industries, they attacked the vast explosives and chemical factory at Ardeer near Stevenston. The explosions were seen and heard all over Ayrshire, and there were many casualties. The morning after the raid my father happened to be calling on a Co-op, predecessor of supermarkets, in Kilwinning. There was a queue, of course, and two typical Ayrshire 'bodies', curlers under head-scarves, carpet slippers, shopping-bags carried near the ground, were in the line having an animated conversation, just in front of my father and a rather stiff-looking English lady, who obviously had a low opinion of these Ayrshire natives.

'Did ye hear it last night?' said Bodie A.

'Aye,' said Bodie B. 'It was that bad, *the pig fell oot the bed!*'

The English lady's eyes bulged in mingled triumph and horror at the image. But 'pig' was and is Ayrshire (and other) dialect for a stoneware hot-water bottle . . .

It is still possible – just – to walk out along the old Ayr harbour breakwater and turn to face inland from the lighthouse, surveying the whole sweep of the Ayr Bay coastline from the Heads of Ayr in the south to the Cumbraes in the north. Then, turning again, you may gaze out over the firth, from Ailsa Craig massively rising out of the sea, and the impressive mountainscape of Arran, to the northern narrows of the estuary, the Holy Loch, the Loch Lomond Hills and the Paps of Jura. It is a spectacular setting that can be enhanced by taking the road to the top of Carwinshoch Hill, the Brown Carrick, which commands a view from the north coast of Ireland and the distant Campbeltown on the Mull of Kintyre to Schiehallion in Perthshire. But for all its romantic beauty, this segment of Britain is nowadays such a mundane and unremarkable backwater that it may come almost as a shock to realise that Ayrshire too has a history, that exciting and alarming events have occurred within its borders, and even that it has not always been a single unit – as Ayrshire – nor always a part of Scotland. Between the northern and southernmost points of Ayrshire – Wemyss Bay to the Galloway Burn – lies a great deal of history.

This history begins far back in the mists of time, long before the integration and realization of Ayrshire itself. Part I of this book tries to give an account of how Ayrshire came about – not just of what happened there once it was in existence. In order to understand the components of what became Ayrshire you have to take into account Strathclyde and Galloway and their long prehistory in the form of Brythonic tribes that may have been in the Ayrshire region since Neolithic times and even before then.

Even in the very deep past, ten or eleven thousand years ago, when the first Mesolithic pioneers crept in their tens or twenties through the silent forests of post-glacial Scotland or came upon the shimmering expanse of Loch Doon, their strategies to make use of the gifts of nature can be recognised – in their industrial chipping of 'microliths' still to be found in quantities on that loch's shores, or in their huge shell-mounds at the edge of the sea, one of which was removed only a century ago near the Castle Hill at Ardrossan. These signs are reproduced all over Britain, showing that human beings were for the first time invading the inhospitable lands of the north and wresting them to their own use. Later, the first glimmerings of state and religious organisation are to be seen in the great row of hill-top cairns that stretches down to the sea from Knockdolian, unmistakably delineating a sacral and royal precinct even if we do not know the names of the people or the kingdom. That little patch of human settlement in the Glen App region endured and still endures – now as an integrated part of Ayrshire.

These apparently forgotten people developed a fully Megalithic culture, perhaps more clearly in places like Arran (on the plain of Machrie) or Orkney, but in Ayrshire well attested by henges, standing stones and cup-and-ring marked rocks. The relics seem anonymous and unresponsive to us, yet present-day place-names, Finnarts Hill, Ayr, Girvan, Loudoun, echoing the names of ancient Celtic deities, may through them preserve a trace of the original Neolithic sense of local divinity and kingly power. Such traces are as worthy of preservation in Ayrshire as in any other part of Britain.

The 'prehistory' of Ayrshire winds through some rather tortuous and gloomy cleughs before arriving at the plain vista of 1371 – the approximate date of integration under Robert II. Yet I have thought it worthwhile in Chapter 2 of Part I to take the reader through some of the linguistic evidence for the pre-1000 period, to display the great melting pot of Cymric, Anglian, Gaelic and Norse influences that can be traced in Ayrshire place-names even today. I have speculated on David I's dismemberment of Strathclyde and his sharing out of the fragments among his Norman colleagues, and I have shown the practical effects of this reorganisation. I have tried to unravel the dynastic rivalries and alliances that in the end led William the Lion to set up his royal castle at Ayr in 1197 and some years later to establish a sheriffdom there with putative powers extending 'on paper' from Cuninghame to Carrick. I have also given, in the Gazetteer, a very brief description of the development of the three principal burghs of northern Ayrshire; Ayr, Irvine and Prestwick – and I should like to give notice here that I have not tried to emulate let alone surpass the meticulous and all-embracing studies of Strawhorn and Dodd, to which I refer all seekers after more information.

I have grappled in a very short compass with the gigantic mess of hesitation, accident, frenzy and misunderstanding that led the Earl of Carrick to renounce his allegiance to the King of England, to make his earldom a base for an adventure which by any standards must have been regarded as crazy, and to come to the throne of a new-minted realm – and by the way to make a Gordian knot of inheritance that, two generations later, by the interposition of a royal house not his own, casually created the integral shire of Ayr. All this with more than one glance over my shoulder at the presiding genius of Bruce history, Professor Barrow.

Newly-made Ayrshire in the fifteenth and sixteenth centuries must have resembled Somalia or Afghanistan in our own day, torn apart by warlords. Montgomeries, Cuninghames, Campbells, Kennedys, Wallaces – all plunged with enthusiasm into fierce rivalry for land and power. The removal or reduction of the threat of English annexation released these chieftains to a seemingly never-ending internecine civil war between families and factions. But once the Reformation had taken hold of Scotland, and the land-hunger in Ayrshire had been to some degree assuaged by the plundering and spoliation of the abbeys of Crossraguel and Kilwinning, the internal enmities began to subside. The people as well as the magnates came together to respond to the challenge of a vaguer, more abstract bogey – one, therefore, that could not be defeated so readily as a flesh-and-blood neighbour: the Church of Rome, and locally, episcopacy, the hated 'rule of bishops'. Ayrshire magnates like the Earls of Cassillis, Eglinton and Loudoun, representing previously irreconcilable interests, rode together against Edinburgh in 1648 to establish a Presbyterian dictatorship, a Rule of Saints. Ayrshire people and rulers controlled Scotland and, for a brief moment, Scots were the Chosen People. But an exclusivist logic had its inevitable effect upon the Covenanters, and they dwindled to a 'suffering remnant' hiding in the hills above Muirkirk and New Cumnock, perpetually divided even against themselves. *Siste viator.*

In the task of compiling this brief record of Ayrshire's history I have had the welcome assistance of many hands, and these must be acknowledged. Dr Richard Oram has been kind enough to read the whole text several times in the course of its development, to make many helpful suggestions and to save me from more than one egregious error. Without the assistance of the Royal Commission on the Ancient and Historical Monuments of Scotland (RCAHMS) I should have been lost – or perhaps even more forwandered. I must thank in particular Mr Iain Fraser, who assisted me vitally in coping with the intricacies of the great database 'Canmore'. The staff at the new Museum of Scotland in Edinburgh and its library have been most helpful in the latter stages of preparation; Mr Andrew Martin and Dr Alison Sheridan have grappled nobly with my anxious queries. In the Dick Institute in Kilmarnock I have been assisted very materially by Mr Bruce Morgan and Mr Jason Sutcliffe. Mr Gordon Riddle and Miss Lorna Cawood of the National Trust for Scotland (Culzean Castle and Country Park) have let me have indispensable information. In addition, the publications of the Ayrshire Archaeological and Natural History Society (AANHS) are completely indispensable for anyone who wishes to master the outlines and detail of Ayrshire's story. So are the section maps (green Pathfinder and red Landranger series) produced by the Ordnance Survey, whose grid references appear at every site entry in the gazetteer. Grateful acknowledgement is made to the Controller of Her Majesty's Stationery Office for permission to include two maps based on Ordnance Survey maps (pp. xxiii and 2), and to Nicolson Street Guides of Largs for permission to modify three local street maps. South Ayrshire and North Ayrshire Concils were kind enough to grant permission to reproduce copyright material, and this is also gratefully acknowledged. I must also thank the staff at Ayr Carnegie Library (in particular Mrs Sheena Andrew) and the Ayrshire Archives Centre at Craigie Estate. I owe a debt of gratitude to the staff at Glasgow University Library, the National Library of Scotland, the Hunterian Museum, Glasgow, and the Museum of the Society of Antiquaries of London (Burlington House). I must acknowledge the kindness of the National Trust for Scotland in granting permission for the reproduction of a detail of the portrait of Sir Thomas Kennedy of Culzean, the Tutor of Cassillis, by an unknown artist. Finally, I must record my great indebtedness to those Victorian heroes, David MacGibbon and Thomas Ross, whose *Castellated and Domestic Architecture of Scotland*, published between 1887 and 1892, provided the superb line drawings which adorn Part II of this book.

Among individuals who assisted me I must mention Mrs Jean Donaldson of the Largs Historical Society, Sir Claude Hagart-Alexander of Kingencleuch and Mr David Hunter of New Dailly. I must also thank my sister Mrs Aase Irvine, Mrs Ann Rayner, Mrs Anne Ross, Mr Charles Sandford, Mrs Carol Wilson and Mr and Mrs Ian Cuthbertson. I also have to thank Mr Hugh Andrew and Mr Andrew Simmons of Birlinn for forbearance and understanding.

Perhaps I shall be forgiven if I give a special place in this list of helpers to two dear friends both very recently dead of the same unspeakable scourge – cancer (one in the flower of her young womanhood). The first, Ian Murray McAllister, helped in two vital ways: I do not possess the skill of driving, but whenever I needed to go to an out-of-the-way site Murray drove down to Ayr and we went off together in his little blue car to take photographs; he also made available his extensive library – and his vast experience and knowledge of Scottish country houses. The other friend, Mary Seaward, assisted me not only in this project but a previous one – by foot-slogging, as it were one of the *pedisequi patrie*, who followed me on foot where it was impossible for a car to go and whose sense of direction and locality invaluably supplemented the Ordnance Survey maps. She acted, too, like Voltaire's old woman who sat by the fireside and criticised every line of his composition, making each successive idea clear to herself and thus to him and his readership. Both these people are irreplaceable in every way.

HOW TO USE THIS BOOK

This book is meant to help you to move around Ayrshire and go to places that you may find interesting. Practical information on sites – how to get there and basic recognition – will be found in the Gazetteer, which is set out in alphabetical order. Background and general historical information will be found in Part I. Names of places in the Gazetteer are printed in Part I and cross-referenced within the Gazetteer in **bold type**.

Each Gazetteer entry has a map reference at the right-hand margin. To make full use of these you should have an Ordnance Survey map, especially for country areas. The OS Landranger series is the most handy, but the green Pathfinder series is more detailed. However it is not essential to carry a map, and many Gazetteer entries give nearby road numbers and the nearest town or village. Each entry tells you what it is for – a cairn, a castle, a church, a burgh. NB Some ways of getting to sites may have changed since they have been visited or may no longer be available even when shown on map. Check local sources of information.

Isolated finds of small Bronze and Iron Age and other objects have often been collected in various museums in Edinburgh, Glasgow, Kilmarnock and elsewhere. The locations are usually given in the site entries.

Places of outstanding beauty or interest mentioned in the Gazetteer are *italicized*. NB however, none of the listed places is guaranteed to be open at any time to the public and some are quite definitely closed, for example the italicized *Rowallan Castle*. The same applies to *Cassillis House*. Except where a house or a location is definitely advertised as being open with or without entrance charge, it is always better to check with the owners before walking across fields or down driveways. In the larger towns there is usually a tourist information centre which is there to be used.

Always follow the countryside code, close gates, and KEEP OUT WHEN TOLD TO DO SO EITHER VERBALLY OR BY POSTER. Some of the places mentioned here are quite dangerous: **Glengarnock Castle** is poised about to fall over a deep ravine; **Lacht Castle** sits atop the Dunaskin Glen in rough moorland where ankles can only too easily be twisted; the Iron Age hillfort on **Castle Hill** above Largs is extremely precipitous. The author of this book does not accept responsibility for the reliability or safety of any of the routes or places described here.

LIST OF ILLUSTRATIONS

LIST OF FIGURES

LIST OF MAPS

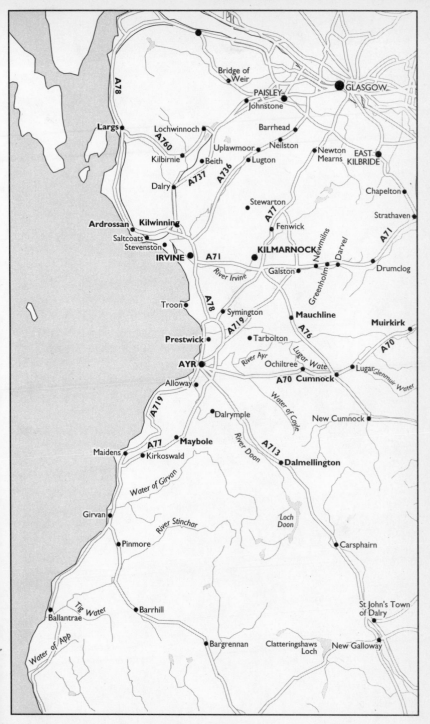

Outline Map of Ayrshire

PART I

Ayrshire from Prehistoric Times
to the Twenty-first Century

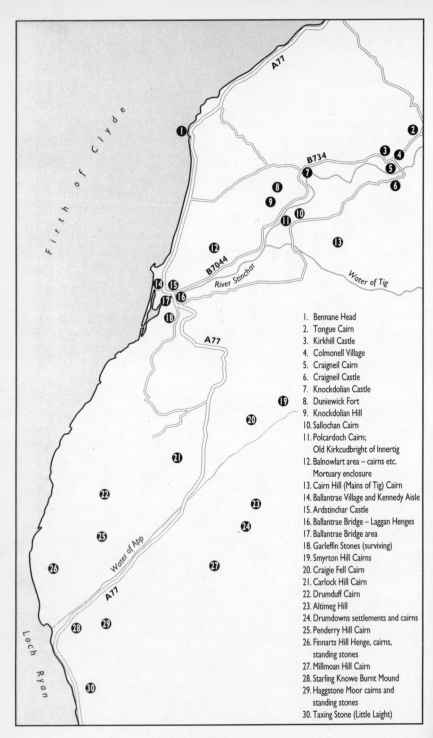

1. Bennane Head
2. Tongue Cairn
3. Kirkhill Castle
4. Colmonell Village
5. Craigneil Cairn
6. Craigneil Castle
7. Knockdolian Castle
8. Duniewick Fort
9. Knockdolian Hill
10. Sallochan Cairn
11. Polcardoch Cairn;
    Old Kirkcudbright of Innertig
12. Balnowlart area – cairns etc.
    Mortuary enclosure
13. Cairn Hill (Mains of Tig) Cairn
14. Ballantrae Village and Kennedy Aisle
15. Ardstinchar Castle
16. Ballantrae Bridge – Laggan Henges
17. Ballantrae Bridge area
18. Garleffin Stones (surviving)
19. Smyrton Hill Cairns
20. Craigie Fell Cairn
21. Carlock Hill Cairn
22. Drumduff Cairn
23. Altimeg Hill
24. Drumdowns settlements and cairns
25. Penderry Hill Cairn
26. Finnarts Hill Henge, cairns,
    standing stones
27. Millmoan Hill Cairn
28. Starling Knowe Burnt Mound
29. Haggstone Moor cairns and
    standing stones
30. Taxing Stone (Little Laight)

Neolithic Sites in South Carrick

1. PREHISTORIC: THE EARLIEST TIMES TO AD 82

The remote past

The first immediately recognisable events to leave their mark upon the Ayrshire region of Scotland took place about sixty million years ago, when cataclysmic volcanic eruptions took place all along what is now the north-eastern rim of the Atlantic Ocean. What caused the cataclysm is not clear. It may have been the latest of a series of geological events originating beneath the earth's crust, or it may have been caused by the impact of an extra-terrestrial body; it was about this time, perhaps, that some such violent global event caused the extinction of the world's dinosaur population. In any case, very large volcanoes erupted, and some of them – Hecla in Iceland, for instance – are still active. East and south of Iceland a chain of extinct volcanic remnants can be traced, noticeably in the Faroes, Shetland and Orkney, and down through the west coast of Scotland – St Kilda, Staffa, Rum, Eigg and Muck, Arran and the Ayrshire coast. Although these volcanoes have been inactive in modern times, earthquake activity is not unknown in Ayrshire, and fault-lines occur in the Kilwinning region and elsewhere in the county. Plutonic forces are still welling up along the North Atlantic ridge and forcing the continents of Europe and North America further apart.

In Ayrshire extensive traces of volcanic activity are to be found where igneous intrusions have forced their way through the granitic cover, from **Loudoun Hill** in the north-east to **Benbeoch** above **Dalmellington**, the **Heads of Ayr** to the south-west of Ayr, and **Ailsa Craig** off **Girvan**. Millions of years of weathering have produced some spectacular effects, for example at Benbeoch, where the characteristic vertical porphyritic crystals form a gigantic cliff-face crowning a dizzy, isolated hill high above the surrounding countryside. At the Heads of Ayr, one half of a large volcano has long ago fallen into the sea, and the remaining half forms a sheer cliff wall, with a wide central cleft marking a vertical vent. At the western end of the cliff, giving on to Bracken Bay, a smaller vent, is as it were, tipped on its side, like a huge ladle in a steel-works, from which lava must have poured in a glowing flood. A similarly slanted vent is situated at the south-western end of Drumadoon Cliff in southern Arran, and from both outlets fault-lines radiate as cracks in a hard lava pavement at the edge of the sea. At Drumadoon the cliff is again formed of great vertical porphyry crystals – a formation also to be seen at Ailsa Craig, as well as at Fingal's Cave in Staffa, the Giant's Causeway in Antrim, Samson's Ribs at the Salisbury Crags in Edinburgh, and other well-known places. Ailsa Craig is a stupendous rock towering more than 300 metres out of the sea opposite Girvan; it, like Loudoun Hill, is a 'volcanic plug' – the cooled lava in the volcano's throat, harder than the crater walls, which have been eroded away over the millennia.

Fire, in the form of plutonic forces, shaped a great deal of Ayrshire's physical form and human destiny. Water, in the form of ice, also contributed to the formation of the land and the fortunes of the inhabitants of Ayrshire. The last great Ice Age, the Younger Dryas period, finally relaxed its grip on Europe about 10 000 BC, and its effects and those of previous Ice Ages on the countryside are still to be seen everywhere. The rounded hills show the effects of the pressure of the ice, and the deep valleys of the rivers – the Doon, the Girvan and the Stinchar in particular – trace the course of glacier tongues flowing from the highlands of the south and east. Striations along the valley sides – notably at Hadyard Hill in the valley of the Girvan – are rubbing marks made by the ice in its slow, heavy progression to the coast. On the other hand, raised platforms to be seen along the Clyde coast – north of **Ardrossan** and south of **Girvan** – are old beaches, testifying to when the sea-level was as much as 30m higher than it is at the moment, following the melting of vast quantities of ice all over the hemisphere. As a consequence of the thaw and the relieving of the heavy pressure of the ice, the land gradually rose again and left the beaches high and dry with their shells and animal remains. Also left high and dry are the so-called 'erratic blocks', large boulders carried along with the slow, strong glacier flow towards the coast and deposited miles from their original home when the thaw came. 'The Baron's Stone of Killochan' in the grounds of **Killochan Castle** is one such boulder, a huge rock perhaps forty tons in weight. Its home was the **Loch Doon** region. Smaller fragments of rock are piled up into great heaps known as terminal moraines, to be seen in the lower reaches of the Stinchar or at **Cuff Hill**, near **Beith**.

According to the latest estimates the ice of the great glaciation first melted in Scotland about 13 500 BC. Some 2,500 years later there was a return of cold, which lasted about 1,000 years. Temperatures have continued to fluctuate irregularly ever since then, but in modern times permanent glaciers have been confined mainly to far northern areas and to high altitudes. With the lessening of the cold the Arctic forms of life gradually retreated northward and the once barren lands of Scotland began to be colonised by plants and animals suited to temperate conditions. At first mere tundra scrub appeared – juniper bushes and low creeping moorland plants like whortleberry. After about a millennium larger trees such as birch and hazel began to form forest areas, which gradually increased in size. Birch covered the whole of Scotland by 8000 BC, quickly followed by elm, and, by 6500 BC, after a significant increase in temperature, by oak. Later still, Scots pine made its appearance in southern Scotland.

Soil is originally weathered rock, and particular kinds of rock give rise to different varieties of soil – both light and heavy, sand and clay. Forests improve soil over long periods by the nutrient-seeking action of tree-roots and the accumulation of organic material from rotting leaves to produce 'brown earth', which is highly fertile. In Ayrshire the rivers which now flow to the coast in the place of the glaciers laid down surrounding plains of productive clay. The great plain of Kyle owes its formation to the action of several rivers flowing west from north and south – the Garnock, the Carmel Water, the Water of Irvine, the Ayr, the Water of Lugar, the Water of Coyle and the Doon. The fertile region east of Girvan follows the course of the Water of Girvan, and the farmlands and forests in the Ballantrae, Colmonell, Barr and Barrhill areas of Carrick lie around the courses and confluences of the Stinchar, Tig, Dusk, Muck and App. Dense forest covered much of the whole area until quite recently; the fourteenth-century chronicler John of Fordun says that in his time the Forest of Selkirk reached as far west as **Ayr Castle**. Extensive clearances, however, were present from a very early period, especially along the coast.

Animals, some of them now unfamiliar, began to roam up into Scotland after the complete sterility of the great Ice Age. Of course, the pre-glacial giants – the mammoth (*Mammuthus primigenius*) and the rhinoceros (*Coelodonta antiquitatis*) – had disappeared. **Sourlie** in Ayrshire is one of only two locations in Scotland where remains of the woolly rhinoceros have been found, and mammoth tusks and teeth have been discovered at **Kilmaurs quarry** and at three other locations close by. But although Scotland has been seen as poor in ancient species by comparison with Europe, the country had become restocked with European animals before the flooding of the 'land bridge' connecting Britain with Europe around 8000 BC. Reindeer (*Rangifer tarandus*) appear to have lived through the Ice Age on the tundra fringes of the glaciation, as witnessed by two Ayrshire sites (near Ardrossan). The wild horse (*Equus ferus*), the aurochs (*Bos primigenius*) and the beaver (*Castor fiber*) have also been recorded in Ayrshire; the last-named seems to have survived in Scotland until recent times. The brown bear and the wolf, also recently extinct, have not so far appeared in the Ayrshire archaeological or fossil record. Other kinds of mammals are fortunately still with us, including the wildcat (*Felis silvestris*) and the pine marten (*Martes martes*), neither archaeologically recorded in Ayrshire. Birds which once abounded in Scotland and the northern hemisphere include the flightless Great Auk (*Alca impennis*), the last of which was killed in Scotland only a little more than 150 years ago. It does not appear to have frequented Ayrshire, though Ailsa Craig would probably have been a suitable habitat for this bird, judging by the populations of other birds which roost on the cliffs of the islet.

With the arrival of these diverse species came another more dangerous animal – man. These tool-using descendants of African forest apes had, of course, evolved hundreds of thousands of years before the great glaciation, had learnt to adapt to conditions other than savannahs and tropical habitats, and gradually colonised most of the land surface of the planet. But although vestiges of the most ancient people – those of the Palaeolithic, or Old Stone Age – can be discovered in southern Britain, they have left no readily identifiable traces in Ayrshire and so will not be considered here. (In Troon, one flint scraper 'of apparently palaeolithic affinities' was discovered in 1985.[1]) In Scotland and in Ayrshire in particular, to all intents and purposes, man appeared only after the great Ice Age, with the onset of a new phase in human culture, the Mesolithic, or Middle Stone Age. The Mesolithic people were represented by small bands of hunter-gatherers who began to trek into Scotland perhaps as early as 10 000 BC.

The Mesolithic period

Mesolithic people in Ayrshire and elsewhere left no surface structures or monuments. They were bow-using nomads, i.e. they wandered from place to place on a seasonal basis. In the immediately post-glacial period, the numbers of people involved were very small – perhaps ten or twenty in a group at a time. Their shadowy presence has had to be inferred either from the remains of the animals they killed for food, from the (tiny) stone and bone implements they used, or from the coastal fish-traps they constructed.

Mesolithic implements, known as microliths, are small fragments of stone that have been shaped or 'knapped' by repeated blows on harder stone to give them shape and direction. Smaller and finer than the corresponding tools of Palaeolithic times, they are often encountered in 'scatters'. Production was intense, amounting to an industry at certain sites, notably at **Loch Doon**. Great quantities of microliths have been found at certain points along both shores of that loch. The types of stone used for these instruments varied quite markedly – flint, chert (flint-like quartz), bloodstone and, in Ayrshire, agate such as that found in the sea off the Heads of Ayr.

Microliths are classifiable by their shapes, but less so in respect of their functions. One may infer that they were used for arrowheads, spearpoints, fish-hooks, harpoons, scrapers, sharpeners, 'burins' (chisels) and even axeheads, used to clear trees and other vegetation. The production techniques of these tools changed and improved at uneven rates throughout the period, the last phase of which was characterised by finely shaped and polished trapezoids. It is thought that in Scotland the early period, from about 9000 BC (or earlier) to 7000 BC, was differentiated from the later (about 7000 BC to 4000 BC) by broad-blade and narrow-blade technology respectively. Broad blades have been discovered at several sites in Scotland, including **Irvine (Shewalton)** in Ayrshire, where, however, a number of narrow blades has also been found.[2]

Other signs of human Mesolithic activity are large mounds of shells from oysters and other coastal creatures. These, as well as bone fragments, are datable by Carbon-14 analysis, as are charcoal traces from fires. But all systems of dating are uncertain. At one point in the fifth millennium BC a massive marine inundation or 'transgression' took place, as a result of which many formerly mainland sites became islands and many islands were reduced in size; later again the water subsided. Mesolithic sites can often be pinpointed as either pre- or post-transgression – but then Carbon-14 dating is often at variance with the expected typology of the stone fragments or stratigraphic dating ascertained in comparison with other sites. Thus confusion arises.[3]

It may be possible to trace some of the movements of the first explorers. Here in the south-west there was clearly exploration by sea along the shores of the firths, and most of the signs of Mesolithic human occupation – stone tools, shell-mounds, middens and camp fires – are found in the coastal regions, at **Ballantrae** at the mouth of the Stinchar Valley and **Irvine** in particular. It is noticeable that many of the sites are to be discovered some little way inland from the present coastline, on or near the 15-metre contour – the beach formed by the raised sea-level following the thaw. The land gradually rose again later, after the tremendous pressure of the ice was lifted. But the impression that the Mesolithic occupation was exclusively maritime, shunning the forested inland areas, is probably wrong. Mesolithic humans seem also to have come overland from the south, from the north coast of the Solway Firth, up into the Southern Uplands and to Clatteringshaws Loch and **Loch Doon**, where the quantity of stone tools found probably represents a long period of temporary occupations rather than large numbers of people. The suggestion has been that the grouping of the sites represents a 'through-way', speculatively traced from the Dee at Kirkcudbright Bay, along the Waters of Ken and of Deugh, the Carsphairn Lane, and down through Loch Doon by the River Doon to the coast; or, to the west, from Fleet Bay by the Big Water of Fleet, Loch Grannoch, the Black Water of Dee, the Cooran Lane, the Gala Lane and the Doon system.[4] It appears that these routes would provide the Mesolithic hunters with game and river fish, and the likely wood cover of these regions (birch, hazel, elm, oak, alder and pine) would provide shelter and resources for fire. All the river routes follow the tracks of massive glacier flows to the coast during the great Ice Age.

Deeper penetration took the explorers northward into the **Muirkirk** region and to the Darvel Valley, through which the Irvine flows to the Firth of Clyde. They also arrived in central Lanarkshire, in the Biggar Common area, and thence to the Forth.

The Firth of Clyde can be looked at as an enclosed sea, open on the south-west to the Atlantic and the Irish Sea. On the west lies the peninsula of Kintyre and on the east the fertile coast of Ayrshire-Renfrewshire. In the middle lies a collection of islands describable as an archipelago,[5] dominated to the north by Arran and to the south by the impressive islet of Ailsa Craig. The Mesolithic peoples after the Ice Age probably used the overland and coastal routes from the Solway to reach the lands of Arran, Kintyre and the near north-western islands, in particular Jura, where extensive mesolithic traces have been found. See **Great Cumbrae Island, Farland Hill**.

The New Stone Age (see p. 2 for Map of Neolithic Sites in South Carrick)

There is no clear cut-off point between the Mesolithic and the Neolithic ages. The meaning of the term Neolithic, 'of the new stone age', refers to a new way of handling stone tools. Of course the basic defining signal of the Neolithic period is a more refined manufacture of such implements, and the use and shaping of stone for construction of walls, dwellings and tombs. But the significance of the period goes further, for it was during the Neolithic times that humans seemed to wake up for the first time to the general possibilities of exploiting nature and nature's gifts constructively, as opposed to merely hunting and gathering. This awakening was a gradual process, uneven and hesitant at times. In Scotland it seems to have taken place during the centuries, perhaps as many as five, on either side of 4000 BC.

Active engagement with nature is most obvious in agriculture – a systematic effort to produce food by cultivating grasses and domesticating animals for nutrition and for traction. These strategies for living involved abandoning the old wandering style of existence and instead settling in one place long enough for crops to grow and be processed and for stock to breed and become useful. The signs of settlement begin to appear round about 4000 BC – the first farms, with fields, fragments of which are often found under peat cover in Britain, and houses, some little better than skin-covered tents, others more substantial structures made of stone, earth and timber. Such traces are barely discernible and none have been found in Ayrshire; fragments of fields dating to before 3000 BC have not been found in Scotland.

Cairns

Early Neolithic humans in Ayrshire and elsewhere did, however, leave very noticeable traces of their presence in another way. Side by side with strategies for sustaining life appeared a systematic attempt to deal with another pressing problem – the disposal of human remains. The solution was the construction of houses for the dead – tombs built of earth, stone and timber. Such tombs, together with the remains and the grave goods inside them, have turned out to be our surest guides to the way of life of our remote ancestors.

Tombs which are covered mainly with heaped earth are called barrows, while stone heaps, which allow more variation in style and internal structure, are called cairns. In addition to barrows and cairns, of course, sub-surface graves and pits were also used at different times, grouped into cemeteries, in which the burials might be laid in cists or under slabs of stone. Secondary indications of corpse disposal include the marks left by bonfires for cremation, and mortuary enclosures, where bodies would be exposed for the flesh to rot away until the residual skeleton could be burnt or buried.

There are a great many cairns the length and breadth of Ayrshire, almost all of them mutilated by modern improving farmers who found the great piles of stone too convenient for wall-building purposes when their original functions had been forgotten. There may also have been an animus against ancient monuments – and this is still with us. It is perhaps significant that the first great age of the grave-destroyers was the rationalistic eighteenth century. And, of course, there had been robbers of grave-goods from a very early time.

Many cairns, then, are represented by ravaged heaps of stone (sometimes of considerable size) in remote places. Many are difficult to date because of the absence of organic (Carbon-14 datable) remains or because grave-goods have been stolen. One group of cairns that seems to be earlier than others is the chambered variety, in which chambers or cells for the dead have been constructed out of stone slabs before being covered with mounds of stone. Some chambered cairns, for instance the 'Bargrennan' group, have a passageway leading from the outside of the cairn to the chamber some metres within the pile of stones; these cairns can have multiple chambers, each with its own slabbed passage, in the body of the cairn.[6] Others, the 'Clyde' group, have entrances opening directly from the exterior into the chamber, which is divided into compartments by low coamings, septal stones set into the ground at right angles to the wall slabs. Some have an elaborate continuous façade of vertical slabs on either side of the entrance, the plan forming a flattened C-shape with 'horns', between which a concourse of flagstones may have provided a space for ceremonial activity of some sort. Differences like these help to distinguish between different groups of people, or separate peoples – or perhaps between different periods of the same people. The Bargrennan group of graves takes its name from the example at Bargrennan in Kirkcudbrightshire just over the Ayrshire border. The Clyde group is centred mainly on the Isle of Arran and examples are to be found in Northern Ireland and along the Solway coast. More widely known are groups beyond the south-west, such as the massively constructed tombs of Orkney.

There are about twelve securely identifiable chambered cairns in modern Ayrshire. They are of only two varieties, while at least six varieties have been identified throughout the whole of Scotland. These tombs appear to have been built and used over the long period between 4000 BC and 2500 BC.

In Ayrshire the only identifiable Clyde-type chambered tomb to have survived even partially is at **Haylie, Largs**. Four Bargrennan-type cairns are also known to have survived into recent times; they were the cairns at **Ar(i)ecleoch, Balmalloch, Cave Cairn (Wee Fell) and Cuff Hill**. All five of these are noted in the Gazetteer together with one unclassified chambered cairn, at **Loanfoot (The Law)**.

By the time that the custom of commemorating the dead in stone came to be practiced by Neolithic people, there must have been a social context in which one person or group of people could command the services of others, for instance in the labour of constructing hilltop or chambered tombs, as well as in farm work. The idea of territoriality may have emerged, including that of tenancy, leading to the subordination of a whole neighbourhood to one land-owning family or individual. Occupational ranking could also have been present: a difference would gradually have emerged between farmers and those in charge of large numbers of animal stock. Historically, herdsmen, owning more land for pasture, tend in time to dominate crop growers.

Apart from the chambered cairns there are dozens of unclassified prehistoric cairns in Ayrshire, undated but certainly later than the chambered variety. There are so many of these that distribution patterns and social organisation may be guessed at even within Ayrshire alone.

By a universal trope, it is a fairly safe conclusion that the people who were accorded burial at the top of high hills were socially exalted – though this does not exclude the occupants of graves at a lower altitude from being socially marked out too. The pharaohs of Egypt were buried in pyramids, artificial hills in a flat plain. In Ayrshire there was no need to build the king a hill for his grave – there were plenty of ready-made hills to hand. So a series of spectacularly sited cairns marches south-west from **Craigie Fell** in Carrick along the western side of Glen App, **Carlock Hill**, **Penderry Hill** and **Drumduff Cairn (Penderry Hill)** to **Finnarts Hill** – high places between the sea and the sombre valley of the App. There is also a clear connection with cairns a little distance from Glen App itself, on the top of **Knockdolian** and of **Cairn Hill, Mains of Tig**, as well as with those on **Drumdowns (Altimeg)**, **Millmoan Hill** and **Haggstone Moor** on the eastern side of the glen.

The Glen App group is wholly within the modern Ayrshire area. Many other groups of hill-top cairns are distinguishable at least partly within the county boundary. Around the Loch Doon / Dalmellington region we find cairns at or near the summits or other prominent features of **Auchenroy Hill**, **Bellsbank**, **Pennyarthur Rig** and **'Bubbly' Cairn**, **Beoch**, **Cairnennock**, **Dalcairnie Cairn (Wee Cairn Hill)**, **Pennyvenie** and **White Laise Cairn**. Further north, in the Muirkirk region, among even higher hills, we find another probably distinct network, including in Ayrshire **Blacksidend**, **Cairn Table**, **Glen Garr Hill**, **Wardlaw Hill I** and **Wetherhill**. In other parts of Ayrshire, both in the north and the deep south, we find yet more clusters of prominent cairns, including of course the Bargrennan group of passage cairns which extends south and east beyond the Ayrshire boundaries. And east of Ballantrae, almost at right angles to the Knockdolian-Glen App group, a series of riverside cairns extends along the course of the Stinchar: **Mains Hill**, **Balnowlart**, the **Colmonell** group – **Polcardoch, Sallochan** and **Tongue Cairns** and the **Craigneil Cairn**.

Some cairn groupings are perhaps not as geographically coherent as the four mentioned above, but all of them give the impression of commemorating lengthy succession lines of local chieftains, whether to be called 'kings', 'warlords', 'land-owners,' 'high priests' or whatever. The Glen App-Knockdolian-Stinchar area of Carrick in particular gives the impression of being a small compact lordship of some sort, perhaps with a sacred significance extending beyond its borders. Another earlier lordship was centred on the eponymous chambered cairn at Bargrennan just outside Ayrshire.

Nearly all the Ayrshire tomb structures have been devastated, but one or two have been overlooked until the present day. At **South Burnt Hill**, during a survey for a windfarm in 1994, researchers discovered the small top part of what may be an undamaged larger cairn poking up from beneath the peat cover near the summit (454m OD). This hill is in the remote upper part of north Ayrshire near the Renfrewshire border (Inverclyde). It is adjacent to the Duchal Moor. There is also a recently discovered ring cairn at **Pennyvenie** near Dalmellington, possibly undisturbed.

Henges, standing stones, cup-and-ring-marked rocks, stone balls etc.

There are other visible Neolithic monuments in Ayrshire besides cairns. These are standing stones (whether single or arranged in fours or rings or arcades), cup-and-ring marked rocks, and 'henge' monuments. One should also remember the characteristic carved stone balls, of which several Ayrshire examples exist. All these artefacts are probably of a later Neolithic period, round about or following 3000 BC.

Henge monuments immediately call to mind the massive structures of Stonehenge, from which the term has been derived. In fact, however, the word 'henge' has now come to mean a ritual circular enclosure within a bank with a ditch running round the inside and with at least one (causewayed) entrance. It may or may not be associated with encircling post-holes or rings of stone or single standing stones, or with burials. These earthworks can be identified by their more-or-less perfect circularity and their siting, often in a high position and always with a clear view over a wide area. There are eight or nine such enclosures in Ayrshire, including one at **Finnarts Hill,** which, by its position and association with cairns and standing stones, would seem to indicate great importance accorded to this site. Two at **Laggan,** closely associated with a burial area at **Ballantrae Bridge,** and the recently destroyed standing stones at **Garleffin,** similarly give the impression of something akin to a temple complex. Ballantrae is of course adjacent to **Knockdolian Hill,** which seems to be pivotal to the little realm whose arms are Glen App and the River Stinchar.

Actual rings of stones in Ayrshire have, however, all been destroyed, some quite recently. **Rig Hill, near Nith Lodge** was obliterated only after

1937 when a dig was carried out. Seemingly there were 15 standing stones in an ellipse on this site. Another ring of boulders may have existed at **Laggish** at the **White Cairn** – an example which makes us think that large circular cairns may have covered over stubby stone rings, as is perhaps the case at Temple Wood, Kilmartin, in Argyll. What was probably a 'four-poster' – four standing stones in a square or diamond-shaped arrangement – still stands in a field at **Cuff Hill,** but the individual stones have been rearranged for the convenience of the farmer. Single standing stones are still not uncommon in the county, and some have been incorporated into urban areas, e.g. in Darvel (the **'Dagon' Stone**) and in **Doonfoot (Ayr)** at **Stonefield Park Road.**

Cup-and-ring marked rocks and carved stone balls are also probably ritual objects, but we do not know what they were for. In both cases we can infer a powerful aesthetic impulse, which leads people to take an interest and pleasure in sheer workmanship, whatever the ostensible primary purpose of the productions.

The most spectacular cup-and-ring markings in Ayrshire are to be found near **Ballochmyle Viaduct** and at **Blackshaw** north of Ardrossan. This kind of rock-carving cannot be Carbon-14 dated, and it has been suggested that the designs go back to Mesolithic times. However, to judge from associated finds, cup-and-ring markings should probably be dated to between 3000 and 2500 BC. The same applies to the characteristic carved stone balls, of which at least three have been found in Ayrshire. The finest example, perhaps, is that found at **Jocksthorn** near Kilmaurs, now in the Dick Institute, Kilmarnock.

Funerary and ceremonial enclosures have been gradually uncovered or discovered in Ayrshire. One of the most (potentially) spectacular sites, at **Ballantrae Bridge,** was revealed only in 1995 by a series of oblique aerial photographs which took advantage of the slanting light of the sun to show up features invisible on the ground.

Mortuary house

A suspected mortuary house has been found at **Courthill, Dalry,** where excavators discovered an apparently rectangular arrangement of posts, roughly 15 by 7m, with, between the long sides, two pits 9m apart, in each of which a very large upright had been planted. This would correspond to the structure at Pitnacree in Fife, in which it is conjectured an open wicker rectangular box was constructed between two large uprights made of a split tree-trunk. Inside the box a body or bodies was exposed for 'biodegradation' or cremation, after which a barrow-mound was constructed to cover the entire arrangement. A cremation was discovered at Courthill between the positions of the two posts, and the structure appears to have been buried under a mound. Pitnacree is dated to between 3800 BC and 3300 BC,[7] and if Courthill is of corresponding date it is one of the earliest monuments in Ayrshire.

Later Neolithic times

After about 2500 BC, cultural changes in Neolithic life appeared in Ayrshire as elsewhere: chambered cairns seem to have gone out of use and from this time onwards it is thought that people began to erect henge monuments and standing stones. Houses became circular in plan, small organised villages appeared in the midst of small cereal fields and pasture-land, and more signs of social stratification can be discerned. In many groups of houses, one house, often larger than the others, stands apart from them – the village chieftain or landowner asserting his status and higher standard of living. 'Roundhouses' can be identified from aerial photographs and crop-marks at **Enoch** near Girvan, at **Ballantrae Bridge** and elsewhere. These are detected by their hut-circles, sometimes double, indicating a central core of stone and soil, sandwiched between wall-faces of wattle-and-daub. There would be a central stone hearth and a conical roof supported by a ring of stout posts. Post-holes have been detected at a large roundhouse in the **Ballantrae Bridge** area and at **Enoch**, where one of the houses is larger than the others and stands a little distance away. Field fragments appear at many, places including **Ballantrae Bridge**.

One feature of Neolithic life that can be identified in Ayrshire and elsewhere is a characteristic way of heating water: the 'burnt mound'. People would heat stones and plunge them into water contained in wooden troughs. When the heating was completed the stones would be discarded into a pile or heap that would gradually form a mound, often crescent shaped, partially surrounding a hearth or site for a fire near a burn or loch. 'Burnt mounds' have been discovered in Ayrshire at **Knockittis Burn** and **Clauchrierob** in Carrick, and elsewhere in the same region. Wooden troughs have been discovered at **Chapeldonan**. It is thought that burnt mounds may indicate camp-sites used in connection with hunting and herding.

What are thought to be fish traps of varying design have been discovered at eight groups of sites on the North Ayrshire coast between Hunterston and Ardrossan.[8] Four are noted in the Gazetteer, at **Ardneil Bay, Bastion Craig** and **Farland Head** – all in the vicinity of **Portincross**. They are lines of heavy boulders across the mouths of small bays below the high-water mark: the tide overlapping the stones carries fish into the bays and leaves them trapped when it recedes. The boulders have often been displaced over the centuries by surf and gales. These devices have not been dated, but it is thought that while originally Neolithic, they may have been in use much later, a conclusion strengthened by the proximity of the eight site groups to eight known coastal fortifications in the area, which include **Hunterston, Portincross, Law, Tarbet, Montfode** and **Ardrossan**.

The Bronze Age

One of the best known of the changes that came about in the culture of the early inhabitants of Britain is the introduction of metalworking, heralding the so-called Bronze Age. Some analysts have down-graded this 'revolution', important though it undoubtedly is. They point out that Neolithic culture is still with us, especially in the matter of building stone houses whether for the living or the dead, and that agriculture, first developed in Scotland 6,000 years ago, is still the mainspring of organised human life. Technological innovation, surprising though it is, has only succeeded in piling complications upon the primary discovery that metal could be wrought. Be that as it may, metal-working first makes its appearance in Scotland about 2000 BC, in the shape of a bronze dagger with a gold band found at Collessie in eastern Scotland. A hoard of roughly the same period containing many bronze ornaments and weapons was discovered at Migdale in Sutherland. The technique of metal-working was probably introduced into Scotland directly from Europe, whether by invasion or by simple exchange of ideas.

Perhaps equally important was the rather earlier introduction of new styles of pottery, indicating a major shift in outlook. Funerary use of pottery may seem a bizarre indicator of cultural trends, but this is one of the major ritual practices by which the development of early peoples can be detected and estimated.

In the early part of the Neolithic period, from about 4000 BC, the farmers seem to have used plain round-bottomed pottery vessels, fragments of which are associated with many Neolithic burials. There seems to have been a ritual practice of smashing pottery into graves together with other domestic refuse. In the later period, from about 3000 BC, different shapes and designs of pottery appear. These include large storage vessels and small elegant drinking-bowls with flatter bottoms, both distinguished as grooved ware, because their bodies are grooved with horizontal lines and bands, some with additional decoration. These are found both at ceremonial/funerary and at what we might call secular sites. But from about 2500 BC onward an altogether different style of pot appears in both kinds of sites: archaeologists call these vessels beakers, by some taken to signify the advent of the famous Beaker People, described as an alien, invading force who conquered the indigenous Neolithic peoples of Britain.

Beakers are decorated pots with rims; they taper below the rim and also toward the bottom, giving an 'S'-shaped profile. They were given their name because they were formerly supposed to hold drink for the deceased, as opposed to what used to be taken for a sub-variety of the design, of various shapes and sizes, but with a more emphatic shoulder and rim, called food vessels. These latter were thought to be provided by the Beaker People to contain solid food for the departed.

However, it is now reckoned that only one of these types, the beakers, represents a genuinely new style of thinking associated with funerary rites and possibly with an incursion of foreigners around 2500BC. The other type, the food vessels, is based upon older indigenous styles of pottery and would provide evidence that the original current or style of ritualistic thought, slightly changed, persisted sometimes side by side with the modification represented by beakers. Neither of these styles of pottery can be taken as proof positive of an 'invasion' of alien people, but only of a current of new thinking. In places in Scotland where beakers and food vessels have been found together it may be guessed that the beaker burials represent a higher status than the food vessel burials.

Beakers and food vessels have been recovered at a number of Ayrshire sites, notably in 1996 at **Kennel Mount** near Culzean Castle, where the pottery has been dated to 2000–1500 BC, but also at **Finnarts Hill** and elsewhere. In Ayrshire there are far more Bronze Age burial sites only with food vessel sherds, e.g. at **Doonfoot, Ayr**, or with a third variety of pottery, the 'Cinerary Urn' style – Bucket-Shaped, Collared and Cordoned. All three kinds have been found at several locations in Ayrshire.[9]

Whether Beaker People actually subjugated British Neolithic native populations or whether the style changes (and metal working) were just the result of peaceful transmission of cultural ideas are still open questions. Some archaeologists have claimed that there was a racial difference between the Beaker People and their predecessors: the Beaker People were brachycephalic, short-skulled, as opposed to the dolichocephalic, long-skulled natives. Evidence for this, however, seems to be questionable. Invasion is a convenient explanation for cultural changes, but it is perhaps even more interesting to contemplate the possibility that since early Neolithic or even Mesolithic times right down to the Bronze and Iron Ages there has been an uninterrupted cultural continuum. Changes such as those between grooved ware and beaker ware, or between sub-rectangular and circular houses – or even between a nomadic and a settled way of life – can be interpreted as changes in fashion or styles of thinking within a single continuum, within one people. Of course, large-scale movements of peoples have occurred throughout history, and various groups have been displaced from time to time. As time progressed, invasions undoubtedly did take place, and settlements of aliens occurred, from the Romans to the Anglo-Saxons, the Danes and Vikings, the Normans and so on. But even these were of comparatively limited effect, and invaders and natives intermingled and settled down together in a gradually strengthening cultural amalgam only occasionally disturbed by intercommunal friction.

Within the native people themselves, however, as Neolithic and/or Bronze Age culture spread throughout Scotland and the population of the territory grew and clustered, differentiation between various groups in separate parts of the country led to the formation of several tribes, and the opportunity for inter-tribal jealousies and warlike antagonisms undoubtedly increased. The evidence for this is in part the variety of cairn types and the geographical groupings of hill-top cairns referred to above. The development of a tendency for one group to war with another is witnessed by the proliferation of killing instruments such as axes, spears and swords. Apart from potsherds, most Ayrshire Bronze Age relics are weapons – an early dagger at **Airds Moss**, a Middle Bronze Age palstave of Irish type from Largs (indicating a possible trade link), or a Late Bronze Age sword from Girvan. The scene is set for the appearance in the Iron Age of the duns and forts of Ayrshire and Scotland, now clearly testifying to the fighting spirit of early human beings.

Hoards of both pottery and metal objects often owe their survival to ritual observance. The circumstances of the hoards found in Ayrshire – at **Lugtonridge**, a set of bronze shields set upright on edge and buried in a ring, and at Maidens, five flat bronze axes and a bronze armlet – seem to indicate a votive purpose, the donor sacrificing these clearly precious objects as an offering or thanksgiving to the gods. A hoard at **Dalduff** may be a bronze-smith's collection of scrap – bronze swords and axes – for recycling, but, as with the similar find in Duddingston Loch near Edinburgh, the possibility of a sacrificial, votive purpose remains open. All of these finds, including the Duddingston hoard, are associated with water or at least marsh 'wetness', and this may indicate that the worship was connected with water deities of some sort.[10] They are perhaps to be dated to the late Bronze Age.

One type of find in Ayrshire reveals a startling reach of trade connections – beads of 'a grey vitreous paste' discovered at Misk Knowes (as well as elsewhere in Ardeer and in Glen Luce). This material is thought to have originated in Egypt in the eighteenth dynasty and to have got here round about 1500 BC.[11] Many Bronze Age finds, from the early period onward, hint at a developed trade between Ireland and Western Scotland. These finds are often ornamental, for instance, 'the somewhat debased herring-bone design on the Cairn Table armlet' which 'resembles the decoration on some Irish Early Bronze Age flat axes'.[12] Trade of this nature had probably been going on since before the beginning of the Bronze Age.[13]

The Iron Age

The Bronze Age is thought to have lasted from about 2000 BC to about 500 BC, when it gave way in Scotland to the Iron Age. This era is signalled in Ayrshire by what may be the remains of a prehistoric iron-smelting site at **Tannahill/Meikle Mosside**, where iron slag has been deposited. A widespread use of iron weapons and other utensils seems to have become common about 500 BC.

The main physical evidence in Ayrshire for the Iron Age is the range of duns and hill-forts which dot the countryside. It is thought that the weather had substantially worsened by the beginning of the period, and this may be the reason for the high elevation of so many buildings assigned to it. The settlements and field fragments of Ayrshire are very often found high in the hills, an indication that boggy conditions in the valleys made them unsuitable for agriculture. These conditions led to what German scholars call *Hohensiedlung* – settlement on the heights. So many of the signs of agricultural settlement of this period are to our minds at an unusual altitude – in Ayrshire at levels now suitable only for hill-farms and sheep-walks; examples are to be found at **High Altercannoch, Gass, Drumdowns (Altimeg)**, and other sites. This tendency to 'high settlement' may also have led to fortification on the heights – and gives this period its characteristic martial flavour of arms and armed camps.

It is from 1000 BC that the Celts are conventionally supposed to have started arriving in Britain and Ireland from the continent in a series of invasions up to about 250 BC. However, the Celts may have been in the two islands longer than that, and it is possible that Brythonic and Goidelic[14] speech may have been in use long before 1000 BC. The use of iron may have been transmitted by trade and peaceful contacts, and the suggestion that it accompanied a conjectured Celtic invasion or invasions of the first millennium BC may not be valid.

In the prehistory of Ayrshire, as in other parts of Scotland, the persistence of the circular style of house-building is one example of a cultural idea – a customary technique – that may have lasted more than 2,000 years. The large huts at **Glenhead**, north of Ardrossan, were originally thought to be a double fort. These twin earthworks are in fact civilian structures and are built upon an earlier level of occupation, also two huts. Beneath the earlier huts were two sets of stone-lined passages which were filled with rubbish including Roman relics: these buildings are unquestionably Iron Age productions. Yet both the earlier and later levels were built in an ancient circular style that may date back to Neolithic times. The larger of these earlier huts had a single internal roof-post support, and the roofs of the later huts were supported by internal rings of posts.[15]

The huts at Glenhead are non-military, but before excavation the structures appeared outwardly to be defensive – two flat-topped mounds separated by gullies from a plateau in the north. It has been suggested that the same circular style of wooden construction may be the predecessor of the stone-built broch style and of its successor, the dun style fortified homesteads. Brochs, looking like miniature dry-stone cooling-towers, are found typically in the north-east and in Orkney and Shetland. If we follow Feachem (and RCAHMS), however, an isolated example is to be found in Ayrshire at **Craigie**, nearly circular, with a diameter of more than 19m and a wall 4.8m thick. Broch building is related, it seems, to dun construction, and other authorities have classed the Craigie structure as a dun.

Some difficulty has also arisen as to the precise difference between duns and forts, and some archaeologists have even proposed to abandon it. The difficulty is shown by the way in which modern analysts have classed as forts or castles some buildings bearing the word 'dun' in their names. **Duniewick** on Knockdolian is classed as a fort; the great motte above Girvan is called **Dinvin**. In the Gazetteer I have followed RCAHMS in the classification of sites.

Duns are to be found in all parts of Ayrshire. It is not always easy to recognise them, such are the eroding effects of time – or of siege and battle long past – or of man's perennial proclivity for quarrying stone. Nevertheless at least fourteen duns have been identified in Ayrshire besides the broch at Craigie.

An Iron Age class of monument which has been extensively investigated over the last century and a half is the crannog or lake-dwelling, of which there are or were several examples in Ayrshire. In the case of one, the **Kilbirnie Loch** crannog originally discovered in 1868, part of a probably associated logboat was discovered in 1952 and sent to Paisley Museum. This specimen had mud in the interstices of the timber, and analysis of the pollen found in this mud suggests that the boat should be assigned to the 'Sub-Boreal' period (pollen zone VIIb), giving dates between 3000 BC and 700 BC, Bronze Age if not Neolithic – substantially earlier than other dated Ayrshire logboats.[16] Most Ayrshire crannogs and logboats, however, appear to be of more recent date, going back only to the beginning of the Iron Age. The crannogs are all roughly of the same kind of construction, artificial islands based on heavy boulders and/or timbers with a brushwood and timber superstructure rising to a platform on which is built (once again) a characteristic round-house with a conical roof supported by a ring of posts. Secondary features include palisades formed of rings of stakes and causeways leading from the shore of the loch. Several levels of habitation are often found – a series of superimposed collapses – and these cover a range of periods from the beginning of the Iron Age to the early medieval period. Most of these structures have come to light through the drainage of a loch, e.g. at **Lochlea** or **Buiston,** and no site in Ayrshire is evident to the eye. The logboats are 'monoxylous', i.e. they are formed from a single piece of wood, a large tree-trunk hollowed out and made sea-worthy with various degrees of expertise. Some of these craft, which are very subject to disintegration on exposure to the air, have nevertheless found shelter in museums such as the Dick Institute at Kilmarnock or Paisley Museum, and they are well worth going to see.

Iron Age forts are perhaps rather larger in the scale of prehistoric buildings than duns, and they are much more obvious to the eye. Often they are simply defensive walls of enceinte on hill-tops, within which, it has been conjectured, village populations and live stock could be gathered for safety in time of war, with a relatively small central organisation of mound and rampart. Some are so large and permanently adapted to civilian settlement as well as military life that, like Traprain Law in East Lothian, they are designated by the Latin word *oppidum,* which can mean either town or fortress, and sometimes both. Perhaps two structures in Ayrshire are *oppida* – **Craigie** and **Harpercroft.** Other structures are prominent by reason of their multiple ramparts, often sculpted into the sides of a hill or knoll, with scarping, terraces and ditches arranged about the summit, which might be taken as the 'conning-tower' in warlike operations.

The Romans

It is at this point in our survey that we encounter the first historically verifiable invaders of Britain – the Romans. In spite of fairly detailed written evidence, much unsubstantiated speculation has persisted about these enterprising imperialists. Many a road or fort has been labelled Roman without a shred of proof. However, the Romans did penetrate to Ayrshire if only for a short period and they recorded the names of the tribes they met here.

When the Romans finally arrived to stay in Britain in AD 43, there was no such thing as a united British nation. Over thirty different tribal areas existed throughout the main island – for instance, those of the Catuvellauni in the south or of the Iceni in what is now Norfolk, from where stemmed the great early (AD 60–1) revolt against the Romans headed by Boudicca ('Boadicea'). Other tribes of the period include the Brigantes (occupying much of the north of England on either side of the Pennines) and the Dumnonii or Damnonii, who held two widely separated areas of west Britain: Devon and Cornwall in the south and Clydesdale and northern Ayrshire in the north.

There was, of course, no division between Scotland and England, but the limit of permanent Roman occupation became stabilized not so very far south of the present English-Scottish border. Hadrian's Wall, built between about 122 and 136, runs between the Tyne (Wallsend) and the Solway (Bowness). Shortly afterwards a further occupation zone was established as far as the Forth-Clyde isthmus, with a northern limit at the Antonine Wall, built in 142–3 and running between Carriden on the Forth and Old Kilpatrick on the Clyde. However, the imperial forces soon found themselves over-extended and, even though the apparent intention had been to enlarge the area of permanent colonization northward, the Romans had to withdraw from what is now southern Scotland, possibly in or soon after 180. A buffer zone may have been in existence for some time after that, but the tribes north of Hadrian's Wall remained unconquered by Rome. North of the wall the Romans were never more than a fleeting presence.

Agricola

After AD 43 the Romans pushed northwards in Britain with caution, thus demonstrating their intention of securing the island thoroughly and permanently. They made sure of their hold on one region of the island – pacifying it, splitting large tribes into smaller units ('*divide et impera*') and establishing the physical and cultural norms of Roman civilization – before probing forward into another. It was nearly forty years after the first invasion when the great general Gnaeus Iulius Agricola pushed his forces into southern Scotland.

Immediately after his arrival in Britain in the spring of AD 78, Agricola had made his mark with the systematic genocide of the Ordovices tribe in North Wales and the conquest of Anglesey, then a centre of the Druidic cult; in AD 79, by contrast, he had proved himself a strong but benevolent 'Romanising' administrator in the territory of the Brigantes. Then, in AD 80, he made his first foray into Scotland, marching up probably in two columns of advance: one on the east from the Tyne and Tweed up to the line of the Forth, and the other on the west by Carlisle and Corbridge to Crawford, and thence north-eastward to join up with the first column at Inveresk. The next summer was spent in consolidating Agricola's grasp on the parts of southern Scotland so far invaded, in preparation for a decisive push to the north beyond the Forth and the Tay. However, before that took place, Agricola investigated the possibilities of invading Ireland. He thought it would not be a difficult operation. The notion may have entered Agricola's mind as early as AD 79 during his operations in Wales and the north-west. Probably in AD 82 he made a reconnaissance in force involving penetration of south-west Scotland and the Firth of Clyde area. He may have crossed the Solway into what is now Galloway and the Rhinns, and he may also have marched up the Nith Valley and down to the Clyde coast, perhaps to Ayr or points south. A substantial Roman camp at **Loudoun Hill** existed just at the Ayrshire border, dated fairly securely to AD 82. This camp has been obliterated by gravel-mining, but the site was efficiently surveyed and described before digging commenced, so that there is no doubt of the characteristic 'playing-card' rectangular plan with granaries, hospital, stores and barracks regularly laid out. Two other camps have been discovered at **Girvan Mains** at the mouth of the Water of Girvan, and a fortlet, perhaps better described as a look-out post, has been identified at **Outerwards** high above Skelmorlie in North Ayrshire. With the exception of Outerwards, no surface feature of these encampments has survived, the Girvan camps being detected as cropmarks by aerial photography in 1976–8.

The Romans, as far as we know, never invaded or colonised Ireland. Instead, the next year, in AD 83, Agricola marched into Aberdeenshire and finally achieved a set-piece victory over the native inhabitants at a place called Mons Graupius, tentatively identified with Mount Bennachie near Inverurie, i.e. in the locality of the Grampians.

For various reasons the battle was not as decisive as the historian Tacitus (Agricola's son-in-law) boasted. The Britons simply continued with the guerrilla tactics they had previously been using and melted away into the hills when the day looked like going against them. Neither Agricola nor any of his Roman successors succeeded in subjugating North Britain. But to his northern campaigns we owe the first historical recognition of the region we now call Ayrshire.

2. GODDESSES, GODS, SAINTS AND PLACE-NAMES

The Ayrshire melting pot

So far, in our brief survey of 'Ayrshire before Ayrshire', we have relied heavily upon archaeology, often arguing from analogous areas, and thus often almost losing Ayrshire amid wide-ranging generalities and generalisations. With the arrival of the Romans, however, the dawn of writing is upon us, and this gives us above all names which can be specific to Ayrshire. With 'Old King Cole' we have at least the first putative name of an Ayrshireman – although of course he himself would have claimed to be only a man of Kyle! We have the names of places, tribes, deities, families, kings and saints. Although Ayrshire itself does not finally take shape until the beginning of the reign of Robert II of Scotland in 1371, we can begin to see the process of the formation of the shire out of the shards of two ancient statelets which in their turn grew out of two contiguous tribes who had lived in the south-west of Scotland through the Roman period and in all probability much further back than that.

Just about the time of the building of the Antonine Wall the Hellenistic (Egyptian) geographer Ptolemy compiled a map of Britain which, though it contains at least one major error (the rotation of northern Britain through ninety degrees), provides confirmable data about the inhabitants of Britain and their respective locations within the island. For our purposes the four tribal names shown by Ptolemy immediately above the 'waist-line' of Britain are of interest: these peoples are respectively the Novantae, the (northern) Damnonii, the Selgovae and the Votadini. The first two shared the area now known as Ayrshire. The name of the Selgovae is probably remembered in the border town now called Selkirk, and the Votadini appear later as the Gododdin, who controlled the fortress now called Edinburgh (a likely echo of 'Gododdin') as well as the great hill-fort of Traprain Law.

The Novantae possessed what we know as Carrick, the southern division of Ayrshire, and the Damnonii the present Kyle and Cuninghame, the middle and northern segments of the modern county. To the south of Carrick, Galloway (Wigtownshire and Kirkcudbrightshire) was also Novantan, and the Damnonii possessed a great swathe of territory to the north and east – the areas now known as Renfrewshire, Dumbartonshire, and the banks of the River Clyde reaching down into Lanarkshire.

Pagan deities in the Ayrshire region

The Damnonii and the Novantae were Brythonic tribesmen and tribeswomen, speaking an extinct variety of proto-Welsh called Cymric, probably but not certainly akin to that other mysterious dead language, a variety of Brythonic called Pictish, which belonged to the north-east of Scotland. The other mainstream Celtic language spoken in these islands was Goidelic, which still survives as Irish and Scottish Gaelic. Cymric has left a surprisingly rich treasury of place-names, and it is through this treasury that we can begin to understand the culture of these ancient Britons.

The Romans of course never affected, let alone succeeded in suppressing British Celtic culture even in the permanently occupied regions of the south. These fierce tribes emerged from the Roman period with their social structures intact. The modification of these structures represented by Christianity was adopted voluntarily by the tribespeople themselves some time near the end of the Roman presence in Britain. But from a study of their place-names a pantheon of pre-Christian British deities emerges triumphantly – as does much else.

For instance, it used to be thought that no evidence for Ayr itself dated from before about 1177 or 1197 (the latter being the foundation date of William the Lion's castle). It also used to be thought that the name 'Ayr' derived from sources that were either Old Norse (*eyri*, 'tongue of land', 'gravelly bank')[17] or pre-Celtic, ultimately derived from a conjectured word *ara,* 'water-course'.[18] However, the Irish scholar Proinsias Mac Cana has pointed out, in connection with the Welsh river-name 'Aeron' (philologically identical with Ayr), that the Celts regularly named rivers and other features after goddesses; Aeron derives from Agrona, one of the Celtic goddesses of slaughter.[19] That this name can refer to the present Ayr district as well as the South Wales river is shown by the fact that 'aeron' and 'vretrwyn' (Troon) as well as 'coet beit' (Beith) are named together, as being in close geographical proximity, in *Cadau Gwallawg* ('The Battles of Gwallawg'),[20] one of the poems of Taliesin originating in the sixth century. Taliesin himself was the court poet of King Urien of the Cymric or early Welsh kingdom of Rheged, the successor state to the Novantae, which probably had its *caput* at Dunragit near Glen Luce on the north coast of the Solway Firth. Another reference to Ayr (Aeron) as a district or settlement rather than a river occurs in the description of the Battle of Catraeth (Catterick) in *The Gododdin* of Aneirin,[21] also originating in Scotland in the sixth century and written in early Welsh.

An identification between the River Ayr and the goddess Agrona fits well with the etymology of the other local river name, Doon, which comes from Devona, the patron goddess of the Damnonii (hence Devon, their southern possession). The Doon marks the southern boundary of the Scottish Damnonian territory, beyond which stretches the territory of the Novantae, Gallovidian Carrick.[22]

All this makes it likely that the name 'Ayr', at least as that of a Scottish river, and probably as that of a settlement at the mouth of the river, certainly existed in the sixth century and perhaps during and even before the Roman occupation. It is clearly older than 'Prestwick', for that is an Anglian name, but the names 'Troon' and 'Girvan' and possibly 'Irvine' have roots at least as deep in the linguistic history of the region as 'Ayr'.

The name 'Girvan' is probably a metathesis from the Celtic Vindogara, a river shown on Ptolemy's map. The element *vindo-*, from the Celtic *vindos*, 'white', occurs in place-names throughout Europe (for instance, Vindobona giving both Vienna in Austria and Vienne in France; there is also a Vindolanda at Hadrian's Wall); it has been suggested by Proinsias Mac Cana that in these instances *vindo-* is used as a deity-name corresponding to the Irish hero Fionn mac Cumhaill,[23] 'Finn McCoull', 'the Fair'. 'Girvan', or rather, 'Vindogara', might then mean something like 'the thicket or grove of Fionn'.

It is suggestive, in this connection, that a great fortress in the hills above Girvan is called 'Dinvin', the Cymric *din-* corresponding to the Gaelic *dun*, 'fort'.[24] One thinks also of the well-attested practice of the early Church of 'christening' local pagan deities by describing them as saints and prefixing the names of associated localities with the tag *kil* or *kirk* ('church' or 'cell'). Thus, the saint of Kilwinning (supposedly 'Uinnianus', 'Findbarr'), and the otherwise unidentified St Inan, who has a well just to the south of Irvine (and a chair in the **Cuff Hills** to the north of Beith), tend to arouse suspicion. The occurrence of the names Irvine to the south and Lochwinnoch to the north, and other instances, increase the probability that in this part of south-west Scotland in pre-Christian times there was a cult of the Brythonic deity corresponding to the Goidelic Fionn.

In this connection it is of interest to consider the names Finnarts Hill, Finnarts Cottage/House and Fintry Bay (the last-named in Great Cumbrae Island). Earlier in this book we have mentioned Finnarts Hill, the south-westernmost of the hills than run down the west side of Glen App in Carrick. This hill, which looks out over the expanse of Loch Ryan and the North Channel to Antrim, was obviously of great importance, a sacred high place in Neolithic times, as witnessed by the henge monument at the summit, the cairns and the standing stones. The name clearly means 'the heights of Fi(o)nn'. (For *-arts* compare the names Newtonards, Ardneil, Ardrossan and other variants.) There are also Finnarts Point, Finnarts Bay, Finnarts Bridge (near the burnt mound at Starling Knowe) and, at the foot of the hill Knockdolian looking into Glen App from the north, Finnart Cottage and Finnart Holm. The suffix *-try* in the name Fintry Bay is likely to have a connection with the Cymric termination *-tref*, a dwelling or habitation: this place-name would mean 'the bay of Finn's house' – in Cumbrae, 'the island of the Cym(b)ri'. All these names reinforce the suggestion of a strong cult of the Celtic God Fi(o)nn in the Glen App area and elsewhere in the region – and perhaps a cultural continuity with the henge builders of the third millennium BC.

Mac Cana has also suggested that Fionn 'may originally have been another name for the god Lugh'.[25] Lugh or Lugus is one of the major deities of the Celtic pantheon, worshipped throughout Europe. His name can be discerned in the place-names Leyden (Lugdunum Batavorum) and Lyon (Lugdunum), in Carlisle (Luguvallum) and perhaps even in London (Londinium). Besides being the Gaulish equivalent of Mercury, he was a formidable god of war, possessing a living spear that always found its mark. This terrifying figure is commemorated in Ayrshire at **Loudoun Hill**,[26] as well as at Lugar and Lugton.

The names of at least two other localities in Ayrshire may be connected with pre-Christian Brythonic deities. The first is **Mauchline**, in origin probably something like *Macha llyn,* 'the pool of Macha'. Macha was one of a trinity of war-goddesses, the Morrighan, Badhbh and either Nebhain or Macha (or one of the three Morrighans or Machas).[27] The other name is the perhaps Christianised **Kilmaurs**, ostensibly the Church of St Maura, who is said to have died in Kilmaurs in the ninth century.[28] The name of the stream that runs through the place, Kilmaurs Water, also appears as Carmel Water. 'Kilmaurs' could be a kind of metathesis (cf. Girvan *supra*). In view of the Celtic habit of naming localities and rivers after deities – and in spite of the existence from the fourteenth century of a Carmelite convent in Irvine nearby – we should perhaps be considering a goddess with the British version of a name like Carman, an Irish war/fertility deity.[29] Just south of Kilmaurs is a place called Carmelgrove, recalling another Celtic practice, that of associating a sacred precinct in the shape of a plantation or grove with the worship of any deity. A so-called Lady Well in the neighbourhood may have originally possessed the same kind of function[30] – a spring associated with ritual washing.[31] The washing appears in many cases to have been that of severed human heads, and the washer to have been one of the fierce red-haired Valkyrie-like Celtic war-goddesses, the Morrighan, the Phantom Queen, 'Morgan le Fay'. **Kyles Well, Kilwinning,** formerly in the precinct of the abbey, was reputed to have flowed with blood in 1184 in time of war.[32] and this tradition, which goes back to Hoveden and Benedictus Abbas, may well reflect a Celtic mythic story or ritual. A pipe leading to the well from the abbey (not, apparently, as a source of drinking water) was discovered in 1826 and it is likely (on Paterson's account) that the monks of the abbey may have actually introduced a red colouring into the well in order to keep up the popular belief.

A further echo of ancient Celtic religious belief in Ayrshire (and elsewhere in Scotland) is provided by the persistence of the legend of the Lughnasa Musician. This legend is associated with the festival of Lugh or 'Lughnasa[-dh]', still celebrated in certain parts of Ireland and carried on in a disguised fashion in Scotland, including Ayrshire. The story in its fullest form is told in connection with the celebrations at Teltown in the centre of Ireland, 'Teltown' being the place of the underworld goddess Tailtiu, whose cult is associated with that of Lugh. According to this version, a piper assembled a large number of young people and while playing on his pipes led them down into a subterranean passage and was never seen again. According to versions which have been collected in Aberdeenshire and Edinburgh, in response to a challenge or dare the piper went down alone, playing his instrument, to face an unknown horror in the basement of some ruined building like a chapel or castle. As his friends waited in trepidation on the surface, they heard the skirl of the pipes come to an abrupt end, and the piper was never seen again. If, however, you listen on a quiet, warm summer's evening in the vicinity of a chapel or other ruin, you may still hear his mournful tune coming from under your feet:

Ah doot, Ah doot,
Ah'll never get oot.[33]

At least two and possibly four or more instances of this ghost story occur in Ayrshire. One is associated with the seaside cave underneath the rock on which **Culzean Castle** stands. The piper is alleged to have gone in to explore a passage reputed to emerge at the Abbot's House at **Crossraguel** Abbey. He never appeared again but his music may still be heard in summer coming from beneath the (present) tarmac of an internal estate road locally known as The Piper's Brae. In Ayr, on the other hand, the passage is alleged to pass under Ayr Bay from the South Harbour region to **Greenan Castle**: it has various starting points, including the eighteenth-century cellars of a well-known and old-established local firm of wine merchants, and the basement of the Old Fort in the centre of Cromwell's citadel adjacent to the harbour. The present Ayr Academy stands almost on top of the citadel site, and I remember as a small boy in the 1950s being dared to venture down into the boiler room to encounter the musical ghost. More recently, I collected a version from a barmaid who served in one of the quayside taverns and who was convinced that the disappearance had actually occurred in the last seventy years, and that the piper's dog had returned to the surface without his master and with all his hair burnt off. The involvement of a dog is not elsewhere unknown but is relatively uncommon. Both the Ayr and the Culzean versions involve high sea cliffs and underwater passages – adding to the impression that this story has something to do with water deities. Other instances may occur in Irvine and at **Dundonald Castle**.

This legend is given its most familiar shape in Browning's poem *The Pied Piper of Hamelin*, and in that version is based upon a supposed actual event in Hamelin in the thirteenth century. However, its provenance lies further back, in the stories of the musician Orpheus and his frustrated rescue of Eurydice from Hades; certain similarities may even be discerned in what happened to Jesus Christ, who (according to some versions) descended into hell, took the infernal punishments destined for mankind on himself, and returned triumphant to the upper world on the third day, the Redeemer. I do not believe that any Christian elements are discernible in the Lughnasa relation, but elements of 'mystery religion' such as were to be found in the

Orphic cult may be cognate with the druidic religion preceding Christianity among the Celts.

Lugh, as mentioned above, was sometimes known as the Gaulish Mercury or Hermes. All three deities performed the functions of the 'Psychopomp', the god who led the souls of the dead down to Hades or Hell or some other abode of the dead.

At any rate, such buried myths exist in Ayrshire to the present day and the Lughnasa festival 'in disguise' continues in Irvine in the so-called Marymass Festival (which includes a significant parade of horses as a central element) and in other guises elsewhere.

Kings and things

In addition to religious or cultic evidences, secular things, events and people of the Brythonic period have left their linguistic traces all over Ayrshire – although one should be chary of attributing merely inert 'thinghood' to any simple geographical feature named in this period. For instance, the name Carrick is given to the southernmost division of Ayrshire, and this name, we are told, means 'rock'. In a very literal fashion the name could be taken, no doubt, as signalising the general character of the indeed very rocky district. But when the element 'carrick' occurs in other place-names, it is very often linked with another word or name, as can be seen in, for instance, Carrickfergus, or Carrickmore – defining and marking out the particular 'carrick' in question. It is unlikely that the Brythonic peoples of the pre-Christian epoch in Ayrshire used the single word 'Carrick' in a sophisticated, modern, abstract way to give a general description of their homeland; they are more likely to have used it to emphasise the particularly striking characteristics of one special rock – its awe-inspiring singularity on first discovery, its tremendous, formidable menace, almost one of the 'Sondergötter', the 'momentary or special gods' described by Usener[34] as typical of primitive consciousness. From its first discovery its supernatural influence would seem to pervade all its surroundings and ultimately characterise the region, which would then adopt the name like a totem. There is, of course, one particular rock which fills this bill: the rock of Ailsa Craig, standing hugely in the sea off Girvan like a frowning sentinel; its radiation of surprising divinity would be sufficient to confer its name, Carrick, on the district. Even today, when the country is no longer wild, lonely and full only of forests and wild beasts, the monstrous shape of Ailsa Craig rising up over the shoulder of Byne Hill is enough to startle the traveller descending through the pass to Girvan by Dinvin and Laggan Hill. How much more of an impression must it have made on the first pioneers seven or eight thousand years ago!

The name 'Kyle' is reputed to have come from none other than 'Old King Cole', Coel Hen, a semi-mythical monarch who seems to have ruled some time during the sixth century. Other 'Kyles' in Scotland can be traced

to other sources, and we might be justified in dismissing the etymology of
the Ayrshire name as apocryphal were it not for the fact that many names in
southern Kyle seem to support it (Coylton, Coilsholm, Coilsfield, Coalhall,
Holebogs, Hollybush etc.). These names are scattered in the vicinity of the
Water of Coyle, which runs at the foot of the Craigs of Kyle. Just at the
point where Kyle abuts on Carrick and Dumfriesshire (Nithsdale), and two
important rivers flow together (the Guelt and Glenmuir Waters), there
stands a single lonely column of ancient masonry called Kyle Castle, the
remnant of a stone castle built atop a probable Iron Age hill-fort which
guards the approaches to Strathclyde from the south and south-east.

King Cole seems to have had much to do with the establishment of
the wider realm of Strathclyde.[35] He was a 'rough'[36] contemporary of
another monarch, Dyfnwal, King of Dumbarton. Dyfnwal was also called
'*Hen*' – a word meaning either 'old' or 'wealthy'. Coel is referred to as *gwledig*
(*Guletic*), a designation which some have seen as a Welsh adaptation of the
Latin *regulus*, 'a kinglet'. In *The Gododdin* he is also called Guotepauc or
Godebog, meaning perhaps 'protector'. He seems to have been an ancestor
of Urien of Rheged,[37] and thus it would not be surprising if he had carved
out a realm for himself just north of Gallovidian Carrick, in what became
'Kyle'. But of this shadowy monarch we know very little. On the farm of
Coilsfield Mains just west of Failford in Ayrshire the remnants of a cairn
are pointed out where about 160 years ago an urn was dug up containing, it
was rumoured, the ashes of King Cole or Coel.[38] He was reputed to have
died in battle near there, and just across the Water of Fail from the site is a
location suggestively called Dead-men's Holm. However, no hard evidence
exists in the form of archaeological finds securely linked to the Damnonian/
Novantan Cymric or Old Welsh period in Ayrshire.

It may be that Christianity in this part of Britain was transmitted first
from a Roman settlement in the Carlisle area. However this does not mean
that a specific Roman agency has been identified. On the one hand, as we
have said, during the long Roman occupation, the British peoples retained
their distinctive social structures surprisingly intact, including aristocratic
hierarchies and methods of war. When the Romans withdrew, British
kingdoms long suppressed suddenly reappeared and resumed their ancient
rivalries – at first unaffected by the menace of the Anglo-Saxons on the east,
and the Scots from Ireland in the west. On the other hand, the Christian
religion somehow took root among these same fierce warriors during the
occupation and spread gradually throughout the Roman province, whether
transmitted by the Romans or in some other fashion.

Christianity: Ninian and Oswald

The earliest British Christian tombstones, discovered at Kirkmadrine
in the Rhinns of Galloway as well as at Whithorn and elsewhere, are

obviously derived from pre-Christian Roman models but as obviously are related to styles of Christian memorials at Poitiers and elsewhere in south-western Gaul (France). Christianity was reported by the third-century Roman author Tertullian to have spread to 'parts of Britain inaccessible to Rome' i.e. north of Hadrian's Wall, although, as Mrs Brooke points out,[39] this does not necessarily imply Galloway. The Kirkmadrine stones are thought to date back to about 450 or even earlier. The British Celts were earlier Christians than their Anglo-Saxon conquerors and probably converted them.[40]

The first British saint that we are aware of in south-west Scotland was Ninian. He had some connection with St Martin of Tours (in south-western Gaul) though he can hardly have been a contemporary. St Martin died in 397 but it is thought that Ninian's time was perhaps a century later. This would still put him earlier than St Columba, who founded his community in western Scotland in 565. We are informed by the Venerable Bede – a Lindisfarne Anglian monk on whose records much of our information about early Dark Age Britain depends – that, 'long before [Columba]', Ninian went to '[a] place [which] belongs to the province of Bernicia, and is commonly known as Candida Casa, the White House, because he built the church of stone, which was unusual among the Britons'.[41] This place was Whithorn in Galloway (Wigtownshire): Whithorn or Hwitærne is an Anglian translation of the Latin Candida Casa, 'white house'. J. B. Johnston has pointed out that the name Whithorn 'was probably taken by [Ninian] from St Martin's community near Poitiers – Locotegiacum, Gaulish *leuc-teg-ac*, "white house place"'.[42] In recent years archaeologists carrying out an extensive dig in the immediate neighbourhood of the medieval Whithorn Cathedral have discovered evidence of very early religious settlements, including whitish stone remnants which may be spoil from the ruins of the original White House.[43]

Very little indeed is known about Ninian. We do not even know that he founded the Christian community in Whithorn; some scholars think that there was a thriving community there by the time of his arrival.[44] His field of missionary activity seems to have been limited to 'the southern Picts', i.e. the Picts who were in control in the neighbourhood of Stirling – as opposed to 'the northern Picts', those in the neighbourhood of Inverness (if in fact the southern Picts were not Cymric-speaking Novantan Brythons from the Whithorn area, nearly related in speech to the inhabitants of north-eastern Scotland).

No trace of genuinely (sixth-century) Ninianic activity has been identified in the Ayrshire area, although the locality name 'Nineyards' in Saltcoats in Cuninghame seems suggestive, given a parallel formation in the Edinburgh (Hopetoun) area, 'Nyniwells', which Mrs Brooke reckons may be a memory of the Pictish form, Ninia, of Ninian's name.[45] The Cymric form of Ninian's name, Nyniau, would of course be used in Strathclyde, but this is not dissimilar to 'Ninia'. There is another explanation of 'Nineyards' in **Saltcoats**, involving property rights of nine original inhabitants of the village, but this has all the appearance of folk-etymology. The place is the south-eastern of two adjacent promontories on the coast of Cuninghame, the north-western being 'Ardrossan'. 'Nineyards' could mean something like 'the heights or the promontory of Ninian'.

There are churches in Ayrshire whose patron is claimed to be St Ninian, but none of these are likely to be older than the twelfth century, when a cult of St Ninian was at its height.[46] Of course, there is also a strong association with St Ninian (a chapel) at Kingcase in **Prestwick**, a former leper 'hospital', which may have been founded much earlier than the time of King Robert I (thirteenth/fourteenth century), the traditional founder.

Next to the Cymric-Brythonic, the greatest linguistic influence upon the post-Roman Ayrshire region was Anglo-Saxon, and this was exerted by means of actual invasion. One suspects, however, that the invasion would have had as little effect upon the Celts as that of the Romans, had it not occurred at the same time as the flowering of a powerful idea – Christianity.

The Anglians from Northumberland succeeded in conquering or annexing by marriage the ancient British kingdom of Rheged, which extended into Galloway and Whithorn, some time in the middle of the seventh century. Their kingdom, Bernicia, was expansionist and they entertained ambitions to control the whole of Scotland. However King Ecgfrith was lured north of the Tay by the Picts and met his match in Pictish territory at the Battle of Nechtansmere in 685. The Northumbrians were beaten back then, but they remained in political control of Galloway until the end of the ninth century.[47] During the seventh century Northumbrian culture was Christianized, effectively by the great King Oswald (635–41), who had come under the influence of Celtic Christianity while in exile in Scotland from 617. In Galloway, including Carrick, under Oswald's brother Oswy (641–71), Northumbrian Christianity replaced that of ancient Rheged and an entirely Anglian bishopric was set up with its centre in Whithorn. This ethnic overlay led to a great blossoming, almost a renaissance, of culture and religion in the Cumbria–Galloway region. This is perhaps best shown in the seventh- or eighth-century Ruthwell Cross, which incorporates in its beautiful carving a version of the great Old English poem, *The Dream of the Rood*.

Little by little the story of the Anglian occupation of these areas has become clearer. A pincer movement from the south coast of Galloway appears to have been aimed at the northern part of Carrick, perhaps homing in on what is now **Maybole**. One route appears to have led up the Glenkens and down through **Straiton** and thence west. Straiton looks like an Anglian name, having to do with a *tun* on a *stræt*, a paved and possibly Roman road; Agricola may have descended on Carrick by this route earlier. The other route, completing the pincer movement, led northward through Glen App and via Ballantrae and Girvan to **Turnberry** and Maybole.

The ending -*botl,* which gives us the second element of the place-name Maybole, carries not only the meaning 'hall', 'dwelling', but also the implication 'mother-town', 'metropolis', a centre from which other settlements spread out.[48] The fact that Maybole is close to Turnberry ('thorn-bush tower'), the military *caput* of the district under the medieval Earls of Carrick and probably an important fortress earlier, may indicate that Maybole was regarded as the civilian capital of an Anglian 'shire' in Northern Carrick, a small administrative nucleus that would co-exist with surviving Cymric areas in Southern Carrick.[49] Mrs Brooke indicates that one of the Anglian Carrick place-names that she has been unable to pinpoint on the map is Coffe (also Cofe and le Coffe; all fifteenth century).[50] However Cove was the original name of the castle now known as **Culzean**, which lies on the coast between Turnberry and (inland) Maybole. Cove would be a third centre in the shire (a different kind of administrative unit from the modern Ayrshire).

A well-known Anglian place-name in Ayrshire is **Prestwick**, 'priests' dwelling', presumably founded after the Northumbrian annexation of Kyle in 752 under King Eadhberht. A puzzling feature, however, of this place-name is that the Northumbrian occupation of Kyle did not last.[51] Strathclyde, of which Kyle was the southernmost limb, was the one British kingdom to survive the attacks of Anglians, Scots and even Norse (in 870) and the short duration of the Anglian presence in Kyle would not, one would think, give time for a place-name to take root. Similarly, other place-names in Ayrshire that have an Anglian flavour to them, such as **Fenwick**, Cuninghame, **Skelmorlie** (? 'lea, meadow of Scealdamer'[52]) and **Eglinton** are dubious examples. The most positive thing we can say about them is, with W.F.H. Nicolaisen, that 'they, in their isolation, only confirm the impression of a thin ruling class of Anglians after Oswy's marriage, rather than of a thorough settlement'.[53] It is also clear that religious settlement did not always go hand in hand with political dominance, and that religious communities often held together and outlasted changes of regime and ethnic balance. The debt of the Scottish language to Anglian influence is manifest in our present 'Lallans' speech, however short-lived the Anglian rule in a province such as Kyle.

We must admit quite openly that our knowledge of this vast tract of Scottish history is fragmentary in the extreme. After all, the period during which the Anglians held Galloway was in the region of 250 years – from the mid-seventh century to 900 at the latest. Whole population movements could have taken place in one of the yawning gaps in our information. We would be none the wiser. It has to be said that although the fact of ethnic and linguistic change is clear, the chronological order in which and the political conditions under which these changes took place are obscure.

Columba

The third great religious, linguistic and ethnic influence upon the Ayrshire region during and after the Dark Ages was, of course, the Gaelic, represented in ecclesiastical terms by the presence of St Columba and the Celtic Church and, politically, by the kingdom of Dalriada. It is a little strange, perhaps, to understand that 'Scots', the name of the people of 'Scotland', originally meant 'Irishmen', even perhaps 'Irish pirates'. Scottish and Irish Gaelic were virtually identical until the fifteenth century. The Gaelic-speaking Scottish kingdom called Dalriada (or, more properly, Dal Riata) had seemingly started as a colony situated on the west coast of Scotland settled from an Irish kingdom of the same name (in County Antrim) about 450.[54]

Columba, the most notable of missionaries to Scotland, was originally an Irish prince. Thanks to one of his successors as abbot, Adamnan (or Adomnan), we have some reliable data about Columba's later life as a holy man and a diplomat, but the first part of his life has had to be reconstructed from fleeting hints and references. Reading between Adamnan's lines, we can conjecture that it was because of some misdemeanour, perhaps in battle, that Columba was in fact exiled from Ireland. He seems to have taken a large company to the bleak and inhospitable western isles of Scotland, with the vigour and leadership which characterised his later career. He also appears to have been a first-rate diplomat with prestige and authority, and travelled back to Ireland on many occasions in connection with state as well as ecclesiastical affairs.

Columba confined his primary religious activities to the south-west of Scotland, notwithstanding his well-publicised efforts to evangelise the northern Picts at their headquarters at Craig Phadraig near Inverness, at the other end of the Great Glen, an expedition along which involved him in the first recorded encounter with the Loch Ness monster. Columba's influence, however, spread far and wide beyond the home monastery of Iona, which he may have established as early as 565 or 563 (although he may have spent some time before the foundation of Iona on another, unidentified island called Hinba). The church that he established or helped to establish is often described as the Celtic Church, as opposed to the Roman Church, which came to Scotland as it were in Anglo-Saxon or Anglian garb, transmitted through the Augustinian establishment.

The Celtic version of Christianity in Scotland competed, then, with the Roman system of belief, and was perhaps unfairly jostled out of position. Columba died in 597. In 664 the ecclesiastical convention known as the Synod of Whitby took place in Northumbria, and during this meeting the Celtic Church, which had derived directly from the Irish matrix, was wrong-footed on a number of theological and ecclesiastical issues – the observance of Easter, the tonsure, and various matters of church organisation. It took nearly half a century for the Celtic Church to adopt Roman practices in these matters (in 712), and in the meantime its influence was diminished. In 717, their 'star pupils', the Picts under King Nechtan, expelled them across the mountains to the west, in favour of the Northumbrian Church. In the west especially, however, the Celtic tradition persisted and traces can be found in Ayrshire as elsewhere.

How are Celtic religious sites in Ayrshire to be distinguished from, say, those where Northumbrian or Anglian influence dominated (remembering that Oswald the Northumbrian Christianiser had formed his ideas under Celtic influence)? The answer is often to be found in the language in which the dedication is framed. Place-names in which the element *Kirk* occurs are often Norse i.e. Christianised Viking in origin, but perhaps Anglian in certain areas of south-west Scotland. Gaelic names originating directly from the Celtic ministry and tradition, on the other hand, often contain the element *Kil-* and refer to Irish saints. So **Kirkmichael** and **Kirkoswald**, both located significantly in Carrick, may well be Anglian-Northumbrian rather than Norse, but in Cuninghame **Kilmarnock** and **Kilwinning** (in its Christian guise) are Gaelic in formation and thus likely to be of the Celtic Church. 'Kilmarnock' is *Kil-mo-Ernock,* where the particle *mo-* is a typically Gaelic honorific corresponding to 'my' i.e. 'my little', 'my dear' or even 'my revered', in fact to the English 'Saint': 'the church or cell of St Ernock or Ernene' – St Ernene being (perhaps) one of St Columba's younger contemporaries.[55] Other Irish saints commemorated in northern Ayrshire include Bridget ('**Kilbride**') and the adventurous Brendan ('**Kilbirnie**').

There are a number of sites in the Girvan valley in northern Carrick which may indicate a Celtic connection: **Killochan** ('the church of Onchu'),[56] Kilkerran ('the church of Ciaran'),[57] and **Kilhenzie** or Kilkenzie ('the church of Cainnech').[58] A recent investigation near Kilkerran has recovered evidence of an ancient church precinct at **Machar-i-Kill**, a name of unusual formation seeming to indicate the patronage of St Machar, another Celtic saint, who is known from a dedication in Old Aberdeen.[59] **Dailly,** the parish in or near which this cluster of sites is found, derived its name from *Dalmulkerane,* 'the valley of the servant of St Ciaran'.[60] But **Kirkdominae**, 'the church of (?Our) Lady', on the upper reaches of the Stinchar in southern Carrick, seems to point by its formation to a Northumbrian foundation.[61]

In the deep south of Ayrshire, on the Water of Tig, is an isolated farm called Kilrenzie. This looks like a 'Cell of St Ringan [St Ninian]' and could possibly be a Gaelicisation of a Cymric Ninianic foundation.[62]

Gaelic farmers

In fact it is with the Gaelic layer of place-names that we begin to have a glimmering perception of 'ordinary' i.e. secular life – as opposed to religious and political developments – specifically in the Ayrshire area. This is mediated through two Gaelic name-elements in particular – the element *baile-*, meaning 'a dwelling', and giving us (in the south) the modern prefix 'Bal-', and the element *achadh*, meaning 'a field', and giving the modern 'Auchen-' or 'Auchin-'. These two elements show a distribution pattern corresponding to that of Gaelic settlements in early times. Below the Forth-Clyde line both elements are virtually confined to the south-west and display variations to their respective patterns corresponding to the administrative boundaries of Carrick of Galloway and Kyle and Cuninghame of Strathclyde respectively. A large number of 'Bal-' names is concentrated in Carrick, but a count of 'Auchen-' names (based on the one-inch OS map) gives a much higher total for the whole of the south-west than that of the 'Bal-' names. The 'Auchen-' names occur frequently north of the Doon, i.e. in the areas which became known as Kyle and Cuninghame, where 'Bal-' names are rare.[63] On the 1:25,000 ('Pathfinder') OS map of the Ballantrae and Colmonell area of Carrick, a casual glance reveals Ballantrae itself, Balkissock, Balrazzie, Balnowlart, Balhamie, Ballaird, Balcreuchan, Ballsalloch and Balloch, but only a few isolated examples of 'Auchen-' (Auchenflower; Auchairne). If, on the other hand, we look at the Ardrossan and Stevenston areas of Cuninghame on the same scale we discover **Auchenharvie**, Auchenmade, Auchenwinsey, Auchenskeith, Auchenkist, but only the single Ballees (north-east of West Kilbride). This sample, unscientific as it is, would help to indicate in the first place that, in the words of W. F. H. Nicolaisen, 'here, at one time or another, people whose language was Gaelic both lived in permanent, non-seasonal dwellings and tilled the soil, brought in the harvest, milled the corn, grazed the cattle, etc.';[64] in the second place it would seem to point to a much greater incidence of settled dwellings of the Gaelic speakers in Carrick in contrast to Kyle and Cuninghame where Gaelic speakers may well have tilled the soil, and have been hewers of wood and drawers of water, but were not the landowning Cymric-speaking farmers. This finding would chime with our historical perception that while (Northumbrian) Galloway was open to Gaelic and Norse penetration from the west and south-west, Strathclyde maintained its national and cultural integrity against all comers – including a seemingly catastrophic raid and capture of Dumbarton itself in 870 by the Norse-Irish Vikings from Dublin.

Vikings

The Vikings began to raid on the west coast of Scotland and further down towards England and Ireland about the end of the eighth century AD. This was part of an expansionist surge that took them as far afield as Russia, Constantinople, the Mediterranean, North America – and north-west France, where they settled and became 'the Normans' who were to conquer England 250 years later. When they first came to Britain in 793 they were entirely pagan and tended to regard the settled communities, and especially the religious foundations, simply as booty for the taking: in that year they sacked Lindisfarne, the monastery that had nurtured the writing of the Venerable Bede.

Much about the Vikings has been debated, whether they were merely bloodthirsty robbers or canny merchants who doubled as settlers. The truth is surely that they were both, depending upon opportunities and circumstances. They have been accused of remaining pagan, 'suckled in a creed outworn' longer than their civilized victims, and raiding, sacking and murdering for plunder's sake. However, in spite of the alleged disadvantages of worshipping Thor, Odin, Freya and the rest, the Vikings developed a legal system that gave the people a coherent identity and sophisticated control even under paganism. This is not inconsistent with a manic, almost psychopathic ferocity in dealings with foreigners and other enemies. The sagas, in fact, bloodthirsty though they are, display a balanced secularity that gives rise to a tragic awareness comparable to that of the literature of the classical Greeks (though admittedly the saga stories were not current among the Norsemen till much later than the period of Viking raids). The lack of Christianity, of course, was very bad news for the foundations at Lindisfarne, Iona and elsewhere. Blathmac and his followers, courting martyrdom in Iona at the hands of the Norsemen, found it in 825 in a particularly repugnant atrocity accompanied by frenzied looting. By then, however, the main community had long withdrawn to Ireland.

Though written sources are silent on the precise area and extent of Norse penetration and settlement in the south-west of Scotland, place-names as ever give us some notion. The great regions of Norse settlement in Scotland are of course the western and northern islands – in the latter of which Norse peasant colonisation was so intense as to obliterate all traces of previous culture. However, substantial settlement appears to have taken place in the Dumfries region, and to some extent along the Solway and Ayrshire coasts (Carrick, Kyle and Cuninghame). If we look at the map of Ayrshire we can see sites with Scandinavian-type names – Busbie, Sorbie and Cumbrae near Ardrossan, Crosby near Troon, three Fell Hills and the Balrazzie Fells south of Girvan. But these examples also show that the Norse elements occur conjoined with words of other linguistic background, and that assignation of any of these names to any one linguistic group is bound to be dubious. Nothing like a clear block of names of one sort or another exists in any district and we must recognise that communities of different ethnic backgrounds existed side by side, in a true 'melting-pot' of nationalities: Anglian, Scandinavian and Gaelic. The Cymric culture and language seem to have had an inner weakness of some sort, because they fade very quickly from the picture except in the north, where the rule of the Strathclyde kings continued in Kyle and Cuninghame.

The impression to be obtained from linguistic evidence in the Ayrshire districts between 650 and 1050 is not so much one of successive inundations of genocidal hordes (in spite of a fairly continuous series of battles and associated political changes) as of a gradual infiltration and peaceful mingling of peoples resulting in a slow metamorphosis of language and culture. In the end the English speech of Northumbria seems to have won out, although Gaelic was spoken extensively, especially in Carrick, until the middle of the seventeenth century. Scandinavian influence, though politically important, has vanished as thoroughly as Cymric, the original speech of the region.

3. THE POLITICAL FORERUNNERS OF AYRSHIRE

Strathclyde

The history of the two northern districts of the later Ayrshire, Kyle and Cuninghame, over the next few hundred years, from about 650 to 1050, is really that of Strathclyde, as the history of Carrick is that of Galloway. However, our knowledge of the political and constitutional history of these districts at this time is not just sketchy – it is nil. Reflections about what is known of Strathclyde's political and dynastic framework down to 1018 will be found in Appendix I. But even in this wider field hard knowledge is scanty in the extreme. The only constitutional fact that we really can be sure of in Dark Ages Ayrshire is that this region of south-west Scotland was ruled by a succession of kings. But we know of no specifically Ayrshire king except, perhaps, King Coel of Kyle.

Kenneth mac Alpin and Alba

A very brief outline, then, is all that we can give of this period of the Dark Ages. It seems that Dalriada, the Gaelic-speaking kingdom in the west, gradually gained hegemony over the Brythonic (Cymric- and Pictish-speaking) Strathclyde and Pictland. Perhaps under Viking pressure, the Dalriadan power-base migrated eastward at some time in the ninth century from Dunadd and Dunollie to Forteviot. Round about 850 a man called Kenneth mac Alpin inherited or conquered the central power of Pictland. The amalgam of Gaeldom and Pictland produced a strong state called Alba, centred north of the Forth–Clyde isthmus. Scone, originally a sacred centre of Pictland, became the place of king-making for Alba.

Strathclyde as a client kingdom

Strathclyde, initially strong in itself and based on the Rock of Dumbarton, 'the Dun of the Britons', gradually came under the influence of Alba. It suffered a devastating blow in 870 when a force of Norse–Irish Vikings from Dublin stormed and sacked Dumbarton and put to death the king, Arthgall. Yet, even after that, Strathclyde seems to have preserved a degree of independence, at least as witnessed by the successive names of Strathclyde kings, which are authentically British until 1018 when the death of King Ywain the Bald was recorded. However, long before that date Strathclyde had been in the position of a client state, and after Ywain was killed, it came completely under the control of Alba and the line of Kenneth mac Alpin. The fourteenth-century historian Fordun suggested that Strathclyde, as a sub-kingdom, was used as an 'appanage', a realm in which the nominated heir of the kingdom could as it were, train for the responsibilities of the major kingdom. Strathclyde became a perquisite of the mac Alpin crown princes of Alba.

The daughter of King Ywain the Bald, who was himself the great-grandson of the mac Alpin King Donald II of Alba, is reported to have married Duncan, Donald II's descendant in another branch; Duncan was apparently the (non-British) king of Strathclyde before graduating to become king of Alba after his grandfather Malcolm II.

Duncan was then killed by the famous Macbeth. Macbeth had married Gruoch ('Lady Macbeth'), who shared with Duncan a common ancestor in King Malcolm I. Macbeth in turn was killed in 1057, whereupon (after the 'interregnum' of Macbeth's son Lulach, who was killed in 1058) Duncan's son Malcolm became Malcolm III Canmore.

Malcolm Canmore and St Margaret

The foundations of Strathclyde's integration with Alba, or Scotia, as it came to be known, were really laid when King Malcolm III Canmore of Alba fell in love with a wise and devoutly Christian foreigner, the future St Margaret. She was half Hungarian and half Saxon, the grand-daughter of Edmund Ironside, brother of the English King Edward the Confessor, whose death in 1066 precipitated the Norman invasion and conquest of England. Edmund's son, Edward, who had been exiled by the Danish King Canute, Knut den Mektige, had married the Hungarian princess Agatha, and their children, including Margaret, had been brought up in the fervently Christian atmosphere of Hungary, which had just been converted from paganism by the great Saint Stephen (d. 1038). Margaret, her sister Christine and her brother Edgar the Atheling, returned to England where, after the 1066 Conquest, Edgar naturally attracted support, especially in the north of England, as a likely contender for the throne against the usurper William of Normandy. When Anglo-Saxon resistance crumbled in the north, Edgar and his sisters and mother fled north to Alba, where Malcolm Canmore, now a widower, married Margaret, probably in 1071.[65]

Margaret took up her new role as Queen Consort with a *mission civilatrice*. In the field of religion she underpinned and began the process of updating the infrastructure of traditional Scottish Christianity. But Margaret's own reforming activities were of relatively slight importance. More important was the fact that her political outlook had been heavily influenced by Norman culture, which had permeated the court of Edward the Confessor: this Norman influence decisively affected the characters and actions of her children, in particular the youngest, David.

Edgar, Alexander, David

Malcolm Canmore and Margaret had no less than six sons and two daughters. Three of the sons succeeded to the throne of Scotia-Alba –

Edgar (the nephew of Edgar the Atheling), Alexander and David. All three kings were heavily dependent upon the support of Norman England, at least at the beginning of their respective reigns. This virtual client status in one sense contrasted with and in another continued the hostility between Malcolm Canmore and the Normans, which culminated in the deaths of Malcolm and his second son Edward following a raid on Northumbria.[66] Edgar, after the elimination of various contenders,[67] was finally established on the throne through English military intervention in 1097. Edgar acceded to the Scottish throne as a vassal of William II Rufus of England, and his sister, Matilda, married William's brother King Henry I of England in 1100. When Edgar died in 1107 his brother King Alexander, a strong man in his own right, was closely tied to England and served under Henry I against Wales in 1114. David, the youngest brother, was a powerful baron at the English court, possessing by marriage large estates in Huntingdon (of which he became earl) and elsewhere in the English Midlands.

Scotland, Strathclyde and the Anglo-Normans

David was the heir apparent after Alexander. Alexander's predecessor, King Edgar, had bequeathed to David a vast tract of land in southern Scotland, including Strathclyde, as an appanage. David got possession of his inheritance about 1113, only after threatening his brother Alexander with invasion from England. Then, when he succeeded as David I to the throne of Alba in 1124, he set in motion Strathclyde's fusion with that kingdom. This integration was implemented by a complete overhaul of the ruling institutions of what was now to become Scotland, involving a heavy infiltration of Anglo-Normans into positions of power, and redistribution of land to the king's Norman friends. The country was brought under feudal control – a system which is historically associated with the Norman conquerors of England and which in both England and Scotland led to the dispossession of native i.e. Celtic and Saxon landholders (though not universally). Feudal lords and their descendants undertook to hold lands in return for military service and the rendering of homage to the king.

The assimilation of Strathclyde, including Kyle and Cuninghame

The process of Norman penetration extended over at least three reigns – that of David I himself, and his two grandsons Malcolm IV and William I ('the Lion'). Associated in particular with David I were the Normans Robert de Brus, Hugh de Morville and Walter fitz Alan. De Morville and de Brus were both Normans by birth, but fitz Alan was was a first-generation Shropshireman whose family was from Brittany. The most wealthy and powerful of these was undoubtedly de Brus, who was a supporter of Henry I of England, and who already had extensive estates in Yorkshire. De Morville had lands in the Honour of Huntingdon. Fitz Alan was a younger son who made his fortune by entering the service of the Scottish king.

Strathclyde, including Cuninghame and Kyle, was divided on a feudal basis between these three men and the king. It is noteworthy how the territory of Southern Scotland was allocated in adjacent strips of alternate ownership. From south-east to north-west the division of territory was (roughly) as follows:

Lauderdale and parts of Tweeddale	de Morville
Annandale	de Brus
Nithsdale (from 1165)	the King
Borgue (from 1165)	(Hugh II) de Morville
southern Kyle ('Kyle Regis')	the King
northern Kyle ('Kyle Stewart')	fitz Alan
Cuninghame	de Morville
Strathgryfe (roughly = Renfrewshire)	fitz Alan.

Some of these district names were probably inherited from Strathclyde, where they may have been given the generic name of *kadrez*, a Cymric term cognate with the English territorial word 'hundred'.

The kings complemented territorial awards with honorific titles confirming the status of the Norman incomers, and some of these titles survive as family names to this day. David I bestowed on fitz Alan the title of Steward of the kingdom, and the style was adopted by the family as a name, Stewart, which later became the surname of the Scottish royal house. Territory on the River Ayr was awarded to a man called Hubertus or Herbertus, the royal chamberlain or *camerarius*: this title is the origin of the name Chalmers. De Morville became Constable of Scotland, but the de Morville line became extinct early and no names were derived from that family or office. Many well-known family names local to Ayrshire came into existence at the period of the Norman feudalisation of Scotland, the most obvious example being Bruce. Others include Lockhart (from Loccard, a Flemish family), Cumming (from Comyn) and Montgomerie (from Mundecumberi, a Norman family whose name includes the element *-cumberi* or *-cymri*, indicating a previous Welsh connection still seen in the old county name Montgomeryshire).

Precise dating of the feudalization of the dismembered Strathclyde, especially at the very beginning, is virtually impossible. The awards of territory indicated above are known to have taken place after 1124 but just when is most uncertain. Probably the award of Annandale to de Brus was the earliest, on or very soon after David I's accession to the Alban throne in 1124.[68] The dating of the awards specific to Ayrshire is much less certain. Fitz Alan came to Scotland in or shortly after 1136, but his territorial awards were made later in at least two separate grants, the second of which, made by Malcolm IV, included North Kyle; his elevation to the status of Steward of Scotland, however, he owed to David I. De Morville, the Constable of Scotland and a close associate of David I, seems to have received Cuninghame and the other territories at some time between these two grants, possibly nearer the beginning of David I's reign. Perhaps we ought to see the division of Strathclyde territory in the light of a series of vacant lots to be taken up by suitable potential magnates as they drifted or were invited north from England, or acquired further merit in Scotland.

Galloway and Carrick

Carrick was not included in this settlement. Galloway, of which Carrick was a part to begin with, was still virtually independent. At the time of the initial settlements Carrick would count as hostile territory, and it is significant that the king reserved for himself for defensive purposes the strip of Kyle that runs along the northern rim of Carrick.

Galloway, it will be recalled, had been under Anglo-Saxon, Northumbrian control until the end of the ninth century. Thereafter rule seems to have passed to people of mixed Scandinavian and Gaelic blood who were associated with the consolidation of Norwegian control over the Western Isles and other territories including Argyll, the Isle of Man and Dublin. It was a mixed force of 'Irish Vikings' that sacked the Rock of Alcluit, Dumbarton, in 870. The name Galloway itself may be derived from the Gall-ghàidhil, the 'stranger Gaels' whose ravages complemented and succeeded those of the Vikings. The language of Galloway became firmly Gaelic, although isolated place-names indicate small pockets of Norse, Anglian and Cymric survivals. Details are sparse and unclear, but it is probably true to say that the first ruler of the region whose name we have, Fergus, prince of Galloway, was of mingled Scandinavian and Gaelic descent, and that the family originated in the Scandinavianised Western Isles of Scotland. The family name was probably MacDowel.

Fergus, Lord, Prince, or even King of Galloway ('*rex Galwitensium*'), reigned from about 1120 to 1160, while his contemporary David I reigned as King of Alba/Scotland only from 1124 to 1153. The territory which Fergus ruled included the modern Wigtownshire and Kirkcudbrightshire as well as Carrick. Carrick became detached from Galloway in the following (complicated) manner.

During the reign of David I relations with Fergus of Galloway had been relatively good. David died in 1153 and was succeeded in the first place by his grandson Malcolm, the fourth king of that name in the line of Kenneth mac Alpin. Malcolm IV was not a strong king, and in 1157 the mighty Henry II of England forced him to give up the southern portion of Cumbria centring round Carlisle, previously in the possession of Strathclyde. This weakened the Scottish king's position regarding Galloway. Then, disagreements arose between the Scottish earls and Malcolm IV, culminating in a siege and showdown between the king and the earls at Perth in 1160. It is possible that Fergus was one of the besieging earls. After and perhaps as a part of a general settlement, Malcolm marched into Galloway at the head of an army and defeated Fergus, who retired and became a canon of Holyrood Abbey, dying shortly afterwards.

This left the realm of Galloway to be partitioned between Fergus's two sons, Gilbert and Uchtred. Uchtred held the eastern portion, including the modern Kirkcudbrightshire. Gilbert held the territory west of the river Cree, that is, the modern Wigtownshire, and north of the Galloway Burn, Carrick, which extended as far north again as the River Doon. The two brothers hated each other virulently. Uchtred, the elder, leant more towards the Anglo-Norman way of life of his Cumbrian neighbours, among whom he still held property although Cumbria had been annexed to England in 1157. He had married off his son Roland to Elena de Morville, sister of the Constable of Scotland. Gilbert seems to have been more conservative, with ambitions to control the whole territory of Galloway.[69]

Malcolm IV died in 1165, to be succeeded by his brother, William I ('the Lion'), who wished to regain Cumbria and to control Northumbria. William saw his opportunity in 1174, while Henry II was preoccupied with the rebellion of his sons, and marched into the north of England. Unfortunately King William was captured by the English. Uchtred and Gilbert, who had marched with him, retreated to Galloway and issued an urgent plea to Henry II to allow them to transfer their loyalty from the Scots to himself. Gilbert then set about the wholesale expulsion of all Scots and Normans from Galloway and, before Henry could reply to the brothers' offer, seized Uchtred's stronghold in the east of the country and mutilated his brother, who died of his injuries.

It is not recorded whether Henry was distressed by the news of the death of Uchtred, to whom he was related, but he was so angry that after concluding a peace on his terms with the Scots (including feudal superiority over King William), he liberated the captive king and ordered him as his vassal to capture and subdue Gilbert. William brought Gilbert to Henry in October 1176, and Gilbert managed to reconcile himself with Henry, delivering his son Duncan as a hostage as well as paying a substantial fine.

Galloway then seems to have continued to be partitioned between Gilbert and Uchtred's son Roland until Gilbert's death in 1185. After this event Roland invaded and occupied Gilbert's territory in the west, massacring the chief officials and nobles. This conduct provoked both King William and King Henry II to mount expeditions against Roland – Henry in the interests of Gilbert's son Duncan – but Roland seems to have managed to keep them at bay until the Bishop of Glasgow succeeded in mediating between them and negotiating terms. In the end both eastern and western Galloway – Kirkcudbright and Wigtown – would remain with Roland as

Uchtred's heir, but Duncan was awarded Carrick in compensation. Carrick thereafter was separately integrated with Scotland, and Duncan, in the next century, was promoted to the status of Earl of Carrick.

4. THE FIRST OUTLINES OF THE SHIRE

Royal control

The next stage in the integration of the south-west came in 1196 after the death of the childless William de Morville, Constable of Scotland and Lord of Cuninghame. Roland, son of Uchtred and Lord of (residual) Galloway, had married de Morville's sister Elena, and de Morville's estates in Scotland, including Cuninghame, devolved upon Roland in right of his wife. A very extensive stretch of the south-western seaboard of Scotland thus came under the control of the grandchildren of Fergus, Prince of Galloway. King William the Lion riposted strategically by planting a new castle in Ayr midway between Carrick and Cuninghame in 1197, one year after de Morville's death, and later, some time between 1202 and 1207, by erecting a royal burgh in Ayr with a sheriffdom. This created a form for Ayrshire, even though it did not have much substance to begin with.

Tightening feudal control in Kyle and Cuninghame

Immediately the primary apportionments of territory had been made, the recipients, now 'tenants-in-chief' of the king, set about the 'subinfeudation' of the land, that is to say, appointing lesser vassals, each with their own charters, to smaller parcels of territory, baronies, for which these vassals had to do service for the feudal superior, within the respective provinces. Each vassal had to erect a motte-and-bailey castle, a large earthen mound surmounted by wooden fortifications, at a conveniently strong point in their district, which coincided with a parish or parishes.

A motte, a typically early-Norman kind of fortification, was basically a mound, either artificial or natural or both i.e. the motte builders could take advantage of a natural knoll or hillock, or of a pre-existing Iron Age fort. The construction may well have been of layers of earth rammed down to leave a level space of varying dimensions at the top. Often, as at **Dalmellington** or **Tarbolton**, the effect would be of an inverted dumpling. There was a palisade surrounding the motte either at the bottom or at the top. On the top of the mound there was a fortified wooden tower, sometimes built on stilts, from which archers could fire arrows in all directions. Sometimes, at one side of the mound, a ditch would loop outwards, with a stockade or other fortification atop the upcast earth, forming a ground-level forecourt for the motte; this was the bailey, which could serve as an advanced fighting position or as shelter for civilians or stock in time of danger. Illustrations of such motte fortifications (without the bailey) are to be found in the Bayeux Tapestry, particularly in the representation of Bayeux itself and in that of Hastings.[70]

Sometimes the motte-and-bailey ground plan would resemble a figure-of-eight; sometimes the bailey would encompass the whole motte with the mound rising at one end of the courtyard. This design of fortress obviously looks back to Iron Age forts such as **Harpercroft** or **Craigie** – or indeed to Traprain Law. It also looks forward to stone-built 'castles of enceinte' such as **Loch Doon Castle,** basically a looping oval or other formation of high stone walls within which wooden or stone buildings stood at one end.

Sometimes we encounter bailey-like structures by themselves, i.e. 'ringworks' such as that at **Alloway**. These are simple circular or subcircular earthworks, with a ditch and upcast rampart and, rather than a mound, a central area at a lower height than the rampart but above the external ground level. Some may have been constructed considerably before the advent of the Normans in Scotland.

The original families can in many cases be identified, although King Robert the Bruce later redistributed territories belonging to families who had chosen the wrong side during the Wars of Independence. Many mottes, as well as later stone castles, still exist throughout Ayrshire, marking off the boundaries between one family feu and another.

Marking off the boundaries

The divisions between the provinces or bailiaries of Ayrshire mostly follow major river lines: South Kyle ('King's Kyle', 'Kyle Regis') lies roughly between the River Doon and the River Ayr, and major tributaries on the upper reaches of the Ayr. North Kyle ('Kyle Stewart') lies between the Ayr and the Water of Irvine. Cuninghame lies between the Irvine and the complicated system of burns and other landmarks that starts in the north-west with the Kelly Burn, the North Rotten Burn and the Calder Water. Carrick lies south of the Doon and north and west of the Galloway Burn, the Carrick Burn and the River Cree (to name but three of many).

The precise delimitation of the four bailiaries is of some interest. One border-post in the east of Carrick was **Dalmellington**, where a very impressive motte-and-bailey castle was built, the mound towering over the town to this day. This was on the south side of the Muck Water, which joins the River Doon from the east about two kilometres below the town. The baron who built Dalmellington motte and was awarded the lands of Dalmellington was Thomas Colville, a vassal of Duncan, Lord of Carrick.[71] The implication of this is that Dalmellington south of the Muck was, at least in the beginning, a Carrick possession, and not in King's Kyle, as would appear from Strawhorn's account.[72] The possibility of a later 'adjustment' in favour of King's Kyle may help to explain or at least to contextualise the fierce contention between King's Kyle and Carrick, of which **Loch Doon Castle**, another sensitive border point to the south of Dalmellington, was the focus for many centuries.[73]

The southern limit of Carrick lies just north of Loch Ryan at the mouth of Glen App at Lacht (Laight) Alpin. Lacht Alpin, 'the grave of Alpin', is the place where Alpin, the father of Kenneth mac Alpin, the unifier of the Picts and Scots, is reputed to have been killed in 841 after a destructive raid into Galloway.[74] The place-name occurs in the charter of the royal burgh of Ayr as that of one of the customs posts assigned to the burgh, and for many years it was assumed to refer to **Laight Castle** in King's Kyle, a remote earthwork north-west of Dalmellington. This would cut Carrick out of the customs area of Ayr, and it was assumed that this was because Carrick was still counted a hostile territory in the early thirteenth century.[75] However, Carrick seems to have been received into the fold perhaps as early as 1186, and it would seem appropriate to have a toll-house just north of the now divided property called respectively Little and Meikle Laight. This idea is strengthened by the presence at **Little Laight** of a very ancient standing stone, which at some more recent epoch was christened **The Taxing Stone**, beside the March or Galloway Burn.[76] It is probable that Carrick would be within the early trading precinct of Ayr, and this precinct, coinciding with the sheriffdom, would be the germ of the modern Ayrshire.

The south-eastern customs post mentioned in the charter of the foundation of Ayr, Crosenecon, may well have been the ancient and mysterious **Kyle Castle** or Dalblair Castle, now a mere column of stone atop an Iron Age British earthwork on a promontory at the confluence of the Guelt and Glenmuir Waters. Kyle Castle was clearly a defensive post and could well have been a customs post monitoring access to the north-west from Nithsdale. It stands today at the junction of (the former) Ayrshire, Lanarkshire and Dumfriesshire, under the shadow of the Three-Shire Hill, adjacent to Corsencon Hill at the head of Nithsdale.[77]

Just west of Dalblair along the Glenmuir Water is **Dornal Motte** (not certainly an Anglo-Norman motte), on the Kyle Stewart bank, for the Glenmuir and the Lugar mark the eastern boundary between the two Kyles. Dornal may have been part of the sheep-farming Melrose monks' estate or 'grange' centred on Mauchline, where their administrative office was called **Mauchline Castle**, although it was evidently not intended as a seriously defensive installation. Further north the eccentric eastern border of Kyle Stewart is marked by the mound of **Main Castle** south of Darvel. South again, at a sharp turn in the border, we come to Distinkhorn Hill – nothing to do with the stinkhorn mushroom, but 'The Hill of the House (-horn) of the Dish-Thegn' – the *dapifer* or steward, who at ceremonial feasts would on bended knee present the king with his golden goblet.

Among the Norman, Flemish and other families that settled in Ayrshire were the Barclays (in Ardrossan and Kilbirnie), the Hunters (in Hunterston), the Rosses (in Portincross, Tarbet etc), the Cuninghames (founded by 'Robertus filius Wernebaldi' in Kilmaurs), the Lockharts (Simon Loccard in Symington, Stephen Loccard in Stevenston, Richard Loccard in Riccarton, and Malcolm Loccard in Kilmarnock) and the Colvilles (in Ochiltree and Dalmellington). Each of these families, and many others, had their own barony with a castle, burgh and parish church and/or a chapel-of-ease.

Religious corporations and parishes in the three deaneries of Ayrshire:
Cuninghame, Kyle (Stewart and King's) and Carrick

Side by side and integrated with the secular regrouping of the lands of Scotland under Norman feudalism, there was a determined and successful effort to bring the country under an even geographical spread of Christian discipline: a parochial system organised into groups of parishes, each with serving priest and local church, supporting and being supported by strategically placed central religious houses. The control exercised by the central abbeys and cathedrals as well as by the parish priests was eminently practical: a system of taxation in kind – tributes of foodstuffs and farming produce, commuted here and there into monetary payments. Secular feudal lords were expected to and did erect parish and other churches and to exercise rights of patronage over them, and, in the case of tenants-in-chief and other magnates, to give large tracts of land to the monasteries or to individual churches. The result was that all the religious 'corporations' became major landowners with considerable political influence throughout Scotland. The grounding of religious bodies in the secular business of provincial land tenure was doubtless intended to weave Christianity securely into the texture of the newly feudalised state, and in this we must see the influence of the energetic and ingenious David I.

It has been claimed that the system of 'appropriation', whereby a sometimes very large proportion of the revenues of each individual church was annexed to the central institutions, led to the impoverishment of the parishes, the downgrading of the serving clergy, and ultimately to the crying abuses which provoked the Protestant Reformation. This may have been the case with the later development of the pre-Reformation Church, where tithing was carried to extremes and where a system of delegation of the individual cures led to a great dilution of the serving clergy.[78] In the beginning, however, it cannot be doubted that the integration of feudal land-ownership and the parish system resulted in a deep, effective Christianisation at the 'grassroots' level, where religion may have had an uncertain grip before.

Christian feudalism permeated every corner of the country, to such an extent that one might say a new state had been born. The parochial framework laid down in Scotland in the twelfth century is still visible and largely intact (though of lesser importance) to this day, despite the Reformation, the later decline in the number of practising Christians, and numerous recent local government reorganisations. In Ayrshire, the principal religious houses exercising control over the parishes – Paisley,

Kilwinning, Melrose and Crossraguel Abbeys, as well as Glasgow Cathedral – were destroyed or transformed at the time of the Reformation, but here as elsewhere the parishes survive to the present day with relatively slight alterations.

The deanery of Cuninghame

The dates of the foundation of the Ayrshire abbeys are in doubt because the original documents have vanished. Timothy Pont, who saw the cartulary of **Kilwinning Abbey** in the early seventeenth century, claimed that the founder was Richard, the second de Morville Constable. If this is accurate, other confirmatory evidence may point to 1187, two years before Richard's death, as the actual foundation date, and 1191 as the date of the papal confirmation.[79]

Kilwinning was a Tironensian[80] foundation, and it speedily became the most opulent religious institution in Ayrshire. All parishes in Cuninghame 'belonged' to Kilwinning,[81] that is to say, each paid to the monastery a tribute in kind, part of which could be leased to a local laird or magnate in exchange for cash payment; in return the monks arranged for a secular priest to take on the actual service of the cure of the parish. The collegiate church in **Kilmaurs** was outside this arrangement, because it paid its tribute to Kelso Abbey.

The deanery of Kyle: (i) Kyle Stewart

Fitz Alan founded Paisley Priory – later Paisley Abbey – in Strathgryfe (which, as 'Renfrewshire' remained outside Ayrshire) in about 1167. Paisley was a Cluniac foundation, with monks drawn from Wenlock in England. It controlled many of the parish churches of Ayrshire. Fitz Alan also granted extensive lands in Mauchline in the east of Ayrshire to the Cistercian abbey of Melrose, and those lands became a large source of revenue to the abbey through extensive sheep-breeding.

The attachment of parishes in Kyle Stewart was more complicated than in Cuninghame; the Stewards – or as they became known, (the) Stewarts – spread their gifts widely. **Auchinleck, Craigie, Monkton** ('Monk's Prestwick') and **Prestwick** ('Prestwickburgh') were all appropriated to Paisley. But Walter II the Stewart attempted to found a convent at **Dalmilling** in the east of Ayr in 1229 and gave the foundation four parishes, **St Quivox, Dundonald, Riccarton** and **Crosby**. The Dalmilling venture collapsed in 1238 – the canons and nuns seem to have disliked the weather in Ayr and to have returned to Yorkshire whence they had come – and the four parishes together with the land and property at Dalmilling went, or perhaps reverted, to Paisley Abbey. With greater success, a monastery at **Fail** or Failford was founded, probably by Alexander the Stewart, in 1252, and it was allocated the parishes of **Galston, Barnweill** and **Symington**. Fail continued to enjoy the revenues of these parishes until the Reformation:

> The Friars of Fail
> gat never oure hard eggs or oure thin kale
> for they made their eggs thin wi butter
> and their kale thick wi bread;
> and the Friars of Fail they made gude kale
> on Fridays when they fasted,
> and they never wanted gear enough
> as long as their neighbours' lasted.[82]

These monks were Red Friars, Mathurines from Paris, and their task in life seems to have been the buying out of serfs held in local and other servitude; they were styled *fratres de redemptione captivorum*. Their function seems to have continued after the Reformation well into the seventeenth century.[83] No trace of the actual monastery remains except in place-names, e.g. the farm-name Spittalside (NS 424 277) north of Tarbolton, marking a hospital run by the Red Friars for the relief of the indigent and ailing.

Tarbolton parish in Kyle Stewart was originally appropriated first to Fail and then to Melrose, but in 1429 it was erected into a prebend of Glasgow Cathedral.

The deanery of Kyle: (ii) King's Kyle ('Kyle Regis')

In Ayr, the **Kirk of St John** itself was under the patronage of the crown and it constituted a 'prebend' of Glasgow Cathedral i.e. a member of the chapter of that cathedral derived his stipend from the fruits of the vicarage of Ayr and was styled a 'prebendary'. The prebend was established in the fourteenth century. Earlier references in legal and ecclesiastical documents indicate that the church had an important connection with Paisley Abbey, as if it had been established by the Stewart. The earliest of these references is dated 1233, less than thirty years after the likely foundation of the royal burgh. The fact that it was the king who chartered the burgh, however, may indicate that he founded the church too. It seems that the church was later gifted to the monks at Melrose by royal charter dated 27 January 1357, which would chime with the known fact that the same monks had long before been awarded fisheries at the mouths of the Rivers Ayr and Doon respectively, at the same time as Walter II the Stewart had gifted his demesne at Mauchline (which included the source of the River Ayr) to Melrose. However, neither the 1357 (David II) charter in favour of Melrose nor its confirmation in 1382 (Robert II) seems to have interfered with St John's long-term connection with Glasgow Cathedral.[84] Later, at the beginning of the sixteenth century, King James IV, who had enlarged the Chapel Royal at Stirling, arranged no less than six prebends for the chapel from the Kirk of Ayr (two of these in fact from Coylton Parish).

A small parish to the south of Ayr, **Alloway**, was also annexed by

James IV as a prebend for his Chapel Royal at Stirling, as were Dalrymple and Dalmellington. Cumnock was a prebend of Glasgow Cathedral and Ochiltree was annexed to Melrose Abbey.

The deanery of Carrick

Due to the political history of the place, the deanery of Carrick had a number of special features. While the integration of Kyle and Cunninghame began soon after 1124 under David I, Carrick had to undergo a number of different evolutions beginning with the abdication of Fergus, Prince of Galloway in 1160 and ending in 1185/6 with the award of Carrick to Duncan fitz Gilbert (see above). Duncan was admitted (later, in 1220) to the establishment of earls of Scotland, and like all post-Davidian lords and earls, he was anxious to set up a monastery in his own bailiary. He gave land near Maybole for the purpose and even erected a small oratory but was frustrated in his endeavours to make a larger institution by the squabbles over status and the general procrastination of the people he had chosen to realize the project: the Abbey of Paisley. In the end he was unable to establish **Crossraguel** as a free-standing autonomous monastery (i.e. not a 'cell' of Paisley) until six years before his death in 1250.

During Duncan's lordship and later, Carrick, with the rest of Galloway, gave allegiance to the bishopric of Glasgow. There were also connections with the priory at Whithorn and the Cistercian nunnery at North Berwick, probably going back to the times when the kingdom of Northumbria extended its rule into Lothian and as far west as the ancient sub-Novantan kingdom of Rheged. As a result, the allocation of parishes was complicated. **Maybole** and the northern parish of **Kirkbride** (now united with Maybole) were both given to the North Berwick nunnery, with whom they stayed until the Reformation. **Kirkoswald** ('of Turnberry'), **Straiton**, and **Dailly** (**'Dalmaolkeran'**) were given to Paisley Abbey on condition that the monks would establish a Cluniac monastery in Carrick. The Paisley monks dragged their feet on this undertaking for half a century, and when Crossraguel itself was built, Duncan transferred these three parishes direct to Crossraguel in spite of the grumbling of Paisley. **Ballantrae ('Old Kirkcudbright-Innertig'** [there was a church of St Cuthbert near the mouth of the Water of Tig in Ballantrae]) and **Girvan** were added to the abbey's estate later, probably in the thirteenth century.[85] **Kirkmichael ('of Gemilstoun')** belonged to the priory at Whithorn. **Colmonell**, however, belonged to Glasgow Cathedral from a very early date.

Some Ayrshire parishes have been split up, like Straiton, Cumnock and Mauchline; others have been combined, like Maybole and Kirkbride. Most of these changes took place after the Reformation, in the seventeenth century. Essentially, however, the parish structure of Ayrshire has remained the same for more than 800 years.

Lesser religious corporations in Ayrshire

A number of smaller institutions also grew up throughout Ayrshire. All the buildings have now vanished save for a few vestigial remains. Besides the hospital run by the Red Friars at Fail, there was a leper hospital at **Kingcase** in Prestwick, possibly of very early foundation, and **St Leonard's Hospital and Chapel** south of Ayr. The **Preceptory of Our Lady Kirk of Kyle** stood near the present Prestwick Airport, and was the scene of a disputed marriage between King Robert II and his longtime mistress Elizabeth Mure of Rowallan in 1347. Of greater importance were the establishments of preaching friars ('**Blackfriars**', Dominican, and '**Greyfriars**', Franciscan, side by side in Ayr on the south bank of the river). The Ayr Dominicans were established by 1250 and the Franciscans in 1474. **Irvine (Fullarton) Friary** was established by the Carmelites (White Friars). Apparently there was also a monastery at **Loch Fergus** in Coylton Parish, perhaps connected with Fergus, Prince of Galloway, but although the remains were reputed to be visible on the wooded island in the loch some centuries ago, nothing is now marked on the OS map.

All these institutions were closely connnected with the secular feudal establishment of Ayrshire. Crossraguel lay in the same parish (Kirkoswald) as the Carrick *caput* at Turnberry; Kilwinning and Irvine are adjacent, as are Prestwick and Dundonald, and Ayr Castle seems to have shared a site with the original Kirk of St John. They were richly endowed with landed property and commercial privileges, yet they do not seem to have been bad or oppressive landlords. Rapacity did not overcome the owners of land until the Reformation. At that time the secular lords decided that if the old system of church ownership was to be dismantled, they might as well claw back the donations which their ancestors had traditionally made to the abbeys and churches. Hence, it seems, the ferocious extortion of the abbey lands of Crossraguel from Alan Stewart, the commendator of the abbey, by Gilbert, fourth Earl of Cassillis in 1570. Cassillis tortured the commendator with fire in the Black Hole of Dunure until he had signed away the property. Admittedly the commendator, being the consummate rogue and asset-stripper he was, had already signed documents with Gilbert and had attempted to renegue upon the agreement. This awareness merely reinforces the impression of overpowering secular greed for ecclesiastical lands unleashed as a consequence of the Reformation.

The burghs

A third element in the administrative remodelling of Scotland under Norman influence was the characteristically Scottish institution of royal and baronial burghs – commercially privileged settlements chartered and designated for urban development. This was the beginning in Scotland of true town life – if not of strictly bourgeois life. There had never been urban clusters of trading activity in Scotland before. Now, besides the military framework represented by the feudal nobles in their castles and the religious presence of the monasteries and parishes, the burghs were established in order to foster economic growth through the conferring of mercantile privileges such as the right to hold markets and fairs and the right to collect customs dues throughout a given area. Urban concentrations of particular professions and trades followed, and were associated with an enhancement of the ancient functions of the sheriff. In these development may be seen the germ of a middle class and of a reformed legal system, as well as of the changed concept of a shire.

Hugh de Morville, or perhaps one of his successors,[86] chose **Irvine** as the *caput*, the military centre of Cuninghame, and Kilwinning as the principal religious community. The choice of Irvine may have preceded its acquisition of burgh status by fifty or more years. The original charters have been lost, and Strawhorn reckoned that the earliest possible date would be no earlier than 1214, i.e. after the accession of Alexander II.[87] De Morville may have selected Irvine because it was within sight of both **Dundonald** and **Prestwick**, the twin centres of Kyle Stewart, as well as of **Ayr**. At any rate, it is known that there was a castle at Irvine in 1184, possibly but not certainly on the site of the later **Seagate Castle**, which still survives in a ruinous state.

Largs, at the north-western extremity of Cuninghame, was originally a separate lordship but in the fourteenth century (1371) was tied in with Cuninghame.

In the case of Kyle Stewart, there is a little more detail. Again, we can see that there were two centres in this province: **Dundonald Castle,** the military *caput* of the region, and Prestwick, the home of the bailiary administration. The original Prestwick ('priests' dwelling') had been what is now called Monkton, a present-day village to the north. Walter fitz Alan, the first Steward of Scotland, founded Paisley Abbey as his principal religious institution and near the beginning of William the Lion's reign (1165) transferred the revenues of the then Prestwick Church to Paisley as part of the income of that abbey. The former Prestwick became known as Monk's Prestwic(k) and then as Monkton. Meanwhile, a burgh was set up to the south by Walter fitz Alan for judicial, administrative and commercial purposes. It had a church, whose revenues were similarly gifted to Paisley Abbey. This burgh was known at first as Prestwickburgh, and in time simply as Prestwick. Monkton and Prestwick churches are still in existence as picturesque ruins, the structures themselves dating from the thirteenth century. Prestwick church in particular is in a splendid situation on a mound of its own, surrounded by an ancient graveyard, just to the east of the railway.

No (baronial) charter for the establishment of Prestwick as a burgh has survived, but it must have been given some time before 1173,[88] which makes this older as a burgh than Ayr, and the oldest burgh on the west coast. On the other hand, there are reasons for thinking that, simply as a settlement, Prestwick is the younger.[89] Both towns reach far back before 1000.

It is known that Ayr Castle was founded in 1197, eight or ten years before the foundation by charter of the royal burgh. The site of the castle remains uncertain. The burgh, administrative centre and military headquarters coincide in this case.

Ayr, Prestwick and Irvine are within sight of each other, but Carrick's *caput* at Turnberry is tucked away to the south behind a bend in the coast-line, and the Carrick Hills form a defensive line to the north, fronted by the River Doon and several castles including Greenan and Newark.

The castle of Ayr, and later the royal burgh, as we have suggested above, were probably set up in order to counterbalance with royal authority the suddenly increased territorial influence of the Gallovidian families of Duncan and Roland. The motive, however, behind the establishment of burghs was as much commercial as military and strategic. The main function of the royal burghs was to provide revenue for the king. In the case of David I, the royal burghs were his only source of income. Burghs of barony were set up with the same purpose for the magnates.

Most royal burghs were grouped along the east coast of Scotland because of the growth in continental trade. Yet the west coast in the thirteenth century was not commercially negligible. We know that there was a substantial trade in corn with Ireland, and Ayr, the first royal burgh in the west, had an important part in this.

Burghs, whether royal or baronial, were usually set up at strategic points for trade, such as a river-crossing or ford or main cross-roads. Ayr was established at the mouth of the River Ayr, where there was a ford, if not already a (wooden) bridge. Two importants roads met at this point also – the north-south coast road and the route from (New) Cumnock and the south to the west coast, possibly an ancient Roman or even pre-Roman road. Irvine similarly lay at the mouths of the Irvine and the Garnock waters (now, if not in the twelfth century, running together south of Ardeer), and also at the 'T-junction' of the coast road and the route to Loudoun Hill, through the Lanarkshire hills and ultimately to the east coast. Prestwick lay between these on the coast road, but there are signs in this case that commercial development did not take place, such as the later (also unsuccessful) chartering of the burgh of Newton upon Ayr in attempted rivalry to the royal burgh south of the river.

All of these burghs shared an additional feature – lying close to the sea – and in two of them port facilities were developed advantageously. The fourth bailiary, Carrick, seemed to have no genuine burgh development. Turnberry, the *caput* of Carrick, was also situated on the coast, and Maidens north of Turnberry could possibly have been developed for some trading purposes but was not. Maybole's foundation was, of course, lost in the mists of the past and the settlement experienced some commercial growth from the twelfth century onward, but it suffered by comparison with the other developing towns through not being on the coast. **Turnberry Castle** itself possesses a sheltered haven for ships within the precincts of the castle, but this would have been strictly for military vessels such as galleys. Two major commercial burgh developments within twenty miles of each other – Ayr and Irvine – were probably enough for the thirteenth century. However, on the west coast the sea had been the main means of communication since prehistoric times, and should still at the time of the Normanisation of Scotland be taken into account in all considerations of settlement, trade and military control.

In order to generate enough income for the king or lord, trade in the burghs had to be stimulated and protected, and the charters relating to their foundation attempted to restrict trading activity to them and to weekly market days held in burgh market places. Goods were supposed to be marketed only within the burgh, and, if they were produced outside the towns, in the 'landward' area within the trading precinct, toll had to be paid on them at the burgh's gate or in the market. Anybody taking goods out of the burgh's trading precinct had to pay toll twice e.g. at the **Little Laight Taxing Stone** – once on leaving a trading precinct and again on entering another. These restrictions and associated privileges were the subject of fierce contention between the burgesses of the different burghs (e.g. between Ayr and Irvine) and were sometimes quite unenforceable.

David I's policy of opening Scotland to immigration centred on the burghs, where numbers of foreigners settled as burgesses, not only as merchants but as skilled craftsmen and as 'local government officers' e.g. *lineatores* who marked out town boundaries and the highly desirable plots of land lining the newly developing high streets. This is when burgh street plans, still in some cases extant, began to take shape.

Merchants and craftsmen from 'a' the airts' – Flanders, Germany, Burgundy, France, Normandy, Lothian, England – flocked to the new opportunities offered by the development of burghs in Scotland. We would now perhaps call it 'inward investment'. Fleshers, tanners, skinners, cobblers, goldsmiths, tailors – all claimed the privileges of burgesses and the security of dwelling within the walls or palisades of a burgh. Burghs were defended and gated. Within the palisades at the foot of the tofts there was often a 'back lane' for rear access (many burgesses possessing land and livestock outside the burgh boundaries), and this arrangement continues in Ayr and elsewhere to the present day, although the defensive stockades have long vanished.

For a more detailed description of three Ayrshire burghs, **Ayr, Prestwick** and **Irvine**, see the Gazetteer.

In ancient Scotland, as in England, the country was often divided up into units of territory, each of which contributed to the upkeep of the king as he moved from provincial centre to centre in the discharge of his kingly functions. These districts even in non-Anglian-speaking parts of Scotland were often called by the English name *scir*, 'shire'. They were controlled by the king's servants or thanes (*thegnian*, to serve), chief among whom was the *scir-gerefa*, shire reeve or officer or '*sheriff*'.[90] He became a kind of principal administrator, to whom gradually accrued legal, military and police powers, as well as duties of collecting rents for the king. The sheriff was the king's representative, exercising the king's rights, and sat in a royal castle on royal demesne.

Apparently no thanages are recorded in the appanage in southern Scotland belonging to David I before he became king in 1124,[91] although a primitive *scir* may have been in existence in the Maybole region not only during the Anglian occupation of Galloway and Carrick in the period up to 900 but afterwards also. Under David there seems to have been no sheriff in the Ayrshire region,[92] perhaps out of deference to Fergus, Prince of Galloway. However, once the reallocation of territory had taken hold, the kings tried to knit the parts of the region even more closely together, and this endeavour lies behind William the Lion's appointment of Reginald de Craufurd as (probably) the first Sheriff of Ayr at the same time as the foundation of his castle ('*opidum*') in 1197.[93] Craufurd's sheriffdom covered and tried to subjugate the turbulent province of Carrick as well as Kyle and Cuninghame.[94]

The whole district constituted the trading precinct as well as the administrative, shrieval, shire, and provincial ('*comitatus*') 'county' of Ayr. It should be noted that, although the ecclesiastical organisation of parishes subordinate to Kilwinning, Paisley and Crossraguel had been well integrated with these secular arrangements, the two sides of David I's dispositions never quite melded and sometimes came into open collision, as in the cases of Abbot Bunche in Kilwinning in 1512 or Commendator Stewart in 1570. David had ingeniously spatch-cocked an essentially transnational power, that of the Church, with his own relatively homegrown but Normanizing constitutional rearrangements. The estrangement of the two domains became more pronounced after the 1560 Reformation.

5. AN INDEPENDENT SCOTLAND, AN INTEGRATED AYRSHIRE

Dynastic background: the descendants of Fergus of Galloway: the line to Balliol

As mentioned earlier, after 1196 Roland of Galloway, son of Uchtred, controlled the whole of Cuninghame and other Scottish lordships in right of his wife (and payment of a considerable fee to the king). He became Constable of Scotland, and possibly, before 1196, the first 'justiciar' of Galloway or even of a very substantial part of southern Scotland: he seems to have decided cases at Lanark and perhaps at Maybole in 1187.[95]

Roland (a Latinised form of the Gaelic name Lachlann) had three children: Alan, Thomas and Ada. Alan, who became Lord of Galloway and Constable of Scotland after his father, had by his first wife two children, Elena and Thomas, the latter of whom died young.[96] Elena married Roger de Quincy, who became Constable of Scotland after the death of Alan in 1234. They had three daughters: (1) Margaret, who married William Ferrars, Earl of Derby, who resigned as Constable of Scotland; (2) Isabel, who married Alexander Comyn, Earl of Buchan, who became Constable of Scotland after his brother-in-law; and (3) Elena, who married William de la Zouche.

By his second wife, Margaret, daughter of David Earl of Huntingdon, Alan had two further daughters: (1) Christina, who married William Earl Albemarle; and (2) Dervorguilla, who married John Balliol, lord of Barnard Castle in England. Dervorguilla and John had one surviving son, John Balliol II, who became King John of Scotland in 1292.

When Alan died in 1234–5, King Alexander forced the formerly unitary principality of Galloway to accept a division along feudal lines.[97] The Comyn, Balliol, Ferrars and Zouche families all shared in the Cuninghame estate at this time.[98]

The line to King Robert I

Roland of Galloway's cousin Duncan fitz Gilbert, Earl of Carrick, had two sons of whom the elder, Neil, succeeded to the earldom. Neil, who died in 1256, had a daughter Marjorie who married Adam de Kilconquhar, who became Earl of Carrick and died on crusade in 1270. Marjorie then became Countess of Carrick in her own right and was in ward of King Alexander III.

One day about two years after her husband's death, Marjorie, an enterprising young lady, went hunting with a party of her friends and servants, perhaps on the beautiful sands that stretch southward from her home, Turnberry Castle. On the shore they encountered a young knight, whom Marjorie recognised as Robert de Brus – in fact the sixth Robert de Brus in line from the time of David I. His father had returned safely from the crusade in which Marjorie's husband Adam had died (at the siege of Acre). Seizing time by the forelock and Brus's horse by the bridle, Marjorie proposed marriage to Robert then and there. With an eye to the king's anger, he at first demurred but, when the other members of her party drew their swords, he yielded and was led off, a kidnapped captive, to the strong tower of Turnberry.

After some days, the gates opened and the young couple emerged to announce to the world that they were happily married. King Alexander III was mightily enraged, and confiscated all the lady's property and lands, but they were returned when a hefty fine was paid. Robert VI de Brus became Earl of Carrick *jure matrimonio*, and on 11 July 1274 his son Robert VII the Bruce, the future King Robert I, was born.[99]

So the family of Fergus, Prince of Galloway, attained the crown of Scotland in two different branches, maintaining through four generations the original rivalry between Uchtred and Gilbert – or, we should say, the battle-lines were drawn: the Balliols and the Comyns on one side, the men of Carrick (and the Kennedys) on the other. In this contest the earldom of Carrick in Ayrshire became gradually supreme, and this is recognised to the present day when in Scotland the heir to the British throne is still styled 'Earl of Carrick': Carrick is his *appanage* as Strathclyde-Cumbria was of his remote ancestors.

The Battle of Largs: the end of the Norwegian claim

The rivalry between Norway and Scotland, which had re-emerged under King Alexander II in the 1230s and in 1249, peaked in 1263. The aged King Håkon IV sailed down the west coast with a very large fleet, intending to re-establish the tributary status of the Atlantic islands, and came to negotiate with King Alexander III at Ayr Castle. After drawing off to Lamlash in Arran, Håkon returned with a large part of his fleet to the Cuninghame coast, took shelter from a massive autumn storm under the lee of the Cumbrae islands to the west of Largs, and the next day descended on the shore to retrieve goods from a merchant ship that had been driven aground during the night. The Norwegians were opposed by a local militia – the *pedisequi patrie*, 'footsloggers of the country' – including a knight from Mauchline, Sir Piers Curry, who was fatally injured but who seems to have taken the lead in driving the invaders off. After what appears to have been a battle of movement, the Norwegians withdrew and sailed off in dudgeon but not defeated. Neither army deployed all its resources in the Battle of Largs, which was a skirmish rather than a full-scale battle.

There has been much controversy over who really won this encounter, and it is interesting to note that the Norwegian king is alleged to have called his men off when people started to get hurt. He died shortly afterwards in Orkney. In the previous year, 1262, the Norwegians had carried out an operation on the same lines against the Icelanders, who were successfully brought back into the fold. Restoration of Norwegian authority in the west of Scotland was a necessarily more difficult operation, but suspicion remains that it was the onset of illness in Håkon rather than the valour of the Ayrshire soldiers that caused this action to be broken off. In any event, two years later the Norwegians came to terms and agreed to a transfer of sovereignty in exchange for a large payment, which King Alexander had been offering for some time.

The Wars of Independence: the claimants to the throne of Scotland, including the Bruces

Twenty-three years after the Battle of Largs, in 1286, King Alexander III broke his neck in a cliffside accident during a stormy night near Kinghorn in Fife, precipitating a succession problem. The resulting power vacuum led ultimately to the Wars of Independence, which dragged on for three generations. The King's two sons had died without issue before 1286. His daughter, Margaret, who also died before her father, had married King Erik II of Norway and produced one daughter, Margaret, the 'Maid of Norway', who was accepted on a temporary or nominal basis as Queen of Scotland. However, the Maid was only three years old, and King Alexander's second wife was rumoured to be pregnant. The prospect that the throne might go to a female was unwelcome to many. The whole future of Scotland rested upon a fluid and uncertain basis, and there emerged a number of competitors to contest the succession. A provisional government was carried on under the authority of a committee of 'Guardians'.

Apart from the Maid of Norway, the two main claimants to the throne of Scotland were Robert de Brus, 'the Competitor', the fifth Robert Bruce in line from the original Anglo-Norman settler of 1124 and John Balliol, the lord of Barnard Castle and ruler of Galloway, a descendant not only of David I but also of Fergus of Galloway, as described above. Balliol was supported by a powerful member of the Guardians, John Comyn of Badenoch, the Red Comyn; Comyn himself was a claimant.

It is perhaps necessary to remember that in the run-up to the Wars of Independence there were no less than three active bearers of the name Robert de Brus ('the Bruce'): (1) the grandfather, Robert V de Brus the Competitor, Lord of Annandale (d. 1295); (2) the father, Robert VI de Brus, Earl of Carrick and husband of Marjorie (d. 1304); and (3) the son, Robert VII de Brus, Earl of Carrick and from 1306 King of Scotland (1274–1329). King Robert I is the man often referred to as '(the) Bruce' and this will be the practice here when referring to Robert singly.

As mentioned above, after King Alexander's death in 1286 and before any decision had been made as to the final form of the succession, the Scots had set up a provisional ruling committee consisting of six Guardians. Excluded from the committee were Robert V de Brus the Competitor and his son, Robert VI de Brus, Earl of Carrick since 1272. This exclusion was probably due to the presence on the committee of the Comyns.

The Turnberry Band: antagonism between Brus and Comyn

The de Brus family and their friends – who included a Guardian, James the Stewart – met at Turnberry Castle in Carrick in September 1286 and signed a 'band', a private treaty promising mutual assistance between themselves, James the Stewart and certain other western leaders, the Earl of Ulster and Thomas de Clare. Although this 'band' was ostensibly to give support to the two Irish participants, and declared the parties' continued loyalty to the King of England (in respect of their English possessions) and to whoever should finally obtain the Scottish crown, it was clearly the formation of a western bloc directed against the regency and in particular against the Balliols and their allies the Comyns. The result was a civil war, in which Balliol's castle at Buittle in Galloway was captured. However the Guardians succeeded in re-establishing their authority.

The King of England as judge

The Scots had thought of Edward I of England as a suitable adjudicator in the event of any dispute about the succession and had made approaches to him as early as August 1286. Edward was the senior monarch and would have been a wise and diplomatic choice as an arbitrator had it not been for his inordinate expansionism and his character, which was both wily and violent. He made acceptance of the Scots' nomination conditional on their recognition of him as 'lord superior' of Scotland. In 1289 and 1290, following a treaty signed at Salisbury and two 'parliaments' at Birgham, the Scots conceded to Edward the right to intervene in Scotland. The principal result was to clear the way for a marriage between the Maid of Norway and Edward's son – with a view to facilitating the absorption of Scotland into the kingdom of England in the future. Edward then proceeded to make piecemeal encroachments upon Scotland and Scottish rights – including annexation of the Isle of Man, formerly a Scottish possession. His agents sought to gain possession of Scottish castles.

All this was building up to the arrival of the Maid of Norway, now six years old, in Scotland, and presumably a ceremony of marriage would have been performed as soon as she was safely on Scottish soil. Unfortunately, by the time the ship carrying the child from Bergen had touched at Orkney, she was mortally ill, and she died in Kirkwall in October 1290. As a result, the succession question became critical. Immediately the de Brus family made a move against any possible attempt by the Guardians of Scotland to set up a king independently, and their neighbour John Balliol sought to re-establish in strengthened form his claim to the throne. Armed men gathered and marched throughout the kingdom and war was an imminent possibility. However, the Guardians seem once again to have re-established control, and this led to peace under the increasingly iron hand of King Edward I.

The Competition

The Scots had appealed to Edward I to settle the question of the succession, and he now promised to do this on certain conditions. Protracted bargaining in 1291 led to a diplomatic package, in which Edward extracted more concessions from the Scots than vice versa. Principal among these concessions were that the Scots should sign a document admitting that Edward was the 'superior lord' and that the royal castles of Scotland, including Edinburgh and Stirling, should be handed over to Edward's agents pending the resolution of the succession problem. Edward thus gained effective control of Scotland without bloodshed. The alternative for the Scots had been at least civil war and armed invasion from England. The scene was now set for the legal wrangling of 'the Great Cause' in a court set up by Edward to determine who should have kingly authority in Scotland.

Not that Edward I was overtly unfair or rode roughshod over the Scots and their problem. Edward's undergame was to become fully apparent only after the vermiculate wrangling of the Great Cause had been brought to a conclusion. As adjudicator in his own court of law, Edward had a great deal of antiquarian research carried out and, after deliberation, recognised Balliol as the competitor with the strongest claim to the throne. This was accepted by everybody concerned – except the de Brus family, who withdrew in dudgeon to their strongholds in Annan, Carlisle and Carrick. Balliol was accordingly crowned king in 1292.

The old Competitor, Robert V de Brus, resigned his claim to his son the Earl of Carrick, Robert VI, husband of Marjorie. Robert VI in turn resigned the Earldom of Carrick to his son Robert VII in 1292. The old Competitor died in 1295, and Robert VI became Lord of Annandale.

Scotland's first revolt (1295–6)

The Scots had been outmanoeuvred by King Edward I, who exploited the acceptance of his suzerainty which had been given when they agreed to submit to his judgment. Now it speedily became apparent that King John Balliol was in a very subordinate and humiliating position *vis-à-vis* the English king, and the Scottish kingdom was in servitude to its southern neighbour. Tensions and hostilities began to boil uncontrollably after the example set by the revolt of the Welsh in 1294 against the service demanded of them by Edward in his quarrel with King Philip IV 'le Bel' ('the Fair') of France. This service was required from the Scots also, but early in 1295 the Scots changed sides and formed an alliance with Philip. To make assurance doubly sure, the magnates took the power of the State out of the hands of King John and placed it in the charge of a new committee of twelve Guardians, who arranged the Franco-Scottish treaty. This was ratified in Scotland by King John and the Scottish parliament on 23 February 1296. The Scots had earlier (22 October 1295) acceded to a treaty signed between the French and the Norwegian king Erik II.

King Erik had married Isabel Brus, the daughter of Robert de Brus VI and sister of the future king, in 1293. This was the way in which Erik sought to increase his friendship with Edward I of England, since the de Brus family were then supporters of Edward. When the Franco-Scottish treaty was signed, providing for offensive action against the English, and when the 'host' was actually called out in 1296 to a *wapinschaw* (muster of arms) and to march south, Robert VI de Brus Lord of Annandale and his son Robert VII Earl of Carrick refused the summons. At that stage they stood by their friendship with Edward I.

The Scots were dismayed at the speed with which Edward responded to their gambit. Their siege of Carlisle was very quickly repulsed by the governor of the city, none other than Robert VI de Brus Lord of Annandale, and Edward I stormed the city of Berwick on the other side of the country, butchering a large number of the inhabitants. Atrocity was piled upon atrocity on both sides. The Scots army was finally broken on 27 April 1296 at Dunbar and the English moved in to occupy and plunder Scotland. It was on this occasion that the so-called Stone of Destiny was taken from Scone to Westminster, and the Scottish regalia and the Black Rood of St Margaret were looted. King John Balliol resigned his kingdom at Brechin Castle on 10 July 1296, and was utterly humiliated there by having all the insignia of royalty physically stripped from him in public. This is how he acquired the nickname 'Toom Tabard' ('Empty Surcoat'). He was imprisoned and the elder de Brus, who had resisted the Scots at Carlisle, was brusquely snubbed when he ventured to ask whether Edward would now support the de Brus claim. 'Have we nothing else to do,' asked Edward, 'but win kingdoms for you?' Edward in effect abolished Scotland and determined to rule the former kingdom as King of England. The de Brus family, along with most leading Scots, were cowed, submitted and did homage to Edward. An occupation régime was quickly and efficiently installed under Hugh Cressingham as Treasurer.

Scotland's second revolt (1297): Wallace and Bruce

In spite of this seeming eclipse of the Scots, a new revolt against English rule developed in 1297, sparked off by the daring actions of the young William

Wallace, a man from Paisley (Elderslie) who now came to the fore under the stimulus of his feudal superior James the Stewart, who controlled the Paisley region. Revolt was also fomented by certain discontented magnates, in particular the 22-year-old future king, Robert VII the Bruce, Earl of Carrick, who broke with his father's timid acquiescence in the English occupation. He first tried unsuccessfully to rally his father's Annandale knights to his cause with the words: 'No man holds his own flesh and blood in hatred and I am no exception. I must join my own people and the nation in which I was born.' By 'my own people' he meant the inhabitants of Carrick, and it was to Carrick and Ayrshire that he made his way after leaving Annan.

The next few years were a tale of almost unrelieved disaster for the independence party. The first effort fell to pieces at once. Bruce and James the Stewart joined with others (including William Wallace) to make head at Irvine, the *caput* of Cuninghame. Alas, strong English forces under Henry Percy and Robert Clifford advanced from their headquarters at Ayr, and the Scots caved in without resistance.

After the Irvine debacle William Wallace joined forces with a young nobleman from the north of Scotland named Andrew Moray, already in revolt. By mid-1297 they had cleared a substantial part of Scotland of English occupiers. They gathered a large army and defeated the English comprehensively at Stirling Bridge on 11 September 1297. Cressingham, the English treasurer, was literally cut to pieces. (The pieces were distributed throughout the country as 'souvenirs'.) However, Andrew Moray, perhaps the stronger man in the Wallace–Moray partnership, was mortally wounded in the battle, and although Wallace and his other associates succeeded in reviving some aspects of Scottish sovereignty, their leadership lacked stability. Wallace raided northern England in the winter of 1296/7 and committed some memorable atrocities but did not reveal wider organising ability.

At some time Wallace is reputed to have captured **Ardrossan Castle** by a trick – luring the garrison out to fight a deliberately-set house fire in the village. Wallace slaughtered the English soldiers and cast their bodies into a pit, the episode being known thereafter as 'Vallace lardner' ('Wallace's Larder'). Ardrossan is not the only place about which this story is told, but the castle appears to have been destroyed roughly at the period of the Wars of Independence.

There is some uncertainty about Wallace's action at Ayr, in which he is reputed to have taken revenge upon the English forces for an act of treachery: the English had summoned Ayrshire notables to a conference in Ayr to be held in the Barns of Ayr, and as each Ayrshireman entered the 'conference centre' he was seized and hanged out of hand.[100] The victims included Wallace's uncle and other named victims, including a Blair from Blair Castle in Dalry. After this foul treachery the English troops caroused and fell asleep in the Barns (? under the dangling feet of their victims).

While they were sleeping Wallace and his men piled straw around the Barns and set the place alight, burning them all alive. Other English soldiers were sleeping in various billets in the town of Ayr and under the encouragement of Wallace the friars of the Dominican establishment there slit their throats or pushed them into the river to drown – whence this atrocity is known as 'The Friars' Blessing of Ayr'. Although these episodes show Wallace in a truly disgusting light there is nothing inherently improbable about the stories, nor would they detract from his heroic reputation either at the time or later.

Edward I was enraged by the Scottish victory at Stirling Bridge and in 1298 came north breathing fire and slaughter. On 22 July he attacked and defeated the Scots under William Wallace at Falkirk. Bruce, then on Wallace's side, galloped straight to Ayr, burnt down the castle ('slighted' it) and drove the people into the fields, so that when the enemy arrived they would find the town empty and in ruins. This was 'scorched earth' policy, and it is typical of Bruce's strategy throughout the war. At and after Falkirk the generalship of William Wallace failed, and he never regained the initiative. But what can be said is that both Comyn and Bruce, in joining Wallace, committed themselves to struggle against the English in the name of King John.

Scots government under jury rig

In spite of defeat and continuing lack of success, the Scots were able to construct a kind of coherent government, taking the form of 'Guardianship of the realm' once again. In 1298 both Robert VII Bruce and John Comyn, now deadly rivals, were elected to the committee, and for some time these two in uneasy alliance led Scottish government 'under jury rig'. However, their co-operation soon began to break down. A meeting in Peebles turned into a brawl, daggers were drawn, and 'John Comyn leaped at the Earl of Carrick and seized him by the throat'.[101]

The dilemmas of Robert Bruce

It is from this point onward that Bruce's allegiance seems to become very uncertain. He resigned from the committee of Guardians of Scotland about the beginning of 1300, and this may well have had something to do with the fact that their proposed scene of military activity was to switch to south-west Scotland, where he and his father held their estates. Not only did Bruce hate the Comyns, who now led the Scottish resistance, but he disliked the idea of fighting for King John Balliol, whose star, in spite of the humiliation at Brechin, was once more in the ascendant. As a result of brilliant diplomatic intervention by the Scots at the court of Pope Boniface, the scales had tipped slightly in their favour, and King John's imprisonment in papal custody was exchanged for a form of house arrest: he was permitted to take up residence at the ancient home of his family, Bailleul-en-Vimeu in France.

At first, Robert VII Bruce fought for the Scots at Turnberry and, after the fall of Turnberry in September 1301, continued to harass the English garrisons there and in Ayr for some time. But after the news about King John had filtered through to him, he came to terms with Edward I. This change of sides was probably dictated by Bruce's calculation of outcomes: if the Scots won, the Bruce claim would fall to the ground, but if the English won and the Bruces were on the defeated side, Carrick and their other very extensive estates in Scotland and England, including the lordship of Annandale, would be lost for ever. Bruce was a slippery customer, and hedged his bets effectively and secretly.

In 1302 Bruce wed the daughter of Richard de Burgh, Earl of Ulster. De Burgh was known to be one of Edward's chief supporters – yet, sixteen years before, he had signed the Turnberry Band with the Bruces. James the Steward, one of the remaining Guardians, was uncle by marriage to Elizabeth de Burgh. Furthermore, in 1304, Bruce signed another secret agreement with one of the most active and important of the Guardians of Scotland, Bishop William Lamberton of St Andrews. Bruce probably had a secret game-plan, to place himself in a position of strength if an opportunity of seizing the throne of Scotland arose – that is to say, if his claim were to be recognised and accepted. That would necessarily involve the removal of the only other serious candidate remaining after Balliol himself: John Comyn, the Red Comyn, Lord of Badenoch.

Meanwhile the war between the English and the Scots had been continuing by fits and starts. The Scots in the south-west had kept the English at bay in 1301. A truce ended in November 1302; the Scots surprised and defeated a strong English force at Roslin in February 1303, but their main resistance ended in the winter of 1303/4. The English captured Stirling Castle on 20 July 1304. Bruce attended the English parliament in October 1302, and in 1303 we find him acting for Edward as Sheriff of Ayr and Lanark. As such he was able to command military resources and men from Kyle and Cuninghame besides his own earldom of Carrick. He remained in the English service long enough to confirm and do homage to Edward I for his inheritance in England after the death of his father, Robert VI, in early 1304. Going by appearances, he was well content to remain under the superiority of the King of England, and continued to be so until 1305, the year of the capture and execution of William Wallace by the English.

An Ayrshire hero: Robert Bruce, Earl of Carrick

In early 1306 it became clear that the old Hammer of the Scots, Edward I, was mortally ill, although still very much and vengefully in command.

After the fall of Stirling he had pursued the task of creating a framework administration for the complete subordination of Scotland to English rule. Both Robert Bruce and John 'Red' Comyn were within the King's peace, and Bruce was apparently in favour with Edward. But on 10 February 1306, while the work of the English administration was continuing in Dumfries, Bruce asked the Red Comyn to come to a meeting in the Greyfriars Kirk in that town. Almost certainly he had some proposal to put to the Comyn about a possible settlement of differences over their respective claims to the throne. Whatever the subject of the meeting, their clearly irreconcilable personal antagonisms came to the fore, and Robert the Bruce stabbed John Comyn with his dagger in front of the high altar of the church. Whether others then ran up to 'mak siccar' is a matter of speculation.

Bruce had killed the Comyn, probably in very hot blood. He may well have been horrified by his own action. Despite that, at this crucial moment he proved a man of action and of quick thought. Without a moment's hesitation he set in motion his plan to seize the crown of Scotland – and proclaimed it openly. After seizing Dumfries Castle he called the country to arms in the traditional way of the Scots – he sent the fiery cross throughout the land. He captured the castles of the south-west, including Ayr and Loch Doon, and provisioned Loch Doon Castle and Dunaverty Castle at the foot of the Mull of Kintyre. He then rode to Glasgow, obtained absolution for the murder as well as whole-hearted support from Bishop Wishart, and went on to Scone to be crowned King of the Scots on 25 March 1306 amid a motley crew of supporters.

Six weeks lie between 10 February and 25 March, but given the state of fourteenth-century Scottish communications, the above operations were carried out at lightning speed. King Edward, on his bed of sickness at Lanercost, was nearer Dumfries than most, but he apparently had not heard of the murder on 16 February. When he finally got to know of it, he at first could not believe his ears. Then, when he was convinced, his wrath was terrible and he issued drastic orders to Aymer de Valence, to 'byrn and slay and rais dragoun'[102] – no quarter, in other words. Valence carried out his orders. Then, on 18 June 1306, Bruce's strategic sense deserted him: hearing that Valence had taken St John's Town of Perth, Bruce prepared for a major fight at that town. Unfortunately for Bruce, he was surprised and utterly defeated by Valence in a pre-dawn attack at Methven. Bruce and a few hundred followers got away by the skin of their teeth. After a second defeat by another enemy, John MacDougall of Argyll, Bruce's force simply disintegrated. Bruce's queen and his daughter and other women were sent north under the guidance of the Earl of Atholl, but were captured and handed over to King Edward.

Edward's vengeance was dreadful. Dozens of Bruce's supporters were hanged, drawn and quartered, or simply beheaded; the women of the waylaid royal party were subjected to savage imprisonment, and two were exposed in cages at Roxburgh and Berwick for years. Loch Doon Castle was captured after a vigorous defence by Gilbert de Carrick and the Bruce loyalist Sir Christopher Seton, an Englishman married to Bruce's sister. Seton, who had taken part in the murder of Comyn and then escaped to the castle, was hanged, drawn and beheaded at Dumfries.

1307: Bruce's return to Carrick and to Scotland

Meanwhile Robert the Bruce vanished, it seemed, from mortal ken, or at least from the view of historians. Theories about where he went abound. Some think he fled to the Norwegian Orkneys or even to Bergen in Norway itself; others that he was in Ulster. It seems fairly certain that he was in the western Highlands and islands, at least in the autumn of 1306. But no real information is on offer. What is known is that, after a long period of lying low and eluding King Edward's vigilance, he slipped into his own earldom of Carrick via Rathlin Island and Arran; he landed on Turnberry shore in late January or early February 1307.

The success of his enterprise was on a knife-edge. His descent on Turnberry was really a mistake. Barbour says that the agreed signal for the landing was to be a fire lit by a spy on Turnberry foreshore if he thought conditions were right. The spy discovered that Turnberry Castle was strongly held by a formidable English force under Henry Percy, the Englishman who had supplanted Bruce as Earl of Carrick. The spy therefore did not light his signal fire. However, somebody else lit a fire on Turnberry foreshore, and Bruce and his party went ahead with the landing. When they discovered the true state of affairs, Bruce fell on the English garrison, many of whom had been billeted outside the castle walls, and killed a great number in an overwhelming surprise attack. It seems likely that the castle itself did not fall to him but the terror inspired by Bruce's sudden appearance out of the night was such that Percy withdrew into his fortifications and held on for dear life, awaiting rescue from Ayr. Bruce meanwhile withdrew into the interior of Carrick and prepared to live off the country and conduct a hit-and-run campaign of harassment against the English. He may have made use of the ancient Iron Age fort on **Maxwellston Hill** (Hadyard) above Dailly as a look-out point. Professor Barrow makes the point that Bruce was a far more able guerrilla warrior than William Wallace, who preferred set-piece battles and weight of numbers.[103]

Bruce's descent on the mainland was actually two-pronged. More or less synchronised with the attack on Turnberry, a force led by Bruce's two brothers Thomas and Alexander and including an Irish element attempted an invasion of Galloway at Loch Ryan to the south. This met with utter disaster. The force was destroyed or captured, and its leaders taken prisoner. King Edward, a year further into his last illness but still absolutely in command, saw to it that Thomas Bruce and the young

Alexander Bruce – the finest scholar of his year at Cambridge – were hanged and beheaded.

In the meantime Bruce had been establishing himself in Carrick and overcoming the fright of the peasantry, who had experience of the methods of the English in repressing resistance. Bruce is reputed to have been fortunate in his relations with the ladies, and one named Christian of Carrick seems to have helped him in the early days with men, shelter, supplies – and perhaps something else. He may also have been helped by supporters in southern Carrick such as the Lord of Knockdolian. Christian of Carrick told him of the fate of the royal women who, he had thought, were by now safe beyond the reach of Edward. This news had the effect of hardening his resolve against the English.

Edward I of England was now rapidly approaching his end, which came at Burgh-on-Sands on 7 July 1307. Before this happened, he had been directing the campaign against Bruce with his usual flair and determination. Bruce's old adversary, Aymer de Valence, had entered the fray again, and a number of attempts were made to murder Bruce, including one using disguised assassins, whom Bruce killed in person when he became suspicious.

The English were not the only foes he had to deal with: the natives of the old Galloway, supporters of Balliol and Comyn and hereditary enemies of Carrick since the murder of Uchtred in 1176, came after him at night in force, probably in the Stinchar valley in Carrick south of Hadyard. He is said by Barbour to have defended the narrow way alone against a force of two hundred, killing several before reinforcements came to his rescue.

With a larger force Bruce battled in Kyle against Sir Aymer de Valence near Cumnock, or possibly New Cumnock, but when he also came under attack from a large number of Highlanders at his rear, he ordered a withdrawal into the western hills, dividing his men into three parties. The Highlanders under John of Lorne had sleuth-hounds with them, and these got on to Bruce's own track, pressing him hard. Bruce's following dwindled under this pressure to one man only, his foster-brother. John of Lorne sent forward five of his most doughty fighters, and these caught up with the dauntless two, only to be outsworded: all five were killed. Still John of Lorne and his men and hounds were in full cry after them, so Bruce used the traditional trick of wading down a river, and this threw the hounds off the scent: John of Lorne abandoned the pursuit in disgust. Sir Aymer de Valence, however, was not so easily put off, and sent another three assassins to pursue the king, who was now in the last stages of exhaustion. Nevertheless, in spite of nearly yielding to sleep, Bruce fought off these three – but not before they had succeeded in killing his foster-brother. He then staggered on until he came to a lonely house on the banks of the River Cree on the Carrick-Galloway border. There he found another lady, who informed him that all travellers were welcome on account of one man. Bruce inquired who that might be, whereupon she replied:

I sall you say,
The King Robert the Bruys is he,
That is rycht lord off this countre.
His fayis now haldis him in thrang,
Bot I think to se or ocht lang
Him lord and king our all the land
That na fayis sall him withstand.[104]

Bruce at once admitted that he was that man, and instantly she drew him in and fed him. While he was still eating, his brother Edward and The Douglas arrived with their men and gave him succour, rest and support.

The above is not untypical of the sort of adventure recorded of Robert the Bruce, and although the story should be treated with caution, since we have really only one source for it – Barbour – it is by no means worthless. All the events are within the bounds of possibility.

After a long period of dodging King Edward's men in this fashion, Bruce began to record some significant successes. In an action at Glen Trool, south-east of Carrick, Bruce inflicted losses on a pursuing force, and during an unsuccessful attempt to capture the treasure train of the English which was travelling under escort towards Bothwell, he nevertheless defeated a large body of English troops near Loudoun Hill, on 13 May 1307. It was not long after this that Aymer de Valence resigned his charge and withdrew to England. But before that happened, King Edward died, and this, more than anything else, transformed the situation.

Edward II and the end of the first War of Independence

The Prince of Wales, now Edward II, while not actually a weakling, possessed none of the hard force of his father. He seems to have been genuinely uninterested in the conquest of Scotland. The initiative, which had been slipping away from the English, now passed decisively to Bruce. Edward I had projected a massive punitive expedition against Scotland for that summer but under Edward II the English had marched only as far as Cumnock in Ayrshire when the new king apparently gave it up as a bad job and went back to England. Bruce was thus left to settle old scores with the supporters of the Comyn family in the south-west before marching off to the North to consolidate his position.

Edward II was, however, still in possession of many strong points in southern Scotland, and these included Ayr Castle and Loch Doon Castle. Ayr remained in English hands at least until 1309 and Loch Doon until 1311. A whole cluster of first-rate castles in the south-east of the country were in the same position – Edinburgh and Roxburgh in particular, along with Jedburgh and Berwick. The Isle of Man was held for King Edward by a succession of commanders, including a previously defeated Gallovidian, Sir Dungal Macdouall, pursuing a hereditary enmity against Bruce and the men of Carrick. The whole of southern Scotland was a patchwork of conflicting loyalties and ruthless (mainly Scottish) blackmailers who raided northern England until Cumberland and Northumberland were desolate and exhausted. In the end, the patriotic party under Bruce began to gain the upper hand. One by one the strongholds retained by the English fell – after daring raids such as the escalades of Edinburgh and Roxburgh Castles carried out by the forces of Thomas Randolph and James Douglas respectively. In 1310–11 Edward II and his favourite Piers Gaveston marched into Scotland with a large army but had to retire, baffled by Bruce's 'scorched earth' tactics and his annoying habit of dodging battle while the English supplies dwindled.

In 1313 Edward Bruce, the king's brother, allowed himself to be trapped into a typical chivalric gesture while besieging Stirling Castle: Sir Philip Moubray, the Governor, pledged himself to surrender unless English forces approached to raise the siege within a year and a day. This meant that King Edward II was bound to march to Moubray's help and Robert the Bruce was bound to oppose him in what Bruce had been sedulously avoiding since 1307 – a set-piece battle. After cursing his brother briefly, Bruce set about making his preparations. Edward marched to Stirling with (it is estimated) at least 15,000 foot-soldiers and 2,000 horse. Bruce came with perhaps upwards of 6,000 foot and about 500 horse.[105] They met at Bannockburn on 23 June 1314. On the first day of the battle Bruce in person had the good luck to fell a single challenger, Sir Henry de Bohun, in front of the two armies, to the rapturous applause of the Scots. After this combat Bruce's soldiers were able to force the English cavalry back beyond the Bannock Burn but were recalled in time by Bruce before they ran impetuously into danger. At the same time an attempt by another squadron of English cavalry to outflank the Scottish position was driven back by a large body ('schiltrom') of spearmen under Thomas Randolph, Earl of Moray. The English forces were dispirited by these two repulses. The next day, 24 June, a second charge by English cavalry again failed to penetrate the massed spears of the Scottish schiltroms and the English bowmen were not deployed efficiently before the Scottish cavalry charged and scattered them. The English infantry do not seem to have been in action at all. The Scots advanced steadily, additional forces came up from behind (including a mob of semi-civilian camp-followers), and the English broke and fell into the Bannock Burn itself in panic disorder. King Edward II barely escaped with his life, but made it back to Dunbar, whence he took ship for Berwick. Such was the Battle of Bannockburn. It won a breathing-space for the Scots but it was by no means the end of the war. King Robert himself drew breath but soon he was back at the grim task of eradicating or neutralising the opposition in the north-east and the south-west, of raiding in the north of England and of attempting to organise a kingdom across the water in Ireland against the determined repression of the English.

David II, the Stewarts and Ayrshire

After Bannockburn there were forfeitures to be made and rewards to be given. The whole question of the succession (the 'tailzie') had to be settled, and this was done at a parliament or council held in Ayr in 1315. King Robert's daughter Marjorie, released from English captivity, was given in marriage to Walter, the young son of James the Stewart, a faithful supporter of Bruce, who had died in 1309. The son of Marjorie and Walter, Robert Stewart, who was born in 1316, was to be heir to the Scottish throne if King Robert I failed to produce an heir and if closer relatives, such as Edward Bruce the king's brother, did not succeed. If Robert Stewart came to the throne, Scotland would become subject to the family of the Stewards of Scotland – the Stewarts of Kyle.

Large swathes of land was redistributed following the dispossession of the Comyns, the Balliols and their supporters. Much of this land was in Cuninghame, which had been in the possession of the Balliols in their capacity as Lords of Galloway and Cuninghame after the failure of the de Morville line back in 1196. Various Balliol vassals and others forfeited their lands, which were chartered to supporters of Bruce. Robert Boyd from Noddsdale near Largs accumulated possessions including Kilmarnock, Ardneil, West Kilbride and Trabboch. Duncan Campbell was awarded Loudoun, and Robert Stewart the lordship of Cuninghame.[106] Other beneficiaries included Reginald Craufurd, Alexander Lindsay and Bryce Blair, all from the Ayrshire region.

After a brief respite, the war continued remorselessly, at first with considerable advantage to the Scots, whose leader conducted himself not only with ruthlessness but also with considerable statesmanship. Things did not go well in Ireland, where the king's brother Edward Bruce, a momentary High King, was killed at Dundalk in 1318. But otherwise pressure was maintained upon the weak and unfortunate Edward II of England, who crowned a career of unrelieved misjudgment by being dethroned and horribly murdered by his wife and her lover in 1327. Robert I had fathered a late son in 1324, and at length, very shortly before his own death in 1329, a treaty with the new English king Edward III was signed in Edinburgh providing for peace and for a dynastic marriage between the infants David Bruce and Joan of the Tower, Edward III's sister. The marriage took place on 12 July 1328.

All seemed set fair, but clouds were gathering on the horizon. The young English king had already been on an expedition against the Scots in 1327 and his youthful spirit had not been lightened by near-capture and complete humiliation at Stanhope on 4 August. He was to prove himself a competent and intelligent war leader, perhaps the most dangerous to the Scots of the three Edwards. Just as ominous, Edward Balliol, the son of King John Balliol, who had died in 1313, had been brought to England from Picardy as a potential successor, and he too was a better and more determined man than his father. The new Balliol, given only unofficial sanction by the English king,[107] set sail with a number of Scottish malcontents on an expedition which landed at Kinghorn on 6 August 1332. This was eight months after the first full coronation with papal authorization in Scottish history had been held for David II at Scone. The Scots were taken off guard and suffered a crushing defeat at Dupplin Moor. Balliol in his turn was crowned king at Scone on 24 September 1332 and in the succeeding months all the gains of the Scots under Robert I were rolled back. The discomfiture of the Scottish government of David II was completed in another total debacle, the Battle of Halidon Hill near Berwick, where five earls and the new guardian regent, Sir Archibald Douglas, fell fighting the English on 19 July 1333. War raged backwards and forwards, first one side gaining advantage, and then the other side. David II went into exile in France in 1334 and did not return until 1341. Thereafter Scottish government staggered on under his leadership – until he compounded his misfortunes by being captured on 17 October 1346 at Neville's Cross, during an ill-considered raid south into England. Apart from a brief visit on parole to try to arrange ransom terms, he did not see Scotland again until 7 October 1357, eleven years after his capture. By then his rival Balliol had given up his claim to the Scottish crown in disgust (20 January 1356) and David could look forward to reigning undisputed in his own kingdom. He did so with comparative success until 22 February 1371, when he died unexpectedly. This event spotlighted yet another potentially disastrous embarrassment for Scotland: the king left no legitimate heir.

At this juncture in history the Ayr *tailzie* of 1315, a subsequent adjustment to it of 1318, and another of 1326 came into play. Failing a direct Brucean heir, the succession to the Scottish throne should pass to the child of Marjorie Bruce, Robert I's daughter, and Walter, the Steward of the kingdom. This child, Robert Stewart, had been recognised as the heir presumptive to the throne if David Bruce should die without an heir. Robert Stewart, now 55 years old, succeeded – not without difficulty – as Robert II of Scotland, crowned on 26 March 1371 at Scone. The Stewart dynasty, which was to last until the death of Queen Anne in 1714, was launched. And this was an Ayrshire dynasty.

The coming together of Ayrshire

The Stewards of Scotland, it will be remembered, had been given Kyle Stewart as their patrimony in the twelfth century, with Dundonald Castle as *caput* and Prestwick as administrative centre. The southern half of Kyle, with Ayr as its *caput*, had been reserved to the king – Kyle Regis. When Robert Bruce as Earl of Carrick had become king, Carrick and Kyle Regis became equally crown lands. As mentioned earlier, the Steward became lord of Cuninghame. And when Robert the Steward became King Robert II, Kyle Stewart and Cuninghame were added to Kyle Regis and Carrick as crown lands. As these four contiguous properties had been under the single jurisdiction of the Sheriff of Ayr since at least 1207, they now amalgamated for most practical purposes as 'Ayrshire', from Robert's coronation in 1371.

In this rather tortuous fashion one of the principal provinces of Scotland was born at last, created from two fragments of Damnonian Strathclyde and one detached segment of Novantan Rheged-Galloway. Thus also the two disparate royal lines of Scotland – that of Kenneth mac Alpin through Malcolm Canmore, and that of Fergus of Galloway – were united in the Ayrshire amalgam.

6. AYRSHIRE AS BATTLEGROUND:
THE CASTLES AND THEIR OWNERS

Families and property

Already, long before 1371, certain families had established themselves in various parts of what was to become Ayrshire. Balliols and Comyns had supplanted de Morvilles in Cuninghame; the Stewarts were in Kyle Stewart, the de Carricks in Carrick. In Cuninghame also there were Boyds, Cuninghames and Montgomeries. All of these came to the fore after Bannockburn, replacing the ejected Balliols and Comyns and subject to the lordship of the Steward over Cuninghame, awarded by Bruce in 1315. In Kyle (both Stewart and Regis) the Wallaces began to extend their tentacles, and in Carrick the Kennedys revealed themselves as a most powerful gang, subject, however, to dreadful internal dissensions. The Craufurds and the Campbells, Kilmarnock and Loudoun folk, also made their presence felt, the Campbells becoming Sheriffs of Ayr from an early time. The Stewarts themselves, of course, were initially the most successful family grouping of all, in spite of their desperately bad luck as the Scottish royal family; they spread webs of influential relationships over the whole kingdom, and the political history of Scotland for the next 350 years is the history of this extended Ayrshire family from Dundonald.

Many of these families, of course, had come in with the Normans, but one or two – the Campbells and the Craufurds, for example – seem to have deeper roots, going back to the Strathclyde era. Robert I, David II, Robert II and Robert III, by issuing fresh territorial charters, placed all the families on the same footing or starting block, to pursue their fortunes through the next few centuries on equal terms, however unequal the outcome. Throughout this race the fluctuating luck of each family is reflected in their territorial acquisitions and retentions – and now, for the first time in the historical record, in the buildings which they have left as monuments in various states of preservation throughout the county.

Perhaps this would be an appropriate place to consider the strongpoints from which all these families operated whether defensively or offensively – the Ayrshire castles, of which there is an extraordinary proliferation.

In the early days, when the motte-building phase had drawn to its close, there were only a few stone-built castles in Ayrshire, including **Loch Doon Castle** (possibly founded on a crannog), **Turnberry, Ardrossan, Dundonald Castle, Craigie, Rowallan, Cessnock,** the stone structures found above the motte at **Portincross, Auld Hill,** and possibly one or two others such as **Terringzean.** These were castles of enceinte, mere circuits of curtain wall initially with wooden buildings facing inward from round the courtyard. Eventually stone towers were built at one end of the circuit, as at Loch Doon. In the later fourteenth century a more formidable style of building was initiated by the Ayrshire royalty, as is shown by the immense tower which they constructed at **Dundonald** on the foundations of the old enceinte structure, and the motte and Iron Age fort beneath that. Grimly defensive structures such as the one at **Dunure** constructed for John Kennedy in about 1367 seem to have been fashionable in Scotland at that time, although the softer life was catered for as well: at **Portincross,** which was used by the second and third Roberts as a stop-over on their way from **Dundonald** to their hunting estates on Bute, two kitchens were installed to look after the needs of a large court party. But the great time of castle-building in Ayrshire seems to have been the fifteenth and sixteenth centuries. A spot check on the (known and approximate) dates of construction or substantial reconstruction of Ayrshire castles listed in the Gazetteer gives a figure of twenty-nine for the fifteenth and forty-one for the sixteenth century. A great many of them are simple square or L-shaped towers (on plan) – like the Clyde fortalices at **Wee Cumbrae, Skelmorlie, Fairlie** and **Law**, which may have been built by the same architect in the late 1460s (one of them, Law, as a semi-royal residence for James III's sister Princess Mary, who married Thomas Boyd, Earl of Arran). In the first half of the sixteenth century, grim, business-like small strengths like **Kingencleuch** or the Ducat Tower at **Newmilns** were still being put up in numbers. Of course even then one or two castles seem to have fulfilled a more ornamental, merely residential function, like **Kerelaw**, which was burnt down, rebuilt and from 1545 used as a winter residence by the Earl of Glencairn. Then, towards the end of the sixteenth century, a new less military and more elegant style of building, suited to rich gentlemen's country seats, asserted itself, with the characteristic 'pepper-pot' upper storeys corbelled out: we find examples of this style in castles such as **Killochan** (1586), **Maybole, Cassillis** (in the extensions) and **Kilhenzie.** This profile in the upper works, giving the typical silhouette by which Scottish castles are mostly recognised, may in Ayrshire have preceded its blossoming in the north-east, in castles like Glamis or Craigievar.

The families who inhabited these buildings profited by their association with the Stewarts and the crown lands of Ayrshire, and not a few of their representatives played dramatic parts locally and nationally. Accordingly the *dramatis personae* should be introduced briefly.

Kennedy

An uncertain attribution traces the Kennedy family back as far as McKenane, an eleventh-century Western Isles chief.[108] It is more certain that Kennedys in the twelfth century fought for Gilbert the son of Fergus in his rivalry with Uchtred before accompanying Duncan fitz Gilbert into Carrick when Duncan was awarded the lordship of the territory in 1187 after losing Galloway to Roland fitz Uchtred.[109] The Kennedys established themselves in a commanding position in Carrick in the succeeding generations, but were not formally recognised as the leading family until they succeeded in supplanting the descendants of the earl's family (de Carrick) in certain traditional offices:[110] that of *kenkynnol* (rights including that of leading the Carrick men in time of war), the bailieship of Carrick and the keepership of Loch Doon Castle.

The assignment of these responsibilities to John Kennedy of Dunure came in three charters of Robert II signed in the first year of his reign in 1372; from then may be dated the dominance of the Dunure branch among the Carrick Kennedys and in Carrick generally, and their territorial expansion to include important nuclei of power. John Kennedy of Dunure seems to have had freebooting and opportunist tendencies. 'By chance' he rescued the Montgomerie heiress of Cassillis from the laird of Dalrymple and carried her off; he fraudulently promised to marry her, and thus induced her to 'resing her landis in the Kingis handis in fauoris off him',[111] i.e. he obtained them by royal charter. Kennedy also acquired first one half of the barony of Dalrymple, and then the other, by charters dated 1371 and 1377 respectively,[112] backed by shocking violence involving the murder of two Dalrymples. This is typical of the behaviour of the land-hungry lords of Ayrshire of the early days. The family acquired more territory by various means in every part of Carrick. Kennedy entries in the gazetteer are **Ailsa Craig Castle, Ardstinchar, Baltersan, Bargany, Blairquhan** (formerly Kennedy), **Brunston Castle, Craigneil, Cassillis House** (as mentioned above), **Culzean-Cove, Greenan Castle, Dalduff,** the **Dalquharrans** (probably including **Lochmodie**), **Dunure Castle, Kilhenzie, Kilkerran-Barclanachan** (Barclanachan was formerly Kennedy: Kilkerran is now Fergusson property), **Kirkhill, Knockdaw, Loch Doon Castle, Newark Castle** (Ayr), **Pinmore,** and **Pinwherry.**

The family flourished in the state, and one of its distinguished early representatives was James Kennedy (1408–65), Bishop of Dunkeld and St Andrews, a leading statesman and diplomat during the reigns of James II and James III and the founder of St Andrews University. The head of the family graduated to be Earl of Cassillis (eventually, in 1831, Marquis of Ailsa).

Boyd

Robert Boyd of Noddsdale near Largs had deserved well of Robert I. He had broken his oath to Edward I, had been out with Wallace, escorted Bruce's queen before her capture in 1306 and fought doughtily alongside the king before and after Bannockburn. He was awarded a great swathe of Cuninghame, including the rich lands of Kilmarnock. He was captured in 1333 at Halidon Hill and died not long after. His eldest son, Sir Thomas Boyd of Kilmarnock, was captured with King David II in 1346 and shared his captivity. His descendants, owning one of the wealthier lordships of south-west Scotland, gradually acquired great power and influence, rising to a peak in the middle years of the fifteenth century, during the mysterious and tumultuous reign of James III.

During the minority of this king, on 9 July 1466 (a year after the death of the previous Ayrshire statesman Bishop Kennedy), Robert, Lord Boyd, and his brother, Sir Alexander Boyd, acting with others, seized the person of the fifteen-year-old monarch, and held him at Edinburgh Castle. Robert Boyd assumed the powers of a regent and arranged for his son Thomas, who became Earl of Arran, to marry the king's sister Mary. **Law Castle** above West Kilbride in Cuninghame was built in 1468 for the young couple. However, on the marriage of James III in 1469, the king and his supporters felt strong enough to accuse the Boyds of treason in parliament, and they fled in different directions – the Earl of Arran and his wife to Denmark and Lord Boyd himself to England. Sir Alexander Boyd, who had previously been ousted by his relatives from his position of power, was unlucky enough to be caught and beheaded on the Castle Hill in Edinburgh. Law Castle, however, remained with the Boyds until the seventeenth century.

Montgomerie

Sir John de Montgomerie had also switched sides during the Wars of Independence and fought alongside Robert I. His eldest son, Alexander de Montgomerie, a man of diplomatic ability, took part in the tortuous negotiations leading up to the release of David II in 1357. His son in turn, another Sir John de Montgomerie, married an Eglinton family heiress, and acquired the great baronies of Ardrossan and Eglinton after her father's death in 1378. This set the Montgomeries on their relentless course of land acquisition in Ayrshire, a course which was to last right up to the eighteenth century. In 1388 Sir John and his eldest son fought at the Battle of Otterburn, where the Scots were victorious but young Montgomerie died. His brother, yet another Sir John, was captured at Homildon Hill in 1402, where the English won. Montgomerie properties in Cuninghame included **Hessilhead (Hazlehead)**, **Giffen**, **Braidstane**, **Knock**, **Skelmorlie**, **Ardrossan**, **Eglinton**, **Stane** and **Seagate Castles**.

Cuninghame

Sir Robert Cuninghame of Kilmaurs was another oath-breaker of 1296, fighting on the Bruce side during the Wars of Independence. Sir William Cuninghame of Kilmaurs, perhaps Sir Robert's son, married Eleanor Bruce some time before 1361 and became Earl of Carrick, a title that did not stay with the Cuninghames. Apart from that, however, they were very acquisitive landowners, though perhaps less successful than their eventual rivals, the Montgomeries. Their properties included **Aiket**, **Auchinharvie**, **Clonbeith**, **Lainshaw**, **Robertland**, **Caprington**, **Corsehill**, **Kerelaw**,

Kilmaurs and **Glengarnock**. Sir Alexander Cuninghame of Kilmaurs, a supporter of James III, was created Lord Kilmaurs in 1450 and was raised to the rank of Earl of Glencairn in 1488 just before the Battle of Sauchieburn, in which both he and his royal patron were killed. His descendant, Cuthbert Cuninghame, was restored to the earldom in 1503 (though the patent was not formally renewed until more than a century later).

Craufurd and Campbell

These families, from the eastern part of Ayrshire, became intertwined at an early stage. They are not Anglo-Norman, and may represent a continuance of the ancient native aristocracy of Strathclyde. Craufurd (Crawford, Craufuird), 'Crooked Ford', is an Anglo-Saxon name which may have come into the Clyde area as early as Prestwick and other place-names contemporary with the Northumbrian invasion of 752. According to Professor Barrow, the name Campbell, 'Crooked Mouth', is of unknown though clearly Celtic origin,[113] and its bearers come into prominence only during and after the Wars of Independence, when Sir Neil Campbell was one of the close companions of Robert the Bruce at the lowest ebb of his fortunes. Sir Neil, who married the sister of Robert Bruce, died about 1316, and his son, Colin Campbell, received the lands of Lochawe from Bruce at about the same time.

Sir Reginald de Craufurd married the heiress of Loudoun (of the original family of James fitz Lambinus, a de Morville vassal) before 1220. He was one of the earliest Sheriffs of Ayr, if not the earliest, and from him sprang a line of hereditary sheriffs continuing down to the time of the Wars of Independence: Hugh de Craufurd, the grandson of the first Reginald, had a daughter, Margaret, who married Sir Malcolm Wallace of Ellerslie near Paisley, and this union is (doubtfully) said to have produced the famous Sir William Wallace, the hero of the first part of the Wars of Independence. The second Sir Reginald, Hugh's son, was one of the Ayrshire notables whose treacherous murder by the English in 1297 was, according to Blind Harry, avenged by William Wallace in the episode of the Barns of Ayr. The third Sir Reginald, son of the second, died in the same year as William Wallace, 1305, leaving a daughter, Susanne, who married Sir Duncan Campbell, possibly a grandson of Sir Colin Campbell of Lochawe. Sir Duncan became proprietor of Loudoun as well as Sheriff of Ayr by a charter of Robert I in 1318. The Campbells, thereafter styled 'of Loudoun', continued the line of hereditary sheriffs. In 1620 Sir John Campbell of Lawers married the Campbell heiress of Loudoun and 1633 was created Earl of Loudoun. Original Campbell properties in Ayrshire include **Loudoun**, **Newmilns**, **Cessnock** and **Kingencleugh**.

Craufurdland Castle has been held by the Craufurd family since very early days. It lies on the Craufurdland Water north-east of Kilmarnock.

They extended their interest into Kyle. Properties of the Craufurds there and elsewhere in Ayrshire included **Drongan**, **Drumsuie**, **Kerse**, **Kilbirnie**, and **Cumnock (The Ward**, or **Lefnoreis)**.

Mure

The fortunes of the family of Mure of Rowallan began, so the story goes, with Gilcrist Mure, who showed outstanding gallantry at the Battle of Largs in 1263 and was rewarded by Alexander III with the hand of Isabel Comyn, the heiress of Rowallan. The family may have chosen the wrong side during the Wars of Independence, for some of their lands seem to have been redistributed to Boyd of Kilmarnock in a charter of Robert I. However the family obviously made a recovery and restored their battered patrimony, including **Rowallan Castle.** Thereafter King Robert II, while still Steward of Scotland in 1347, married Elizabeth Mure of Rowallan – probably after seducing her and having several children; the legitimacy of this marriage (solemnised in **Our Lady Kirk of Kyle** near Prestwick) was later questioned with regard to the right to the throne of the whole Stewart dynasty. The properties of the Mure families in Ayrshire included **Auchendrayne** and **Cloncaird**.

Wallace

Paterson[114] is of the opinion that the famous Sir William Wallace was born in Ellerslie near Paisley but spent much time in his youth in Riccarton near Kilmarnock. The Wallace family had been in possession of Riccarton at least since the time of Alexander II, no later than 1249. John Wallace of Riccarton married the Lindsay heiress of **Craigie** in the year of Robert II's coronation, 1371, and from that time onward dates the strong influence of the Wallaces in Kyle. They remained in possession of Craigie till 1600, when they moved to Newton-upon-Ayr and Craigie Castle was allowed to fall into ruin. After 1371 Sir Duncan Wallace was granted the barony of **Sundrum**, having married Eleanor Bruce, Countess of Carrick. Sir Duncan appears to have been her second husband, the first having been a Cuninghame who married her before 1361.

Other Wallace properties included **Carnell** (probably built by Adam Wallace before 1510) and **Auchencruive**. The family became possessed of the hereditary Bailieship of Kyle Stewart and owned extensive property there, in Newton-upon-Ayr and Prestwick. There was a long dispute about the feudal superiority of both burghs, which in the end the Wallaces won in 1599 and 1603. They held control of Prestwick and Newton until the end of the eighteenth century.[115] The influence of Wallace is seen to this day in place-names in Newton ('Wallacetown' and 'Craigie').

The losing side

What of the families who were dispossessed after the Wars of Independence? The Rosses come to mind as principal sufferers, having supported the Balliol-Comyn faction. They were based at a castle called **Tarbet**, now entirely vanished, on the south-eastern outskirts of West Kilbride on the Cuninghame coast. They seem to have controlled the Barony of Ardneill on the Hunterston Peninsula, with **Portincross Castle.** The Rosses also held land further south, including **Trabboch** (a nearly obliterated castle) in Kyle. All this was given to the Boyds. It is of interest to note that the names Trabboch and Tarbet contain the same Cymric element *tref-*, a dwelling, and that these similarities may indicate that the Ross superiority went back to the time of the Cymric-speaking kingdom of Strathclyde. Trabboch and Portincross were transferred to the Boyds of Kilmarnock by Robert I from Godfrey de Ros.

The Ayrshire feuds and other matters

The two centuries following 1400 were stirring times for Ayrshire, as the various families fought for supremacy both at home, in Edinburgh and in the wider nation. Murder, lynching, arson, cattle-rustling and sheep-stealing, simple theft, assault, kidnapping and treason all figure largely in the complicated web. Perhaps the best comparison would be with the nineteenth-century American Wild West, although that did not last as long as the Ayrshire troubles.

The rate of castle-building may indeed have been accelerated by the statute passed by Parliament in 1535 ordaining 'that each man possessed of lands valued at £100 "in the inland or upon the bordouris" was to build a barmkin or enclosure "for the ressett and defens of him, his tennentis and their gudis, in trublous tyme, with ane toure in the samyn gif he thinkis it expedient," and men of less substance were to build "pelis and gret strenthis" for the same purpose.'[116] That 'tymes were trublous' had earlier been amply demonstrated in Ayrshire in the aftermath of the Battle of Flodden (1513), when the widows and families of Ayrshiremen killed in the battle were summarily ejected from their properties by greedy relatives. Robert Colville, laird of Ochiltree, for example, was slain, and relatives took violent possession of the castle; Colville's widow and immediate family were expelled until the Privy Council restored them. The same trauma was experienced in the case of David Dunbar of Cumnock and others.

Colville-Auchinleck

Inter-family feuding, however, had been going on for a long time before Flodden, as may be seen in the case of the Ochiltree family themselves. **Ochiltree Castle** was a little more than a kilometre upstream on the

River Lugar from **Auchinleck Castle**, which lies at the confluence of the Lugar and the Dippol (Dupal). At first there was friendship between the Ochiltrees (Colvilles) and the Auchinlecks, who communicated by means of a pulley, drawing a basket backwards and forwards between the two buildings on a kind of primitive ropeway. Relations, however, deteriorated to such an extent that in 1449 or 50 the Auchinlecks sent the Colvilles a sheep's skull by the basket, as a deadly insult. The Colvilles then attacked and took Auchinleck Castle by surprise and slew James Auchinleck of that Ilk then and there. Unfortunately for the Colvilles, the Auchinlecks had a powerful friend, the Earl of Douglas, who promptly laid siege to Ochiltree Castle and burnt it to the ground, killing Colville himself and his sons. The tit-for-tat killings and disturbances continued afterwards beyond the turn of the century and to the time of the Battle of Flodden.

That kind of vendetta seemed to be endemic in Ayrshire in the post-1400 period. The greatest feuds, however, erupted round about the turn of the fifteenth and sixteenth centuries, and the cause of most of them was the control and ownership of land.

Cuninghame-Montgomerie

In the case of the Bailiary of Cuninghame, the original cause of dissent appears to have been the award of the (hereditary) bailieship to the Montgomeries, possibly as early as 1448 or even 1425. If so early, this particular dispute appears to have hung fire until 1488, the year when James III of Scotland was defeated in the Battle of Sauchieburn by the forces arrayed under the leadership of his son, the future James IV, who thereafter had him assassinated as he fled. A fortnight earlier Alexander Cuninghame, Lord Kilmaurs, had been created Earl of Glencairn by James III – and slain along with his royal patron in the battle . It was in 1488[118] that Cuthbert Cuninghame, Alexander's successor, created an affray in the streets of Irvine against the Montgomeries, who in retaliation burnt down **Kerelaw Castle**, a Cuninghame stronghold. From then on it was war to the knife between the two families. In 1499, for instance,we hear of a street battle in Irvine involving Cuthbert Cuninghame and others, during which Irvine tolbooth was captured, and, in 1511, another outrage committed by the Montgomerie Earl of Eglinton and others, including what we now might call 'false imprisonment' of a burgess of Irvine in the same tolbooth. Murder followed murder, raid followed raid. **Eglinton Castle** was burnt down by the Cuninghames in 1527, and the Montgomerie family withdrew to Ardrossan Castle for security.

Outside Ayrshire, too, on the national stage, the Cuninghames played an important and some would say a dastardly part after James IV's death at Flodden, and in this case the motive was not so much the grabbing of land as simple, naked lust for power. The curse of a royal minority fell once again on Scotland, and the young James V was tossed between waves of faction-fighting among the various parties of the nobility. The English under Henry VIII did their best to intensify the trouble, and large sums of English gold helped to sow dissension and strengthen the opposition to the unhappy regent, the Duke of Albany. The Cuninghame Master of Kilmaurs, the future fourth Earl of Glencairn, was prominent in this opposition, and in 1524 personally scaled the walls of Edinburgh with the Earl of Angus at the head of 400 armed men, imposing their will upon Parliament and helping Angus to get possession of the young king. Glencairn, however, fell from favour, joined another army in opposition (this time against the Earl of Angus), was defeated along with Cardinal Beaton and, in 1526, got away with it by giving an undertaking to stay out of trouble in the future. He seems to have celebrated this escape by setting fire to Eglinton.

Campbell-Kennedy

The Cuninghames did not rest after this crime but had their fingers in many pies. In 1527 a Cuninghame of **Glengarnock** was one of the army-sized gang indicted for assassinating the chief Kennedy, the second Earl of Cassillis, on Prestwick Sands under the direction of none other than the Sheriff of Ayr. As Sheriffs of Ayr the Campbells found themselves in close and sometimes uncomfortable contact with the great Carrick family, the Kennedys. Despite several inter-family marriages, the Campbells continued to feud with the Kennedys and other families. The feuding rose to a climax in 1527 when the Sheriff of Ayr, Sir Hugh Campbell of Loudoun, organised a huge force of 1,400 men, including representatives of many of the leading families of Kyle and Cuninghame, to waylay and 'slaughter' Cassillis on his way to Edinburgh, on the sands at Prestwick. It is thought that the sheriff was urged to this deed by his wife, a Wallace, whose family were in control of Prestwick.[118] Sir Hugh absconded after the murder, and there was a period of open warfare in Ayrshire. The Kennedys are reputed to have marched upon the then **Loudoun Castle** and burnt it to the ground, but this outrage does not show up in contemporary records. Paterson says that the Sheriff 'had, in 1544, a remission for all crimes prior to that date',[119] and there is a strong impression that Campbell had been living normally at liberty and in enjoyment of his possessions long before 1544, if not immediately after 1527.

In spite of the alleged involvement of the Wallaces in the Cassillis assassination, it is suspected that the principal instigators of the crime were in fact the Craufurds, whose relations with the Kennedys had reached rock bottom. The Craufurds had property at Kerse marching with the Kennedy lands at Dalrymple which, as related above, John Kennedy of Dunure had acquired by skullduggery. The story of Kerse which well illustrates the death-and-glory spirit of the times. The exact date of the episode is unknown and it is not impossible that it is a pack of lies . . .

Craufurd-Kennedy

It was near **Skeldon** that the famous 'flittin' o' the soo' is supposed to have taken place. Old David Craufurd of the now entirely vanished **Kerse Castle** had been feuding with his Kennedy neighbours south of the River Doon for so long and so vindictively that they sent a cartel of war to him, declaring that they proposed to tether a sow upon his land as the ultimate insult, and to defend the position against all comers. Came the stated day and the sow was duly tied to a stake north of the river near Skeldon Haugh, and hundreds of brave Kennedy warriors ranged themselves in front of it. Craufurds came from all parts of Kyle and Cuninghame, and marched in warlike array to confront the perpetrators of the outrage, without, however, old Craufurd, who was no longer capable of riding a horse. All day long the battle raged and the Doon ran red with the blood of the desperate heroes. At length a solitary horseman covered with wounds was seen approaching Kerse Castle, outside which the patriarch of the tribe was sitting in splendid state awaiting news. The horseman said, 'Ah hae terrible news for you, Dauvit Craufurd. Your eldest son is deid and the floor o' the Craufurd men o' weir wi' him!' Old Craufurd interrupted him: 'Is the soo flittit?' . . . 'A' the Kennedy clan's sodgers are deid or fleein', and the soo is pit across the Doon . . .' 'Ma thumb for Jock!' cried the old villain in triumph. 'The soo's flittit!'

Se non è vero, è ben trovato . . . Sir Alexander Boswell, the son of James Boswell the biographer, produced a ballad in the early nineteenth century about the event, and it was published as an appendix to the seventeenth-century *Historie of the Kennedyis* printed by Pitcairn in 1830. This work, a very curious manuscript, has proved to be correct in so many details that 'the flittin' o' the soo' might be an accurate record of a real event too.

Cuninghame-Montgomerie again

Eventually, nearly sixty years after the burning of Eglinton, the Cuninghames reached the height of their anti-Montgomerie fury at **Lainshaw**, south-west of Stewarton. In April 1586, sixteen years after the estate of 'the Langschaw' had been bought by the Montgomeries from the Stewarts, Hugh Montgomerie, fourth Earl of Eglinton, was travelling with a small party of servants to Stirling where King James VI was holding court. On his way he stopped for a meal at the Tower of Langschaw, then the home of Sir Neill Montgomerie. During the earl's stay, his hostess, no less, climbed to the topmost tower and hung out a white tablecloth as a signal that the earl was in the house. Thirty-four murderers, including John Cuninghame, brother of the Earl of Glencairn, David Cuninghame of **Robertland**, Alexander Cuninghame of **Corsehill**, Alexander Cuninghame of **Aiket**, and John Cuninghame of **Clonbeith**, thereupon assembled beneath a bridge over the River Annick. The good earl, unsuspecting, was passing over the bridge, 'when, alace! all of a sudden the whole bloody gang set upon the earl and his small company, some of whom they hewed to pieces, and John Cuninghame of Clonbeith came up with a pistol and shot the earl dead on the place'.[120] The involvement of the lady of the house in the plot is explained by the fact that she was a daughter of the Cuninghame house of **Aiket**, and still preserved her family loyalty. The whole assassination was probably arranged by the seventh Earl of Glencairn, but he maintained for years afterwards that he had had nothing to do with it – and of course everybody believed the Earl of Glencairn!

In fact the feud between the Cuninghames and the Eglintons had been in some abeyance for a number of years, but after this deed 'the horror of the fact struck every body with amazement and consternation, and all the country ran to arms either on the one side of the quarrel or the other, so that for some time there was a scene of bloodshed and murder in the west that had never been known before.' John Cuninghame of Clonbeith, the actual murderer of the earl, fled to Hamilton, but John Pollock of that Ilk traced him to a house there, and 'in a fury of passion and revenge, found him out within a chimney; how soon he was brought down, they cut him to pieces on the very spot'.[121]

This feud at length seems to have petered out after a non-fatal squabble in a parliament in Perth and a formal reconciliation, in 1606. But the treacherous lady Langschaw is reputed to have been compelled to hide until the end of her days.

Cassillis-Bargany

The last of the Ayrshire feuds which we shall mention here is the complicated struggle between the two principal branches of the Kennedy family, **Cassillis** and **Bargany** respectively. In 1570 Gilbert, fourth Earl of Cassillis, had, as previously mentioned, extorted the lands of Crossraguel from the commendator of the abbey, Alan Stewart, by torturing him with fire in the cellars of **Dunure Castle**. The laird of Bargany, who wished to have the abbey lands himself, captured the castle and rescued the commendator – but the earl retained the lands. This caused bad blood between Bargany and the earl, exacerbated by Bargany's retention of Dunure Castle for some time.

Earl Gilbert died in 1576. During the fifth earl's minority he was under the guardianship of his uncle, Sir Thomas Kennedy of Culzean, known as the 'Tutor of Cassillis', an evil, devious man. The old laird of Bargany died in 1597, to be succeeded by his son, also called Gilbert. There arose a complicated dispute about the ownership of land in which a lady called Blak Bessy Kennedy, a widow for the third time and a large property-owner, was wiled away from the Bargany side by the tutor, who also took advantage of Gilbert Bargany's ignorance of the law to make him liable for large sums of money. This trick created unappeasable resentment in Bargany who, on the other side, relied upon the friendship of John Mure of Auchendrayne, an evil genius in his own right.

The dispute was apparently about money but was in fact about supremacy in Carrick. Positions became entrenched and reconciliation became more and more difficult. In 1600 an armed confrontation between large bodies of supporters of the two factions all but gave rise to a battle, and a plot in 1601 to shoot the Earl of Cassillis as he rode up from **Craigneil Castle** nearly succeeded. This provoked the young earl to lay his own plot to have it out with Gilbert Bargany. In December 1601 the two men and a large number of their respective supporters encountered each other at the Brockloch outside Maybole. Gilbert Bargany's men were hopelessly outnumbered, and Gilbert was killed. In revenge, on 12 May 1602, John Mure of Auchendrayne shot Sir Thomas Kennedy of Culzean as he rode from **Greenan Castle** towards Ayr. Mure and his son were eventually brought to justice, having committed another murder in an attempt to suppress evidence. They were both beheaded in Edinburgh in 1611. But the Kennedys of Cassillis retained the Kennedy primacy in Carrick.

Other contentions

These are just a few of the feuds that beset this district in the sixteenth century – by no means the most strife-torn part of Scotland at the time. In Ayrshire we have not mentioned the struggle in the Kilmarnock area between the Cuninghames and the Montgomeries acting together on the one side and the Boyds and the Mures of Rowallan on the other, nor the vendetta between the Shaws and Fergussons of Kilkerran. There was the capture of Loch Doon Castle from Sir David Kennedy by the Craufurds in 1510, and the murder in 1512 of Patrick Dunbar of Corsencon in Cumnock Kirk by William Craufurd of Lefnoreys and others. In the same year a fierce quarrel broke out during which the last Tironensian abbot of Kilwinning, William Bunche (later slain at Flodden), was assaulted in the precincts and physically restrained by the earls of Glencairn and Angus and their men, in an endeavour to make him resign in favour of John Forman, precentor of Glasgow. These are all testimonies to the weakness of the central power in Scotland and to the unbridled territorial ambitions and power-lust of unregulated men.

7. AYRSHIRE AND THE REFORMATION

The Lollards of Kyle and the Reformers

Before the turn of the fifteenth century Ayrshire had its first taste of the new force in religious thinking that was to shatter European Christendom into fragments. In 1494 the so-called 'Lollards of Kyle' had been arraigned and admonished for various heretical opinions including denial of the Real Presence, and a general hostility to church officials including bishops and the pope. They included Reid of **Barskimming,** Helen and Isobel Chalmers of **Gadgirth**, Campbell of **Cessnock,** Stewart of **Ochiltree,** Mure of Polkelly and about twenty-five others, all from the same region of Ayrshire.

The philosopher and theologian John Major, under whom John Knox the reformer studied, and who wrote in support of the right of the people to depose an unjust (or 'ungodly') monarch, was vicar of **Dunlop** in Cuninghame between 1518 and 1523. Later, under Henry VIII, it was to the advantage of the English to encourage the spreading of heretical opinions among the Scots as a spoiling tactic against the religiously conservative Scottish establishment. George Wishart, the English reformer who was later burnt at the stake, preached in **Barr Castle** in 1545. John Knox, an 'accessory after the fact' in the murder of Cardinal Beaton in 1546 and later a galley-slave until 1549, would probably have been burnt under Queen Mary Tudor of England, but she had little objection to his spreading heresy in Scotland. He slipped back into Scotland in 1555 (to marry) and preached his reforming doctrines in many locations in Ayrshire, including **Barr Castle, Kingencleugh Castle** south of Mauchline, **Carnell** near **Craigie, Ochiltree** and **Ayr.**

When Queen Elizabeth acceded to the throne of England in 1558, she let it be known that the author of *The first blast of the trumpet against the monstrous regiment of women* was not welcome in England – and so England lost a reformer and Scotland gained one. On 10 May 1559 Knox preached in Perth and Dundee against idolatry – and in less than ten days Ayr Town Council prohibited the celebration of the Roman mass.[122] Events gathered pace after that in Ayrshire and five local magnates – the Cuninghame Earl of Glencairn, Sir Hugh Campbell of Loudoun, Robert Lord Boyd of Kilmarnock, Andrew Stewart third Lord Ochiltree, and James Chalmers of Gadgirth – rode from Craigie at the head of 2,500 men to join the so-called Army of the Congregation at Perth which enforced Protestant worship in Scotland in 1560. In August of that year the Scottish Parliament decreed the end of papal authority in Scotland and prohibited the celebration of mass. In 1561, under the urging of John Knox and the Privy Council that 'all places and monuments of idolatry' should be cast down, the Earl of Glencairn took it upon himself to supervise the destruction of **Kilwinning Abbey**, putting his son in as commendator and thereby appropriating to himself the broad acres that had formerly been under the control of the abbey. Also destroyed were **Crossraguel Abbey, Fail Monastery,** the precincts of the **Blackfriars** and the **Greyfriars** in Ayr and many other institutions which could not readily be converted for Protestant use. In 1562 seventy-eight Ayrshire magnates came together in Ayr and signed a covenant to defend the Protestant way of worship.

Also in 1562, the distinguished and learned Abbot of Crossraguel, Quintin Kennedy, conducted a vigorous debate in Maybole with John Knox and seems to have won on points – but the disputation was officially declared inconclusive, the aged abbot diplomatically and probably wisely claiming physical exhaustion. In 1563, after the celebration of mass had been made a capital offence, it was in fact celebrated in **Maybole Collegiate Church** in the presence of a congregation of 300 armed Kennedy retainers. But Quintin Kennedy died in 1564 and after that it was felt that the old faith had been snuffed out in Carrick.

John Knox became mighty in the land – and, in 1564, at the age of nearly fifty, came to Ayrshire in search of a second wife. He wooed and married Margaret, the daughter of Andrew Stewart of **Ochiltree**. She was only seventeen years old and the opponents of Knox slanderously imputed to him the assistance of the devil in enticing her. It is said that Mary, Queen of Scots was affronted by the match, not because of the disparity of ages but because of Knox's impudence in allying himself with a member of the (royal) Stewart family.

Adjustment to the new order of things

Scottish Presbyterian Protestantism, based on the doctrines of Calvin, was not fully realised for several generations. Although the fundamental tone of the Scottish Reformation was undoubtedly anti-clerical and even rationalist, the function of bishops in the Church – perhaps the major practical bone of contention in the ecclesiastical quarrels of the Reformation – was not even quasi-formally abolished until the time of the Glasgow Assembly of 1638 and it was more than fifty years after that tumultuous gathering before the question was finally settled.

Not that every individual bowed to the inevitable. Some were in surprising circumstances. Captain Alexander Montgomerie of **Hessilhead**, who died in 1611, was born before the Reformation and remained a Catholic all his life, although he was a member of the so-called 'Castalian group' of poets around the young King James VI. He was sometimes engaged, not happily, in secret Catholic affairs, and died a disappointed and embittered man. Another poet, Hew Barclay of Ladyland in Kilbirnie, seized and fortified **Ailsa Craig** in 1597 – or perhaps 1588 – 'in the Spanish interest' and was promptly killed or committed suicide after his machinations had been exposed by the Rev. Andrew Knox. (He appears to have fallen into the sea after being 'discovered while laying in a store of provisions'.[123])

Inter-family feuding started to go out of fashion about the time of the Union of the Crowns in 1603, and as the Reformed religion took hold in Scotland, Ayrshire soldiers of fortune became aware of the new Elizabethan-Jacobean spirit of 'adventuring'. A whole new world of potential plunder opened up for Ayrshiremen and others. One example is given here.

Montgomeries in Ireland

The Barony of **Braidstane** in Cuninghame was possessed as a separate unit by John de Lyddale in 1452. A charter for this barony was granted to a cadet member of the Montgomerie family in 1468. A descendant of this Montgomerie was Sir Hugh Montgomerie, born in 1560. After travelling and taking service in the Netherlands with the Scots Guards under the then Prince of Orange, he accompanied King James VI of Scotland to London when the latter assumed the English crown. There Montgomerie met his only surviving brother, then Dean of Norwich, and the two discussed how to increase their fortunes.

They decided that one of the best ways to do this was to take advantage of the 'waste condition and unsettled state of Ireland'. After the defeat of native Irish resistance in Ulster and elsewhere at the end of Elizabeth's reign, many Irish people became demoralised, and their chiefs, including the great Hugh Roe O'Donnell and Hugh O'Neill, were so badly frightened by English persecution that they fled abroad. Many of the people of O'Neill were imprisoned or badly treated. One of these unfortunates was a certain Con O'Neill. Hugh Montgomerie, writes Paterson, '[rescued Con O'Neill from Carrickfergus and] obtained a third part of the forfeited O'Neale [*sic*] district in Ireland, and led over a colony of Scots, whose descendants people Ireland to this day'. Paterson continues:

> It is to be regretted that the castle [of Braidstane in Cuninghame] was taken down, as it was a kind of land-mark, and must have been the building in which Con O'Neil was sheltered on his escape from Carrickfergus, and in which the indentures and agreements were entered into, by which he gave away two-thirds of his estate to Hugh Montgomerie and James Hamilton. Perhaps the treatment of Con O'Neil may appear harsh, yet it conferred great benefits on Ireland; for James VI, with much wisdom, took Montgomerie and Hamilton bound to settle the estates with Protestants from England and Scotland and specially prohibited them from admitting any native Irish; so that these estates were settled with industrious farmers and labourers from the west of Scotland, who introduced those new and industrious habits into the district, which have tended to make Ulster so superior to the rest of Ireland.[124]

Hinc illae lacrimae. It was thus, perhaps, that James VI and I earned his title of the 'wisest fool in Christendom' – if folly is the right word.

Kings and Presbyterians

In the meantime, from the 1570s the Scottish Church, under the influence of one Andrew Melville, the author of *The Second Book of Discipline*, entered on a prolonged period of readjustment within the episcopalian framework and the assertion of its own independence of – or, some would say, supremacy over – the state. After the Battle of Carberry in 1567, when Mary, Queen of Scots was defeated and deposed, and civil war resulted in the emergence of the Earl of Morton in 1572 as regent for the infant King James VI, the Scottish church struggled in vain for a purer kind of religious governance against those supporters of the state who were wary of a presbyterian-clerical dictatorship. Even after the fall of Morton the government set its face against the setting-up of presbyteries – ruling committees of parish ministers of the Church – and against the condemnation of bishops. Andrew Melville fled to England in 1584 and the so-called *Black Acts* passed by the Scottish parliament in effect declared the king's supremacy over the Church, reasserted episcopalian powers and cried down presbyteries. Ultimately, in 1592, presbyteries were permitted by parliament, but bishops remained unaffected in their positions of strength. The 'ultra-protestants', however, continued sublimely unaware of the limitations of their power and kept on interfering in secular affairs of state, usually negatively, as when they succeeded (temporarily) in stopping trade with Spain or when Melville (restored to favour) denounced the king to his face as 'God's silly vassal'. This could not but lessen Presbyterian prestige and power even in the short run.

The result was to make James VI of Scotland very wary indeed of any kind of Presbyterian influence, and when in 1603 he additionally became James I of England he was reinforced in his attitudes by the vast increase of wealth and power that the united monarchy conferred upon him. 'No bishop, no king!' was his cry. Ayrshire and the west, by then resolutely Presbyterian, experienced the smack of strong government and law enforcement. John Welch, minister of Ayr, John Knox's son-in-law, who had exercised vigorous physical control over his unruly parishioners,[125] was himself banished in 1606 for preaching against bishops.

The Covenanting episode (1638–88) and the Civil War (1642–9)

King James VI and I was a canny man, who had an eye to the preservation of royal authority. His son Charles, born in 1600, was much rasher and more intolerant. King James had an abiding belief in the divine right of kings, but he also had realism, flexibility and humour. Charles, who succeeded to the throne of Great Britain in 1625, was much more inclined to stand on his rights, including divine right – and to be devious and faithless in his dealings with any opposition. He had an unquenchable dislike of Presbyterianism, and was determined to impose the Anglican form of worship on his Scottish subjects. By royal fiat he introduced 'innovations' into the Scottish liturgy, including an English-style Prayer Book, and regulations for the dress of clergy. These alien elements in the service were regarded with horror, as 'Romanizing'. An attempt to enforce them in 1637 led to tumult in Edinburgh, and in 1638 a National Covenant – a manifesto asserting the rights of the Scots to their own way of worship – was drawn up and signed by most influential people in the country. The result was the abolition of episcopacy by the General Assembly of 1638, which met under arms in Glasgow Cathedral. This defiance led to open warfare in Scotland – twice, in 1639 and 1640; on both occasions the king was worsted and had to make heavy monetary reparations to the Scots, who set up their own independent government run by a series of committees under the patronage of the great men of the country – the earls and other magnates. When the king's obstinacy provoked his English subjects in their turn to war, the English invited the Scots to join in on the parliamentary side, and they did so to some effect. Thus Britain became infected with the religious and military turmoil of the Thirty Years War that was tearing the whole of Europe apart at the time – although the British did not become directly involved in continental warfare, and took up arms rather later than the other participants.

In order to regularise the situation, the Scots and the English Parliamentarians signed a treaty of mutual assistance called the Solemn League and Covenant in 1643. At the same time the delegates devised what they called The Westminster Confession, whose 39 articles form the basis of the way of worship of the Presbyterian Church of Scotland to this day. The Presbyterians were often referred to as Covenanters in view of the two Covenants, National and Solemn League, which they had now signed up to.

While the king was fighting his losing battles against Oliver Cromwell, his lieutenant in Scotland, the Earl (later Marquis) of Montrose, was winning a string of victories against the Presbyterian government. What saved the Presbyterians was a savage outbreak of plague that prevented Montrose from occupying Edinburgh. Then the Scots under General Leslie caught Montrose off guard at Philiphaugh in the Borders, and the royalists were scattered. The Covenanters found themselves in command of Scotland. General Leslie went on and defeated the Irish MacDonnel invaders who had been fighting an almost private war against the Campbells in an endeavour to recover the ancient MacDonald lands of the west. When in 1647 he finally captured the fortress of Dunaverty at the southern extremity of Kintyre, he drove the entire Irish garrison to their deaths over a nearby cliff, at the urging of the army's chaplain, Rev. John Nevoy of **Loudoun Kirk** in Ayrshire.

In the meantime King Charles I had been conclusively defeated at the Battle of Naseby in 1645, and, faced with a choice, surrendered to the Scots at Newcastle. The Scots came to a financial arrangement with Cromwell and handed the king over to the Parliamentarians in exchange for a large down-payment. They then withdrew to Scotland, to audible sighs of relief from the English. The Scots had not made themselves popular south of the border. The king was immured in Carisbrooke Castle while the New Model Army and the Westminster Parliament decided what to do with him.

After having betrayed Charles I in this manner, the Scottish authorities also betrayed astonishing volatility: there rose to power a party which made an agreement or Engagement with none other than the defeated and captive Charles to restore him to the throne in return for token concessions to Presbyterianism. They set about levying an army to carry out their project.

Most of the weary population of Scotland simply refused to join the Engagers' army. The centre of defiance was Ayrshire. On 12 June 1648 a large party of horsemen gathered to resist the levy on **Mauchline Moor** south of Kilmarnock. Their leadership was incoherent, although it seems to have included Rev. William Adair from Ayr, and Rev. John Nevoy mentioned previously. A party of soldiers came down from Glasgow and easily scattered them. The Engagers carried their project, gathered a force, and marched south to do battle for King Charles. Oliver Cromwell met them at Preston and defeated them between 17 and 19 August 1648.

Immediately the news of the Engagers' defeat filtered through to the west of Scotland, the forces scattered at Mauchline reunited and, under the leadership of three Ayrshire magnates, the Earls of Loudoun, Eglinton and Cassillis, marched upon Edinburgh in what became known as 'the Whiggamore Raid'.[126] They took over the capital and instituted a clerical dictatorship which characteristically started to purge its own supporters in an attempt to make both Government and army acceptable in the sight of God. They called the legislative instrument with which they carried out this purge the 'Act of Classes'.

The Covenanters passed the Act of Classes on 23 January 1649, but on 30 January Charles I was beheaded in London. In Edinburgh the whole outlook altered kaleidoscopically again. Charles I was, after all, a Scottish king born in Scotland in 1600. The Covenanters broke off diplomatic relations with London, and proclaimed the Prince of Wales, a young man aged nineteen, as King Charles II. They then entered negotiations to bring their new king to Scotland, and actually did so on 23 June 1650. Immediately he was made a virtual prisoner and subjected to a prolonged course of Presbyterian brain-washing: the Covenanters were determined that the king should sign the Solemn League and Covenant.

The Commonwealth in Scotland and Ayr

Oliver Cromwell marched north in a hurry, despite being in poor health. He defeated the Scots at the Battle of Dunbar on 3 September 1650 and occupied Edinburgh. The Scottish government withdrew to Stirling and Perth, where they continued the attempted indoctrination of Charles II. Charles was indeed nearly driven insane by the determined efforts of his captors, and managed to escape in what was known as 'the Start' in early October, but was caught and brought back. In the meantime a section of extreme Covenanters came together in Dumfries and formed what became known as the Western Association; this body produced a document called a Remonstrance, complaining about the conduct of the war, which, they reckoned, had been lost because the Scots were still ungodly. They held that the purging instituted by the Act of Classes had not gone far enough. The Remonstrance was rejected by the Perth authorities, whereupon a large number of Presbyterian ministers walked out of the government, splitting it from top to bottom. The Western Association then proceeded to attack General Lambert, one of Cromwell's more seasoned veterans, at Hamilton. The General demolished them thoroughly at the Battle of Cadzow on 1 December 1650.

Nothing daunted, the rump Scottish government finally crowned Charles II King of Scotland at Scone on 1 January 1651 – the last monarch to be inaugurated there.

They repealed the Act of Classes, gathered back into the army all the elements that had been purged, and prepared to march against Cromwell. The king accompanied them, under duress. He had been compelled to subscribe the Solemn League and Covenant, and a document accusing his father and mother of wrongdoing. He never forgave the Presbyterians for their treatment of him, and after the Restoration took his revenge. But now he had no choice, and marched south with his army, to be defeated at Worcester on 3 September 1651, the anniversary of Cromwell's victory at Dunbar.

The king escaped, but the Scots had now to submit to English occupation and virtual integration with England under the Commonwealth. Cromwell set about subduing the country, building a series of fortresses throughout Scotland to keep the rebellious natives in check. One of the most formidable was the Citadel at Ayr, completed in 1654, incorporating the sites both of the large Kirk of St John and of the ancient Ayr Castle near the river. The garrison of this citadel provide one of the first pictures of ordinary life in Ayr, in their letters home.[127] One of the most abiding impressions is of the treatment of witches, several of whom were burnt in Ayr during the period of occupation. Cromwell himself provided a Witch-Finder General for England (one Matthew Hopkins) but ordinary Commonwealth soldiers do not appear to have given universal approval to these severities.

Charles II, James VII and II and the Covenanting resistance

After Cromwell's death and the collapse of the Commonwealth, Charles II was restored to the throne of Great Britain and Ireland with remarkably little bloodshed. He was a diplomatic and cautious character, intelligent, with his grandfather's sense of humour and the insight gained through danger, sorrow and exile. There was one exception to his leniency: Scotland. His chief persecutor had been the Campbell Earl of Argyll; he lost his head, and other principal Presbyterians were hanged. Charles II was as determined as his father had been that all his subjects should conform to Anglican-style church governance. In this, the king was assisted by the venality of the Presbyterian's chief negotiator, Sharp, the minister of Craill in Fife: this man allowed himself to be bought by the promise of the archbishopric of St Andrews, and deceived those whom he represented in dealings with the king before and after the Restoration.

By the time that the Scottish Presbyterians woke up to what was happening it was too late. Presbyterian assemblies, from presbyteries to the General Assembly, were forbidden; each minister had to be confirmed in his post by the local bishop before he was allowed to continue his functions. Over 300 ministers chose to be deprived of their livings – to be 'outed' – rather than conform to the new rules. Popular discontent and suspicion, especially in the west, was intense. The church historian Wodrow recounts that when the Earl of Middleton rode down to Ayr to enforce conformity, members of his entourage gathered at the market cross in the town at midnight on Christmas night 1662 to drink a health to the Devil.

As time went on it became clear that the character of Covenanting Presbyterianism had changed from being a party led by aristocrats to a more popular movement, in which small lairds, merchants, doctors, farm labourers, landless people and even women could take part. As such it became very much more dangerous to the central government authorities, and their alarm rose with the spread of 'conventicling'. Conventicles were irregular religious services held by 'outed' ministers, sometimes in private houses, and sometimes out of doors, when they could develop into vast assemblies of worshippers lasting several days, addressed by relay teams of preachers and even guarded by armed men. It was at this time that figures of Protestant legend arose – Alexander Peden, the schoolmaster from **Tarbolton** who became a charismatic preacher, John Blackadder from Troqueer in Dumfries, John Welsh from Irongray, and others.

Thus, when in 1665 Britain went to war with the Netherlands, where many exiled Presbyterians had taken refuge, the nervousness of Archbishop Burnet of Glasgow led to the imposition of martial law in the Lowlands of Scotland. This in turn led to a spark of rebellion in 1666. Soldiers had been maltreating a peasant in the small Kirkcudbrightshire village of Crossmichael, and others forcibly disarmed them. These peasants then gathered a small army, marched to Dumfries, and captured the local government commander, Sir James Turner, in his nightgown. They then gathered more forces and trekked northwards through Ayr, led by a Colonel Wallace of **Dundonald and Auchans**. They decided to go to Edinburgh, perhaps with no more hostile intention than to present a petition against the oppression of the times. They marched through Muirkirk and across country to the Penicuik area, from where they could see Edinburgh. Since Muirkirk they had been haemorrhaging deserters. The famous General Sir Thomas Dalziel came on them at a place called Rullion Green and defeated them easily as the November night fell. Large numbers of prisoners were taken, and of these some were sent to their home towns to be executed as an example to the public. Seven men were hanged in **Ayr**, and two in **Irvine**. Two were taken as spies near Lanark and hanged; their heads were sent to **Kilmarnock**, where they were buried. Others were sent to Glasgow and Dumfries to be hanged. This was the story of the Pentland Rising.

The troubles of 1666–88 in Ayrshire and elsewhere

After Pentland, moderate Scottish governments under the Duke of Lauderdale tried to cool the religious situation by adding a few 'carrots' to the big stick of official repression: they offered Indulgences, licences to preach on terms, to certain ministers who had previously been 'outed'. This policy had a limited success, but a hard core of resentment remained and intensified, especially in the west, in Ayrshire and Galloway. Side by side with the policy of Indulgence, governmental repression grew harder, and was enforced by draconian laws against illegal conventicling. It became a capital crime to preach at a conventicle, and landowners on whose property conventicles had been held were liable to heavy fines. A particular cause of resentment was a statute holding men liable to fines in respect of any of their women-folk or dependants who attended conventicles. The government devised a method of holding whole districts to account if conventicling was reported from them: they billeted soldiers on the inhabitants of the area and allowed them to plunder and destroy at will. Dalmellington in Ayrshire suffered particularly badly in 1678, under the so-called 'Highland Host'.

The assassination of the archbishop; Drumclog and Bothwell Brig

At length the inevitable explosion occurred. James Sharp, the perjured Archbishop of St Andrews, was assassinated by extreme Covenanters in front of his daughter and servants in Fife on 3 May 1679. The murderers, headed by one Sir Robert Hamilton, took refuge in the west. The apparatus of government reprisals swung into action. One of the government commanders in the region, John Graham of Claverhouse, got on to the track of Hamilton near the town of that name. While following him, Claverhouse came upon a very large conventicle at Drumclog just next to **Loudoun Hill** on the Ayrshire border, on 1 June 1679. He attacked the conventicle, but the young fighting men in the congregation, ready and armed for just such an emergency, repulsed Claverhouse's small force of dragoons and killed many of them. Claverhouse had to run for it and lost several more soldiers while retreating through Strathaven. This was the first – and only – defeat of a government force by armed Covenanters, a crisis for government policy.

All the Covenanters of the western territories now came together under the leadership of Sir Robert Hamilton and marched north towards Glasgow against the gathering forces of the government. They encamped beside the River Clyde at a crossing called Bothwell Brig. Divisions started to appear in their ranks, and they spent the next three weeks in bitter quarrelling, when they should have been organising for a battle. Shortly the government troops started to arrive on the other side of the Clyde, under the generalship of the Duke of Monmouth, King Charles's illegitimate son. On 22 June 1679 Monmouth fell on the Covenanters at Bothwell Brig and routed them dismally. Large numbers of prisoners were taken. Some few were hanged in revenge for the assassination of the archbishop, others were released or escaped, but a hard core refused to accept terms, and were deported in November 1679. The ship in which they were travelling to the Barbadoes hit rocks off Orkney on 10 December, the captain refused to open the hatches to allow the men to escape, and about 200 drowned.

The Cameronians and Airds Moss

After Bothwell Brig morale among Covenanters in the west of Scotland fell to zero, but in October 1679 a young firebrand, Richard Cameron, returned to Scotland from the Netherlands, where he had been studying for the ministry. He was violently outraged and excited by the presence in Scotland of the Duke of York, the king's Catholic brother, who was conducting a strong campaign of repression. Cameron preached inflammatory sermons against York, the future King James VII and II. In 1680 the Queensferry Paper was brought to light, a manifesto in which Cameron's plan for a clerical dictatorship on the lines of the 1648 Scottish government was set forth. Then, on 22 June 1680, the anniversary of Bothwell Brig, Cameron and his associates made an actual declaration of war against the King and the Duke of York, at the market cross in Sanquhar just south of Ayrshire. They then galloped off into Ayrshire, trying to raise rebellion. Alas, the authorities had been informed, and at **Airds Moss** east of **Muirkirk**, Bruce of Earlshall and his dragoons caught up with the Cameronians. There was a brief battle – the last ever fought in Ayrshire – and Cameron and eight of his men were killed. Others were taken alive, including David Hackston of Rathillet, one of the original party that assassinated Archbishop Sharp. He and others were taken to Edinburgh and executed.

The defeat of the Cameronians might have spelt the end for organised Covenanting in the west, but the Government's repression was redoubled and a system of oaths was introduced, designed to enforce loyalty to the crown and its system of church government, and to ensure the succession to the throne of the king's brother, James, Duke of York. One of the remaining Covenanting leaders, a man called Donald Cargill, who had been preaching at **Maybole** and who had previously pronounced sentence of excommunication on the king and the Duke of York, was taken and hanged. A hero of the Covenanters for fifty years, Captain John Paton of Meadowhead near **Fenwick,** was taken in his old age and hanged in the Grassmarket in Edinburgh in 1684. The same year the aged Sir Hew Campbell of **Cessnock,** descendant of a long line of Ayrshire Protestants, was accused of giving aid and comfort to the rebels at Bothwell Brig and, in spite of the breakdown of the star prosecution witness in open court, was sent to the Bass Rock, used as a prison island in those days.

James Renwick and The Killing Times

It was no surprise, then, that Covenanting feeling in Ayrshire in particular began to rise towards boiling point once again. Another young firebrand from the Netherlands, James Renwick, arrived in September 1683, and found a complete underground resistance network ready for use again. The hard-core extremists, now reduced to a self-styled 'suffering remnant' numbering a few hundred, had formed themselves into an interlocking system of praying societies constituting a 'correspondence union' based on the remote Logan House near Lesmahagow. This house was only a few kilometres from **Priesthill Farm** in Ayrshire, the base of the legendary and mysterious John Brown, 'the Christian Carrier' i.e. the correspondence union's postman.

After further repressive measures and executions, James Renwick decided to issue what he called an Apologetical Declaration from his hideout (probably at a remote hill-farm just outside Ayrshire called Friarminnion, in the Nithsdale hills). This threatened death to spies and collaborators and was posted on church doors throughout the region on 28 October 1684. Then, on 28 November, two soldiers notorious for their persecution of Presbyterians were assassinated as they left a tavern near Bathgate in West Lothian. The paranoia of the government rose to new heights and the Scottish Privy Council allowed themselves to take a step which can perhaps best be described as totalitarian: they devised and issued a loyalty oath directed against anybody who supported the violence threatened by James Renwick and his ideas. Any person who, on demand, did not abjure Renwick and his threats of violence could 'lawfully' be put to death in front of two witnesses. The Abjuration Oath was administered by servants of the crown such as John Graham of Claverhouse. It was from November/

December 1684 that the period described as 'The Killing Time' can be dated. One of the earliest victims was a Ballantrae man named Andrew McGill, who was hanged at Ayr in November.

The promulgation of this oath was followed by a Covenanting atrocity (the murder of the curate of Carsphairn) and a prison break at Kirkcudbright Jail, carried out by a large body of Covenanters, followed by a skirmish between those raiders and dragoons under Claverhouse at the Bridge of Dee. Claverhouse barely won that encounter on 18 December. From then onward executions multiplied.

The deaths of King Charles II and John Brown of Priesthill

On February 12 1685 King Charles II died unexpectedly in London and was succeeded by his brother, James, Duke of York. This man, who now became James VII and II of Scotland and England, was determined to honour the secret Treaty of Dover signed in 1670, in which the French king had made a large subvention available in return for the English king's undertaking to re-Catholicise his kingdoms. King Charles II, who had engineered the treaty, was far too wily to do more than take the French gold and temporize about the re-Catholicisation. King James, arrogant, obstinate and over-ingenious, was all for pressing ahead with implementation in full and was quite open about it. Panic seized numbers of British Protestants, and plans for rebellion were hastily advanced by two conspirators in particular – the Duke of Monmouth, who had crushed the Covenanters at Bothwell Brig, and the Earl of Argyll, the exiled son of the man who had lost his head after the restoration of Charles II.

In the meantime government repression rolled on in the west of Scotland. One of the centres of repression was the garrison at the **Ducat Tower, Newmilns Castle** in the east of Cuninghame. The garrison commander was a man called John Inglis, and his son, Peter or Patrick Inglis, was in his command. Peter was in the habit of taking out roving patrols in order to track down and surprise conventicles and the like and apprehend prisoners. In April 1685 Peter Inglis came upon suspicious activity – probably reported by a spy – at a farm named Little Blackwood south of **Fenwick**. He surrounded the premises and the soldiers started to close in. Twelve covenanters were inside, including the farmer, James Paton, and his new wife. When they became aware of the approach of the soldiers, a Covenanter named James White seized the only gun in the house and fired it. The light of the shot gave him away and he was immediately shot dead by the soldiers. Two other Covenanters succeeded in getting away but the dragoons rushed the farmhouse and arrested the other men. Peter Inglis then beheaded the corpse of White with an axe and took the prisoners back to the Ducat Tower. They would have been executed there immediately, but some difficulty arose about getting authorisation from Edinburgh. Peter Inglis was sent to get it. The next day the dragoons played football outside the tower with James White's head. As the tombstone in Fenwick churchyard puts it,

> This martyr was by Peter Inglis shot,
> By birth a tyger rather than a Scot,
> Who, that his monstrous extract might be seen,
> Cut off his head and kick't it o'er the green;
> Thus was that head which was to wear a Croun
> A football made by a profane Dragoun.

In the meantime the two Covenanters who had got away raised the country and gathered a large force under the leadership of John Browning of Lanfine (near Darvel). They raided the smithy at Darvel, stole the forehammers, and broke down the doors of the Ducat Tower, releasing the prisoners, killing two of the guards (one of the football players was put over the parapet at the top of the tower), and losing one man, John Law, whose sacrifice is commemorated in a tablet on the outside precinct wall of the tower to this day. Old Captain Inglis, who is said to have spent the period of the raid hiding under his bed, was in paroxysms of rage and two innocent men, one of whom may have been John Smith of Threepwood near Galston, are said to have been shot during the following dragnet operation. A Kilmarnock doctor named Jasper Tough, who had treated some of the raiders for gunshot wounds, was thrown into a dungeon beneath **Dean Castle**. But the raiders and their released prisoners had vanished into the heather, and Captain Inglis lost his command.

At this point, however, on 1 May 1685, John Graham of Claverhouse and his troop of specially-trained roughriders were called in. Between Darvel and Muirkirk these dragoons became aware of being under observation and immediately went after the spies. They captured them and it turned out that they were none other than John Browning, the leader of the Newmilns raid, and his uncle John Brown, the Christian Carrier. Claverhouse marched them to Brown's cottage at **Priesthill**, where he set about interrogating them in the presence of Brown's wife and family. While this was going on the dragoons had been conducting a search of the neighbourhood and discovered an underground 'vault' or cellar containing weapons and treasonable papers, besides accommodation for twelve men. Claverhouse proferred John Brown the Abjuration Oath, which Brown rejected with cool contempt. He said that he knew no king, that is, that he was entirely devoted to the heavenly king, Jesus Christ. Claverhouse then ordered Brown's summary execution in accordance with the conditions of the oath, and, after taking an affecting farewell of his wife and children, Brown died with studied indifference. The execution was intended to break the nerve of the younger man John Browning, and, in order to save his life, he confessed to his part in the raid and to other matters, such as taking part in highly illegal military training exercises in the hills with James Renwick. Claverhouse then sent him down to a holding centre at **Mauchline**, where he was hanged together with four other suspects on 6 May. This is the story of the martyrdom of the Christian Carrier and his associates, perhaps the high – or low – point of The Killing Time of 1684–5.

Most of the victims of The Killing Time were Ayrshire people. Between 28 April and 13 May 1685 no less than twenty people were shot or otherwise disposed of in various parts of south-west Scotland. After 13 May the flow of executions stops as if turned off by a tap. Only a very few isolating shootings at long intervals occur after that date.

The reason for this sudden cessation, and indeed for the clusters of executions preceding was probably the fear of the authorities that the south-west was going to burst into rebellion in support of the Earl of Argyll's invasion force then sailing from the Netherlands to raise Scotland against the Catholicising project of the new King James. On 28 May, a fortnight after the last execution, James Renwick and his associates issued a declaration which can be interpreted as an undertaking not to support the Earl of Argyll. The government seem to have kept their side of a bargain. Not a Covenanting finger was raised in support of the Earl of Argyll, whose invasion failed miserably, and on 30 June 1685 he was beheaded in Edinburgh, as was his equally unlucky co-conspirator the Duke of Monmouth in the south.

From that time onwards the harsh measures taken against Covenanters fell away almost to nothing, except at the beginning of 1688, when James Renwick was taken and hanged with great cruelty on 17 February. One final martyr, George Wood, at sixteen the youngest victim of the Killing Times, was shot during the dragnet operation following Renwick's capture and is buried at **Sorn** in Ayrshire. At the end of that year, James VII and II over-reached himself, and had to go into exile. His successor, William of Orange, a very cool and calculating man, reckoned that suppressing the Covenanters would be more trouble than it was worth and shortly thereafter the Presbyterian Church became officially recognised as the Church of Scotland, which it has remained ever since. The episcopalians suffered the temporary indignity of being declared illegal and John Graham of Claverhouse, created Viscount Dundee in one of King James's last acts, was killed at Killiecrankie in 1689 while leading what might have been a successful rebellion against the usurper. But the rebellion to pieces in the absence of the driving personality of its leader.

8. EPILOGUE: AYRSHIRE IN
MODERN TIMES: 1688–2003

With the death of young George Wood at Tincorn-hill outside Sorn at the hands of 'Bloody John Reid trvper' in 1688 the heroic age of Ayrshire comes to an end. Ayrshire people suddenly found better things to do with their lives than to give them up in defence of a particular religious orientation, which in any case appeared to have triumphed. Voltaire recommended cultivation of gardens. Ayrshire turned to cultivation of root crops and stock-breeding.

After the Union

The Union of Parliaments in 1707 meant that the Edinburgh-based General Assembly of the Church of Scotland, at last established after so much trouble, could no longer hold local politicians in leading strings, because the men of real power all migrated southward and the practical influence of Presbyterianism diminished radically. After all, the Kirk's anti-Erastian position, sternly rebuking state interference with matters of religion, had the converse result of isolating the General Assembly from day-to-day secular government. Religious disputes lost their attraction, as previously had the secular feuding of the sixteenth century. And, with the declaration of peace and the removal of vital pressure, splits developed within the fabric of the Kirk itself and half a dozen factions separated themselves and set up rival churches – Seceders, Burghers, Anti-Burghers, Auld Lichts, New Lichts, Relief congregations and so on.

Sanguis martyrum semen ecclesiae, 'the blood of the martyrs is the seed of the Church' – but if the flow of blood stops, the church withers and loses a sense of direction.

The eighteenth century was a time of steadily growing sceptical indifference to the message of religion. For Ayrshire this is shown by the case of the poet Robert Burns (1759–96), whose trenchant satires are balanced by his powerful use of folk tradition – demonstrating a continuing and vibrant Scottish cultural vitality. On the other hand, basic religious instability is exhibited in a characteristic messianic outbreak in Irvine: in 1783, a local landlady, Mrs Elspeth Buchan, persuaded herself and the minister of the Relief Church, Hugh White, that she was the woman described in Revelations xii:1. Part of the congregation, as 'Buchanites', followed Mrs Buchan and the Rev. White into exile from Irvine, first in Cumnock and then in Kirkcudbrightshire, where they waited in vain for a second coming. Poor Luckie Buchan tried on several occasions to jump from hilltops in the expectation of being drawn physically up to heaven.

In Ayrshire, then, as in the other parts of southern Scotland, the douce burghers were growing up into modern secularity and had no taste for the desperate fiasco of the '45 and the slow fade of the house of Stewart. The Earl of Kilmarnock, the one Ayrshire magnate who was foolish enough to take up arms in the cause of Bonnie Prince Charlie, lost his head. The others, the Earls of Cassillis, Eglinton and Loudoun, improved the occasion by rapidly developing into landed gentlemen of taste and fashion. (The line of the Earls of Glencairn, perhaps ranked fifth in terms of local prestige, came to an end in the late years of the eighteenth century.) And, as enlightened despotism became fashionable in the macrocosm of European politics, so in the microcosm of British politics the mighty aristocrats transformed themselves into improving landlords and farmers.

After a brief period of near-famine at the end of the seventeenth century and the beginning of the eighteenth, Ayrshire began to prosper. New methods of farming were experimented with by principal landowners, including the Earl of Eglinton, who was assassinated in 1769 for his pains. Both Eglinton and Loudoun encouraged the Cuninghame stockbreeding that from about the 1770s produced an Ayrshire breed of cattle notable for improved milk yields. Cheese production seems to have improved around the Dunlop area of Cuninghame. Farming was reorganised and new crops, in particular root crops such as potatoes, began to appear. Industrial production in towns increased, particularly in such fields as fine textile and lace manufacture in Kilmarnock and the Darvel valley. Coal had of course long been extracted in Ayrshire, but mining was not organised on a large scale before the eighteenth century, when certain landowners, such as Sir William Cunninghame of Caprington, took it in hand. Before the full blossoming of Glasgow, Irvine and to a lesser extent Ayr became wealthy through overseas trade in the eighteenth century – and Ballantrae became notorious for smuggling. The penalties of mercantilism were also visited upon Ayrshire, and the Ayr Bank crash of 1772 was one of the more painful scandals of the time. But landowners often remained wealthy and became connoisseurs of the arts, patronising architects like Robert Adam. The transformation or rebuilding of houses like **Culzean, Kelburn, Blairquhan** and others (including the lamented **Montgomerie House,** and **Dalquharran, Eglinton** and **Loudoun Castles**) belongs to the second half of the eighteenth and the first of the nineteenth centuries. Lesser houses too, like Belleisle or Rozelle (south of Ayr), owe their present appearance to the improving taste of wealthy landowners or parvenus who had made their money through trade in this period.

Industrialisation

The principal transforming factor in Ayrshire during the nineteenth century was perhaps transport. Roads had already been improved as a result of the agricultural reforms already mentioned, and by the technical innovations of John Loudoun McAdam, an Ayr man who had been born in **Lady**

Cathcart's House in Sandgate, went to New York, made his fortune and returned to experiment successfully with tar, setting up a company with the Earl of Dundonald to exploit the new techniques. Roads previously had been in an atrocious condition, and farmers had used wheel-less sledges to convey produce. Now wheeled carts appeared on the scene in greater numbers, and passenger transport by coach became a practical proposition. Then the technological revolution overtook Ayrshire, with steam transport both by land and sea. Rail carriage, initially by horse-drawn vehicles, had already proved the best solution for moving coal in the great quantities now beginning to be required, and the introduction of efficient steam-driven locomotives greatly increased the versatility of this mode of carriage. Railways were ideal for moving large numbers of passengers and quantities of goods at speed from point to point. It became possible to bring perishables such as vegetables to distant markets, making it economically viable for farmers to produce at more than subsistence level. Market gardeners started to flourish. Ayrshire developed its own rail network, starting in 1839 with a link between Ayr and Irvine and in 1840 one between Glasgow and the old North Harbour Street station in Newton-on-Ayr. The interior of the county was opened up by lines from Dalry to Kilmarnock and from Kilmarnock to Troon, Irvine, and the Darvel Valley. A link between Kilwinning and Ardrossan led to the opening up of the latter as a cargo and passenger port for steamships. Steamships had been first practically developed on the Clyde with Henry Bell's *Comet* in 1812, and by 1840 they were regularly plying Ayrshire coastal waters from Glasgow. In succeeding years they co-operated with the railways to provide a service between Glasgow and London, and the Clyde networks were greatly expanded to connect with Ireland and the Isle of Man.

All this, and the development of a long-distance railway through Kilmarnock to the south together with ancillary lines opening up the south and east of the county, meant a very significant expansion in heavy engineering and in the extraction industries dependent upon it. Muirkirk and Dalmellington in particular were vast sources of ironstone as well as coal, and ironworks of various types began production all over Ayrshire after about 1850 – not only in Muirkirk and Dalmellington but in places like Ayr, Stevenston, Glengarnock, Lugar, and Kilmarnock. In Kilmarnock specialist plants began production of railway locomotives (at Hurlford) and hydraulic machinery (Glenfield and Kennedy). In 1873 the Swede Alfred Nobel established his dynamite factory at Ardeer near Stevenston. Export industry included whisky production ('Johnnie Walker' – Sir John Walker's distilleries in Kilmarnock), ceramics, textiles, and footwear. From the 1880s steel production began at Glengarnock.

Embourgeoisement

North Ayrshire rapidly became intensively industrialised, and the original movers and shakers, the landed magnates, receded in importance. The increasing irrelevance of the aristocracy is aptly symbolised by the dismal failure of the Eglinton Tournament, a 'medieval' entertainment including knightly jousting in the old style dreamt up by the Earl of Eglinton at colossal expense in 1838. Everybody who was anybody was invited to the spectacle, including the Duke of Wellington and Louis Napoleon. It rained heavily and incessantly for the three days of the event, which ended up beggaring the Eglinton family, whose fortunes never recovered. Yet, of course, there remains to this day one memory of the tournament, whose survival almost makes up for the failure: the **Eglinton Trophy** itself, a man-size hillock or chess-castle of a confection incorporating ladies at windows, knights in armour, caparisoned destriers, banners, trumpets and spears, all done in solid silver and worth a king's ransom, fit to satisfy the keenest medievalist – or reader of Sir Walter Scott. After all the grumbling about vulgarity and lack of taste has subsided, I at least think it is a fabulously beautiful example of the silversmith's art. It may be seen in the offices of North Ayrshire Council at Cuninghame House in Irvine

The aristocracy were slowly but surely dwindling into insignificance – though it was a long dwindle. Yet Ayrshire's social status improved markedly. Ayr, Prestwick, Kilmarnock, Troon and to a lesser extent Girvan became known as suitable retirement places for wealthy businessmen, and the large and beautiful stone-built private houses that still adorn these towns were built in the middle and latter half of the century. The tourist trade was born, and day trippers from Glasgow ventured 'doon the watter' both by steamship and by rail. The ethos of the towns changed: the old Scottish élite of merchants, tradesmen and local magnates gave way to a more cosmopolitan, wealthy bourgeoisie – doctors, lawyers, industrialists, journalists and other professionals with horizons wider than the state of herring catches and disputes over theology or land.

Politics, religion, administration

The nineteenth century in Ayrshire began with repressed revolution and riots, as a consequence of the widespread economic distress following the French Revolution and the Napoleonic Wars. Rioting took place in Ayr in 1816, and in 1817 two Kilmarnock men were imprisoned for sedition. Then, following the Reform Act of 1832, which began the extension of the political franchise, the People's Charter sought to hasten and deepen the process of democratisation in accordance with the agenda of those who called themselves Radicals. In the same year as the Eglinton tournament, 1838, several meetings took place in Ayrshire and the Chartist movement briefly took hold of a large section of public opinion, with Chartist associations all over the county. In order to combat what the authorities saw as dangerous revolutionary fervour, a local militia, the Ayrshire Yeomanry, had earlier been set up, and at least once saw real (although apparently non-fatal) action, in 1854, at the Battle of Balloch Brae near Maybole. The yeomanry separated the two parties which have continued to menace civil order since then – the Orangemen and Irish Roman Catholics (who were increasing in numbers astonishing to Ayrshiremen whose ancestors had died in the Covenanting struggles).

Chartism was a short-lived phenomenon. But in 1887, at meetings held at Craigie Hill and Irvine Moor, the newly-formed Ayrshire Miners' Union adopted resolutions advocating 'the formation of a Labour Party in the House of Commons'. These were the resolutions which laid the foundations of the Labour Party in Britain. They were taken under the advice of James Keir Hardie, a lay preacher and former Liberal, who became the first Labour MP in 1892.

In the meantime the Church of Scotland had continued on its fissiparous way, division reaching a peak in 1843, when a large part of the ministerial establishment in Scotland withdrew from the General Assembly of the Church of Scotland in what was known as the Great Disruption. Sixteen of the fifty-six Ayrshire ministers voluntarily 'outed' themselves, giving up charge, stipend and manse, and helping to form a new Free Church. Local separations and reconciliations continued until Christianity itself began to collapse in the twentieth century and the principal disputant bodies came together again in 1929 for self-protection in a new-old national Church of Scotland.

In the nineteenth century the administrative framework of the county was modernised. The population increased and a new style of urban organisation, the 'police burgh', was instituted in thirteen different locations in Ayrshire that had not been considered populous enough to be granted burgh status in the past, or whose ancient 'burgh of barony' status was considered insufficient for modern conditions. These included Cumnock, Stewarton, Ardrossan, Troon and Prestwick. In 1889 Ayr County Council was set up by Act of Parliament, with overall responsibilities within the landward area of the county. In 1929, however, a much more radical reorganisation took place resulting in greatly increased powers for the county council in education, main roads, public health, planning and other areas. A new headquarters for the council was built in 1934, one of the few really handsome twentieth-century buildings in Ayr. As the welfare state increased in scope after the Second World War, its raft of new functions and heightened expenditure naturally resulted in even greater responsibilities for the council, and it became one of the biggest employers in the county, with a maximum of 12,000 employees in 1974, the year before the new reorganisation.[128]

The twentieth century

The period of the two wars is perhaps problematic for the historian of Ayrshire. Here is a century occupied by two of the most devastating conflicts in the history of mankind, occurring in quick succession, with profound consequences for the survivors – so that in retrospect, in spite of the relatively short duration of the two major wars, the whole century seems to consist of unrelieved conflict. Yet Ayrshire, for all its turbulent history, passed through these agonising crises almost unscathed. It remained a quiet backwater, an island of tranquillity amid the tremendous events that raged around it. During the First World War there was an invasion scare, as a result of which the seafront esplanade at Ayr was fortified with crenellations and a gun platform was built at the north end. The curved rail for traversing the weapon is still to be seen embedded in the old concrete. But the Germans stayed away.

Even in the Second World War we remained relatively unscathed physically – but hardly undisturbed. I remember as a small child in Ayr being carried in my father's arms down to the dugout shelter at the bottom of our garden as the Heinkels and Junkers throbbed overhead on their way to destroy Clydebank. Later that night my father, a special constable patrolling the deserted streets, emerged on the Low Green and saw the flames of the stricken shipbuilding town rising high in the air forty miles to the north.

Earlier, in April of that year, my Norwegian mother had wept for a fortnight, listening to the radio as the Norwegian forces retreated before the German onslaught. The Norwegian transmitters played the National Anthem over and over again, and fell silent, one by one, northward along the Scandinavian peninsula. Indeed I remember the BBC broadcasting their frantic appeals for small boats to hasten to Dunkirk in May 1940, in answer to which many Clyde craft went south, including a paddle steamer called *Waverley*, the predecessor of the now solitary surviving Clyde pleasure steamer of the same name.

That summer my father, fearing invasion, took his family to a remote farm south of Colmonell in Carrick. I went peat-cutting with the young men of a neighbouring steading and looked over to the blue hump of the Merrick, highest in the Southern Uplands, amid the perfect stillness of an Ayrshire morning, with distant waterfalls cascading lazily down the sides of the valleys. Back at home I saw long columns of similar young men marching past our front windows to Ayr Railway Station, conscripts going to the wars in silence. Memorials to them are to be seen in many places in Ayrshire.

And later I remember being with my mother in a shop in Newmarket Street in Ayr when the young assistant started to place flags in the window. My mother asked her why this was being done. The assistant said, 'Have you not heard? We've won the war!' We hurried home and my father took out a huge Norwegian flag that we had kept furled all through the war, and stretched it out above our front porch. The next thing we knew was that an entire contingent of Norwegian sailors from Neilston camp at the Heads of Ayr was parading in our front garden singing.

My father had a cask of brandy, obtained from some undisclosed source, and the Norwegian boys drank it dry – and tried to run away with my mother.

At the beginning of the twentieth century Ayrshire was a prosperous agricultural and industrial province of the United Kingdom. At the beginning of the twenty-first, its status is rather more in doubt. According to a survey taken in 1910, more than four million tons of coal were extracted yearly, and 319,000 tons of iron ore. Today the coal-mining industry is no more and iron-mining has long disappeared. The great industrial concerns of the nineteenth century have in some cases survived: Alfred Nobel's explosives factory, for instance, still exists, buried somewhere in the enormous works of Imperial Chemical Industries at Ardeer. But the metal industries of Ayrshire have vanished almost without exception. Agriculture itself is threatened, fishing has disappeared from the coastal ports of Ayrshire and the great highway that is the Clyde has been deserted since the closure of most of the ship-building industry and the ending of Glasgow's function as an international emporium of trade.

The upper reaches of the Doon Valley used to be home to a great cluster of mines, and Dalmellington was pre-eminently a coal- and iron-mining town. Even long ago small mines were run into the sides of hills, producing good coal from seams near the surface, and leaving a round hole visible from the outside, an 'ingaun ee' (an 'in-going eye'), for instance on the side of Benquhat Hill (NS 466 091 and 468 093). Alas, both the great and the small, the old and the new, have departed. The Dalmellington Iron Company, Houldsworths, Bairds, the mines at Waterside, Minnivey, Pennyvenie, Polnessan, Burnfoot, all are closed down, some for generations past. The enormous slag-heap at Waterside (NS 438 085), that used to have a spur railway line into its side, crossing a bridge over the main Dalmellington Road, has been 'landscaped' out of existence: it was a foul old monster resembling some apocalyptic toad, imperishable-seeming, but mortal like the rest of us. Bairds' great overhead cable-way, which used to span the head of the valley, visible from afar, with its stately, slow-moving procession of hutches, has vanished, and with it a kind of gritty, steamy, mephitic, industrial feeling that used to pervade the entire district. Dalmellington, I suppose, is one of the remoter parts of the British Isles; life as a worker for one of these companies, or even the National Coal Board, was crude, harsh and isolated – as may be understood by anyone who climbs up to look at one of the ghost mining-villages that are now sinking back into the grass, for instance, at **Corbie Craigs** or **Lethanhill** above Patna. But the impression felt at least by a relative outsider was one of industrial pride, even of metropolitan importance.

Some open-cast mining, with a vastly reduced work-force, has appeared in the Auldnaw Glen (NS 515 095) and points north, right over to the Burnock Water and beyond. But for Dalmellington itself the outlook is not encouraging, however bravely conservation trusts and similar bodies may try to stimulate tourism and interest in 'industrial archaeology'. Not that the theme-park approach is to be decried. Conservationists have converted a row of eighteenth-century weavers' cottages in **Dalmellington** into the **Cathcartson Interpretation Centre**. **The Scottish Industrial Railway Centre** has taken over the ex-colliery at **Minnivey** (NS 475 073) and operates steam locomotives as an attraction, and the **Dunaskin Heritage Centre** at **Waterside** is justly proud of its achievements. But perhaps the most impressive monuments in the district are just the two white-painted stones at the side of the A713 commemorating the unemployed of the 1930s (NS 431 091).

The heroic role of **Prestwick Airport** during the war as the country's only all-weather landing facility seemed to presage air transport as the replacement for maritime travel and trade, but the history of Prestwick since 1945 hardly gives confidence in the airline industry as the answer to the problems of Ayrshire. No more do the enticements of the tourist trade, which we have recently been told is more important in terms of Gross National Product than farming.

The agricultural sector is still just with us, but Ayrshire has recently had hair's-breadth escapes from the disastrous British epidemic of foot-and-mouth disease and from a totally unexpected horror, bovine spongiform encephalopathy.

Light industry, often provided by 'inward investment' is often suggested as a solution to the problem of unemployment, but this form of investment is subject to the vagaries of the international money market and of over-production, as shown by the closure of several computer factories in Ayrshire and elsewhere recently.

Another solution is said to be provided by education, but the twentieth-century methodological transformation in schools has, it is said, resulted in a higher national percentage of illiterates than in 1912 – even, according to darker rumours, a functional illiteracy rate amounting to three out of every four adults. Large areas of Ayrshire have become blighted with local authority housing which contributes to the 'ghettoisation' of the unemployable. Unskilled labour is no longer in demand and too many of our young men and women are unemployed.

Ayrshire is still a beautiful and wealthy province, fortunate in escaping the worst ravages of war, but its future is uncertain. It is not helped by a loss of identity. In 1976, a 'local government reorganisation' was brought in which deprived Ayrshire of its unity: in the place of the single county four 'districts' were set up, Kyle and Carrick (including Ayr), Kilmarnock and Loudoun, Cumnock and Doon Valley, and Cuninghame. These four and others were placed under the aegis of a Glasgow-centred region, to which the reorganisers whimsically gave the name Strathclyde. Ironically, Strathclyde Region embraced the territory not only of the ancient kingdom but also of its rival Dalriada in Argyll. It was the largest such region in the United Kingdom, with overall responsibility for trans-district services such as transport.

Ayrshire people and others grew to like Strathclyde, but someone in government felt that the 'two-tier' system implied by its existence was unwieldy. So Strathclyde has disappeared again, and since 1996 Ayrshire has been re-subdivided, into three 'single-tier' authorities, East Ayrshire, South Ayrshire and North Ayrshire, each with its own control over roads, transport, education, lighting and so on. *Divide et impera*, as Agricola might have said. Whether this present state of affairs will be any more permanent than its predecessors remains to be seen.

Part II

Gazetteer of Sites in Ayrshire

GAZETEER OF SITES IN AYRSHIRE

Abbot Hunter's Tower   NS 497 272

See **Mauchline**

Aiket Castle   *NS 387 487*

The first version of this castle, a plain tower-house of four storeys, was probably built soon after the Cuninghame family acquired the land in 1479. In 1586 the owner, Alexander Cuninghame, was himself murdered for his part in the murder of the Earl of Eglinton, and the house was virtually destroyed. Cuninghame's widow, however, had it rebuilt in 1592, with an extension towards the Glazert Burn, which flows close by. When it was sold in 1734 the new owners took away the top storey and 'demilitarised' the building, clumsily remodelling it to conform with their idea of a Georgian semi-classical country house. Thus it remained, latterly as a simple farmhouse, until it was entirely gutted by fire in 1957. However, once more, new owners purchased it and restored it, with meticulous attention to detail, to its pre-1734 condition, which involved rebuilding the top storey. This process took place between 1976 and 1979. The interior fitments, including authentically-styled roof beams and flagged internal pavements, were accurately restored, the staircase tower was reconstructed and a turret between the two halves of the building was rebuilt. The whole building was harled in white on the outside and the interior walls were recoated with antique-style plaster. The barmkin enclosure was made into a courtyard and the rear of the house has a splendid garden. This outstanding castle restoration was awarded a Diploma of Merit by Europa Nostra in 1987.

Aiket Castle is situated in a strong position on a bend in the Glazert Burn 2km from Dunlop. The nearest major road is the A736, about 1km to the west.

Ailsa Craig Castle   NX 023 994

The history of this airy fortification is obscure. Ailsa Craig itself belonged to Crossraguel Abbey from 1404, when it was included in a grant from Robert III presumably as an addition to the abbey's exploitative property holdings, i.e. rights of fishing and seabird-taking from the cliffs. The castle is supposed to have been built by the Kennedys, perhaps in the early sixteenth century and to have been in ruins in 1580. Thereafter, at the Earl of Cassillis' instigation, Thomas Hamilton, whose arms appear on a plaque above the doorway, refurbished the tower, which has remained in a fairly stable condition since.

The castle stands about 100m above the shoreline on one of the few footholds on the cliff-face. The building probably had three storeys, but

Fig 1. Castle, Ailsa Craig, from the south-east.

only two have survived, as has a forbidding vaulted subterranean chamber, as likely to have been a storeroom as a prison, accessible only by a dangerous trap on the stair landing at the entrance on the east side. The outside stair leading to the ground floor on the east side has long vanished but the marks of where it stood are still visible. The internal dimensions of the rooms are tiny. The second story, which is reached by a straight stair, has two apartments. The larger has a wide fireplace the length of the wall, and an oven at one corner. The vanished top storey may have had bartizans at its corners. There is a very small barmkin on the north side.

There is naturally no transport to the now uninhabited Ailsa Craig, but Girvan boat-owners occasionally ferry visitors, depending on the state of the tide. The scramble even to the level of the castle is very arduous, that to the castle well or the Garra Loch much more so.

Airdsmoss Covenanting Memorials   NS 642 259

The scene of a battle, the last on Ayrshire soil, fought between followers of Richard Cameron and dragoons under Bruce of Earlshall is marked by memorials to nine Cameronians killed on 22 July 1680. Nearest road: A70 west of Muirkirk. Access over rough moorland.

Aitnock Dun   NS 279 508

This dun is very much reduced. It has been built at the angle of a deep ravine, the Hindog Glen, in a good natural position for defence over the Rye Water – protected on its east side by a high cliff, and on the north by steep slopes; the two remaining sides, on which the approach is on a gentle rise, are defended by a double arc of walls and a deep outer ditch. Finds within the structure have included a lump of sandstone bearing two pecked cup-marks, burnt bones, fragments of Samian pottery from the 1st or 2nd century AD, a sandstone cauldron, quern fragments, and, in an upper layer of debris denoting a later phase of occupation, four Roman denarii, two of Antoninus Pius, one of Vespasian and one of Hadrian. The Hindog Glen region may be reached through a network of side-roads north from the B780 and west of Dalry.

Alloway: Cairn Crescent cairn   NS 330 186

The original cairn here was removed in 1963 and a modern cairn erected in the street which bears its name. When the original owner excavated it, more than a hundred years before, it is reported that he discovered urns and human remains. The modern structure has a plaque to commemorate the Burns connection with a suitably sanitized but, as it stands, enigmatic inscription from the poem *Tam o' Shanter*: 'And thro' the whins, and by the cairn.' When, six months after the removal of the real cairn, the mechanical excavators started to gouge out the earth round where it had stood, the remains of a small cist beyond the cairn's original edge were uncovered, together with minute scraps of bone and modern wood shavings. The full Burns quotation is as follows: 'And thro' the whins, and by the cairn, /Whare hunters fand the murder'd bairn.'[129] This would doubtless be unsuitable for a douce modern housing estate, but the question must arise – did the eighteenth-century hunters find a genuine, recently murdered bairn – or did they find the remains of the original inhabitant of the cairn – and, in either case, did they rebury him/her on the spot in a modern wooden box? But the scene of the possible crime is now buried, perhaps for ever, under tons of concrete and tarmac.

Alloway and Burns   NS 334 186

Ayr in the eighteenth century became noted for the pre-eminence of one man, Robert Burns the poet, whose birth in the then separate village of Alloway has been annexed for the greater glory of Ayr and Ayrshire. The 'auld clay biggin' (**Burns Cottage NS 334 186**) which is now exhibited as the birthplace of Robert Burns was certainly the local 'howff' or inn in the Alloway neighbourhood in the eighteenth and nineteenth centuries; whether this particular biggin actually witnessed the birth of the poet is perhaps a moot point. Charmingly thatched, it now gives a very clear picture of the way of life of the Ayrshire peasantry. It is a long house on one floor, with the south-western end divided off as a byre for animals. The human end of the house is provided with authentic furniture of the period. The niche beds in particular give a sense of the cramped conditions in the living quarters. At the rear, a museum houses Burnsiana of every variety including manuscripts, letters and early editions.

Alloway, Auld Brig o' Doon   NS 332 178

This bridge joins Kyle and Carrick on what is probably a very ancient route. The presence of two fortifications on the River Doon here – **Alloway motte** or **ring-work** on the Kyle bank and **Brigend Castle** on the Carrick bank – testifies to the sensitivity of this frontier. The present version of the bridge was probably built about the same time as the **Auld Brig o' Ayr**, towards the end of the fifteenth century, before 1466, if Bishop Kennedy built it. A graceful, single-arched hump-backed span with rubble spandrels and wing walls, it has now been by-passed by a modern road bridge and is reduced to the status of a garden or park feature, a footbridge used infrequently. This is the scene of the climax of Robert Burns's famous Ayrshire poem *Tam o' Shanter*; Tam made for this bridge on his way from Ayr because Shanter was and is a farm in Carrick above Turnberry, beyond Maybole and Kirkoswald.

For Alloway's 'auld haunted kirk', see the entry for **Alloway Kirk** below. The **'Tam o' Shanter Experience' (NS 332 181)**, formerly within the ex-railway station but now inhabiting a building of its own, gives a treatment of the life and times of Robert Burns using film loops and models and sound/visual commentaries. About fifty yards further on, to the left of a recently refurbished hotel, **Burns Monument (NS 332 179)** rises on a knoll on the right (north) bank of the River Doon. This is a splendid reproduction on a large scale of the choragic Monument of Lysicrates in Athens, and dates from 1822/3. The architect was Thomas Hamilton, who also designed Ayr Town Hall.

Alloway Kirk   NS 331 180

This ruined parish church is dedicated to St Mungo. Although the building is reputed to have been erected in 1653 (or in 1516) it incorporates many elements of earlier buildings, such as the possibly thirteenth-century double lancet window in the east gable, and a fourteenth-century cross on the lintel of a window in the south wall. The doorway at the west end of the north wall has a pointed arch which is also probably medieval. The bell which still hangs in the belfry is dated 1657. The first mention of Alloway parish is in 1236. The church was probably a pendicle of Ayr but in 1501 it became a prebend of the Chapel Royal at Stirling and the king was patron of both prebend and church – an arrangement which continued even after the Reformation and the severing of the Stirling connection. The parish was too poor to continue independently and so in 1690 it was united with the parish of Ayr; this building was allowed to fall into ruin. In 1860, however, Alloway was re-erected as a separate parish, when the present Alloway church was built on the opposite side of the road.

Alloway Motte   NS 338 179

According to Talbot's classification, this is an early medieval ringwork.[130] It sits on a steep bluff on the east bank of one of the pronounced meanders of the lower Doon not far from **Brigend Castle** (on the west bank) and the **Auld Brig o' Doon**. This is a typical 'hollowed-out' ringwork, with a D-shaped central area protected on the landward sides by a rampart. An external ditch can still be made out on one side. If there were any defences on the river side, they have fallen away; the bluff there is very steep.

Ardneil Bay Fishtraps   NS 191 475, NS 190 478

(1) NS 194 475. A line of massive boulders running north-east to south-west and designed to trap fish carried across the barrier at high tide and unable to return to the sea with the ebb.

(2) NS 190 478. An arc of large dolerite boulders dams off a pond of seawater below high water mark, presumably leaving fish penned within when the tide goes back.

Both sites are on the shore between West Kilbride and Portincross.

Ardrossan, Cannon Hill: former shell mound   NS 231 418

A large shell-mound existed until the end of the nineteenth century at this point on the inner curve of the Ardrossan (northern) peninsula, where a rock shelter overhung most of its length. On excavation it was found to consist mainly of periwinkle and limpet shells, as well as animal bones. Artefacts included a bone chisel and two needles, and some human bones were also found. No trace of this mound now remains. It stood just beside the railway.

Ardrossan Castle   NS 232 422

The ruins of Ardrossan Castle, a one-time stronghold of the Montgomerie family, still crown a prominent hillock in the south-west of Ardrossan.[131]

Although the building is very ruinous, it has been possible to detect four successive phases of stone-work. (There may also have been a previous phase of wooden building corresponding to a twelfth-century motte.) The first stone-built phase, consisting of a forward-facing gatehouse block and a rectangular curtain-wall as a 'castle of enceinte', seems to have been erected in the thirteenth century and destroyed at the end of that century, probably during the Wars of Independence. This might be the Ardrossan castle captured by William Wallace.

The second phase represents the rebuilding after that episode, when the gatehouse was restored. In the third phase the gatehouse was heightened and made into the towerhouse or keep, whose remnants are still the tallest elements on the site. Also in the third phase a south-western tower was erected, represented by the tunnel-like arch or vault that now stands open to the air. This, with the erection of stone buildings along the curtain-wall including perhaps a chapel in the north-west, is dateable to the late fifteenth or early sixteenth century. At the wall is a passage leading to a well.

In 1528 the Montgomeries took refuge here after the Cuninghames had burnt down **Eglinton Castle**. Phase four, consisting of the blocking up of an entrance and the insertion of a large gun-loop, may date from this time. The whole building was ruinous by 1689 – perhaps because Cromwell's troops had removed stonework for the building of **Ayr Citadel** in 1654 – and in 1911 the Town Council had some of the more dangerous rubble removed and the rest repointed.

Ardrossan Old Parish Church   NS 232 424

The first parish church in Ardrossan stood on the Castle Hill east of the castle itself. The foundations of the building, perhaps as early as 1270, are still traceable, since the wall-footings have survived. There appear to be two entrances on the south side. Kilwinning Abbey owned the church, and the Archbishop of Glasgow had the patronage. It had at least two altars, one to the Blessed Virgin Mary and another to St Peter. When the church was excavated in 1912, a possibly thirteenth-century stone coffin with a carved lid was dug up; it is now in the North Ayrshire Museum in Saltcoats.

This building was finally blown down in a fierce gale in 1691 or 1695. The parochial functions were translated to another church at **NS 238 434**, now completely gone, and thence in 1744 to Saltcoats.

Ardstinchar Castle   NX 087 824

The fragments of this castle stand on an irregular four-sided platform high above the south end of Ballantrae village. Two early towers survive – the most complete, in the east, being a mere corner. It was originally three storeys high, and a fourth was probably added as early as the fifteenth century, when a courtyard was also constructed. The castle dominates the approaches to Carrick through Glen App and from the Stinchar Valley (now by the A77 and the B7044 respectively).

The Ardstinchar property is said to have been bought about the year 1400 by an early Kennedy, who returned after a distinguished military career in France, settled down and founded the branch of the family that later took the territorial designation of **Bargany.** Rivalry persisted between this branch of the Kennedys and the senior Dunure or Cassillis line, culminating in 1601, when the Earl of Cassillis slew Gilbert of Bargany at the Battle of the Brockloch. Bargany's body is contained in the ornate mausoleum in the **Kennedy Aisle** in **Ballantrae.**

Ariecleoch chambered cairn   NX 174 782

This cairn, most probably Bargrennan-type, has now disappeared completely. The place was very remote, about 7km south-west of Barrhill.[132]

Assloss Castle   NS 446 401

Built into the structure of the farmhouse at Assloss is the lower part of the old 'toure [and] fortalice' of Auchinloss (cf. Auchinleck > Affleck). It now has a modern tiled roof with four slopes instead of an upper storey, but it is still recognisable as a very small tower-house. Its interior is vaulted. Assloss Farm is not to be confused with the nearby Assloss House close to the Fenwick Water in the north-east of Kilmarnock.

James Assinloss of that ilk is mentioned in a criminal case in 1562. '*Jacobus Auchinloss apparens de eodem*' had a charter from Queen Mary in 1543.[134]

Auchans Castle   NS 354 346

This once-impressive castle, now a complete wreck near **Dundonald Castle**, has gone through several phases since it was first built, probably in the late sixteenth century. Then it was an oblong block three storeys high, running east to west, with a stair-tower in the middle of the south side, thus exemplifying the T-plan. Probably shortly after 1640 or 1644 a north-running wing, three storeys and a garret in height, was built on to the west end of the main block, converting the castle to the L-plan. A square stair-tower with a Renaissance doorway was built in the re-entrant angle. A further extension came in the shape of a block built on to the north end of the first extension, with towers at the north-west and south-east corners. The south-east tower was round with a tall conical roof, and the north-west tower, like the original southern stair-tower, was corbelled out square with a crow-stepped gable, so that the whole ensemble gave a typically late sixteenth-century Scottish 'haunted-castle' silhouette. The garret storey had a fine gallery lit by a large traceried Gothic window to the south and dormer windows at each side. The building, however, is now irreparably ruined.

The estate was acquired in 1527 by the Wallaces of Auchans, who sold it in the seventeenth century to Sir William Cochrane of Cowdon, later Earl of Dundonald. Later still it passed to the Montgomeries of Eglinton.

Auchencloigh Castle   NS 494 166

On a mound at the side of the Burnton Burn, a few columns of masonry can be seen half-buried in scrub and bushes. The remains are difficult to date, but Coventry is of the opinion that they are of the fifteenth century.[134] There seems to have been a rectangular structure, fragments of whose walls still rise from the ground. Nothing is known of Auchencloigh Castle, which is now both difficult and dangerous to approach: it lies within the purlieus of a vast open-cast coal mine, where huge earth-moving vehicles trundle among signs warning of deep water. The nearest public road is the B7046.

Auchendrain (-drayne) Castle   NS 334 151

The original Auchendrayne Castle was the den of the fearsome John Mure, the henchman of Gilbert Bargany and the 1602 assassin of the equally villainous Tutor of Cassillis. It is described by Abercrummie as 'an high tower, with laigh buildings, surrounded with good orchards and gardens, parks, and good cornfields.'[135] The present nineteenth-century house was built upon the last vestiges of the old tower. It lies to the east of the A77, on the banks of a loop of the River Doon, a little more than 3km south of Alloway.

Auchenharvie Castle   NS 362 442

This ruin, probably dated to the sixteenth century, was a simple keep resembling Law Castle and Barr Castle in the shallow continuous corbel course, which is still visible on the south side, though the parapet itself and corner turrets have gone. The hill on which it stands has been all but quarried away and most of the structure has collapsed. There were three storeys, the ground floor with a semi-circular vault, the hall on the first floor with a lofty vault and fireplace in the south wall, and the third floor gaining width by means of thinning the walls. Two sides are all that remains, with a few vestiges of internal organisation. The Cuninghames of Auchenharvie originally owned the property, but abandoned it in 1708 when they moved to Stevenston. The castle lies east of the A736, about 4km north-east of Irvine.

Auchenroy Hill cairn   NS 450 050

This cairn, atop Auchenroy Hill (360m OD), is one of a series of summit cairns around Dalmellington and Loch Doon. The B741 runs past it to the north.

Auchensoul Hill cairn   NX 263 945

A summit cairn underlying the triangulation pillar on Auchensoul Hill
(314m OD), which dominates Barr village from the west. An arduous track
leads up from Auchensoul Farm on the B734 to the shoulder of the hill,
from which one must scramble.

Auchinleck Castles   NS 499 232, NS 500 231, NS 507 230

At least three versions of Auchinleck Castle have existed at different
locations within the estate, which is about 5km north-west of Auchinleck
town. The first one, properly called Auchinleck Castle, sits on a high rocky
point overlooking the gorge of the Lugar Water at its confluence with the
Dippol Burn. The Lugar represents the frontier between Kyle Stewart, in
which the castle lies, and King's Kyle to the west. The castle's date cannot be
ascertained, but the land was held by the Stewards of Scotland before 1241.
We know that the name of one Nicol de Achethlec occurs in the Ragman
Roll of August 1296. It is not impossible that this castle was his stronghold
or that of his successor. The remains consist of a few courses of walling with
an arched opening.

A few hundred metres to the east the second castle, known as the [Old]
Place or Palace of Auchinleck, is now nearly as ruined as the first. At one
time it was clear that the building, a seventeenth-century L-plan structure,
had a square stair-tower with a doorway in the re-entrant angle. This tower
had a corbelled-out caphouse without a parapet walk, and there might have
been three storeys beneath. Since 1789, when Grose made a sketch of it, the
tower has disappeared, and all that is left is isolated stretches of wall, with
two whole barrel-vaulted rooms on the ground floor.

Finally, the eighteenth-century mansion built for the lawyer Lord
Auchinleck, father of James Boswell the biographer, is a good example
of pleasant Georgian classical style in a rural setting. It is three storeys
in height, has pilasters on a projecting entrance front and a decorated
pediment (with a corresponding, plainer, garden front), and has a balustrade
running right round the top of the building. Alas, it too is derelict and has a
most uncertain future. It is set back again from the Old Place, and the view
from it down to the river is superb.

Auchinleck Old Parish Church   NS 551 215

The original parish church of Auchinleck was a possession of the monks of
Dalmilling near Ayr. When their venture collapsed in 1238, the church and its
pertinents passed to Paisley Abbey, and remained so until the Reformation.
The 1754 renewed church building probably occupies the place of the original
thirteenth-century structure. In 1843 this was superseded by the present
Auchinleck church, and the older building was allowed to fall into ruin;

it remained de-roofed until 1978 when it was reopened as the Auchinleck Boswell Museum. It is a small, rectangular building with 5m-high walls and 6m-high gables. It has a lintel dated 1683 over the west doorway.

Auchtitench   NS 181 719

The ruins of Auchtitench farm steading, just within the eastern border of Ayrshire high above Kirkconnel in Nithsdale, are probably now untraceable in the recently afforested Penbreck area. It is not impossible that the farm was used as a safe house by Covenanters like James Renwick during the later part of the Covenanting emergency (1679–88).[134]

Auld Brig o' Ayr   NS 338 221

See **Ayr Royal Burgh**

Auld Brig o' Doon   NS 332 178

See **Alloway, Auld Brig o' Doon**

Ayr Auld Kirk   NS 339 219

See **Ayr Royal Burgh**

Ayr Carnegie Library   NS 337 222

This institute is located just across the New Bridge in Newton-on-Ayr. It houses a very important local collection of manuscripts, books and other archive material. A Covenanting flag and other relics are also stored there. Associated with the library is the **Ayrshire Archives Centre** in Craigie Estate at **NS 344 217**.

Ayr Citadel NS 333 221

See **Ayr Royal Burgh**

Ayr Covenanting memorials   NS 338 219

There are memorials in the churchyard of the Auld Kirk to seven Covenanters executed in Ayr on 27 December 1666 after the Battle of Rullion Green (November 1666). There is also a tomb incorporating the effigy of William Adair (against north wall of church), minister of Ayr Kirk until 1682.

Ayr Royal Burgh   NS 338 222

The first beginnings of Ayr (chartered as a royal burgh *c.*1205) took the shape of a very small settlement in the shelter of a fairly substantial mound, on the south bank of the river near the mouth, at the principal ford, a position now occupied roughly by the line of the present New Bridge. From the ford a track mounted the rise southward, leading into a wide rectangular market place lined on the north-west and the south-east by dwellings. At right angles to the market place a passage between two rows of houses ran west along the line of the present Academy Lane, and this issued at what is now one side of Fort Street, the western boundary of Ayr in the thirteenth century. The north-west side of the market-place ran on southward past another opening and the site of what is now **Lady Cathcart's House** (sixteenth/seventeenth century) to a narrower outlet to a track leading out to the sand-dunes and a coast road to Carrick. The south-east side was appreciably shorter than the north-west, stretching only between a position just west of the present Town Hall to what is now the opening of Newmarket Street. Behind this line to the south-east lay an irregular group of dwellings receding in three or four steps from the north-western end towards the south. The whole ensemble could not have exceeded 300m square.

The river ran north-west past this primitive settlement to meet the Firth of Clyde coast at an acute angle. West of the settlement, towards the other leg of the isosceles triangle thus formed, there was a church in the position later held by the Kirk of St John. Between the burgh and the sea there was an inlet in the river-bank forming a 'haven'. This was a base for trading and fishing activities. It is thought that the 1197 castle occupied a position further out on the peninsula to the north-west, protecting both haven and town from sea-borne attack. (The other theory, that it occupied a site at Castlehill, 2km further up the river but supposedly on the coast in the twelfth century, would perhaps involve too violent a revision of current thinking not only about the castle but also about the position of the town itself.)

Above the settlement, on the south bank of the river, roads converged from the south and the east and ran along the line of the river to meet the approach to the ford very approximately at the junction of what are now Sandgate and High Street.

Such may have been the layout of Ayr when the *lineatores,* the equivalent of modern town planners, made their appearance at the end of the twelfth century. They came at the behest of the king to plant and develop an official trading post defended by a royal castle and controlled and supervised by a king's man – a sheriff whose writ would run from the Maich Burn to Laight i.e. from the north of Cuninghame to the south of Carrick. This was the trading precinct of the burgh. Ayr was suitable for the purpose, being

1. Ayr Harbour pierhead
2. First World War battery
3. The Ratton Hole (Old Ayr Harbour)
4. Miller's Folly
5. Ayr Carnegie Library
6. Newton Cross
7. Loudoun Hall and Ship (Boat) Vennel
8. Possible site of early Ayr Castle
9. Approximate centre of Cromwellian citadel
10. St John's Tower
11. Auld Brig
12. Malt Cross (site) and Town Hall
13. Second burgh market (now Fish Cross)

14. Auld Kirk o' Ayr; earlier site of Greyfriars
15. Auld Tour site (now Wallace Tower) and Blackfriars
16. Lady Cathcart's House and Tolbooth site
17. Crenellations on Promenade wall
18. (Probable) site of Newton Castle
19. Approximate position of Sandgate Port
20. County Buildings (1935) and Courthouse
21. Mill Wynd Area
22. Carrick Street
23. Cow Wynd area (Kyle Street)
24. Fauldbacks (Burns Statue Square)
25. Burrowfields Area

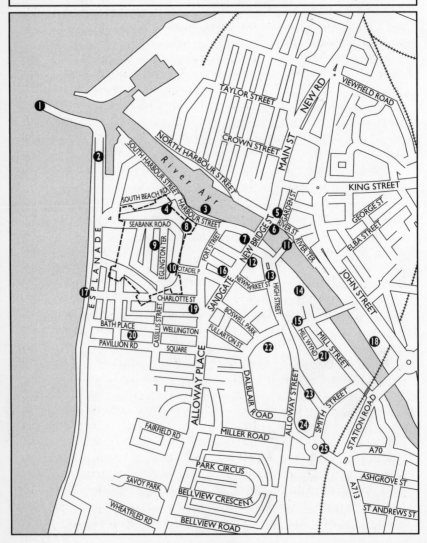

Street Map of Ayr

possessed of a market place and close to the mouth of a fordable river at the convergence of several routes – east from the Kyle hinterland, south from Carrick, north from Cuninghame.

What the *lineatores* did, here as elsewhere, was to mark out burgage plots or tofts and to expand and make coherent the limits of the town itself, with such additional roadways as seemed necessary. The tofts were long rectangular plots of land, contiguous, with the short side fronting the street, serving as homesteads and business premises combined. They were offered for sale to prospective burgesses – tradesmen and merchants who would make a living in the burgh and in return make over a proportion of their gains to the overlord, in this case the king, via the sheriff. The king set up the market anew, with strict rules and privileges respecting rights of buying and selling within the precinct of the burgh. Initially this was a highly profitable arrangement.

It was soon found that the original position for the market in Ayr was unsuitable for south-westward expansion because of sand blown by the prevailing wind. The position of the first market is witnessed by the width of the modern Sandgate (perpetuated by the building of a now-vanished tolbooth in its centre), but the expansion of the burgh now was to the south-east, with a new or supplemental market place just opposite the southern approach to the Auld Brig (then probably a timber structure). Burgage plots stretched south-eastward along the line of the river-bank and lined both sides of what was to become the High Street.

These plots were also extended to the north and west, covering much of the area of the former settlement, and filling up the approaches to the Sandgate market place from the ford. The continuous façade of commercial premises which is characteristic of the streets of central Ayr to the present day – as in most other Scottish towns – has its origins in the close-packed frontages of these tofts. The 'dog-leg' layout of the Boat Vennel in the space between Academy Lane and the ford dates from this period, when two or more tofts of horizontal and vertical plan respectively collided. The Boat Vennel led to the haven, a widening of the river on both sides, later to be christened The Ratton Hole. This gradually developed into a regular harbour with a common quay just to the north-west of the Boat Vennel. An extensive trade developed, dealing in raw sheepskins, wool, hides, salted fish and cloth.

Another street whose dog-leg pattern first arose from the same cause is now called Newmarket Street, formerly New Yard or Trinity Vennel, connecting the Sandgate Market (and St John's Kirk) with the new market area in the middle reach of High Street. The widening of the street to accommodate the market may still be seen at the small transverse street called 'The Back of the Isle', where buildings now jut into High Street. The southern boundary of the burgh followed the line of the present Carrick Street westward at right angles to High Street and, slightly further south, at the site of the nineteenth-century Wallace Tower, eastward along the line of Mill Street. This represented a considerable southward reorientation as well as expansion of the town.

Historical records tell us of 'ports' or entrances to the burgh at various points on its periphery. Six names that have survived are the Auld Tour Port at the Mill Wynd (at the site of the Auld Tour, where the Wallace Tower now stands); the Sea Port at the west end of the Boat Vennel; the Kirk Port on St John Street, which led out of Sandgate on the way to St John's; the Over Port in Kyle Street (then the Townhead); the Cow Port on the Cow Vennel; and the Sandgate (Carrick) Port, which would control the south-western egress from the burgh. These ports could double as blockades in time of need, with hinged gates or zareba (thorn hedge) fences as required. Their positions indicate early foundation, probably contemporary with the thirteenth-century charter burgh or the fourteenth-century medieval burgh. None of the ports have survived, but the later remnants of a guard-post of some kind still stand at the north end of the Auld Brig.

In order to increase security the burgage plots were uniformly tailed off and possibly palisaded where they would otherwise give on to the open countryside beyond the burgh limits. The now putative line of the Back Dykes indicates the alignment of these rear toft ends, looping round from the Boat Vennel in the north-west to the river-bank beyond the Over Port in the south-east. Internally a primitive chicane may be detected in the deliberate misalignment of the openings of Mill Street and Carrick Street on to High Street still to be seen at the Wallace Tower: armed marauders or mounted thieves would not have a clear passage through the centre of the burgh and there would be an opportunity to trap them. (This feature would also serve to deflect the strong south-westerly winds, which would otherwise funnel right through the town bearing quantities of sand.)

Besides the internal burgage plot arrangements, the original charter made provision for each burgess to have a certain area of land, about six acres, outside the burgh in what was known as the Burrowfields. This was in order to supplement the limited space and poor soil available in the burgage plots. The Burrowfields were situated beyond a cultivable area known as The Fauldbacks – now Burns Statue Square – adjacent to the Cow Vennel beyond the southern boundary of the original burgh. The Fauldbacks and the Burrowfields correspond to the 'indale' and 'outdale' encountered in early **Prestwick**.

Under royal patronage Ayr speedily developed into an important centre. The Kirk of St John the Baptist was probably founded at the same time as the (undated) burgh charter, and is known to have enjoyed much influence and many benefactions. Excavations on the site show the now demolished building to have been substantial. The nave seems to have had at least twelve piers. And, although the church has been utterly demolished for at least 250 years, a ghostly kind of impression or 'raggle' of the west gable and rose window still remains in the east wall of the tower of St John's at Bruce Crescent in Ayr.

Why the tower – a typical defensive fortification of the sixteenth century – was ever built in that position, blocking out the west end and window of the church, and why, when the church was demolished, the tower was allowed to remain, are two of the minor mysteries of Ayr's history. The ancient castle of Ayr, not far away, was by that time presumably in deep disrepair if it had not disappeared altogether after the Wars of Independence, and perhaps the lack of fortification was felt even before Cromwell came on the scene. In Slezer's drawing of 1693 the whole church can be seen distinctly, with the tower in position. This was nearly forty years after the end of the Cromwellian occupation, during which the entire building had been incorporated in Tessin's Citadel as an armoury.

A wealthy friary of Dominicans, the **Black Friars**, was set up in 1230 by Alexander II on the southern boundary of the burgh on the bank of the river, perhaps the first of eight such royal foundations throughout Scotland. The king commanded a grant of £20 per annum to be paid from 'firms' (feu fermes) of the mills and from the Burgh of Ayr. The grant was supplemented over the years by gifts of property from individuals in Ayr, and the corporation became very wealthy. The dedication of the friary church was to St Katherine of Siena, and there were also altars dedicated to the Trinity and to St Duthac. A St Katherine's Well (now lost) was reputed to have healing properties 'for seik maidens'. After the Reformation Mary, Queen of Scots transferred the entire property to the burgh but, characteristically, made the donation conditional on a nineteen-year lease to one of her servants. This was confirmed the following year by the Regent Moray. The stones were later pillaged for a municipal project, and all that remains is a high stone wall extending northward along Mill Street from the Wallace Tower.

The **Greyfriars** (Franciscan Observantines) arrived in Ayr only in 1472 or 1474. They were a popular order, who remained faithful to their original vows of poverty. No trace of the buildings now survives, although archaeological investigation of the site to the west of the Auld Kirk suggests that they may been more opulent in the matter of glazed windows than their vows were supposed to permit.[137] These friars too were the recipients of both royal and local benefaction. At the Reformation their property reverted to the Burgh of Ayr and the site of their monastery was occupied from 1654 by the **Auld Kirk of Ayr**.

With such a variety of ecclesiastical institutions in Ayr, choristers were an important part of the establishment, and had to be educated for the purpose. A 'sang schule' was established from an early date, and the schoolmaster of Ayr was named, obviously as an important ecclesiastic, in a document relating to a legal dispute in 1233.

The medieval burgh, succeeding the charter burgh after the Wars of Independence, continued to expand to the south. The vennel which later became Carrick Street had led in from the south-west, in fact from the coast road ultimately leading to Carrick. Building began to creep westward along the line of Carrick Street. And as the built-up area in High Street extended itself further along the river-bank (leaving a wide space between itself and the bank for the rear of the tofts) it joined the two roads which later became the urban thoroughfares Kyle Street ('Townhead'), from the east, and Alloway Street from the south. The latter was originally known as the Cow Vennel or Cow Wynd, and this name has recently been revived for a section of the primitive street rediscovered in the gradual refurbishment of the rear premises of the Burns Statue Square area. Also at the junction of these three streets was the Mill Wynd leading to the burgh mills, which were operated for and ultimately by the Blackfriars as part of their income. Mill Street, running from High Street at the Wallace Tower to the river and south-eastward along the bank, partly retraces the course of the Mill Wynd.

As the name indicates, the Cow Wynd led to the cattle-market, which was early one of the major commercial successes of Ayr – given the backing of the Royal Burgh Charter. A cattle-market and a separate slaughter-house (not on original sites) were still located in the vicinity until late in the twentieth century. Directly adjacent to the Cow Wynd and the Burrowfields was the Gallows Hill, one of a number of gallows sites in Ayr, now the site of the railway station. The Cow Wynd was, as indicated, the main road from the Alloway–Carcluie area, an extensive piece of land to the south which was later given to the burgh as additional grazing.

As Ayr developed in stature, substantial stone buildings began to appear, and some of them have remained in use until the present day – such as the building now known as **Loudoun Hall (NS 337 221)**, located at the angle of a lane still known as the Boat Vennel, running from just opposite the Town Hall on New Bridge Street down to Ayr Harbour. Loudoun Hall is now known to have been erected in the late fifteenth century; its first owner was probably Thomas Tait, a merchant burgess of Ayr (*fl.* 1480–1512), but the building derives its present name from Sir Hew Campbell of Loudoun, Sheriff of Ayr in the sixteenth century, who purchased it to use as 'the schirefis tenement' and whose female descendant Margaret married Sir John Campbell of Lawers, created Earl of Loudoun in 1633. Loudoun Hall is three storeys high, with a jamb or wing; in typical style the main hall is on the second storey, with vaulted cellars on the ground floor. Sleeping accommodation would be on the top storey. Although these features are commonly found in defensive structures throughout Scotland, this building is not fortified and appears to be purely civilian in character. After the Loudoun family lost control of the house in 1652, it passed through the hands of a series of owners, deteriorating during the process until, just after the Second World War, it was a mere wreck. It was rescued by the Saltire Society, who restored it to its present condition, and the building is now run for a board of trustees by the local authority, as a centre for concerts and other cultural activities. The restoration has never been quite completed.

Lady Cathcart's House probably dates from some 75 or 100 years later. An elegant and very characteristic Scottish building at the corner of Cathcart Street and Sandgate, it was recently rescued and painted yellow. The house was associated with the Cathcart family, who owned **Killochan**, **Carleton** and **Camregan Castles** as well as other properties in Carrick.

Loudoun Hall is possibly contemporary with the first stone-built version of the Brig of Ayr, now the **Auld Brig**, which connects King's Kyle and Kyle Stewart as the **Auld Brig o' Doon** connects King's Kyle and Carrick. There has been a bridge in this position at least since 1236, when King Alexander II provided revenues *ad sustentationem pontis* (for the upkeep of the bridge), but this was probably a wooden structure like the early (1285) Clyde Bridge at Glasgow. The stone-built version is late fifteenth-century. The initial construction perhaps dates from 1491 when King James IV, an indefatigable pilgrim to Whithorn via Ayr, gave money to masons working on the bridge. That date would agree with the style of architecture, which resembles that of certain parts of **Crossraguel Abbey** built at that time. It should be noted that the king was ferried across the river on his outward journey and it was on his return that he gave ten shillings to the masons; was the stone bridge newly opened on the 11 November 1491?[138]

Since then it has had various vicissitudes, including major repairs carried out in 1588, in 1732 (when the north arch fell), and again in 1907-10, when it was in danger of being demolished: the water could be seen flowing beneath through the gaps in the deck of the roadway, and the entire assemblage was on the verge of collapse. A subscription was raised and the bridge was secured. Its characteristic outline can be seen in the Slezer print of 1693 – a graceful if slightly sway-backed four-span structure with elephantine triangular cutwaters.

On the eastern parapet of the bridge there used to be a sundial of the rare horizontal attached variety i.e. it was set into the stonework on two bracket-stones which protruded a little over the water, but it has long gone. A gruesome feature of the bridge are the two deck cobblestones set at right angles to the others near the north end of the bridge opposite a set of notches in the west parapet: these mark the place where the wooden gallows framework was set up for a public execution. But today the Auld Brig is a beautiful component in the architecturally distinguished group of buildings forming the northern entrance to Ayr burgh, including the nearby Auld Kirk.

Ayr has two market crosses, neither of which survive in original form. The Malt Cross is marked by a cross let into the tarmac in Sandgate opposite the Town Hall. The Fish Cross, now identified by a handsome statue of a boy holding a fish in his hands, is about 100m east of the Malt Cross in the area

ANNO VICESIMO QUINTO

Georgii III. Regis.

C A P.   XXXVII.

An Act for rebuilding the Bridge across the
River of *Ayr*, at the Town of *Ayr*.

WHEREAS the Bridge across the Preamble.
River of Ayr, which is of great
publick Utility, being the only Communication for Travellers going for
Ireland, by the great West Road,
through the County of Ayr, and for
the March of His Majesty's Troops
to Ireland by that Road, is not only very incommodious,
being steep at each End, and so narrow, that it is with
Difficulty that Two Carriages can pass each other, but
also the same, from its great Age and natural Decay, is
become insufficient; it is therefore absolutely necessary
either to have the said Bridge taken down and rebuilt,
or to build a new Bridge near to it; but the same cannot be effected without the Aid of Parliament: May it
therefore please Your Majesty that it may be enacted;
and be it enacted by the King's most Excellent Majesty,
by and with the Advice and Consent of the Lords Spi-
ritual and Temporal, and Commons, in this present
Parliament assembled, and by the Authority of the same,
11 M 2   That

*Fig. 2. The condition of the Auld Bridge of Ayr in 1785, as described in the Act of Parliament
for its replacement or rebuilding.*

of the former market in High Street at the foot of Newmarket Street (near
the Back o' the Isle) opposite the south end of the Auld Brig.

Up to the Reformation and beyond, Ayr was a comparatively compact
small urban unit, filling up the gaps in the previous plans, and cautiously
expanding. The Sandgate extended itself to the line of the present Boswell
Park – that is, to the south-west, creating more built-up areas abutting on
the rear of the original burgage plots.

Fig. 3. The rare sundial on Auld Brig o' Ayr (no longer in situ).

After defeating the Scottish army at Dunbar (1650) and Worcester (1651), Oliver Cromwell set up an army of occupation to hold down the Scots, who were by no means prostrate in front of the conqueror. He established a chain of fortresses throughout Scotland to deter rebellion, and one of the most impressive was **Ayr Citadel**, hexagonal in plan, with six bastions and six curtain-walls. The designer was one Hans Ewald Tessin, a Dutch fortification engineer, and what he produced was very unlike previous Ayrshire military works: it was massive, with no fancy turrets or battlements, but squat, forbidding, six-legged and dourly prepared for assailants on all sides. Not that there were no towers: for the focus of his fort Tessin seized upon the most strategic site in the neighbourhood – the high tower of the Kirk of St John was ideal for a look-out post. The congregation of the church were unceremoniously turned out and their old church became the centre of the citadel, used as an armoury.

A replacement parish church, now known as **Ayr Auld Kirk**, was built in 1654 on the site of the former **Greyfriars**, largely with money provided by the Commonwealth (1,000 merks). This building is still in use today, although the original severely Presbyterian internal fitments have mostly been removed or replaced. The trades galleries are still in place. The site is on the south bank of the river. Access is gained to the kirk and kirkyard through a seventeenth-century lich-gate leading from what is now called the Kirk Port, an ancient vennel off High Street.

In 1663, after the Restoration, the area of the fort was designated as a burgh of barony i.e. one separate from and in competition with Ayr. This creation was intended as a reward to the Earl of Eglinton for loyalty, but as a commercial venture the burgh, called Montgomerieston, failed. The old church was brought back into use as a place of worship only from 1687 to 1689, and it was demolished except for the tower in 1726. In 1727 the citadel area came into the ownership of the celebrated beauty Susanna, Countess of Eglinton, who set up a whisky distillery and later brewery within the precincts of the fort in 1734. She sold it in 1755 to her kinsman Sir Thomas Kennedy, later ninth Earl of Cassillis. The Kennedy family retained the citadel until 1854, when the fortifications were still more or less intact.

Thereafter it was seen as a desirable plot for building, and by 1906 the existing quiet pleasant residential area was in place, only the street names testifying to its history as a rival burgh: Eglinton Terrace, Montgomerie Terrace, Ailsa Place – and Cromwell Road. The housing, however, is very evidently built on top of fortifications, which show themselves starkly along South Harbour Street in particular, 4 to 6m high, and to the west and south-west, along to Cromwell Road. On the interior of the wall at Ailsa Place a grass-grown bank or platform is to be seen, 4m wide and 1.2m high. The upper part of the main gateway is still visible as an arch built into the rear of a garden giving on to a back lane running along behind the present buildings of Ayr Academy. Further to the north this lane rises to surmount more buried fortifications and, in a deep welter of building levels directly behind the Cromwellian wall, old stonework survives at the back entrance to a public house. This is near the place from which, in 1976–7, very old pottery was recovered by members of the Ayrshire Archaeological and Natural History Society. The pottery was older than the seventeenth century, perhaps of twelfth/thirteenth century date, and it may indicate that this in fact is the site of the original Ayr Castle, which has otherwise completely disappeared.[139]

In the nineteenth century an eccentric called Miller, perhaps deeming the Cromwell wall insufficiently romantic, built a grotesquely oversized bartizan with huge corbels on top of the north-west bastion. **Miller's Folly** glares down upon Ayr Harbour to this day.

After the Restoration Ayr languished economically to the point at which it became depopulated and almost ruinous, but after the 1707 Union of Parliaments developments in trade, stock-breeding, agriculture, mineral extraction and industry brought a revival in the town's fortunes. In the nineteenth century the development of steam travel both on land and sea brought changes in the Ayr's status: from being a predominantly market centre, it now became not only an early tourist destination but a favoured place for the retirement of the wealthy middle classes – and, in the north across the river in Newton, an industrial centre. Elegant building began to spread outward and southward from the railway station and the Sandgate area, in three prongs – the Carrick Road, Midton Road and Racecourse Road. Ayr burgeoned in size, becoming in the end a large burgh absorbing Alloway in the south and Newton and other settlements across the river. Its central area, however, under successive layers of modern development, retains its original plan as laid out by the servants of King William the Lion at the beginning of the thirteenth century.[140]

Ayr, St John the Baptist (Parish) Church   NS 333 220

See **Ayr Royal Burgh**

Bain's Hill standing stone   NS 204 078

A monolith stands above John o'Groats Port (a natural inlet among rock shelving) west of Maidens, Ayrshire. This standing stone is very close to the site of the discovery of the possibly votive Bronze Age hoard at **Maidens, Port Murray**.

Balchriston Dun   NS 257 111

Balchriston Dun is built on a small promontory above the confluence of two unnamed burns in a gully reaching north-west to the Rancleugh Burn. It seems to have been circular. In the author's opinion, it is possible that Balchristian was a broch, unusual though these are in Ayrshire. The wall is now represented by a broad band of tumbled stone. It may have been protected to the east by a deep ditch, but this has been damaged by rain and can hardly be told from a natural gully. An extension to the defences may have projected south-westward, and access may have been gained from the north. The dun is situated east of the disused railway in the valley that slopes towards Culzean Bay north of Culzean Castle.

Balig Farm cup-and-ring marked stones   NX 094 839

This detached small sandstone boulder has two shallow circular cups with inscribed circuit lines around the top and the bottom. It was found against the east wall of the paddock at Balig Farm and is now held at Corseclays House to the north. Two other stones were also found but are now lost. Another is still held at Balig Farm.

Ballantrae: Mesolithic Microliths   NX 085 817

An area of about 25ha., centred on the above OS reference, is said by RCAHMS to be the most productive for not only Mesolithic but Neolithic microliths in the Ballantrae vicinity. This area is also noted for standing stones and other signs of intense Neolithic activity. It is south of Ballantrae village and west of the A77.

Ballantrae Bridge funerary/ritual site   NX 086 817 to NX 086 821

This large and complex site was revealed only in 1995 by a series of oblique aerial photographs taking advantage of the slanting light of the sun to show up features invisible on the ground. NB There is nothing currently to be seen at Ballantrae Bridge, but the various subdivisions of the site must be recorded in view of the central importance of the place for archaeological understanding of the Ballantrae region.[141]

The site is immediately adjacent to the former site of the standing stones at Garleffin, and, on the other side of the bridge, the suspected henge and other sites at Laggan. Also, stretching inland from Ballantrae along the course of the Stinchar as far as Colmonell, are a number of cairn sites, including **Balnowlart Hill**, **Mains Hill** and **Knockdolian**, all overlooking Ballantrae. The whole system (excluding the Stinchar cairns) is detailed as follows:

(1) Garleffin Standing Stones   NX 0873 8172

There were originally eight standing stones arranged in the arc of a circle with an outlier and one recumbent within the circle. All except two have been removed, some buried in a ravine by the owner of the land in January 1992 after notification of Historic Scotland's intention to schedule the site. In spite of this determined frustration of archaeological conservation, two stones remain, designated 'E' and 'F' by OS **(NX 08719 81635** and **NX 08726 81616)**: their sites fell within the garden of a private house.

(2) Pits   area centred on **NX 0865 8199**

Cropmarks of a large number of pits south-west of Ballantrae Bridge, suggesting a small community's inhumation burials.

(3) Cropmarks   NX 0872 8208

Cropmarks of a round house, two pits and a souterrain (underground structure), south-east of Ballantrae Bridge (towards the Laggan side).

(4) Cropmarks   area centred on NX 0868 8192

Cropmarks of a souterrain; a possible circular enclosure and two square enclosures: all approximately 350m south of Ballantrae Bridge.

(5) Field boundaries   area centred on NX 0860 8217

Immediately south-west of Ballantrae Bridge, the cropmarks of old field boundaries.

(6) Garleffin   NX 087 818

Approximately 500m south of Ballantrae Bridge, the following cropmarks: at **NX C0874 8178**, a 'four-poster' stone circle; at **NX C0874 8180**, a round barrow and (to the east) a possible ring ditch; at **NX C0878 8175**, a large pit with a small ring-ditch to one side.

(7) Laggan (Ballantrae Bridge area) (1) NX 091 821 and (2) NX 102 824

These sites are to the east of Ballantrae Bridge: two ring ditches approximately 1km apart along the south bank of the River Stinchar, one on each side of the modern Laggan farm complex; both plotted on a 'distribution map of henge monuments and penannular ring-ditches covering southern Scotland'.[142]

(8) Balnowlart   NX 097 832

At precisely **NX 0973 8325** oblique aerial photographs have shown up the cropmarks of a possible rectangular mortuary enclosure south-east of Balig Farm.

(9) Holm Park   NX 082 817

This site is on the south bank of the Stinchar where the river takes a wide sweep south near its mouth. It is not certain that this discovery has anything to do with the Ballantrae Bridge complex or even that it dates from the same period, but it is in the same area. The story goes that in 1879 or 1880 a Ballantrae man was raising an embankment to prevent soil erosion by the river when he came across no less than eight skeletons laid out side by side on their backs with legs together and their hands closed over their stomachs. Their heads were all pointing to the west. They lay upon shingle under layers, first about 1m of sand, then a layer of flat pebbles, a layer of sea-shells about 0.3m thick and a final layer of sand. The burials were left in situ and they have never been re-excavated. A number of scenarios could be constructed to account for the inhumations if they were later than the prehistoric complex, but they must remain mysterious for the present.

Ballantrae: Old Parish Church (Kennedy Aisle)   NX 083 824

This building, at the south of Ballantrae, was built in 1604, originally as a monument to Gilbert Kennedy of Bargany, who was killed in the Battle of the Brockloch in 1601. In 1617 it was erected into the parish church of Ballantrae. It was largely demolished in 1819, leaving standing only the 'aisle' or burial vault, with a fine monument to Gilbert Kennedy.

Balligmorrie cairn   (1) NX 221 907 (2) NX222 908

Balligmorrie farm lies on the south side of the B734 2km from Pinmore. (1) A big circular cairn stands on a hillock between the road and the River Stinchar. It has been subject to peripheral stone-robbing but appears intact in the centre, on top of which lie large stones cemented together. (2) A smaller oblong mound, which has been damaged, sits on the slopes of Shillmore Hill east of the farmhouse, on the Balligmorrie side of the road.

Ballochmyle Viaduct   NS 508 253

This is one of the great achievements of the early railway age. It was built in 1846–8 and is still in use. It spans the gorge of the River Ayr – itself one of the more spectacular natural features of eastern Ayrshire – the highest railway bridge in Britain, with a gigantic masonry arch flanked by three arches on either side; the arch is the longest single railway span ever built. The finely-jointed red ashlar-work is beautiful. The A76 runs close to the viaduct, and there are steep but negotiable paths down to the River Ayr from where good views may be had.

Ballochmyle Viaduct cup-and-ring markings   NS 511 255

These are spectacular. There are two groups of them on a sandstone cliff face a short distance north-east of the Ballochmyle Viaduct in the Ballochmyle Gorge. This can be reached by a footpath from South Lodge, which is on an old loop road west of the A76. The carvings are more varied than usual, with complicated whorls and lines, and recently discovered designs resembling trilithons.

Balmalloch chambered cairn · · · · · · · · · · · · NX 263 845

This round Bargrennan-type cairn is situated 4km north-east of Barrhill, just north of the Black Loch. There may be three chambers in the cairn but only two are visible. The eastern chamber appears to have been square while the northern chamber is round. A human skeleton reportedly discovered in one of the chambers has been lost from Balmalloch farmhouse, where it was kept.[143] A footpath from Balluskie next to Barrhill leads or used to lead to Balmalloch.

Balnowlart Hill · · · · · · · (1) NX 101 835 (2) NX 103 836 (3) NX 102 835

Balnowlart Hill (60m OD) stands above the B7044 and the River Stinchar 2km north-east of Ballantrae. (1) On a ridge on this hill a line of three cairns stretches from north-east to south-west. They appear to be undamaged in spite of a stone scatter down from the midpoint cairn. (2) At the summit of the hill stands a single cairn. (3) 100m south-west of cairn (2) lie what appear to be the remnants of yet another cairn, now appearing as a mere ring of cairn material.

Baltersan Castle · NS 284 087

About 1km north-east of **Crossraguel Abbey** about 100m from the A77 stands the ruin of Baltersan Castle, originally owned by Crossraguel and in the sixteenth century tenanted by Lady Egidia Blair (*d.* 1530). As part of the post-Reformation settlement of lands the property was acquired in 1574 by David Kennedy of Pennyglen, who is said to have erected the present L-plan tower-house in 1584. An unusual square staircase tower is corbelled out in the re-entrant, although the main stair is in the wing, at the base of which is the doorway. The basement is vaulted and the great hall is on the first floor. The walls stand three storeys high with an attic and a garret, and there are ashlar angle-turrets. The top storey of the wing is square and corbelled out with crow-step gables and a projecting window again corbelled out, with shot holes at the side.

Some years ago (1996) proposals to redevelop this building were put forward, but they seem to have fallen by the wayside and the future of the castle is now in doubt.

Bank Viaduct · NS 574 205

This viaduct is to the north of Cumnock, crossing the Lugar Water at Holmhead. It was designed by John Miller of Granger and Miller, who was also responsible for the great Ballochmyle Viaduct, and it is as impressive in its own way. It has nine arches between panelled pilasters and was built between 1848 and 1850. The main line from Glasgow to the south runs across it.

Fig. 4. Baltersan Castle, from the north–west.

Barclanachan Tower   NS 304 030

See **Kilkerran Castle**

Bargany   NS 247 002

The original Bargany Castle – 'a hudge, great, lofty Tower, in the center of a quadrangular court, that had on each of three corners, fyne well-built Towers of freestone, four story high' (Abercrummie) – has long gone, and no trace of it can now be discovered, except that some of its sixteenth-century window casements appear to have been re-used in the present Bargany House. This was built in 1681, originally a single block of three storeys and an attic, with a handsome double row of five windows towards the back, and with two projecting single-storey wings forming a U-plan surrounding the front door. During the eighteenth and nineteenth centuries this simple and elegant arrangement suffered much distortion: putting the front door at the rear in place of the central window of the five, and then reverting to the previous arrangement; building two storeys on top of one only of the previously single-storey wings of the U-shape; and finally tacking on to the other end of the main block a large Victorian extension accommodating a drawing-room with bay windows. In spite of all this the house remains beautiful and visually striking in well-landscaped grounds. Bargany was restored recently.

Originally held by the Kennedys of Bargany, the property passed to the Dalrymples of Stair, and, via a tenancy of nineteenth-century French aristocracy, to the Dalrymple-Hamilton family.

Barnweill Motte   NS 406 300

This motte (Talbot's classification[144]) is part of the complex of fortifications in the neighbourhood of **Craigie Castle**. It is oblong or sub-rectangular rather than circular on plan, sitting on the edge of an escarpment near Barnweill Farm. It is protected on three sides by a rock-cut ditch. There is no sign of a bailey.

Barnweill Monument: folly   NS 406 295

This Victorian structure marks the spot where William Wallace allegedly drew rein after one of his anti-English exploits and, gazing back to the flames of Ayr, remarked, 'The Barns of Ayr barn weill.' The atrocity which he had just committed (see pp. 65–6) is well matched by the atrocity of the pun which is supposed to have given the name to the place: but 'Barnweill', (*Berenbouell* 1177–1204, *Brenwyfle* 1306) is derived from a Cymric word incorporating the element *pren-*, 'a tree'.[145]

Barnweill Parish Church   NS 406 299

The remains of the church of the Holy Rood stand on a hillock (135m OD) about 3km north-west of Tarbolton. It is a small rectangular building. As with so many smaller church ruins in Scotland, the gables have withstood the passage of years better than the other parts, although here they are unstable. A segmental arched window high in the east gable may be of fifteenth-century date. Apart from that the building looks seventeenth-century in style. It stands in a walled kirkyard. The parish of Barnweill, which before the Reformation was in the possession of the monastery at **Fail**, was suppressed in (perhaps) 1653, when its territory and income were divided between Tarbolton and Craigie, with a part of the revenues going to Stair. The site may be approached by a network of side roads north-east from the A719 at Bourtreebush.

Barr Castle   NS 505 360

Barr Castle in Kyle is still in good repair and is in use, although not as a fortification. A tall single block five storeys high without wings or other extension, it now has an incongruous modern roof, the construction of which involved the disappearance of most of the typical 'top-hamper' of Scottish towers – although the continuous corbelling of the parapet and the base-part of the angle turrets are still visible. The castle is strongly and massively built, probably of the fifteenth century. If we believe that William Wallace took refuge here at one time, there must have been an earlier castle on the site, which is a small rocky knoll on the bank of the Burn Anne on the southern outskirts of Galston (near the B7037). Whether the earlier building was identical with the ancient Galston Tower, otherwise unidentifiable, is open to conjecture. Barr Castle was built for the Lockharts, the original grantees of the barony. They were enthusiastic opponents of the Roman Church, and a plaque above the present door of the castle records that the reformer George Wishart preached in Galston in 1545 and John Knox in 1556 (at the invitation and under protection of John Lockhart of Barr and others). Later, in 1670, Barr Castle was bought by the Campbells of Cessnock.

Barr Covenanting tombs   NX 276 941

Tombstone in churchyard of Barr Village in Carrick to Edward McKeen, shot 28 February 1685. Another stone to John Campbell, returned deportee, *d.* 1721. Both stones painted white. Churchyard in centre of village (B734).

Barrhill Covenanting memorials   NX 232 818

A fragmented stone to two Covenanters captured and shot in 1685 survives in a grave enclosure some way west of Barrhill Village (A714), on the Cross Water of Duisk. Access by woodland path from bridge in village.

Barskimming, Old   NS 482 251

Barskimming, New   NS 482 253

Barskimming – that is to say, Old Barskimming, which lies on the south bank of the River Ayr, in Stair Parish – is in King's Kyle. New Barskimming was erected opposite this, on the north bank in Tarbolton Parish in Kyle Stewart. The two are linked by a bridge spanning the spectacular gorge through which the Ayr passes at this point. The ancient castle of Barskimming, apparently existing in 1612, is said to have vanished completely. There are, however, ruins close to the lip of the gorge.

The mansion house of New Barskimming, which in its latest version dates from 1883, is elegant and scenically landscaped. The original building was erected in 1771, and it was enlarged by the addition of two wings in about 1816, but after a fire in 1882 the house was completely reconstructed. An impressive stable block exists across the river. Barskimming House is still privately occupied.

Access to Barskimming is difficult and limited, but highly scenic footpaths along the banks of the River Ayr are accessible both from the B743 and from unlisted roads south out of Mauchline.

Bastion Craig Fishtrap NS 192 477

Between the two sites noted for **Ardneil Bay** there is an inlet formed by the rock shelving known as the Bell Stane and a parallel shelf jutting from the land. An intertidal wall has been constructed across the mouth of this inlet so that it can retain water and fish when the tide ebbs from high water. The wall has now suffered storm damage.

Beith: Old Parish Church NS 349 538

Only vestigial remains survive of the original parish church of Beith. All that is visible is a front gable and a belfry. This building, which was demolished in 1810, stood on ground occupied from a very early date by the Chapel of St Inan, who is also commemorated at **Cuff Hill** (a well and a 'chair') and elsewhere in Cuninghame. Before the Reformation the parish was one of the possessions of **Kilwinning Abbey.** The first Presbyterian minister is mentioned in 1573. The site of the old kirkyard with the remains is in the centre of Beith not far from the police station.

Bellsbank: 'Bubbly' Cairn NS 490 035

Somewhere amid the recent Bellsbank Plantation, probably more than 265m OD, lie the remains of a large cairn, called by some the 'Bubbly' Cairn. It was pillaged for building dykes before the middle of the nineteenth century, and human bones were then discovered. Before the plantation it would have overlooked the Muck Water to the east and Loch Doon to the south.

Bellsbank: Pennyarthur Rig cairn NS 485 038

Another big cairn almost lost amid an area of intensive forestry. It has been reduced to a 'shapeless mound of disturbed stone obscured by long grass and trees'.[146] Pennyarthur Rig is 277m OD, about 0.5km north-west of the 'Bubbly' Cairn, overlooking Dalmellington from the south

Beoch cairn NS 522 084

Before the area was afforested this cairn was a conspicuous object at 325m OD on the slopes of Meikle Hill on the south side of the B741, facing Benbeoch. When it was excavated in 1937 three cists were found, as well as a beaker, three cinerary urns and a ring-marked stone. The cairn kerb and a double cist are still visible. The site is about 5km from Dalmellington.

Blackfriars, Ayr NS 338 218

See **Ayr Royal Burgh**

Blackshaw cup-and-ring markings (1) and (2) NS 231 483

(1) A flat rock surface 15m long and tapering from 6m to 1m in breadth with a large number of cup marks, cup-and-rings, spirals etc. The rock is weathered and portions are covered with turf so that it is difficult to make out exactly how many of these designs there are, or what they are. On the other side of a field wall the exposed part of another flat rock surface has at least two cup marks. (2) A cuboid gritstone slab, found nearby and displaying broken segments of rings, including one with a cup in it, and another unringed cup, is now in the Hunterian Museum of Glasgow University.

Blackshaw is about 5km north of Ardrossan. The B781 runs north of the site.

Blackshaw Farm Park NS 231 491

This is a demonstration working farm with visitor/children's facilities. Contact Mrs Todd on 01563 534257. The farm is 2km east of West Kilbride, just south of the B781 on a side road.

Blair NS 304 480

The Blairs held land in Dalry at least as far back as the beginning of the thirteenth century (possibly as early as 1165), but the date 1203 appearing here and there in Blair Castle is fictitious. The present still-inhabited castle is a very large L-plan house built around a core tower possibly of the sixteenth century. There is a square stair-tower in the re-entrant, with a main doorway dated 1668, and a smaller square turret built on to the former, also with a doorway dated 1617. The core tower is a simple keep of four storeys with very thick walls. Built out to the west from this core is the main seventeenth-century wing with dormer windows at the third storey and a garret above this. To the south is the later (post-Restoration) wing. The whole house is built slightly on the curve above the course of the Bombo Burn, from which it has the towering, complex appearance of Edinburgh Castle. It is a very beautiful and impressive building, set in superb woodlands.

Blair Castle is in the Garnock Valley, about 1km south-east of Dalry (on the east side of the railway).

Blairquhan *NS 365 054*

The present mansion near Straiton, built in the 1820s, incorporates in its service court some fragments from a very much older building, which was demolished at

Fig. 5. Details of Blair Castle: entrance doorway, date on doorway in turret, two dormer windows.

the same time. This older building may have begun life as a tower built by the McWhirter family in 1346. It had passed to the Kennedys by 1573, when it was incorporated into one of two parallel palace ranges on either side of a courtyard; the old tower may have been used as one of the limbs of a typical Z-plan block. By the early nineteenth century the originally magnificent palace complex was ruinous. A plan for a new building prepared for the new owner, the famous Sir David Hunter Blair (a printer and publisher), which retained the two towers of the forward range, probably proved impractical. An entirely new scheme was finally adopted, based on the designs of William Burn. This was grandiose but effective, with a hollow lantern tower rising 20m through two floors. Galleries run round the well. The tower stands between two symmetrical wings of two storeys and is fronted by a massive porte-cochère. A rather lower extension runs out on the same axis from the end of one of the wings towards a lower tower adjoining the service area. This extension deliberately and pleasingly unbalances the regular symmetry of the main building profile. The relics of the earlier palace are within the service courtyard: an ornate doorway and windows and other decorations including a framed coat-of-arms.

Still owned by the Hunter Blair family, the mansion today is run as a 'stately home' as well as museum and art-gallery open to the public (during one summer month) with some holiday-home and other facilities in and around the building itself. It is situated at the end of a very lovely 5km drive beside the Water of Girvan, in which may be seen both waterfalls ('linns') and swimming otters.

Bower Hill Fort (Heads of Ayr)   NS 284 187

A small fort at the western tip of the Heads of Ayr, overlooking Bracken Bay. From the landward side it is defended by two separate ditches (visible only as cropmarks). The internal space is divided in two by a broad natural gully. A very steep precipice to the shore forms the western and northern defences.

Boydston Dun   NS 219 448

This small oval dun is oriented towards the south, perched on an eminence with precipitous sides on east, west and south. It has a very broad ditch on the north, as well as (the remnants of) a stone wall. There may have been an outwork towards the north-east. The fortification is situated immediately beside the railway at Boydston Braes, overlooking the coast road (A78) between Ardrossan and West Kilbride.

Brae Hill Dun   NX 209 979

South-west of the television mast on Brae Hill is what appears to be a fortification, taking advantage of the naturally defensive features of the terrain. A small isolated hillock on Brae Hill has two terraces below its flat summit, which is surrounded by a barely traceable wall. The lower of the two terraces expands to a wide platform on the west.

Brae Hill is 2km east of Girvan, above the Water of Girvan. It is not far from the structures on **Saugh Hill** to the south (cairns, barrow).

Braidstane or Broadstone Castle NS 362 531

At the farm of Broadstone, south-east of Beith on a side road between the B706 and the B777, there may still exist a few grass-grown hummocks or even exposed masonry, the last vestiges of Braidstane Castle, once a part of the Barony of Giffen. The Barony of Braidstane was possessed as a separate unit by John de Lyddale in 1452. A charter for this barony was granted to a cadet member of the Montgomerie family in 1468. The estates of Braidstane were sold to Sir John Shaw of Greenock in 1650. It appears that material from the castle was reused to rebuild Broadstonehall farm steading at the beginning of the nineteenth century.

Brigend or Bridgend Castle NS 333 176

The ruins of a very small sixteenth-century tower sit on a promontory high above the River Doon on the Carrick side near Alloway. The bridge referred to is the **Auld Brig o' Doon.** The tower, which retains only the ground floor cellar and fragments of the first-floor hall, is relatively inaccessible on Doonside estate. Nothing is known of its history, but it is reputed to have been owned by the Montgomeries.

Bruce's Well NS 346 244

See **Kingcase** in **Prestwick Burgh of Barony**

Brunston Castle NS 260 011

The vestigial remains of Brunston Castle are slowly crumbling to dust in the centre of a golfcourse on the north bank of the Water of Girvan just west of Dailly, next to the Bargany policies. It was a T-plan mansion of the seventeenth century, enlarged from an original structure of the early 1500s. It was the home of a notorious thrice-married lady named Blak Bessie Kennedy, whose matrimonial exploits led to one of the bitterest territorial feuds in Ayrshire.

Buiston Crannog and Logboats NS 415 435

This crannog (precisely **NS 4155 4352**) was first excavated in 1880 and then in 1989–90. The nineteenth-century finds included a crude forgery of a seventh-century Anglo-Saxon gold coin, itself an imitation of a Roman model, as well as stone, bone and iron implements and weapons, two gold spiral finger rings (?Roman), a piece of second-century Samian ware and pieces of Roman glass.[147] Scientific investigation more than a century later discovered four levels of occupation. Carbon-dating has shown that the phases in the structure's history covered a period extending from AD 1 to 525 – from before the Roman occupation, through the Damnonian ascendancy, to the early life of the Kingdom of Strathclyde.

Log boats have been discovered in association with the crannog at Buiston. The first was recovered by the nineteenth-century excavator Munro, who donated the craft to the Dick Institute at Kilmarnock. Unfortunately this specimen was destroyed in a fire in 1909. A second logboat was found in 1992 by Dr B.A. Crone, who had been responsible for re-excavating the crannog in 1989–90. This boat was reburied after measurements had been taken. A third logboat was reportedly discovered, perhaps by Munro, but it is unknown when. It was seemingly unearthed on Lochside farm, directly to the north of Buiston farm and the former loch. Its first resting place after recovery was the Dick Institute in Kilmarnock but – perhaps before the 1909 fire – it may have been taken to the Hunterian Museum, where there exists a very fine specimen (not on display at the moment) of unknown provenance, the 'River Clyde' logboat. This may be the identical boat.[148]

Buiston is on the east side of the A735 half-way between Kilmaurs and Stewarton. Lochside (also **NS 415 535**) is directly adjacent to the loch and the main site. Nothing now appears on the site itself.

Burns Cottage   NS 334 186

See **Alloway and Burns**

Burns Monument   NS 333 179

See **Alloway, Auld Brig o' Doon**

Burnton Viaduct   NS 372 153

The Ayr to Dalmellington railway used to cross the Purclewan Burn by this bridge north-east of Dalrymple. It is a magnificent structure of sixteen lofty slender arches, and can be seen from far and wide.

Cairn Hill, Mains of Tig: cairn   NX 132 836

Cairnhill, 166m OD, is about 1km east of the Mains of Tig, and overlooks the Water of Tig as it flows through its gorge at Craig Wood. The cairn is at the summit, and is one of a number of hilltop cairns south of Ballantrae. It has a hollowed-out centre, without kerb or ditch.

Cairn Table: cairns   NS 724 242

Cairn Table (592.5m OD) is one of the giant hills, visible from afar, that line the eastern horizon of Ayrshire, and the East Cairn at the summit is one of the finest in the neighbourhood. It seems to have escaped the attentions of the stone-robber and/or the grave-robber. A bronze armlet was recovered in 1933 from its margins, and this may be dated to the early Bronze Age.[149] The West Cairn might have been its equal, but it was pillaged to construct a nearby memorial. Cairn Table, through whose summit the Ayrshire boundary runs, dominates Muirkirk and Glenbuck.

Cairnennock cairn   NS 508 007

This, the White Cairn of Cairnennock, is one of a series of hill-top cairns in the Loch Doon and Dalmellington areas. The hill in question is Little Eriff Hill, and the White Cairn is situated on the summit plateau at about 320m OD. It has been much robbed for stone dykes, and it is reported that human remains were found during the pillaging, which took place before 1857. A footpath up from the Dalmellington area passes close by it, above the line of the A713 Carsphairn road. NB this should not be confused with a number of other 'White Cairns' south of here. There is also a White Laise Cairn almost exactly opposite this cairn on the west side of Loch Doon.

Camregan Castle   NX 215 987

This remote and little-known castle is represented today by a few fragments of walls situated on a ledge on the steep eastern side of the Camregan Glen overlooking the Killoup Burn. The wall footings are the remnants of three separate buildings, perhaps of different dates. The position has been a strong one, defended not only by ditching and external banking but also by the steepness of the natural slopes. The castle is said to have been a Cathcart stronghold from the thirteenth century but the surviving buildings are not likely to be so old. The B734 runs past the mouth of the glen, and Girvan is about 3km to the west.

Caprington Castle   NS 407 362

The Tudor Gothic remodelling of this castle, undertaken in the 1820s and '30s, includes some features intended to rival **Blairquhan**, such as the lofty first-floor entrance hall with a well three storeys high encased in a prominent tower, a formidable porte-cochère and an asymmetrical service wing . The tower, round and central, is also reminiscent of **Culzean Castle**. However, the remodelling has a character of its own perhaps best described as 'mock-baronial', with high corner turrets and a crenellated rather over-size parapet right round the building. The façade conceals the original old tower, which survived earlier Georgian alterations, and now contains a fine library.

Caprington Castle sits beside the Todrigs Burns about 100m from the south bank of the River Irvine 2km west of Riccarton (Kilmarnock).

Carleton Castle   NX 133 895

Carleton Castle, in the yard of Little Carleton farmhouse, is the stone-built successor of **Little Carleton Motte** on the opposite side of the road. Both were possessions of the Cathcart family. The castle is a tall (five-storey) single-block ruined keep, perched on a shelf between two hillside streamlets overlooking the tiny coastal settlement of Lendalfoot. The north-east corner has entirely collapsed, probably taking with it the entrance, which would have been at the hall-floor level i.e. above the basement. There are signs of a small barmkin between the the two burns to the north-east.

The castle is probably fifteenth-century in date. Like other coastal forts in Carrick – Dinvin, Dow Hill, Duniewick – it guards a pass from the east/south-east to the littoral strip. The Cathcarts also possessed **Camregan Castle, Little Rigend Castle**, in the east of Ayrshire, and **Killochan Castle**.

Fig. 6. Carleton Castle, from the south-east.

Little Carleton motte has been mutilated by roadworks and by ploughing but is still prominent, with a level summit and surrounding ditch. The whole site is on a very steep hill and is bisected by a minor unlisted road which runs between Lendalfoot and Garnaburn east of Colmonell. It overlooks the A77 and Carleton Bay.

Carlock cairn   NX 085 772

Carlock Hill (OD 319m) stands at the northern entrance to Glen App from Ballantrae. It is one of a series of high hills which form a massive western wall for that glen from north-east to south-west, down to Finnarts Hill. Almost every one of those hills has a summit cairn. The Carlock Hill cairn was pillaged mercilessly for nineteenth-century stone dykes. During the stone robbing, which took place before 1856, it is reported that human bones of enormous size were found.

Carnell   NS 467 322

Still a private residence, this building incorporates a fifteenth-century tower-house with a parapet and corner bartizans supported by continuous-course corbelling. A stair-tower with crow-step gables was added in 1576. The castle was adapted and extended in Victorian times, first by William Burn in 1843 and then by Charles Reid in 1871, to form a typical, pleasant Scottish baronial mansion. Decorations include crowstep gables, an ornate doorcase and dormer windows, and recognizably Burn-type square turrets with tall pyramidal roofs.

This tower stands on the south bank of the upper Cessnock Water, east of the A719.

Cassillis House   *NS 340 128*

This is one of the most magnificent houses in Ayrshire, and still belongs to the Kennedy family, powerful in Carrick since at least the fourteenth century. The present structure appears to date back in parts to that time. The very thick walls of the core rectangular building argue for great age. It rises four storeys to the parapet, above which is a garret storey. A projecting stair-tower was added probably in 1673 or 74, making the building L-plan in formation. It is likely that this formed part of a general remodelling of the building on the advice of the designer Sir William Bruce, when the characteristic 'top-hamper' was added – roofed turrets and garrets replacing the former parapet walk, on whose continuous corbelling these units were built out, with balustrading in between. The spiral staircase in the seventeenth-century tower has a hollow newel with stone step-like projections on the inside, as well as slits at intervals for light. The slits would not help to conceal a secret inner staircase, if that is what the stone projections amount to, and it is more likely that they would have provided a form of stair lighting, with

Fig. 7. Cassillis House, from the north-east.

candles or the like mounted inside. A prison-like apartment is built into the north wall of the old tower.

Cassillis House is situated on the south bank of the River Doon, south-west of Dalrymple. It is not open to the public, but an excellent view of it may be had from the upper road, the B742, leading from Dalrymple. Just across the B742 from the viewpoint rises an abrupt green slope, **Dowan's Hill** or **Dunree,** topped by an Iron Age fort.

The property originally belonged to the Montgomerie family but was acquired by the real founder of the Kennedy dynasty in Carrick, John Kennedy of Dunure, in or around 1367. Cassillis House is still the main residence of the recognised Kennedy chief, the Marquis of Ailsa.

TOP
Ailsa Craig

BOTTOM
The cairn on Finnnarts Hill

TOP
Tarbolton Motte

BOTTOM
St Nicholas Church, Prestwick (13th century)

TOP
Kilwinning Abbey

BOTTOM
Crossraguel Abbey

TOP
The Auld Brig of Ayr

BOTTOM
St John's Tower (The Fort), Ayr, with raggle

TOP
Loudoun Hall, Ayr (15th century) with the Town Hall steeple (19th century)

_____

BOTTOM
Lady Cathcart's House, Ayr (16th century)

_____

TOP
Dean Castle, Kilmarnock

BOTTOM
Rowallan Castle (not open to the public)

TOP
Miller's Folly, Ayr

BOTTOM
The prospect of the town of Ayr from the east (John Slezer)

Cave Cairn (Wee Fell): chambered cairn   NX 183 792

This round Bargrennan-type cairn is south-west of Barrhill, about 1.5km north of the former chambered cairn site at **Arecleoch**.[150] It is situated in a clearing in the Arecleoch Forest on the northward-facing slopes of Wee Fell. It has been robbed for sheep-fanks, which have been built on top of it, but enough has been left to allow the structure to be made out. Two chambers are visible. The first one has a large capstone still in position. A mostly unroofed passage 'bulges' out into this chamber in characteristic Bargrennan style. The north-east chamber is choked with rubble.

The vicinity of this and the Ar(i)ecleoch Cairn is called the Arecleoch Forest area and must be distinguished from the other Arecleoch Forest area, also containing (non-chambered) cairns, which lies to the north-east about 11km away, beyond Barrhill and Balmalloch.

Cessnock Castle   NS 510 355

Like **Blair Castle**, Cessnock extends itself along a ridge above a stream, the Burn Anne. Like Blair also, it is a massive and complex structure of

Fig. 8. Cessnock Castle. Staircases in the quadrangle and a detail of an ornamental plaster ceiling.

several periods, the earliest perhaps going back to 1296, that is, just before the Wars of Independence. The earliest part of the structure is reckoned to be the basement of the tower-house at the south-east of the courtyard. The other three storeys seem to be no later than the fifteenth century. The extensions to the tower-house, forming three sides of a square or open courtyard, were probably begun shortly after 1578, and additions were being made into the late seventeenth century. These were less defensive than the previous structure, and converted the castle into a civilian mansion, some parts of which are in good condition. These include the great hall, where in 1890 restorers discovered a ceiling covered with Renaissance paintings in panels; ornamental plaster ceilings were found in other rooms. Exterior Renaissance-style ornamentation takes the form of elaborate dormer pediments and doorcases.

Cessnock Castle was one of the centres of pre-Reformation religious agitation, and a Campbell of Cessnock was one of the 'Lollards of Kyle' arraigned but dismissed by King James IV in 1494. Nearly 200 years later another Campbell of Cessnock was a leading supporter of the Covenanting movement after the Restoration of King Charles II, and was imprisoned.

This castle is about 1km south of Galston and 0.5km south of **Barr Castle,** which was purchased by the Campbells of Cessnock in 1670. Both castles stand on the Burn Anne, and the B7037 runs past both.

Chapeldonan burnt mounds (water heating)   NS 195 003

No less than six burnt-mound deposits were identified here recently (1996–7). A wooden trough (for water) was discovered in association with one deposit.[151] The site is just north of Girvan.

Clauchrierob burnt mounds (water heating)   NX 314 848

This site is east of Black Clauchrie Farm on the path to Fardin near the remote south-eastern border of Carrick. Two burnt-stone mounds are situated west of a tributary to the River Cree. They are recognisable by their horse-shoe appearance, facing a stream.[152]

Clonbeith Castle   NS 338 455

This is one of the many remnants of castles, in Ayrshire and elsewhere, that are relegated to the status of a shed or something similar in the yard of what was once their own home farm. (*cf.* **Dalduff, Knockdaw, Kersland, Assloss etc.**) The structure has been a small rectangular country house, with an unusual corbel for a window (no longer extant) directly above a central doorcase dated 1607. The site was probably occupied by a castle prior to that date. The ground or basement floor is all that has survived, open to the air and now used as a dump by the owner of Clonbeith Farm. Clonbeith was a property of the Cuninghames, and its owner in 1586, John Cuninghame, took a leading part in the assassination of the Earl of Eglinton that year: he held the pistol to the Earl's head and pulled the trigger.

Clonbeith is situated on a side-road south of the B778 not far from the equally exiguous remains of **Montgreenan Castle.**

Cloncaird Castle   NS 357 076

After a recent period of use as a convalescent home, during which the name was changed, this is once more Cloncaird Castle, a private residence. A sixteenth-century castle, modernised and well-preserved, is incorporated into a castellated Regency façade which gives it the appearance of a miniature Windsor. At the entrance to the courtyard is a stone dated 1585. This building is about 2km downstream on the Water of Girvan from **Blairquhan**, whose policies march with those of Cloncaird. The castle may be seen from the B7045 and also from the long approach road to Blairquhan.

The old property of Cloncaird, which is recorded as far back as the late fifteenth century, belonged to the Mure family. Patrick Mure of Cloncaird died at Flodden in 1513.

Coal Hill Dun   NS 245 469

This is a subrectangular ridge fortification built on the narrow summit plateau of Coal Hill, with steep natural slopes to east and west. There are traces of ramparts on the north and south as well as two rock-cut ditches on the south and at least one on the north. Coal Hill is just at the northern extremity of Busbie Muir reservoir 4km north of Ardrossan, at the side of the B780.

Coilsfield Mains, King Coil's Grave   NS 446 262

This cairn, much reduced, is situated on a hillside close to Coilsfield Mains farmhouse. It was opened nearly 200 years ago and a number of urns filled with burnt bones, as well as 'warlike implements' were found. It was at this site that the legendary King Cole or Coil (Coel Hen) is reputed to have fallen in battle about 500, but the cairn is much earlier than the Iron Age.

Colmonell Parish Church   NX 144 857

St Colman Eala, a nephew of St Columba, is supposed to have died in about 610. There was a church here from at least 1178, annexed to Glasgow Cathedral until the Reformation. The present building, which replaces one demolished in 1771, stands at the west end of Colmonell village (A765) and has some fine woodwork.

Colmonell Covenanter's grave   NX 144 857

Blue-painted grave-stone in churchyard. Front has inscription to James McCracken; rear is inscribed to memory of Matthew McIlwraith. McCracken was buried with permission in the pre-existing grave of McIlwraith, a Covenanter shot in 1685 by John Graham of Claverhouse.

Colmonell: Polcardoch, Sallochan, Tongue
NX 118 842, NX 121 844, NX 154 862

Two of these cairns, Polcardoch and Sallochan, are on the south bank of the River Stinchar opposite Knockdolian Hill, and the third, Tongue, is on a bluff on the north bank east of Colmonell village. All of them have been well-nigh obliterated by stone-robbing: Polcardoch and Sallochan cairns, in the middle of low-lying fields (on the 75m contour shelf), are barely distinguishable as rings of cairn material. Polcardoch and Sallochan are the names of adjacent farms.

Connor Hill henge monument   NS 715 201

Connor Hill is a twin-topped eminence (415m, 416m OD) overlooking the sources of the Glenmuir Water. In a dip to the east of the two summits, at about 375m, lies an almost perfectly circular enclosure with an inner bank, ringed by a ditch, a berm and a palisade trench; an entrance ramp rises through the rings on the west. Because of its near-perfect circularity and situation it has been considered a ritual site or possible henge. The Mesolithic chipping floor at the Thorter Burn on **Glenmuirshaw** is less than 1km to the west, and the possible Covenanting site at **Auchtitench** is less than 2km to the south east in the Penbreck forest area. The proximity of these sites does not diminish the lonely isolation of Connor Hill, which is 7km south of Muirkirk and 8km north of Kirkconnel, amid some of the wildest hill-country in the south-west.

Corbie Craigs   NS 457 091

A deserted mining village above the Dunaskin Glen (2km east of Waterside and the A713, across rough country east of **Laight Castle**).

Corsgellioch (Carsgailoch) Hill Covenanting memorial   NS 547 147

Memorial to three Covenanters caught while on the run from Dalmellington and shot by dragoons in 1685. Probably connected with similar memorials at **Cumnock** and **Waistland**. This stone is difficult to access, probably now in the midst of new forest, but it can be reached on foot from Dalgig Farm, which is 3km west of Afton Bridgend (New Cumnock).

Corshill Castle   NS 416 465

Just north of Stewarton, in the narrow strip between the railway and the A735, there are two bits of massive wall, all that remains of the Cuninghame stronghold of Corshill. Two centuries ago the ruins were much more extensive, showing a gable end and a basement vault. Patrick Cuninghame of Corshill was another of the party of murderers who made away with the Earl of Eglinton and his entourage near **Lainshaw** in 1586. Patrick in his turn was assassinated by vengeful Montgomeries shortly after the earl's death.

Cove or Coif Castle   NS 232 102

See **Culzean Castle**

Coylton: Old Parish Church   NS 421 192

Judging by the fragments remaining, this was a richly decorated building. Salter believes that the west gable may be as early as *c.*1200. The surviving decorated archway is about 1400. The belfry atop the west gable is seventeenth-century in date. The small roofed building is an eighteenth-century burial vault.

Craighead Dun   NS 222 012

A small much-robbed dun on Craighead Hill above Killochan Castle to the north. It is situated on a rocky prominence on the western slopes of the hill, above the railway and the B741 near the mouth of the valley of the Water of Girvan.

Craigie Broch   NS 427 327

This feature, in the midst of the heavily fortified Craigie area, has been classified as a broch by Feachem and RCAHMS, but as a dun by others. Irregularly-shaped facing-stones are visible here and there, five on the inside and several more on the outside. This is one of several fortifications north and west of Craigie village. **Craigie Castle** is 2km away to the south-west.

Craigie Castle   NS 408 316

Research into this castle is still incomplete. The castle itself is now very unstable and is little more than a heap of rubble. Nonetheless it is possible

Fig. 9. Craigie Castle. Details of the hall.

to see that there has been a magnificent large hall, the structure of which has been raised to accommodate an equally large first-floor hall and probably another storey on top. MacGibbon and Ross thought that the hall would date no further back than the fifteenth century but Stuart Cruden has voiced the opinion that the main part of the castle was a hall-house dating to the twelfth or thirteenth century, and further, that this incorporates an earlier building.[153] The fifteenth-century addition consisted of the raised upper storeys. The fragments of the hall that remain display unusual magnificence of structure and decoration. This includes a vaulted roof in three bays, each with three ribs springing from corbels set at the level of the base of the window openings, which were splayed massively towards the interior. Two courtyards existed, the one to the east being perhaps the earlier. Ditches defended the northern and southern sides of the castle, and a third ditch to the north-east cuts the ridge on which the castle sits to form a bailey.

Cruden's early date for the main hall-house puts this erection back to the time of the Anglo-Norman takeover of Strathclyde, when northern Kyle was given to the Steward of Scotland, Walter fitz Alan. The previous building, of which Cruden has detected signs, might have belonged to the Strathclyde predecessor of Walter Hose, recorded as possessing the fief of Craigie under fitz Alan in about 1155–60.

Later the property passed to the Lindseys, and from them it passed by marriage to John Wallace of Riccarton in 1371 (the year of the accession of King Robert II, a Stewart descendant of fitz Alan). The Wallaces remained in possession of Craigie till 1600, when they moved to Newton-on-Ayr and Craigie Castle was allowed to fall into ruin.

The remains of Craigie Castle are on the lands of Craigie Mains, north of the B730.

Craigie Fell cairn   NX 097 783

Craigie Fell is one of the series of great hills in a north-east to south-west range which forms the very steep west wall of Glen App in Carrick. This one is north-east of the gap through which the A77 enters the glen. There is an oval cairn at 200m OD on the west-facing slope, overlooking the pass.

Craigie Fort   NS 428 325

Craigie fort, directly above Craigie village in Kyle, is a large enclosure, the boundaries of which follow the contours of the summit (about 152m OD). The defensive rampart is much reduced. There is an entrance on the south side, and the ground falls away sharply on the other sides. The impression is as much of a defended settlement as of a fort, and this feature should perhaps be styled an *oppidum*. Compare the entry for **Harpercroft**.

Craigmuir Mote (Dun)   NS 337 161

This dun sits on a knoll overlooking the River Doon, protected by steep slopes on the east, south and west and by the wall to the north and north-west. There is perhaps a ditch as well. It is south-west of Blairston Mains about 2km south of Alloway. The A77 runs alongside the River Doon to the east of the position.

Craigneil Castle   NX 147 853

This fourteenth- or fifteenth-century castle is a simple keep with two main floors. It stands on a height over a quarry, into which the north-western corner fell in 1886. The only vaulted room is the great hall on the second main floor, as can now be seen from the outside. The castle stands above the

Fig. 10. Craigneil Castle, from the north-west.

south bank of the River Stinchar, opposite Colmonell village and **Kirkhill Castle.** An unlisted road runs beneath Craigneil rock.

Craigneil Cairn NX 146 854

This is another almost obliterated cairn on the south bank of the Stinchar (*cf.* **Colmonell: Polcardoch, Sallochan** and **Tongue Cairns** above). Craigneil Castle is to the south of the site, opposite Colmonell village.

Craufurdland Tower NS 455 407

There are three main elements in this still-inhabited castle complex – a fifteenth- or sixteenth-century tower-house, a mansion dated 1648, and, connecting these two originally separate units, a vast Gothic front or façade of the early nineteenth century. The old tower has three storeys and an attic as well as a stair-tower rising beyond the attic in a caphouse with crow-stepped gablets. The seventeenth-century house has only two storeys, and has a fine plaster ceiling in the principal room. The Romantic–Gothic frontage has an enormous portal, ecclesiastical windows, dummy bartizans and a parapet. The whole building was well restored in the 1980s.

This castle has been held by the Craufurd family since very early days. It lies on the Craufurdland Water about 1km north-east of Assloss on the outskirts of Kilmarnock, some way east of the A77 (east from the B7038 for the Borland Bridge and Broombrae).

Cromwell's Fort, Ayr   NS 333 221

See **Ayr Royal Burgh**

Crosbie Castle (Troon)   NS 343 300

Crosbie, now represented by a few fragments between Monkton and the present Troon, was granted by the Steward of Kyle to one Henry Croc in the twelfth or thirteenth century. Bits of the castle, which have been attributed to the thirteenth or fourteenth century, survived in the grounds of Fullarton House (off B749) until 1969; vestiges may still survive. Until 1745 this was the residence of the Fullarton family.

Crosbie Castle (West Kilbride)   NS 218 500

This castle, about 3km north-east of West Kilbride, is just on the verge of the high moor but is situated in pleasant enough policies, now a caravan park. Still visible is a T-plan fortalice dated 1676, with two storeys, an attic and a stair-tower, built as usual on the lip of a deep ravine. It is surrounded by Victorian extensions and additions and is privately owned. The castle was formerly owned by the Craufords of Auchenames, and the celebrated William Wallace is reputed to have taken shelter in an earlier structure.

Crosbie Chapel (Frognal)   NS 344 294

This small chapel was briefly a parish church after the Reformation, before which it had been a pendicle of Dundonald. The chapelry of Crosbie was first mentioned in 1229, in which year it was transferred to the convent of **Dalmilling** by Walter II fitz Alan, the third Steward. When the Dalmilling venture collapsed in 1238 Crosbie was signed over to Paisley Abbey together with Dundonald itself, and they remained tributaries of the abbey till the Reformation, when Crosbie was erected into a parish before being united with Monkton parish. The present ruined building between Monkton and Troon is seventeenth-century in date, rectangular and gable-ended.

Crossraguel Abbey

This abbey was founded later than Kilwinning and Paisley, perhaps because of the lateness of its founder's reception into the fold of Scottish earldoms. Obeying the precepts of his mother and other influences, King David I set a fashion for endowing large ecclesiastical institutions, which every magnate within his realm was expected to follow. De Morville set up Kilwinning Abbey, fitz Alan set up Paisley, both probably in the latter part of the twelfth century. Duncan became lord of Carrick in 1190 and earl only about 1220, and it was not until twenty-four years later that he was able to establish the promotion of Crossraguel from its original (1214) status as a small oratory to a full-blown abbey, independent of Paisley. In this way he 'joined the club' of earls – considerably later than his cousin Roland, Lord of Galloway, who founded Glenluce Abbey in Wigtownshire in 1192. The abbey may not have become fully operational until 1286, when the first abbot is recorded.

The original cruciform abbey church was destroyed during the Wars of Independence, and all that remains of this building are two angles of the nave. The new nave, rebuilt in the fourteenth century, is relatively unusual in that it is long and narrow, without aisles or transepts, and its apse is three-sided, following a continental model. It has prominent buttresses, boldly thrown out. In the sixteenth century, the abbey church was divided in two, the western part becoming a lady chapel.

Relatively more survives of this abbey than of its sister institution at Kilwinning, and the cloister here is magnificently preserved. In the east range the sacristy and the chapter-house, both fifteenth-century rib-vaulted chambers, have survived intact, with a glorious acoustic. There are interesting conventual buildings, including a frater (refectory) and an infirmary block, as well as rare details, such as a reredorter *(monastic lavatory) drain. Provision was made within the abbey precinct for housing* corrodiars *i.e. lay pensioners.*

At the time of the Reformation in 1561 the buildings were partially destroyed, though subsequent stone-robbing may have contributed to the present-day appearance of the ruin. Monks continued to occupy the abbey at least till 1592, and one was still alive in 1607. In its heyday Crossraguel was a very wealthy institution, plentifully endowed with lands and parish revenues by the founder Duncan of Carrick and his successors, who included Robert the Bruce (Duncan's great-grandson) and both Robert II and Robert III.

That the times were warlike is shown by two additional buildings, the abbot's tower and the gatehouse, both clearly defensive fortifications built into the precincts of the abbey. The tower, which is much more of a ruin than the gatehouse, sits on the south-eastern corner of the complex. It is, perhaps, a conversion (about 1530) of an earlier abbot's house to a secular residence for the third Earl of Cassillis when he was under the guardianship of Abbot William Kennedy. The tower-house had four storeys and an attic with a corbelled parapet. The ground floor basement is vaulted and there was a great hall as usual on the first floor. The private apartments were on the top floor, where the remnants of an elaborate fireplace are to be seen. There are gunloops of the inverted keyhole type.

The gatehouse, almost intact and recently restored, is a very interesting structure, perhaps a little later than the abbot's tower conversion. It is another tower-house, built over a gateway and passage, with a circular stair-tower rising above the level of the parapet and corbelled out to a square caphouse adorned with crowstepped gablets and chequered corbelling of its own. The main tower has three storeys, an attic, a corbelled parapet walk and rounded bartizans. The gate passage has a small 'porter's box' let into the thickness of the west wall, and the apartments above are adapted to a gate-keeper's lodge with fireplaces, garderobes and stone seats.

The dovecot is completely undamaged. It is also sixteenth-century in date.

The name 'Crossraguel' probably means '(at the) cross of Riaghail (the Irish saint Regulus or Rule)'. This indicates that there was a standing cross on the site before the foundation of the original oratory in 1214, if not an actual chapel or cell. The abbey ruins are a prominent landmark on the left of the A77 as you leave Maybole for Girvan.

Cuff Hill chambered cairn   NS 386 551

The Cuff Hill cairn is an outlying member of the Bargrennan group some 70km north of the Barrhill area, in 'undulating agricultural land' in Beith parish, a (now) more inhabited area.[154] Larger and longer than the other cairns, it has been mutilated and disturbed over nearly two centuries, first by those industrious agricultural utilitarians in 1810 who thought they had a much better use for the cairn material, namely road metal, and later by excited antiquarians, who probed and turned over the surviving stones in an endeavour to find more chambers. Despite all this, at the northern end the cairn is relatively undisturbed and reaches its greatest surviving height. One chamber may still lie intact in the undisturbed part. Only one discovered chamber, the east (found in 1810), preserves one of its capstones intact in its exact place. It is on the south side of Cuff Hill. A north-eastward spur from the B777 runs close to the foot of the hill.

Cuff Hill standing stones   (1) NS 379 550, (2) NS 386 552

(1) is a site between Lochlands Hill and Cuff Hill at about 195m OD. Four stones were arranged in a square as a 'four-poster', but the two smaller stones (the south-western and south-eastern) have now been dislodged and placed leaning against the two larger ones. The site is in level pasture land. (2) is a single earthfast boulder, probably a broken standing stone, on Cuff Hill itself, 150m north of **Cuff Hill Chambered Cairn (NS 386 551)**. An unlisted road between the B777 and the B776 passes both sites, which are about 5km east of Beith in North Ayrshire.

Culzean Castle: Kennel Mount Bronze Age cairn   NS 241 098

A low stone cairn was recently (1996) identified at the Kennel Mount on the Culzean estate, associated with burnt bone. In 1998 further excavations took place and a Yorkshire Vase-type food vessel was retrieved, which dated the cairn to 2000–1500 BC.

Recently (October, 2001) the discovery of three Neolithic axes was reported from Culzean Country Park. The axes may date as far back as 4000 BC, and were possibly used by farmers to clear woodland. They may have been imported from the Lake District or from Antrim in Northern Ireland. The discovery indicates the likely presence of a Neolithic settlement in the area. Aerial photography has revealed 'a large circular ditched enclosure over 30 metres in diameter'. The discovery was made during a field walking exercise carried out by park rangers under the supervision of the National Trust for Scotland's West Region Archaeologist, Mr Douglas Alexander.

Culzean or Coif (Cove) Castle   NS 232 102

Culzean Castle was originally called Coif or Cove Castle. The existing eighteenth-century mansion was built around Cove Castle, which was one of a number of Kennedy strongholds in Ayrshire, dating from very early times, perhaps the fourteenth century or before. In fact the name 'Coffe' is recognised as that of one of the seventh- or eighth-century Anglian settlements in their shire in Carrick dependent on Maybole.[155] *The name 'Culzean' or 'Kuillein' belonged to another now-vanished mansion which, according to Blaeu-Pont, was probably situated east of Turnberry beyond the Milton Burn (approximately NS 23 06). Sir Thomas Kennedy – later shot on the shore at* **Greenan Castle** *– owned both Cove and Culzean in the 1590s and lived at Cove, but preferred to be known by the more prestigious territorial designation, Culzean, and this in time came to be applied to Cove or Coif.*[156]

A descendant of this man, also called Sir Thomas Kennedy and later ninth Earl of Cassillis, inherited Cove-Culzean in 1744 and began to convert it from its original military and defensive functions to those of a gentleman's country residence. The next earl, David Kennedy, invited Robert Adam in 1777 to tender for a complete reconstruction and conversion not only of the castle but of the surrounding policies. Over the next ten to fifteen years, Adam's scheme for a harmonious complex of buildings designed in a uniform style was realized. He enveloped the older building in an eighteenth-century modification of an Italian Renaissance style which was entirely alien to the previously very Scottish architecture of Cove, but which became famous as Adam's own trademark here and in England. He reoriented the castle to make it stretch along the cliff face with wings on either side and, in 1785, built the great round tower that stands at the edge of the cliff. In 1787 the exquisite oval staircase was 'dropped into' the well between the tower and the original Cove castle block. This was now converted to form one of the principal saloons ('The Eating Room') of the remodelled structure.

On the outside of Culzean Castle there are corbels, towers, crenellations and dummy bartizans enough to satisfy the heart of the most feudal romantic, all realised in beautiful fawn-coloured local sandstone. Inside, the furnishings and fitments are meticulously designed to harmonise with the architecture: the circular saloon in the tower overlooking the sea and the cliff has curved doors and other fitments agreeing exactly with the curvature of the room. Each room has its own style of decoration, and the Wedgwood 'Jasperware' theme in the plasterwork of the ceilings and surrounds is breathtaking. All this has recently been restored with great attention to authenticity, as has the exterior stonework, which was beginning to deteriorate due to exposure to the sea air.

In addition to the castle itself, gardens, stables, home farm and entrance way (under a tall 'romantic-ruin' arch) are all designed in the same characteristically smooth Adam style, making this one of the most elegant groups in Scotland. It is popular with the public, who come in numbers to visit the castle and the grounds. The National Trust for Scotland, who have run Culzean as a tourist attraction since 1945, have converted the home farm into a highly successful visitor centre. Excellent guidebooks are available.

Culzean Castle may be approached from Maybole on the B7023, from Ayr on the A719 or from Girvan on the A77 giving on to the A719.

Cumbrae Castle (Wee Cumbrae)   NS 152 513

This is one of a group of four castles situated round the mouth of the upper Clyde estuary of closely similar design and roughly the same date (the second half of the fifteenth century). The other members of the group are **Law, Fairlie** and **Skelmorlie.** In this castle part of the first-floor great hall

Fig. 11. Little Cumbrae Castle, from the south-west.

is divided off by a stone partition to form a kitchen with a fireplace as big as the kitchen itself. The entrance door is on the first floor, reached by an outside stair. Both basement and great hall are vaulted. The second floor is divided into two chambers. At the top there is a single course of continuous corbelling below an arrangement of chequered corbels. There are three round angle-turrets and a single square one. Gables and chimneys have collapsed with the roof and garret chamber. It was surrounded by a rampart and ditch.

The castle is situated on a small islet off the east coast of the Wee Cumbrae facing the Cuninghame shore. It is probably not the first castle on this site, since Wee Cumbrae was part of the royal game reserves from very early times and was under the control of the Hunters of **Hunterston Castle**. It was burnt by Oliver Cromwell in 1653 after one of his opponents had taken refuge in it, and since then it has been a ruin.

Cumnock: Baird Institute   NS 568 202

This institute, now a small museum, contains an extensive local collection including Covenanting relics. It is in Bank Street near the Square.

Cumnock Covenanting memorials   NS 571 203

Monuments (1) to Alexander Peden (three stones), fugitive Covenanting minister died 1686 of natural causes, (2) Thomas Richard, farmer, shot 5 April 1685, and (3) three Covenanters probably taken at **Corsgellioch** and shot in 1685. The graveyard fronts the A70 leaving town eastward.

Cumnock Market Cross   NS 567 201

Cumnock was granted the right to have a market cross of its own in 1509, but this cross, which has been moved at least once, is dated 1703 (repaired 1778). It has a sundial and a ball finial. It stands in Cumnock Main Square.

Dagon Stone, Darvel   NS 563 374

Now re-erected in Hastings Square, Darvel, this is probably an ancient standing stone. The small round boulder at the top is a joke fixed on by a local blacksmith with an iron bar in 1821. There is a tradition that newly-weds had to walk round the stone for good luck, and this could reflect an ancient pre-Christian marriage ritual.

Dalcairnie cairn   NS 462 042

The Dalcairnie Glen lies south-west to north-east, pointing in the direction of Bogton Loch and Dalmellington. On the flat summit of the Wee Cairn

Hill (239m OD) to the north of the glen stands the mutilated Dalcairnie cairn, one of a number of hill-top cairns in the Dalmellington–Loch Doon area.

Dalduff Castle NS 320 069

Dalduff farmhouse is reputed to be built over and out of fragments of Dalduff Castle. A slit window and thick walls in parts of the house may be survivals from the old structure. Hector Ferguson of Dalduff is mentioned in a Crown charter of 1557, and his grandson, John Ferguson of Dalduff, came into the property in 1615, but it seems to have been sold to the Kennedys of Cassillis before 1622.[157] Apart from this, nothing is known of Dalduff Castle. The farmhouse is less than 1km west of Crosshill, close to the Water of Girvan.

Dalduff hoard NS 320 069

In 1846 a Late Bronze Age hoard was unearthed here, possibly during building operations. It consisted of bronze swords and axes and other fragments in a pot. Some of the bronzes were lost, but others are in the collections of the National Museums of Scotland (NMS X. DQ 92–98A) and are currently on display in the Museum of Scotland, Chambers Street, Edinburgh (Early People section, 'Glimpses of the Sacred' area in the basement). Still others are retained in Kilkerran House. Four socketed axes and two sword-fragments in various states of preservation were given to the museum, and seven axes were held at Kilkerran. Also found were cauldron staples and rings, and another sword fragment. See p. 16.

Dalgarven Mill NS 296 458

This is a heritage centre based on a mill erected in 1640. It is a wheel-operated watermill powered from the River Garnock with French burr millstones and cast-iron gearing. The premises also house a country life museum and an extensive costume collection. The centre is almost 2km north of Kilwinning on the A737 between the river and the main railway-line.

Dalmellington: Cathcartson Interpretation Centre NS 482 059

This is a converted row of weavers' cottages (just off the Square) displaying aspects of past local industry including weaving, mining and railways. The cottages are dated 1744.

Dalmellington Motte NS 482 058

Dalmellington Motte towers above the B7013 and the Muck Water, at the east end of Dalmellington. Much of the motte is obscured by vegetation as well as by intervening buildings, but from certain angles the characteristic 'truncated cone' profile still stands out sharply. The original builder of the motte was Thomas Colville of Lincolnshire, who was granted Dalmellington by Duncan, first Lord of Carrick to guard against incursions from Galloway.[158]

Dalmilling   NS 36 22

There is really no indication of where this monastery stood, if it was ever developed. Walter II fitz Alan the Steward in 1229 intimated to the master of Sempringham his intention of planting a colony of Gilbertines on his land north of the River Ayr. A grant of territory was made and some canons appear to have come to Ayr on a scouting expedition to spy out the land, but there is no evidence that the English order of Gilbertines ever succeeded in establishing a house at Dalmilling, and in 1238 the two residual canons were ordered to return to Yorkshire. It appears that some property in the neighbourhood of the area now called Dalmilling was transferred about that time to Paisley Abbey.

Dalquharran Castle (Old)   NS 272 018
Dalquharran Castle (New)   NS 270 021

Two spectacular ruins, one on the north the bank of the Water of Girvan near Dailly, the other near the first but on high ground, overlooking the whole Girvan Valley.

Old Dalquharran Castle, a Kennedy property, has gone through many phases in its history. Probably first built in the fifteenth century, it was originally a rectangular block with a hall on the first floor. This would have been divided in two, giving a private room at the east end with access to a further apartment in a round tower at the south-east angle. At the top of the building, corbels and parapet walk have survived, showing unusual ogee arches between each pair of corbels. Only one of the angle bartizans still exists, the others having been built over. In 1679 a northern extension was added with a round tower at the north-eastern end (balancing the appearance of the castle seen from the river), and two northward projections on the northern side of the original tower block. These two projections were square stair-towers with gables. The tower at the re-entrant angle still has a doorcase with a pediment.

Old Dalquharran Castle is now extensively ruined and most of the north wing has collapsed. But even in its present state it presents a more cheerful appearance than New Dalquharran Castle, a huge eighteenth-century Adam mansion standing above it on the slopes of Quarrel Hill. The new castle incorporates some features very similar to those of the highly successful design at Culzean, including the central round tower and a fine

Fig. 12. Old Dalquharran Castle, from the north-west.

staircase. Unfortunately the building fell on evil days and was deroofed in 1970, massive deterioration setting in thereafter. The interior is now a complete wreck and, viewed from Dailly, the exterior has rather a macabre, skull-like presence, heightened by the ruined windows resembling eye-sockets. See also **Lochmodie Castle**.

Dalry, Courthill: probable mortuary house NS 292 495

This structure, now buried under a slag heap, has been identified as a prehistoric barrow, covering a rectangular structure built of stakes and containing evidence of inhumation as well as cremation. This site has been alternatively interpreted as a much later Norman motte.[160] See pp. 12–13.

Dean Castle, Kilmarnock *NS 437 394*

This castle falls into three separate parts corresponding to three different phases of construction. The first was a motte, represented by a large tree-covered mound some distance away from the stone buildings. This was presumably erected by Malcolm Loccart, the twelfth-century grantee of the Kilmarnock barony from de Morville, Lord of Cuninghame.

The second part is a tall stone tower-house with a parapet walk but no projecting corbel table. It has the usual vaulted basement and first-floor hall, also vaulted, with a musicians' gallery. A second-floor hall contained private apartments and a chapel. This tower dates from some time after 1316, the year in which Robert the Bruce confirmed his grant to Robert Boyd of this part of the forfeited Balliol inheritance.

The third part is a palace range with another first-floor great hall and a five-storey tower. It has a corbelled-out parapet and the tower cap-house has kept its original stone roofing slabs. This part of the castle was erected in the 1460s, when the Boyd family was at the summit of its influence with the royal family, and required a more opulent residence. The range has no internal connection with the old tower, but sits on the seventeenth-century defensive wall that surrounds the entire complex. There is also a very fine gatehouse

The castle was virtually destroyed by fire in 1735 but between 1908 and 1946 the buildings were meticulously restored by a new owner, Lord Howard de Walden, who subsequently gifted the entire property to Kilmarnock Burgh. It now serves as a museum, with collections of musical instruments, medieval arms and armour and Covenanting relics. Among the features provided by Lord Howard de Walden were very fine early seventeenth-century plasterwork ceilings acquired from Balgonie Castle in Fife. These now adorn the great hall and another chamber in the palace range.

The castle is situated in the north-eastern quadrant of Kilmarnock, on the west bank of the Fenwick Burn just north of its confluence with the Craufurdland Water.

Diamond Hill cup-and-ring markings and ? standing stone   NS 213 539

Receding from the Hunterston peninsula the coastal cliffs go up in three 'steps' to Kaim Hill at 387m OD. The first 'step' is Diamond Hill (148m OD), along whose top there runs a track from south to north. Near the northern extremity of this track, just south of a patch of woodland, is a cup-and-ring-marked rock with probably in excess of twenty cups and one or two rings. It is largely covered in turf, and there may be more marks. At **NX 215 539** there is a possible standing stone.

Dinvin Motte   NX 200 931

Dinvin Motte, on a southern shoulder of Dinvin Hill, is massive and in good shape. From the summit of its knoll the steep central mound stands out, belted by two rings of ramparts and ditches. A causeway crosses the inner fortification from the east. The motte occupies a commanding position covering the hill pass from the interior of Carrick to the Girvan area, and both the railway and the A714 road run close to it today. It can be seen from the shore-line and from well out at sea.

Doon, Auld Brig (Alloway)   NS 332 178

See **Auld Brig o' Doon**

Doonfoot (Ayr): Stonefield Park Road standing stone   NS 322 186

This stone stands at present in a housing estate at the north end of Stonefield Park.

Dornal Moat or Motte   NS 632 194

The Ordnance Survey inspector in 1981 termed this an 'enigmatic earthwork' – which is at least an advance on Christison, who was sure in 1893 that it was nothing more than a 'natural eminence'.[160] It is uncertain whether the name refers to a moat, meaning a water-channel round the base of the 'eminence', or to a motte, meaning that the mound has been at least in part artificially structured as a defensive station. It is a very odd large mound on what might almost be called the flood plain of the Glenmuir Water, cut off from the surrounding countryside by a miry meadow which is inundated in winter. Some parts of the water channel are artificial. Although nothing like building foundations or earthworks have been detected on the mound, it might be revealing to investigate further. It may be significant that the Glenmuir Water forms the frontier at this point between Kyle Stewart and King's Kyle, and that Kyle Castle, about 2km to the east of Dornal, is on the King's Kyle side, while Dornal is in Kyle Stewart.

Dowan's Hill Fort   NS 347 124

This fort is on the summit of Dowan's Hill (134m OD). It has been identified as the original Dun Ree, the name of an adjacent farm being Dunree. The fort is circular, with two stony ramparts, the inner one having an internal ditch. The external rampart is a continuous terrace with a scarp. The entrance is to the north-west. Dowan's Hill overlooks **Cassillis House** to the west and Dalrymple to the north. The B742 runs past its foot.

Dow Hill Fort, Girvan   NX 192 960

This is a prominent fortification above the southern part of Girvan. It appears to be a dun erected within the defences of an earlier fort, although the dun-like structure could simply be the primary nucleus of a fort. The structure has a western rampart on the edge of a broad level terrace. A rock-cutting leads from this terrace up to a flat space; another break in the scarp behind this platform leads to the hill-top, where fortifications are represented by a curving earth and stone bank on the west and traces on the east above a number of decayed ramparts on the eastern instep of the hill. Before a coherent archaeological picture can be gained the whole structure would have to be subjected to detailed examination.

Dowhill Mount   NS 202 029

Near the alginate factory on the east side of the A77 coast road north of Girvan rises a structure which has been variously claimed for a dun, a motte and (most recently) a 'homestead'. The central mound, sitting on the edge of a steep bluff, is surrounded on all sides except the west by a double rampart and ditch. The summit of the mound is flat. Within this area is a subcircular enclosure defined by a reduced drystone dyke. The structure might well be a twelfth-century motte, but this would not exclude the possibility of a previously existing dun on the same site.

This possible motte should not be confused with the preceding entry, **Dow Hill Fort**, which is in the south of Girvan.

Dreghorn Parish Church   NS 352 383

The first mention of Dreghorn Parish Church is in 1406, when Robert Storm was confirmed in possession of the perpetual vicarage of Dreghorn by the antipope Benedict XIII of Avignon. Apart from that, little is known of the early history or buildings of this church. It is assumed that the earliest church building, probably of the twelfth or thirteenth century, lies underneath the present unique octagonal structure, which was built in the 1780s. Like other parish churches in the neighbourhood, the church was early appropriated to Kilwinning Abbey, with which it remained until the Reformation. In 1668 it was united with **Perceton** parish.

Drongan Castle   NS 449 178

If the traveller follows the B730 past the village of Drongan, he or she will meet the Water of Coyle just at Drongan Mains, where the faintest traces may be made out of the thoroughly demolished Drongan Castle, an ancient fortified residence of the Craufurds. This building was probably of the fifteenth century.

Drumclog battle memorial   NS 625 397

Scene of defeat of John Graham of Claverhouse and his dragoons at the hands of enraged conventiclers (Covenanters) interrupted at their Sunday devotions on 1 June 1679. See pp. 97–8. Drumclog monument is just outside Ayrshire east of Loudoun Hill north of the A71 on a side road.

Drumdowns, Altimeg: settlement
NX 103 753 to NX 105 751, NX 105 755

Altimeg is one of the higher hills (392m OD) which forms an eastern wall to the narrow gorge or glen of the south-flowing Water of App. There is a high pass, a footpath out of Glen App at Altimeg and over the hill's south-west shoulder, which is itself called Drumdowns. Immediately to the south-west of this shoulder, straddling the footpath, are a number of features which have now been interpreted as a prehistoric settlement or village. The features are now thought to comprise (1) a hut-circle (**NX 1048 7530**), (2) an unclassified feature (**NX 1051 7520**), (3) a rectangular structure (**NX 1053 7518**), (4) an enclosure (**NX 1047 7519**), (5) another hut-circle (**NX 1048 7530**), (6) cairns (**NX 1050 7517** and **NX 1043 7533**) and (7) another enclosure (**NX 1045 7518**). These have all been exposed in old peat-cuttings, and more excavation might show up more structures. There is also (8) a cairn at **NX 1051 7550** and (9) an enclosure at **NX 1047 7519**. All this area may now, however, be afforested and further investigation may be impossible.[161]

Drumduff cairn (Penderry Hill)   NX 068 762

This cairn is situated on the lower, north-westward-facing slopes of Penderry Hill, overlooking Glendrishaig farmhouse and the sea. It has been heavily robbed. Penderry Hill (309m OD) is one of the north-east to south-west range of high hills that constitute the west wall of Glen App south of Ballantrae.

Drummochreen Dun   NS 285 035

At Captain's Bridge, which is east of the modern Drummochreen, there is an oval dun on the summit of a knoll. A wall has been partially destroyed by a quarry on the north-west, but in other parts it can be seen as a line of rubble. Facing-stones are visible. The site is just north of the B741 and the railway half-way down the valley of the Girvan.

Drybridge standing stone   NS 359 364

A large and impressive standing stone near the crossing of the railway and the B730, in a field behind a row of houses at Drybridge hamlet, which lies along a curve in the River Irvine south of Dreghorn.

The Ducat Tower   NS 536 373

See **Newmilns Castle**

Dumfries House   NS 541 204

The name of this gracious Palladian building, still the seat of the Marquis of Bute, is slightly misleading. William Dalrymple, fourth Earl of Dumfries, commissioned the present mansion near Cumnock from the brothers Adam, and it was built between 1754 and '59. It is built in palatial style, with a grand central block and wide staircase rising to an impressive entrance, and two wings completed as late as 1905.

The former castle or tower on the banks of the Lugar Water seems to have been called The Ward, and the property, owned by a branch of the Craufurd family, was known as Lefnoreis or (in some versions) Lochnorris. In the early part of the seventeenth century the Craufurds disposed of Lefnoreis (partly through the other great Cumnock family, the Dunlops) to the up-and-coming Creichtons of Sanquhar; William, seventh Lord Sanquhar became Viscount of Ayr in 1622 and Earl of Dumfries in 1633. The earldom and later marquisate of Bute came into the family by marriage in 1814. No trace of the ancient tower called The Ward appears to survive, although Lord Bute is said to have found old walls and a causeway during excavations (now untraceable) in 1897.

Dunaskin Industrial Heritage Museum (Waterside)   NS 440 086

This is a Victorian ironworks, opened in 1848 and finally closed after two conversions (to coal and brick production respectively) in 1976. Preserved installations on display include engineering workshops, the Craigton mine, an engine house and a furnace. Visitor facilities including audio-visual commentaries are available. See also **Laight Castle.**

Dundonald Castle   *NS 363 345*

A gigantic earthwork or motte initially surmounted by wooden buildings, Dundonald Castle stands in a strong niche of the Clavin hills surveying the whole north-western firth and territory up to and beyond the Cuninghame border.

*It may be rather difficult to think of this remote and secluded building as the centre of royal power, though it may not inspire the hilarity it provoked in Dr Johnson when he visited the site in 1773. In fact it is a huge bleak fortress, scowling down towards Irvine and the Cunninghame coast – with a glance over its shoulder in the direction of Kilmarnock. The west coast was far more important in the life of Strathclyde in the Dark and Middle Ages than it is now, and this hillock in northern Kyle was occupied long before the Stewards of Scotland identified it as a strong point from which to dominate the countryside. The strategic importance of the site is shown by the Iron Age fortifications that surround it, on **Wardlaw Hill (NS 358 327)**, **Kemp Law (NS 356 336)** near Hallyards, and **Harpercroft (NS 360 325)**. At Dundonald itself an older fortress was built over in the twelfth century. Perhaps this was done as a gesture of 'Norman Scottish' dispossession of and mastery over original Strathclyde owners.*

The present structure shows signs of repeated rebuilding after the destruction of the Wars of Independence. Under Robert II in the 1370s an enormous tower-house was constructed upon the still visible ruins of a slighted 'castle of enceinte' of the thirteenth century. This earlier structure, itself a considerable building, may well have belonged to Walter II fitz Alan the third Steward, who died in 1241. It was preceded by two structures, a vitrified Iron Age fort, and a Norman motte, whose bailey may be traceable some distance from the fifteenth-century barmkin wall. Two very large drum towers forming a gatehouse were demolished, probably in the fifteenth century, to make room for the barmkin, and an extension to the south and a courtyard on the east were added.

The sheer scale of the fourteenth-century rebuilding is surprising, and has been clearer since the partial reconstruction by Historic Buildings and Monuments (Scottish Development Department). The ground plan is rectangular, and there are two principal storeys. The ground floor is a hall with a pointed arch, and the great hall on the first floor was probably larger, with ribbed vaulting. The enceinte or barmkin wall survives in places. The exalted status of the owner was emphasised by a line of shields on the west external wall, armorial bearings of himself as Steward and as King of Scotland. It is rather a terrifying place, lowering above the peaceful village of Dundonald like a thundercloud, and squatly visible from afar like a symbol of oppression.

Access is from the B730 running north through Dundonald. There is now a visitor centre below the castle mound with a display showing important details of the successive occupation layers on the site.

Dundonald Parish Church   NS 366 343

The first mention of Dundonald Parish Church is in 1229, when it was donated to the convent at **Dalmilling**, which had been set up by Walter II fitz Alan the third Steward. When the Dalmilling venture fell through in 1238, Dundonald, together with other tributary parishes, was reassigned to Paisley Abbey, with which it remained until the Reformation. The present building was built in 1803.

Dunduff Castle   NS 272 164

Above Dunure to the north-east is a cluster of hills including the Brown and Green Carrick Hills and lesser heights such as Blacktop Hill and Fisherton Hill. Near the summit of Fisherton Hill is Dunduff, a late sixteenth- or early seventeenth-century L-plan tower-house, north-east of Dunduff farm steading. The building had two storeys only, although a third storey was clearly intended. There was a three-storey stair-tower with an entrance in the re-entrant angle, and the ground floor had three barrel-vaulted rooms. The second-storey hall had splayed window embrasures and a fireplace.

Dunduff was recorded as incomplete in 1696. It has now been converted into a dwelling-house. Not far away is a suspected motte or Iron Age fort.

Duniewick Fort   NX 116 851

On the north-eastern shoulder of Knockdolian, a fort sits atop a craggy protuberance. It is very conspicuous, especially from its eastern approaches from Colmonell. Its earthen rampart, circling the high point of the crag, encloses a wide, flat area. The access path is very steep and rocky, rising to an entrance on the west. The fort commands the passes from the interior of the Stinchar valley to the coast represented by the modern B7044 and B734.

Dunlop   NS 404 494

The earliest mention of Dunlop parish church occurs in the cartulary of Paisley Abbey, where it is stated that one John de Reston occupied the vicarage (perpetual) of Dunlop in 1265. Like other parish churches in Cuninghame, Dunlop was granted to **Kilwinning Abbey**, which received its revenues until the Reformation. The noted philosopher John Major or Mair, the preceptor of John Knox the reformer, was vicar of Dunlop between 1518 and 1523. The present church is an 1835 rebuilding of a church of 1765, itself a rebuilding of a structure of 1641, which presumably replaced an even earlier building. The north aisle has traces of Jacobean architecture (strapwork). In the kirkyard stands the burial vault of Hans (Johannes) Hamilton, the first Protestant minister of Dunlop, who was appointed in 1563. The vault was erected by Hamilton's son, who became Viscount Clandeboye.

Dunree   NS 347 124

See **Dowan's Hill Fort**

Dunure Castle   NS 252 158

The substantial polygonal enclosure walling running round the edge of the up-reared rock that is the basis of the fortification may have been built before the Wars of Independence. A tower-house of two or three storeys was fitted in at the summit of the crag within the walls. The defences were extended to the east in the form of an open tower with an internal stair giving access to the upper parts of the main building. In the fifteenth century all this was further improved by covering over the whole remaining area enclosed by the early wall of enceinte, to create a 'donjon' of two storeys. A further extension to the east over falling ground enabled the construction of a three-storeyed range, and the whole extended building was furnished with a machicolated parapet. An internal defence was a shallow masonry staircase rising against the east face of the original tower-block to a short drawbridge. There was a siege in 1570, when Bargany rescued the Commendator of Crossraguel from the clutches of Gilbert fourth Earl of Cassillis. (See pp. 54, 87) This resulted in substantial destruction including that of a chapel, fragments of whose smashed ecclesiastical glass have been recovered from a debris dump. Over this dump was constructed the last improvement, a kitchen range extending to the landward. In the seventeenth century the castle was subjected to systematic robbing of building materials such as slates, stone, lead, glass and window frames. Perhaps this was done by Cromwell's troops salvaging materials for the construction of **Ayr Citadel**, as they are reputed to have done at **Ardrossan Castle**. Whoever was responsible, the castle was a total ruin by 1696. It has remained in its perilously insecure condition until 1998, when the Strathclyde Building Preservation Trust and other agencies combined forces to stabilize the structure.

Even in its ruined condition the castle dominates the village and tiny harbour of Dunure. These may be reached by a spur road descending the cliff face from the A719 at Fisherton.

Eglinton   NS 323 422

Historically this castle was surrounded by extensive grounds, now divided by the A78, which runs to the south of the ruins. The latest building was an ambitious eighteenth-century palace designed by John Paterson. It was vacated in the early twentieth century, deroofed in 1925, used for target practice during the Second World War, and in 1973 done away with altogether except for a corner tower and a few pieces of masonry. Thus passed the chief glory of the Montgomerie family.

The earlier buildings had their share of violent vicissitudes. Presumably the first stone castle on the site was placed there by the Montgomeries after the displacements of the Wars of Independence in the fourteenth century, and it was this building which was burnt down by the enraged Cuninghame family in 1527 or '28, only twenty years after Montgomerie had been created Earl of Eglinton, and thirty years after his acceptance of the bailieship of Cuninghame. The next castle – the one that was demolished unceremoniously in 1796 to make way for Paterson's design – was a solid four-storey tower with the conventional parapet-walk, corbelling and attic storey, added to and altered throughout the years.

Eglinton Trophy (Cuninghame House, Irvine): folly   NS 318 387

This gigantic specimen of the silversmith's art is a monument to the folly of one of the Earls of Eglinton, who ruined his family with a colossally expensive extravaganza called the Eglinton Tournament in 1838. Housed within a glass case and standing in the meeting chamber of the North Ayrshire Council, it shares a quality which all good follies should possess – that of being striking and handsome, and worth preserving for itself. Cuninghame House is that building resembling a beached whale opposite the northern end of the down platform at Irvine railway station. I suppose that the North Ayrshire authorities can be persuaded to let visitors gaze at the amazing thing. See p. 106.

Fail Monastery   NS 421 286

This was an establishment of Red Friars or Trinitarians – originally a
French order called Mathurines (after a locality in Paris). The monastery
was established in 1252, north of Tarbolton at the present Fail Mains (Fail is
a small river running ultimately into the River Ayr). The ruins of the house
were finally demolished as recently as 1952, and some traces can still be seen
in the neighbourhood of Fail Mains. Further south, on the west side of the
B730 opposite the former Tarbolton Loch, a farm called Spittalside testifies
to the former existence of a hospital, a place run by the Trinitarians for the
reception of the indigent and homeless as well as the sick.

Fairlie Castle   NS 212 549

This isolated castle is the most decayed of all the sea-cliff castles of North
Ayrshire, except of course **Knock**, which is only preserved as a romantic ruin.
The wayfarer plodding up Fairlie Glen comes upon Fairlie Castle suddenly,
where it looms among the trees on the north side of the forbidding gorge of
the Fairlie Burn. The shell of the building itself is fairly complete, although
the stonework is deteriorating, and someone has been kind enough to keep
the greensward at the base of the tower in good condition. Once again the
kitchen can be identified as occupying the first floor together with the great
hall. (*cf.* **Cumbrae**, **Skelmorlie** and **Law**). The corbelling at the top of the
building is chequered and there are round angle turrets at each corner. It is a
relatively massive structure four storeys high, perhaps from the late fifteenth
century. The first owners were the Fairlie family (supposed to be descended
from the family of Ross of **Tarbet**). The Boyles of **Kelburn** bought Fairlie
Castle in 1650.

  The path that runs past the castle shows traces of very old stone paving,
and it is likely that this was a main road in former times, crossing the moor
from the Dalry region.

Farland Head Fishtrap   NS 179 485

At the north-west end of Ardneil Bay on the south of the Hunterston
Peninsula a shallow pond has been dug out so that its east end is open to the
high tide; 30m from the east end a cross wall has been erected with a gap in
the middle. Fish can swim in at high tide and be dispersed into a series of
side-ponds, but not swim out again when the tide drops.

Fenwick Parish Church   NS 464 434

This church was called The New Kirk of Kilmarnock for some time
after it was made into the parish church of the northen part of the

former Kilmarnock Parish (divided in two in 1642). The building had a disastrous fire in 1929 but was fully restored in 1931 and is still in use. The jougs for confining scolds and other malefactors are still to be seen on the wall outside.

Fenwick Covenanters' memorials   NS 465 435

A large concentration of Covenanters' tombstones and memorials in the churchyard: to (1) Captain John Paton, hanged Edinburgh 9 May 1684; (2) James White, shot 1685 (for story and inscription see p. 100–1); (3) Peter Gemmel, shot 1685; (4) John Fergushill and George Woodburn, shot 1685; (5) Buntine and Blackwood, hanged respectively 19 and 21 December 1666 (see also **Irvine Covenanters' Grave**); (6) William Guthrie, (d. 1665); (7) James (d. 1691), John (d. 1755), and John (d. 1793, author of *Scots Worthies*), Howie of Lochgoin, *et al.* Also within the church a Covenanting battle flag and Bible used by Captain Paton on the scaffold in Edinburgh. Fenwick Village is on the B751 off the A77 north of Kilmarnock.

Fergus Loch   NS 393 182

There may have been a 'monastery' on the island in Loch Fergus, and from the shore 'totally formless low mounds of boulders' have been seen on the island, but no definite information is available. Loch Fergus is 6km east of Alloway, and the nearest road is the B742.

Finnarts Hill henge etc.
(1) and (2) NX 053 742, (3) NX 055 745, (4) NX 051 740

This hill, at the south-western extremity of the 'western wall' range of Glen App, carries a cluster of sites of various types. (1) is an almost perfectly circular mound surrounded by a ditch and a bank. A causeway leads across the ditch into the inner circle. The suggestion that this was a Roman signal station is now discounted, and the site is plotted on a distribution map of henge monuments and penannular ring-ditches covering southern Scotland (1997).[162] *It is reported that a funerary urn containing human bones was discovered at the 'bottom' of the 'fort'.*[163] *At the same site reference i.e. at the summit of Finnarts Hill (183m OD), (2) is a robbed and wasted cairn now appearing as a circular enclosure, with an inner and outer ditch. At (3) there is one tall standing stone and another, a mere stump surviving (precisely* **NX 0553 7454** *and* **NX 0553 7455**). *(4) is another cairn, partially built into the rock, with a short cist. A food vessel discovered in this cairn is now held in the collections of the National Museums of Scotland (NMS X.EE 138), currently in the Archaeology Department Study Collection, Leith. The unusually arched capstone of the cist can still be seen in the centre of the cairn.*

Gadgirth   NS 412 225

Old Ha'   NS 406 219

The now demolished Gadgirth House is said to have incorporated the remains of Gadgirth Castle, a fourteenth-century tower. The name Gadgirth probably refers to the dimensions of the plot of land, on the south bank of the River Ayr. The Chalmerses were the original owners of Gadgirth.

About 500m downstream in a southward direction are to be found the traces of an even older building (the 'Old Ha'), reputedly the first Gadgirth. On a high promontory jutting into the river from the south bank is a stretch of masonry built against a rocky crag, and another bit seeming to form the corner of a building. The promontory is defended by a ditch.

The nearest road to the locations of both Gadgirths is the B742, which crosses the river by the Gadgirth Bridge and runs north to the Annbank area.

Galston Covenanters' gravestones and memorials   NS 501 364

Tombstones in churchyard to (1) Andrew Richmond, shot June 1679 (after Battle of Bothwell Brig); and (2) John Richmond of Knowe (hanged Glasgow 1684), James Smith of East Threepwood, shot 1685 (see also **Hillend** and **Mauchline**), James Young and George Campbell (deportees drowned 1679) and Rev. Alexander Blair (imprisoned 1673, *d.* 1674). Galston is on the A71 east of Kilmarnock.

Gass: settlement   (A) NS 421 055, (B) NS 415 052, (C) NS 412 054

Gass is a lonely farm midway between Straiton and Dalmellington on the B741. (1) A little short of 1km east of this farm, on the south side of the road, the following features have been identified: (A) (1) a subrectangular building with two compartments and turf walls; (2) a rectangular enclosure next to the building; (3) three huts to the north-east; and (4) a single hut further on in the same direction. (B) About 0.5km south-east of Gass farmhouse, (1) a crescent-shaped structure, possibly a building divided into three compartments, built on a stony bank; (2) immediately to the north-west, a circular mound which may be the remnants of a hut; (3) to the south-west, another possible hut. (C) again south-east of Gass, the traces of a farmstead close to an area of rig-and-furrow cultivation. These settlement features are grouped above or to the west of the Lone Glen close to the source of a tributary of the Lone Glen Burn, on the north-east slope of Gass Hill.

Giffen (Giffin)   NS 377 507

Three or four fragments of rubble masonry are all that is left of this ancient

Montgomerie castle (fifteenth century). It collapsed into a pile of rubble in 1838 and was finally cleared away in the 1920s during quarrying operations. The bits of stone surviving are used as parts of a garden rockery.

Girvan: Enoch: settlements   (1) NX 208 993, (2) NX 209 993

Air photographs have revealed the cropmarks of (1) half of a circular settlement with two parallel palisades and a break for an entrance to the south-west; the ditch-marks of at least two and perhaps four circular timber huts are to be seen, the westernmost with an internal concentric ring of what look like post-holes; (2) superimposed on or underlying the first, half of a ditched and palisaded settlement with a wide ditch, and inside the enclosure, at least one timber house (uncertain which period of settlement). These enclosures are on the edge of a steep scarp or bluff running northwards 350m north-east of Enoch farmhouse. Also at **NX 208 993** and slightly south-west of the sites described above are the marks of a single apparently timber house with a surrounding ditch and an internal concentric ring of post-holes, rather larger than normal. This settlement area is clearly multi-period.[164]

Enoch, 350m south-west of these settlements, is a farmhouse on the north bank of a meander of the Water of Girvan east of Girvan town.

Girvan: Enoch: fort   NX 207 991

The putative fort here is also revealed only in cropmarks photographed from the air, and it is directly south-west of the marks indicating settlements of different periods at **NX 208 993** and **NX 209 993**. All three areas are on the north bank of the Water of Girvan. The fort cropmarks indicate the north-east end of what may be an earthwork with three ditches crowning the bluff just to the north-east of Enoch farmhouse.[165]

Girvan Mains Roman Camps   NX190 991, NX 187 990

There are two camps here, neither with any surface detail. They were brought to light in the first place by aerial photography of cropmarks in 1976–8 and confirmed by a variety of means including trenching and geophysical magnetometry, as well as more aerial photography. Both camps may have extended right to the sea-cliff and high water mark, which would indicate an intention to use them as beach-heads for possible combined operations along the British western coast. They are both legion-size temporary marching camps and may have been constructed for the Roman general Agricola's projected but abandoned invasion of Ireland in or about AD 82. The discovery in the western camp of a piece of Roman glass datable to the late first century AD has strengthened this assumption.[166]

Glaisnock Viaduct   NS 598 214

The Ayr–Muirkirk–Edinburgh railway was discontinued after the Second World War, and this bridge was closed, but is now used as a footpath from Cumnock to Barshare. It has thirteen arches.

Glengarnock Castle   NS 310 573

This is one of the more spectacular ruins of Ayrshire, situated above the River Garnock at the mouth of the most deep and gloomy portion of the gorge. A very large building, the keep is in a dangerous condition and could collapse at any time; it has been poised on the verge since 1839, when a large part was blown down in a storm. A portion of the wall of the tower-house survives up to the level of a string-course which doubtless supported the corbels and parapet. A portion of vaulting hangs like a bridge at a great height between this and the opposite wall, and was clearly the top of a tall second-floor hall. Behind the keep to the east there is a courtyard containing traces of many buildings, including a kitchen and a substantial gatehouse. The whole complex sits on a promontory jutting out over the river, defended on the landward side by a ditch. MacGibbon and Ross place the castle in their Third Period i.e. any time between 1400 and 1542.

Glengarnock Castle is north of Kilbirnie, up the unlisted road to Ladyland from the A769 via Langlands, turning west at Glengarth and climbing the gradient to Blackburn.

Fig. 13. Glengarnock Castle. View from the north-east angle of the courtyard.

Glenhead settlement   NS 214 453

Originally thought to be a double fort, these twin earthworks have no
military detail in their construction and on excavation proved to be two
large wooden huts, whose roofs were supported by internal rings of posts.
This site appeared as two flat-topped mounds on a cliff edge overlooking
the ravine of the Gourock Burn between the railway and the sea-coast
midway between Ardrossan and Seamill (on the A78). The impression of
defensive works was strengthened by the gullies separating the northern
plateau and the northern and the southern mound. The whole location is
overgrown with trees.

Glenmuirshaw: Mesolithic chipping floor   NS 706 204

This site is at the side of the Thorter Burn, a tributary of the Glenmuir
Water. The microliths gathered here are generally unretouched, typical
of the Scottish Mesolithic. The MacFadzeans, the discoverers of the site,
reckon that this was a chipping floor because of the amount of flaking waste
present.[167] Glenmuirshaw, a remote hill farm slightly south of the Thorter
Burn, can be reached by a track from Kyle Castle and High Dalblair east of
(Old) Cumnock.

Great Cumbrae Island, Farland Hill: Mesolithic camp site   NS 172 545

Farland Hill juts south as a peninsula, forming the eastern horn of the Bay
of Millport. A cave in the inner cliff face opening on to the raised beach and
the bay was excavated, showing signs of seasonal occupation. Finds included
two bone needles and some pieces of lignite. These appeared to be of the
Obanian culture, i.e. Early Post-Glacial, indicating a connection with the
nearer Western Highland mainland.

Great Cumbrae Island, Millport: crosses (1) NS 167 551, (2) NS 162 549

(1) Now held at Millport Cathedral are three cross fragments recovered from
the parish kirkyard. Three others are at Millburn House (**NS 1586 5480**),
one of them cemented on top of a wall. They may date from the seventh
or eighth century. (2) is another stone cross (head only) found in 1823 at
NS 1625 5492 in association with a stone cist, now destroyed. The shaft of
the cross was recovered but has also disappeared. The cross head is now in
the cathedral.

Great Cumbrae Island: standing stone   NS 176 564

At Craigengour, a standing stone was pushed over by hooligans but it has
been set upright again in concrete.

Greenan Castle NS 311 193

This ruined castle at present forms a conspicuous landmark, perched high on a shore cliff south-west of the mouth of the River Doon, with its high gable resembling an upward-pointing forefinger. How long it will remain on its badly-eroded pinnacle is anybody's guess, and the visitor may see by the tumbled masses of masonry on the westward slopes the fate that awaits the rest of the building. It can be seen that the main building was rectangular, and that there were three storeys and a garret but no parapet or walk. There were, however, four corbelled and roofed angle-turrets, slightly less decayed in the time of MacGibbon and Ross than in our own. It appears to have been at least refurbished and possibly extended in or around 1603 by its owner, John Kennedy, who acquired it from its former owners, the Davidson family, in 1588. His initials J.K. appear on the door lintel with a date 1607. The Davidsons had held the fortalice since the fifteenth century.

Fig. 14. Greenan Castle, from the south-west.

Previously there had been a motte and bailey castle there, owned by Roger de Scalebroc in the 1190s. This represents the northern defences of Carrick in the days of Gilbert of Galloway before the assimilation of Carrick into Ayrshire and Scotland. Gilbert's grant of land here to a Norman knight may be seen as unusual and possibly unique in view of Gilbert's attitude to non-Gallovidians. The arrangement was continued when Duncan, son of Gilbert, became Lord of Carrick later on.[168]

The bailey can still be seen on the south with an outer ditch . An additional defensive ditch cuts off a wide area of the promontory on which the castle stands.

It can be seen that both the motte and the stone castle(s) built on the motte stand within the defensive area of a typical Iron Age fort, with four ditches cutting across Greenan promontory. An entrance cutting across these ditches on the north-east has a defensive chicane, and there are at least two palisade trenches.

Greyfriars Monastery, Ayr   NS 339 219

See **Ayr Royal Burgh**

Guiltreehill: possible henge monument   NS 353 109

As one pulls up the long rise from Dalrymple on the hill road to Kirkmichael, one's eye is caught by a prominent earthwork on the skyline to the west. At about 165m OD, it is a raised circular platform with a surrounding ditch and traces of additional internal and external ditches. Because of its circularity, and the magnificence of the views to be had from it, I would suspect this to be a henge (notwithstanding the apparent absence of an entrance causeway) and not a settlement. The earthwork has been ploughed regularly but has retained its shape.

Haggstone Moor Neolithic cairns   NX 057 725, NX 058 721

A large, much-reduced cairn with kerbstones on the south-west, and another cairn, better preserved, south of the first, overlook Glen App from the westernmost corner of Haggstone Moor nearly at the southern extremity of Ayrshire.

Haggstone Moor standing stone   NX 065 726

A large standing stone near the summit of Haggstone Moor (206m OD), now apparently lost amid the recent afforestation. This may be the stone from which the moor derives its name.

Hallowshean Fort NS 244 061

This hilltop fort sits on an flat oblong summit area on the verge of a steep slope to the south. The entrance was probably on the west where a moulded natural scarp curves in from the north side. The east side is protected by four ramparts. Hallowshean overlooks Kirkoswald village and the main coast road to Girvan from Maybole.

Harpercroft Fort NS 360 325

This is an *oppidum*, a defensive station that could act as a shelter for civilian populations and animals in times of emergency and in some cases (e.g. Traprain Law in East Lothian) permanently. It consists of two concentric (though not precisely circular) ramparts on the top of a hill (145m OD). The inner ring circles the summit area itself, partially surviving as a rampart. The outer area could have been used to hold cattle. The fort, which crowns one of the Claven or Clevance hills south of Dundonald, overlooks Prestwick Airport.

Hawking Craig: Mesolithic remains NS 179 507

Hawking Craig is a site on the west coast of the Hunterston peninsula, south of the power station and about 1.5km north of Portincross Castle along a cliff-foot path. A rock shelter was excavated in 1879 and three levels of flooring were exposed, each formed of layers of sea-shells on top of ash on trodden sand. Animal bones were found at all levels, as well as a bone implement, a flint tool and other objects, some of which are now in the collections of the National Museums of Scotland (NMS X. HM 3–4), currently in the Archaeology Department Study Collection, Leith.

Haylie (Largs) chambered cairn NX 209 586

This is the only identifiable Clyde-type chambered tomb to have survived in Ayrshire: that is to say, the chambers opened directly into the exterior without a connecting passage.[169] All that now survives is the internal 'skeleton' of one chamber. Thousands of cartloads of cairn material were removed with pride (they were counted) from the useless pile of stones. This took place in 1772, prior to which the chamber was covered by a massive mound known as 'Margaret's Law'.

In 1772 five compartmentalized chambers were apparently discovered in the tomb, but only one has survived, divided into three by transverse septal stones, and only the westernmost (innermost) compartment remains relatively intact with its capstone. At the east end of this compartment two human skulls were discovered in 1954. In 1772 five skulls and a quantity of bone were discovered (it is said) in each of two chambers.

Haylie tomb is situated in Douglas Park north of the Largs cemetery on the lower slopes of Castle Hill.

High Altercannoch: settlement
(1) NX 242 802, (2) NX 243 789, (3)NX 243 795, (4)NX 244 797, (5) NX 244 798, (6)NX 245 788, (7) NX 245 805, (8)NX 249 807

This cluster of eight sites at High Altercannoch comprises cairns, a barrow, hut-circles, a turf hut and other buildings unspecified, enclosures and field-systems. In order of site reference, these are (1) many small cairns and piles of stones on a small north-facing hillside 1km south-west of High Altercannoch farmhouse; (2) more small cairns and the traces of a circular house within a field system; (3) two circular houses and two rectangular buildings, all within a surrounding wall with facing boulders on the south-facing slopes of a small hill south-west of the farmhouse; beyond the wall, at least fourteen cairns, the largest of which is oval; and on the crest of the hill a barrow; (4) a circular enclosure resembling a house; (5) small cairns and piles of stones on the north-eastern flanks of Eyes hillock; (6) a peat-buried enclosure and three small cairns; (7) a circular mound perhaps representing a collapsed turf-built hut; and (8) on a slope a circular enclosure within a stony bank.[170] All this is less than 2km south of High Altercannoch, which is at the west side of the B7027. It is not far from the **White Cairn** at **Laggish**.

Hillend cairn   NS 531 353

This cairn, considerably reduced, is now surmounted by a modern marker cairn commemorating the death of a Covenanting martyr in 1685. Human bones were said to have been found when the stones were removed. This cairn sits on a conspicuous promontory overlooking Galston and the Darvel valley.

Hillend Farm Covenanting memorial   NS 531 353

In consequence of uncertainty about the precise position of the grave of James Smith of East Threepwood, striking miners sympathetic to Covenanters in 1926 erected a marker to his memory at this point, overlooking the Threepwoods. It sits atop a Neolithic cairn (see preceding entry). Please observe directions on gate if the visiting site. Hillend is on a farm track north of an unlisted road which runs between the B7037 south of Galston and the A71 east of Darvel. See **Galston** and **Mauchline**.

Hindberrybank   NS 517 377

See **Loudoun Castle**

Holms: possible henge monument   NS 359 369

A suspected henge enclosure was reported to have been found here in early 2000.[171] The site is about 0.5km north of the standing stone at **Drybridge.**

Howmoor Dun   NS 277 118

This dun is circular with a concave interior. The sides are not precipitous except to the south, so that a bank and a ditch have had to be constructed on the rest of the circuit at the base of the knoll. It is situated 2km north-west of Maybole, beyond the B7023.

The Hunterston Brooch   NS 178 505

This Dark Age adornment was discovered in the open just beneath **Hawking Craig** north of **Portincross Castle.** Like all other archaeological finds in the neighbourhood, it was at first taken for a relic of the Battle of Largs (1263), and even thought to be a possession of King Håkon IV. In fact it is datable to the later 600s. It is a large silver casting richly mounted with gold, silver and amber insets. Secondary runic inscriptions of the tenth century read 'Melbrigda owns this [brooch]' and 'This brooch belongs to Olfriti'. It is now in the collections of the National Museums of Scotland (NMS X.FC8) and is currently on display in the Museum of Scotland, Chambers Street, Edinburgh.

Hunterston   NS 192 514

This is a small-scale fortalice at the north end of the Hunterston Peninsula, not far from the nuclear power station with its Magnox reactors and the so-called ore terminal. The castle's date may be earlier than 1500. The old tower-block is small, with three storeys, a garret, crow-stepped gables, and a massive parapet without angle-turrets. A two-storey wing, also with an attic storey, was added in the seventeenth century, the effect being to double the area of the great hall. A stair-tower projects into the rear courtyard, and the circular staircase gives access to both wings. The courtyard is old and intimate, and the castle complex makes a beautiful group with the adjacent farm buildings. At one time situated in a marsh, it is now surrounded by cultivated or wooded land.

Hunterston Nuclear Power Station   NS 185 515

This mighty venture, inaugurated in 1964, may come to the end of its useful life in the next few years, although arguments both for and against its continuation still generate controversy. Whatever the outcome, these massive buildings are a fact of Ayrshire history likely to remain on the scene

Fig. 15. Hunterston Castle, from the south-west.

for decades if not centuries. A visitor centre shows off the technological features of the installations.

Irvine Royal Burgh   NS 320 390

Irvine's primitive outlines are harder to make out than Ayr's, partly because of major changes in the coastline over 800 years and partly because of lack of information. The burgh of Irvine was not a creation of the king but of the local magnate and we have no early charter and no clear date for the foundation. A charter from Alexander II is known to have existed, and this implies a date between 1214 and 1249 – rather later than Ayr's charter. If the initiative for the foundation came from the local lord, this might have been Alan of Galloway, who had married one of the last de Morville heiresses, a descendant of the original Lord of Cuninghame.

The first radically different feature of early Irvine from the present-day town was a large inland loch to the east of the site. In addition, the River Irvine curved round to the south of the town as it does today, but it did not have the complicated northern loop that it has now: the sea came right in over the Marress and Bogside to lap the Town Moor bluff – then the open sea-coast, now the north-east bank of the river. Hence the name 'Seagate' for the street which dips down westward from Eglinton Street to the present river level, and contains the ancient **Seagate Castle** on its eastern side. Whether this fortification is the same, or in the same place, as the castle of 'Hirun' near the church of St Vinin [Kilwinning] mentioned by Benedict of Peterborough in 1184 is a moot point. We can be relatively sure that the 'Strathyrewen in Galwegia' mentioned in charters before that

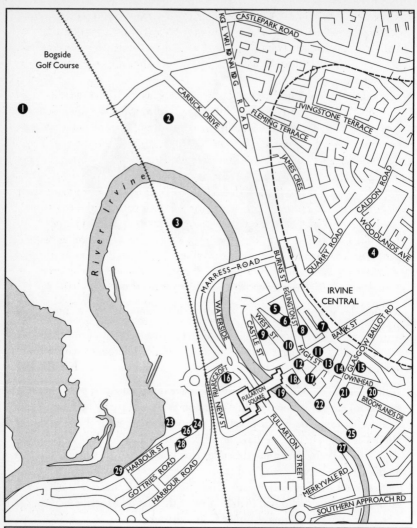

1. Bogside
2. Town's Moor
3. Maress
4. Line showing part of primitive Irvine Loch
5. Seagate Castle
6. Vicus marinus/via que ducit ad mare (Seagate)
7. Eastbackside (East Road)
8. Possible site of Townend Port
9. Monte arenosa/ly Sandgat (Westbackside: West Road)
10. Grip/Gruipe Gutter (Chapel Lane) (NB 'Wee Gryp' Public House)
11. Possible site of Western Burgh Port
12. Bridgegate
13. Town's House and market cross (now war memorial)
14. Vicus Fori/Vicus Regius (Market or King's Street): modern High St
15. Smethy Bar (Glasgow Vennel)
16. Friars' Croft
17. Vinella dicta Monkmosart (Hill St)
18. Vinella que ducit ad aquam de Irwin (Puddleford)
19. Site of Puddlie Deidlie/Daidlie Ford (with 'Granny Stone')
20. Possible site of Townend Port
21. Venella ecclesiastica (Kirk Vennel)
22. Irvine Parish Church
23. Maritime Museum
24. Approximate site of Irvine (Fullarton) Friary (Carmelites)
25. Chapel Brae and possible site of St Mary's Chapel
26. The Halfway (Montgomerie St)
27. St Inan's Well
28. Linthouse St area
29. Irvine Harbour

Street Map of Irvine

date (*c.*1130) means 'the valley of the River Irvine', and it is fairly certain that there was a small settlement here or hereabouts on the isthmus between the loch and the sea in the twelfth century and before. But its topography does not start to emerge into daylight until well after the supposed date of the burgh charter.

The attractive feature for the burgh-makers, as with Ayr, was Irvine's situation at the junction of important routes next to the sea at the mouth of a river. As with Ayr, the pre-existing settlement had a rectangular market-place on an elevation, on the site of the present High Street to the east of the river. The burgh which developed in the thirteenth century centred on this rectangle, referred to in the fourteenth century as the Street of the Market (*Vicus Fori*), and as the Royal Street (*Vicus Regius*) in the fifteenth century. Into this street led routes from across the Irvine ford from the coast road and the south, other routes from the south and south-east, from Dundonald and Kyle, and, round the top of the loch, a road from Kilwinning, which converged with one from the east of Ayrshire.

Settlers were invited to take up burgage plots, rectangular areas of ground with their narrow fronts crowding each other around the broad market street and creating a secure line of building on either side of the commercial focus of the burgh. If Seagate Castle was the original castle of Irvine, it would have defended this central area from attack from the sea, as well as enforcing the overlord's regulation of trade. There may have been a wooden palisade behind the uniformly aligned plots, and associated with the palisade there may have been a ditch and a back lane. These lanes would be used for access for stock and similar purposes. The Town Moor to the north was common ground on which animals would be grazed. Also made available to the burgesses were areas of cultivable ground on the Back Riggs to the west and east of the tofts, bounded respectively by the open sea-coast and the inland loch.

The Townhead Port seems to have stood at the east end of the High Street near the Kirk Vennel, and there may have been a western port somewhere just before or just after the opening of the vennel now expanded to the Bridgegate. The northward expansion of the town was limited for some time by a stream running from the loch west to the sea, called the Grip or Gruipe Gutter. The stream dried up with the loch, but its course is partially marked to this day by a narrow passage along the side of the King's Arms Hotel called Chapel Lane; a public house at the lower part of the lane is currently called the Wee Gryp. As this barrier was overcome and the tofts pushed on towards the castle and Kilwinning, the port was resited along the route of Eglinton Street, probably just beyond the top of the Seagate, and called the Townend Port. Two tracks approaching Seagate, respectively the Westbackside and the Eastbackside, ran parallel to the future Eglinton Street and in time became the West Road and the East Road. (West Road graduated in the fifteenth century from being a back lane to *monte arenosa*,

Sandymount, or the equivalent of Ayr's Sandgate, *ly sandgat,* but the name did not last.)

The burgh extended itself down towards the ford, which was apparently referred to as the 'Puddlie Deidlie' or 'Puddlie Daidlie', with obscure reference to an alleged passage of arms here between William Wallace and the English in 1297. There were stepping-stones at this ford, and one of them, the so-called Granny Stone, can still be seen at low water beneath the modern trans-river shopping mall. The pathway or vennel leading down to this ford from the Kirkgate area is still in existence (now the 'Puddleford'); it can be identified in a fifteenth-century document as *vinella que ducit ad aquam de Irwin.* Above this area and behind the Mizard Hill (the site of the present Trinity Church building) is *vinella dicta Monkmosart,* now called Hill Street. The Kirkgate itself is mentioned in the fourteenth century as *vicus ecclesie,* and the Kirk Vennel is *venella ecclesiastica* (fifteenth century). Also in the fifteenth century the street now called Glasgow Vennel (containing several well-restored eighteenth-century buildings) was known as 'Smethy Barr'. *Vicus Marinus,* or *via que ducit ad mare,* is clearly Seagate. These are all names from areas of central Irvine that have been relatively untouched by modern development.

On the Irvine side of the river a church had been established since the earliest days, on a hillock originally outside the eastern boundary of the burgh, on the site now occupied by the modern (1773) parish church. Nearby was a St Mary's Chapel, now vanished but recalled by an ancient vennel called the Chapel Brae, leading from the modern churchyard down to a still surviving **St Inan's Well** on the river-bank. See **Irvine Parish Church**.

Opposite the Kirkgate entrance in High Street is the Town's House, on the site of the 1386 tolbooth, and in front of this is the site of the market cross. Irvine Cross is first mentioned in 1260. The latest version was taken down in 1694, and its position is marked by a design in the cobbles in front of the Town House. In the twentieth century a typical Scottish market-cross-style monument was put up nearby as a replacement and as a war memorial.

The main factors affecting the later development of Irvine town were the draining and reclamation of the inland loch, and the extension of the burgh beyond the river into the territory of Fullarton, a part of Kyle Stewart towards the west. This had been established by the Fullarton family in the fourteenth century as a home for a Carmelite priory and was created a burgh in 1707. The religious holding is recalled in the name 'Friars' Croft' for the tract of land which now includes Cunninghame House and the railway station. They grazed sheep on the Maress and had a kiln for malt at Dyet's Temple to the south-west of their property. They also seem to have owned property – despite restrictions on their order – in Irvine itself, in the Kirk Vennel.

To the east of Irvine, the loch first dwindled into three separate sheets of water and then was drained altogether at the end of the seventeenth century. The burgh had already owned a large part of the parish of Irvine itself, including most of the remoter north-eastward sections, and the gradual disappearance of the loch made more territory available for use, letting and disposal by the town. The loch seems to have covered an area stretching from the present-day positions of Ravenspark in the north-west to Thornhouse Avenue in the south-east and from (roughly) the Kilwinning Road in the west to Livingstone Terrace in the east. Reclaiming this land added considerably to the town's wealth and opened the possibilities of burgh development as far east as Stanecastle. However, quite a large part of the original Trindle Moss/Scotts Loch area is still retained as open space, including several sports grounds and allotments.

The sea receded as a result of the process of silting up (and of land reclamation) so that the river had to loop up beyond the Town Moor and to the west where it was joined by the River Garnock flowing down from the north. Enclosed within the new loop of the Irvine is the promontory known as the Marress, across which the railway now runs; on the outside of the curve on the west is a tongue of land called the Bogside and on the other side of this the Garnock cuts down through the Stevenson (Ardeer) sandflats and the modern ICI industrial sites bordering the sea. This river joins the Irvine in an estuary just at Irvine Harbour, which has migrated more than 1km west from a tiny haven at the Seagate. In 1677, after unsuccessful attempts to establish a harbour at Little Cumbrae and at Troon as well as at the Marress, a harbour was successfully laid out on the south bank of the estuary.

Irvine was connected with its new harbour by a long straight street called 'the Halfway', later rechristened Montgomery Street. A bridge had spanned the Irvine near the 'Puddlie-Daidlie' ford perhaps as early as the twelfth century, though there are no records to that effect. This joined Irvine with Fullarton: the Halfway Street cuts right through the northern part of Fullarton to the harbour. The resiting of the harbour proved to be its good fortune, since it prospered greatly in the eighteenth century in both exports and imports, in spite of the rivalry of Ayr and Glasgow. However, after a long period of decline from the nineteenth century, accelerated by the post-1945 disuse of the Clyde as a shipping lane of any sort (except naval) and the disappearance of virtually all of Ayrshire heavy industrial production, Irvine harbour has now reverted to a sleepy anchorage for pleasure craft – offset by the establishment of a popular **Maritime Museum**, the refurbishment of the Montgomery Street area and the bringing back into use of several magnificent eighteenth- and nineteenth-century buildings in the Linthouse Street district.

Irvine (Fullarton) Friary   NS 317 387

This site is known; walls were discovered about 50m west of the Old Place of Fullarton, but the area has been built on and no trace is visible. A settlement of Carmelites was made in the fourteenth century as the result of an arrangement between the order and Reynald Fullerton of Fullerton, confirmed by a charter of Robert III. The Carmelites were an order of mendicant friars sometimes called White Friars from the white cloak they wore over their habits. The priory was dedicated to the Virgin Mary, and, although restricted as regards property rights by the conditions of the order, the friars appear to have prospered in Irvine/Fullarton through bequests and gifts, including some from King James IV. At the Reformation all the properties etc. reverted to the burgh of Irvine.

Irvine: Glasgow Vennel   NS 323 388

This is one of the more untouched streets in the older part of the town near the Town's House. The vennel has been refurbished to give a seventeenth/eighteenth-century feel. Robert Burns worked in a 'heckling-shop'(combing out flax) in the street and lodged in an attic here. Residential accommodation here is good.

Irvine: Old Parish Church   NS 322 386

An eighteenth-century preaching box, perhaps larger and more elegant than many of its contemporaries. It was built on the site of a very much older (?cruciform) church first mentioned in 1233. It was a tributary of **Kilwinning Abbey** and must have been wealthy in its own right, with many grants and 'mortifications' from local magnates and burgesses. There were up to fifteen separate altars or at least dedicatees of altars, with seven chaplains assisting the parish priest.

Irvine Covenanters' grave   NS 322 386

Table gravestone to James Blackwood and John McCoul, hanged 31 December 1666 after Battle of Rullion Green; Blackwood also memorialised in **Fenwick** parish churchyard in south central Irvine.

Irvine, Seagate Castle   NS 318 393

The present Seagate Castle probably overlays the original (twelfth-century) Irvine Castle, which has otherwise completely disappeared. What is now on the surface is sixteenth century, built for that Earl of Eglinton who was murdered by Cuninghames in 1586, and it represents a civilised rather than a defensive mode of existence, with elegant architecture and stonework exemplified for example by window-mouldings and a Romanesque doorway. It may have been built at the time of the earl's marriage to Agnes Drummond in 1562, but whether Mary, Queen of Scots stayed there after the Battle of Langside in 1568, as stated on a plaque next to the doorway, is perhaps a moot point.

Fig. 16. Seagate Castle, Irvine. View in the courtyard from the south-east.

It is a substantial building, with an extended street front (to Seagate). The ground floor is the only part of the building in a reasonably complete state – two principal rooms to the south, and, on the other side of an entrance archway with two guard-rooms, another two rooms, one of which is the kitchen. All these rooms are vaulted, and the entrance passageway has a flat vault with moulded ribs. One feature that we might regard with horror nowadays is the cesspool located just outside the kitchen door with piped connections to the garderobes upstairs, as well as a channel connecting directly with the kitchen fireplace. There were three towers, one of which is now just a stump. The northernmost is triangular, something which has been dictated by the shape of the ground. These towers are all at the back of the castle overlooking a wide courtyard.

Irvine, Shewalton: flints etc.
NS 325 372, NS 349 368, NS 350 370, NS 364 371

Shewalton Moor and district constitute the *locus classicus* for finding Mesolithic flints and other stone implements in Ayrshire. These sites are all in the vicinity of the River Irvine and are on the edge of the 15m OD contour on the flood plain – i.e. they were actually on the beach before the land was raised following the withdrawal of the ice after the great glaciation. The first OS site reference above is the approximate location of the recovery in 1938 of a celebrated Mesolithic non-flint barbed tool, an antler point, from the bed of the river just at the northward turn of the meander that takes the flow through Irvine. The antler point is now in the collections of the

National Museums of Scotland (NMS X.HLA 1), currently on display in the Museum of Scotland, Chambers Street, Edinburgh (hunting, gathering and fishing section).

Flint scatters continue northward to Stevenston and Ardeer.

Irvine, Stane Castle   NS 338 399

This is a plain tower, resembling other north Ayrshire fortalices of the sixteenth century. Now roofless, it has two storeys, surmounted by a corbelled-out parapet with open corner rounds. Because of its present position – isolated, in the east of Irvine, in the midst of a tangle of motorway junctions and roundabouts – it may be hard to appreciate that it was taken over as an adjunct to the Eglinton Castle pleasure grounds, on the edge of which it stood. In about 1750, long after its defensive usefulness was past, Alexander, tenth Earl of Eglinton, decided to make it into a garden folly, and to heighten the medieval effect, pierced the walls with grotesquely oversized Gothic windows. The original building was erected about 1520 by Montgomerie of Greenfield, a cadet of the family. It was stabilised by Irvine Development Corporation when the only alternative was demolition.

Jocksthorn: carved stone ball   NS 417 410

A sandstone ball 6.5cm in diameter, ornamented with six equal discs slightly projecting, was discovered on this farm and donated to the Dick Institute, Kilmarnock, in 1887 (KIMMG: item number JT400 on display). Jocksthorn is about 0.5km east of the centre of Kilmaurs village.

Keirs Castle   NS 430 080

On the Carrick (south-western) side of the Doon Valley, 1km from Waterside, the Keirs Glen reaches upwards into the hills. Near the isolated Keirs Farm, a few fragments of masonry may be discovered on a shelf in the hillside. These are all that remains of Keirs Castle, a fortalice without a history. Paterson says that in his day 'enough remain[ed] to show that it had been a house of considerable size and strength'.[172] A stone bearing the coat of arms of Shaw of Keirs was reputed to have been built into the farmsteading nearby.

The nearest access-point is on the A713, which runs along the valley beside the River Doon.

Kemp Law Dun   NS 355 336

Here there is a high narrow promontory where a mound of rubbish lies at the centre of an enclosure formed by a wide wall that runs round the promontory's edge. Some stones in the mound have been fused together by intense heat – vitrified into a glassy mass during some fierce Iron Age siege. This is a very characteristic feature of many duns and forts, and it is just possible that the defenders or even the builders of Kemp Law themselves set fire to the reinforcing timber-lacing in order to increase the strength of the fortification by bonding the stones. The site is very near the extensive quarry-workings at Hallyards, and close to the A78.

Kelburn Castle   NS 217 566

Uniquely among the cliff-line castles of the north Ayrshire coast, Kelburn has been properly exploited as a tourist attraction, although it is still privately owned by the original family, the Boyles, who are now Earls of Glasgow. Unlike the other examples (Skelmorlie, Knock, Law, Fairlie), the initial plain rectangular castle block (with two round towers at diagonally opposite corners of the block, earning it the designation 'Z-plan'), has been added to throughout the centuries since 1581, when the present building seems to have been commenced. The principal addition is dated 1722, although it seems to have been built not later than 1692. This is a fine mansion attached to the main block, and a further wing was added in the late nineteenth century. The building is thrown open to the public in July and August only, but the grounds are open all the year round. The stables have been converted to a visitors' centre of a type rapidly becoming standard to theme-park-type enterprises throughout Scotland. As ever, the castle has been erected high on the lip of a precipice overlooking a stream gorge, in this case the Clea Burn. The whole site gives magnificent views over the north Clyde estuary and surroundings.

A tree-covered mound in Kelburne Park at NS 212 562 may be the original motte of the locality.

The Boyles, who have held these lands since the twelfth century, have been active participants in many historical events – for instance, the Battle of Sauchieburn in 1488, when John Boyle of Kelburn was killed. David Boyle, the 1st Earl of Glasgow (1703), was one of the commissioners concerned with the Union of the Parliaments in 1707.

Kerelaw ('Kerila') or Stevenston Castle   NS 268 429

This building is now in ruins, having been converted to a mere garden folly in the nineteenth century, with fake Gothic windows not dissimilar to those which also disfigure Stane Castle in Irvine. One complete side remains – the eastern – with parts of the north and south, giving the effect of a wooden film-set façade propped up for a Western, in the middle of a Scottish housing estate. It has been two storeys in height, with a round-arched doorway in the centre of the wall. Other surviving features include a fireplace and traces of an angle-turret. An earlier castle was burnt down in 1488, but it must have been rebuilt, since we hear of the Earl of Glencairn using the building as a winter residence in 1545. This version of the castle was probably put up in the late sixteenth century, at roughly the same period as **Seagate** in Irvine, with which it may have certain affinities. It is situated east of the Kerelaw road on the northern outskirts of Stevenston, on the west bank of the Stevenston Burn.

Kerse Castle NS 432 144

A few stones may still mark the stronghold of David Craufurd of Kerse by the banks of Kerse Loch not far from Kerse Park beside the Craigs of Kyle. An unlisted road runs past the site, between the A713 and Drongan.

Kersland Castle   NS 306 508

Kersland Castle still survives as part of the farm buildings of Kersland on the east side of the railway north of Dalry, on an unlisted road running north from the A737. A substantial part of the original L-plan tower has been built into the farmhouse: there are two barrel vaults. The barmkin wall, now a garden wall, still has a strong defensive corner tower visible from the railway. Above the door of the farmhouse is an original stone inscribed 'D Ker 1604'.

Kilbirnie Crannog and Logboats   NS 323 535

As a result of slag-dumping into Kilbirnie Loch from Glengarnock Ironworks in 1868 the lake-bed sediments were displaced upwards and what had been known locally as a small loch island, 'The Cairn', rose higher and was shown to be artificial. There were four probable levels of occupation. This crannog was entirely destroyed subsequently by the slag dumping. Pieces of log-boat were discovered close by.

One piece, discovered and donated to Paisley Museum in 1952–3, had mud in the interstices of the timber. Analysis of the pollen found in this mud suggests that the boat should be assigned to the 'Sub-Boreal' period (pollen zone VIIb), giving dates between 3000 BC and 700 BC – substantially earlier than other Ayrshire logboats.[173]

Kilbirnie Loch lies between the small towns of Kilbirnie and Beith in North Ayrshire. The steelworks have gone although there is substantial industrial activity in their place. The site of the crannog is at the south end of the loch, where the slag-dumping took place.

Kilbirnie, The Old Place   NS 303 541

The word 'place' is here a Scots contraction of 'palace', and at one time the building, now so dilapidated, was undoubtedly palatial. It is in two

Fig. 17. Kilbirnie, The Old Palace. View from the south-west.

parts. The old tower may have existed in some form before 1470, but it was improved or built at that date for Malcolm Craufurd and Marjory Barclay, the last of her line. It had four storeys with two vaulted floors and a corbelled parapet walk. An additional wing, long and narrow, was built in 1627. This was joined to the old tower by a stair-tower in such a way that the first-floor great hall of the older building was retained as a dining room, with the corresponding room in the new wing en suite as a drawing room. The entrance to the wing has an unusual projecting porch in the south front. There are turrets with dog-tooth ornamentation typical of the period. Alas, the building was gutted by fire 130 years later and the Craufurds abandoned it. Still standing today, cracked, ivy-covered and with trees growing up out of it, it has deteriorated past the point of no return.

Kilbirnie Parish Church   NS 314 546

Kilbirnie was presumably originally the cell of St Brendan, who had a spring in the neighbourhood. We have no information about the site of his cell or chapel, which may not have been occupied by the saint himself (?fifth century) but only dedicated to him. The parish may have been founded before 1127, when the first mention of it appears. The present church building is apparently late sixteenth century in date. The Glengarnock aisle was built in 1597 and extended about 1642, which date appears on the building. Before the Reformation Kilbirnie was annexed to **Kilwinning Abbey.**

Kildoon Fort   NS 298 073

This is a vitrified fort, one in which the setting alight of the timber lacing of the ramparts has generated heat intense enough to fuse the boulders into a strong glassy mass. It sits on a hill that juts into the valley with precipitous slopes on three sides, the west side being defended by three external ramparts barring the way along the ridge top. The perimeter wall has been completely robbed but its course is still traceable round the verge of the jutting hill and behind the innermost western rampart.

South of Maybole, the fort looks out across the valley floor to Kirkmichael and Straiton in the east. It has been partially mutilated by the erection of a monument to a local dignitary on the eastern ramparts. Vitrified material has been noticed beneath this monument and at the south-east corner of the rampart.

Kilhenzie Castle   NS 308 083

This is a small, beautifully restored sixteenth-century L-plan tower-house, visible from the B7023 south of Maybole. The original castle was rectangular, with two storeys, an attic and corbelled-out angle turrets but apparently no parapet. A three-storey wing was added to the east later. As with Maybole Castle and Cassillis House, nineteenth-century 'Scottish Baronial' treatment has given the building a not-inappropriate 'fairy-castle' atmosphere, with plenty of turrets and finials. Kilhenzie was a complete ruin early in the nineteenth century, but someone took it in hand about 1850 and made a very good job of restoration. The original owners were a family called Baird, well-known for feuding, but it passed to the Kennedys in the seventeenth century. It is still inhabited, but not by Kennedys.

Kilkerran, Mote Knowe: possible motte   NS 298 001

This is a mound on sloping ground at the head of a valley about 0.5km further upstream on the Lindsayston Burn from **Kilkerran Old Castle**. The mound resembles a motte but it has not been investigated.

Kilkerran, Old   NS 293 005

Kilkerran, New   NS 304 030

Barclanachan Tower   NS 304 030

A high wall, rising to a crowstepped gable, is all that is left of the first stone castle of Kilkerran. (The original motte of the locality may be **Mote Knowe** to the south-east.) The existing stone remnants, probably of the fifteenth century, indicate that the castle had four storeys and an attic with a corbelled-out parapet but no angle turrets. The ruin is poised precariously

Fig. 18. Old Kilkerran Castle, from the north-west.

over a deep pool in the Lindsayston Burn but looks much the same today as it did more than a century ago when MacGibbon and Ross sketched it.

The new castle or mansion of Kilkerran, built in the early eighteenth century, incorporates an old tower-house called Barclanachan, date unknown. The present building, still the home of the Fergusson family, is a model of classical restraint and elegance, three storeys high with a central pediment; it has been improved and added to since the eighteenth century almost to the present day. The house stands in extensive and well-wooded grounds, some of which have been adapted to commercial use; there is now a camping and caravan site in the old gardens themselves.

Killochan Castle   NS 227 003

Killochan: either *Coil Lochain*, 'wood by the little loch' (Johnston) or *Killunquhane*, 'Onchu's church' (Watson). The present Killochan Castle, whose policies, on the B741, march with those of Bargany to the east, is an exceedingly beautiful building, bearing the date 1586. This is on the L-plan, with an unusual round tower at the outside angle of the L. A square stair-tower occupies the inner re-entrant angle. The main block has five storeys, with a higher wing extending north from the east end. The 'top-hamper' of the building includes corbelled-out turrets with conical caps, but there is no balustrade or parapet: it is a forerunner of the classical 'pepperpot' style of the great castles of the north-east, such as Crathes (1596) or Glamis. Also compare **Maybole Castle**. The great hall has seventeenth-century panelling. A new-style scale-and-platt staircase (square steps with wide landings) reaches up to the first floor in the main building; above this level there is a spiral stair in the stair-tower. There may have been an earlier tower on the site, and this is supported by certain features such as massively thick masonry. However Tranter mentions a 'general belief . . . that the earlier Killochan stood a little way off, higher up the river'.[174]

Kilmarnock, Laigh Kirk   NS 427 379

There must have been an older building here, but no traces of any ancient structure meet the eye. The church precinct, elevated and nearly circular, may however indicate a very early original *Cil-mo-Ernoc*. The present church was erected after 'a melancholy accident' in 1801 when, after a cracking sound was heard in the roof of the preceding building, a panic rush to escape ensued and twenty-nine members of the congregation 'were killed on the spot'[175] and eighty were injured. Consequently, this version of the Laigh Kirk has seven exits.

Kilmarnock Covenanting memorials (Laigh Kirkyard etc.)   NS 428 380

(1) Laigh Churchyard in central Kilmarnock (Bank Street): tombstones to John Ross and John Shields, hanged and beheaded 27 December 1666 after Battle of Rullion Green, and to John Nisbet, hanged 14 April 1683; also (2) at King Street (shopping precinct): execution site (14 April 1683) marked by concrete plug let into circular steel seat on concourse (NB 2001: this marker has vanished). Another Laigh Churchyard stone, to five drowned deportees (see p. 93) and to John Finlay (hanged 15 December 1682), has been vandalised and is no longer on view.

Kilmarnock: The Dick Institute   NS 433 387

The neoclassical Dick Institute in the centre of Kilmarnock houses perhaps the most important museum collection in Ayrshire as well as an art gallery and a library. It has overflowed to **Dean Castle**.

Kilmarnock, Soulis Cross NS 433 387

This cross is dated 1600 and seems to commemorate the murder of Lord
Soulis in 1444. It used to stand at the entrance to the High Church in
Kilmarnock, but has been removed to the Dick Institute Museum, where
it is held in store. It is an octagonal pillar in two pieces atop a stepped
base, surmounted by a floriation and a gilt vane. It seems to have been last
restored in 1825, at which date an earlier original may have been entirely
discarded.

Kilmaurs Cross NS 410 412

The original cross, which was in need of repair in 1678, has now gone and a
modern pillar dated 1830 stands in a small enclosure near the Tolbooth.

Kilmaurs, Glencairn Aisle NS 414 407

The church here was apparently dedicated to St Maura. See p. 26. It
was granted to Kelso Abbey in 1170 by the founder of the Cuninghame
family, *Robertus filius Wernebaldi*, and was further endowed as a college of
secular canons in 1413. At the Reformation it was seized by the fith Earl of
Glencairn, whose descendant the seventh earl erected the Glencairn Aisle
in 1600. In this there is a monument to the ninth earl, Lord Chancellor of
Scotland (*d.* 1644).

Kilmaurs Quarry: Mammoth tusks NS 405 396

Remains of prehistoric elephant (mammoth) have been found here, as
well as at three unidentified sites nearby. The B776 runs along the south
end of the site, which lies to the south of Kilmaurs village, not far from
Kilmarnock.

Kilmaurs Tower and Place NS 412 411

Kilmaurs Castle or Tower has disappeared, though Davis thinks it may have
been sited where there is a small rise in the fields east of Jocksthorn Farm
(Jocksthorn, itself a possible site, is at **NS 417 411**). The historical residence
of the Glencairn (Cuninghame) family was the seventeenth-century
Kilmaurs Place, a still inhabited crow-stepped T-plan mansion. This is
adjacent to a ruined palace (hence 'Place') range dating from the sixteenth
or seventeenth century, and possibly built upon an earlier castle. Part of the
range is treated as a (single-storey) farm outbuilding and has a roof. The
western part is open to the air and seems to have been vaulted.

Kilwhannel High Plantation: settlement
NX 120 804 – NX 122 800, NX 117 804

Four houses are situated within or at the side of a group of small cairns on the north-west side of Benawhirter. The traces of the houses, three in a group and a single house, show that they were circular. There are traces of stony terracing or banking amongst the cairns, and a field system is discernible lower down the hill. Close to the isolated house the remains of a single cairn (**NX 1173 8048**) are visible. It has been dug into.[176]

The site is about 4km south-east of Ballantrae.

Kilwinning Abbey   *NS 303 432*

The establishment of this abbey was a part of the drive towards Christian and feudal reorganisation in the former Strathclyde and Scotland generally, instituted by King David I and his successors from the second quarter of the twelfth century. The cartularies of the two principal Ayrshire abbeys, Kilwinning and Crossraguel, have disappeared, and we have no clear date for the foundation of either, but in the case of Kilwinning it is taken, on the basis of other documentation, that the abbey was founded by the de Morville family, who were awarded the lordship of Cunninghame in about 1136. It was a Tironensian foundation.

Hugh, the first de Morville, established his caput *(administrative and military centre) in Irvine perhaps as early as 1140. The abbey at Kilwinning was not founded until some time later – perhaps 1157, or possibly 1187 or 1191; if the latter two dates are considered, this would assign the foundation to Hugh's son Richard, who succeeded his father in 1162. It is known that the abbey was in existence by 1202/7, when an abbot of Kilwinning witnessed a legal document. In any case, the phases of the building at Kilwinning can be dated roughly to within decades by careful examination of building styles in sequence.*

Only fragments of the great structure are still standing, most of it having been pulled down in 1562 by Alexander, Earl of Glencairn at the instigation of John Knox during the Scottish Protestant Reformation. From what remains, though, the following phases may be deduced. A church may have been constructed as early as 1157 – making the founder the first Hugh de Morville. This dating has been arrived at by examination of the long stretch of walling and satellite structures to the west and south of the great surviving gable, and by comparison with other dated building styles elsewhere. This stretch of walling may have been the south side of an early nave, bordering the cloister to the south again.[177]

The remnants of a chapter-house bordering the cloister to the east, and a passageway between the chapter-house and the foot of the gable end were probably built during the 1180s.[178]

A great processional arch between the gable and the wall gives stylistic signs of having been constructed roughly during the decade 1190–1200 – perhaps a gift or bequest from Richard de Morville, who died in 1189.[179] *Then came a major building phase, or perhaps reconstruction, during which the towering south gable, pierced by three tall windows and an 'oculus' (round window), was built as part of an eastern transept, stylistically dated to the 1230s. By that time the male de Morville line had died out, but it is thought that one or other of Richard de Morville's daughters – one of whom had married Roland of Galloway, Lord of Cuninghame and Constable of Scotland – completed the monastery up to that point (or perhaps her son Alan of Galloway, who died in 1234). Finally the nave – the main body of the church – was reconstructed and a west transept, which had two towers, was added on perhaps during the 1250s. One of these towers, the north-west, survived until it was struck by lightning in 1809 and then in 1814 was finally demolished by gunpowder.[181] A modern louvred clock tower was then erected in its place. Meanwhile, in 1775, a plain modern parish church was built to the north-west, obliterating all that remained of the north-eastern quadrant of the old abbey.*

The surviving parts of this abbey are fragmentary but enough remains to impress the visitor. The gable with its three lights and oculus still dominate Kilwinning, as the centre of an extensive complex. The abbey became extremely wealthy, possessing the revenues of no less than thirteen parish churches in Cuninghame beside those of Kilwinning itself. All these tributary churches seem to have been donated to the abbey foundation in the late twelfth or early thirteenth centuries. Large estates belonged to the abbey, including Monkcastle to the north and Monkredding to the north-east of Kilwinning. Towards the end of the monastic period in Scotland covetous eyes were cast upon the rich revenues of Kilwinnning as of other abbeys, and in 1512 a fierce quarrel broke out during which the last Tironensian abbot, William Bunche, was assaulted in the precincts and physically restrained by the Earls of Glencairn and Angus and their men, in an endeavour to make him resign in favour of John Forman, Precentor of Glasgow.

The abbey stands on a prominent rise overlooking the River Garnock in the centre of Kilwinning. The A737 passes the site on the north, and access may be obtained directly from the street.

Kingcase (Kincase or Kilchais): St Ninian's Hospital   NS 346 243

See **Prestwick Burgh**

Kingencleugh Castle and House   NS 503 256, NS 504 258

Old Kingencleugh is perched high on the lip of a sombre gully at the bottom of which a turbulent burn rushes down to the River Ayr. Access to this gully may be had from the south-eastern side of the A76 (on the Mauchline side of the Catrine road-head) via a farm road signposted Kingencleugh: those who venture through a style into what may be an ancient right of way are advised to beware of dangerously slippy conditions and a precipitous path; it is also difficult to see the castle from this angle through the screen of trees. It is better to make an appointment with the owner of Kingencleugh House[182] (first on the right on the farm road before the farm entrance) to gain access over the field at the rear of the house: the castle stands high on the left-hand side of this field.

The old castle is now represented by two tall and extensively ruined corners of a four-storey block with a crow-stepped gable: the east and the south walls are relatively intact. The date has been given as around 1600 or 1620. Salter says that the 1620 building replaced an earlier structure.[183] An earlier date would fit the tradition that John Knox preached in Kingencleugh Castle in the mid-sixteenth century. The reformer Knox was active in the neighbourhood, both in Mauchline and in Galston – in territory then controlled by the Campbells of Loudoun, who had infiltrated from Cuninghame into Kyle Stewart. Kingencleugh was one of several castles erected as border markers for the Campbell feus in the neighbourhood. It also forms part of a chain of castles bordering the River Ayr from the north. The Campbells of this region had been in the forefront of the movements leading to the Scottish Reformation since at least 1494, when a Campbell was among the 'Lollards of Kyle' (see p. 89) arraigned before King James IV.

A short distance from the castle stands Kingencleugh House, built about 1765 and refurbished in 1957, a two-storey building with two wings, recently painted pink.

Kirkbride Old Parish Church   NS 264 158

The most northerly parish in Carrick, Kirkbride was gifted by Duncan then Lord of Carrick in about 1197 to the Cistercian nuns at North Berwick. The building here is enclosed in a burial ground south-west of Dunduff Farm, across the Dunduff Burn. As usual, this parish church was a plain rectangular building. Doorways are set in the parallel long walls towards the west end, and an aumbry (recess) is found in the south wall. Part of a probable sanctuary consecration cross, possibly dating from the twelfth century, was discovered in the ruins in 1927 and then lost again. The parish was united with Maybole, perhaps before the Reformation.

The site overlooks Dunure and the A719, which runs 200m to the west.

Kirkdominae (Kildomine, Kildamnie, Kirkdandie)   NX 253 928

In spite of the name, which means on the face of it 'the church (or chapel) of (Our) Lady', this ruined chapel, first mentioned in 1404, is said to have been dedicated to the Holy Trinity. It was pillaged for stones in 1650 or 1653 in order to build the new church at Barr. The west gable stands more or less complete but the east end has disappeared and the north and south walls are only footings. The entrance is in the north wall. **Struil Well** a few metres away (**NX 2512 9291**) was the water supply for the chapel. It gushes between two stone walls from the bottom of a perpendicular rock.

Immediately adjacent to the chapel is the ruined farmhouse of Kirkdominae. The B734 runs past it to the south.

Kirkhill Castle   NX 145 859

This castle, though ruined, is elegant and compact in outward appearance. The interior has fallen in completely and the building is roofless. Sixteenth century in date, it is L-plan, with three storeys and a garret. There is no parapet but two corbelled-out bartizans survived until recently (one has now

Fig. 19. Kirkill Castle, Colmonell. View from the south-west.

collapsed). There are shot-holes for defence. Some skew-putts are decorated with carved faces, and the gables are still crow-stepped. The building stands on a lawn next to the modern Kirkhill House at the west end of Colmonell on the B734.

Kirkmichael Parish Church   NS 345 089

The present building at the east end of the village stands on the site of the old church, which it replaced in 1787. The original church with its emoluments etc. was granted to the prior and canons of Whithorn by John de Gemilstoun, and confirmed to them by Robert I in May 1325, as well as by James II in 1451. This building is still in use, surrounded by a high kirkyard wall.

Kirkmichael Churchyard Covenanter's grave NS 345 089

A Covenanter named Gilbert McAdam, shot in 1685, is buried in the churchyard here. The original 'Old Mortality' gravestone (with characteristic ligatured lettering) is now housed in an elegant small monument like a pavilion.

Kirkoswald NS 238 075

This church was dedicated to Oswald who, as king, was one of the heroes and martyrs of early Northumbria, which absorbed south-west Scotland as far as this and beyond, before the formation of independent Galloway. The present building, built in 1777 and now ruined, replaced an earlier church which was originally granted in 1227 to Paisley Abbey by Duncan, Earl of Carrick but was transferred by him to Crossraguel when that abbey became independent of Paisley in about 1244. In the kirkyard are the graves of Douglas Graham ('Tam o'Shanter') and John Davidson ('Souter Johnnie'), both characters in the poem *Tam o' Shanter* by Robert Burns.

Knock Castle NS 194 631

This is a coastal cliff-top fortalice in north Ayrshire situated next to a deep ravine through which runs a stream. Part of the old castle has been retained and prettified as a garden ornament for the larger Victorian Knock Castle nearby; the remaining portion consists of mere fragments of masonry. The old structure is early seventeenth century (1603–4: mentioned in Timothy Pont) but dating has been rendered difficult by later faking. From the fourteenth century the property was held by the Fraser family until it went to Sir Robert Montgomerie of Skelmorlie nearly 300 years later (*cf.* **Skelmorlie**). The surviving half-building has two towers, one of which at least is of doubtful authenticity, perhaps having been rebuilt in the nineteenth century. It is about 3km north of Largs on the coast road (A78).

The Knock Fort NS 202 628

Another vitrified fort, this one on top of The Knock hill at 217m OD. The fort is oval in shape, surrounding the summit of The Knock with a single stone and turf rampart. A shallow ditch has been cut in the rock below the top of the rampart. Vitrified sandstone has been found on the north-west side of the hill.

The Knock is 2km north of Largs. It can best be reached by taking a side road north from Largs to Brisbane Mains farmhouse, whence a winding track leads up to the summit of the hill. It overlooks the Firth of Clyde. Further up the same road is the farm of **Outerwards** in front of the Roman fortlet of that name.

Knockdaw Castle NX 151 897

Knockdaw is a contender for the title of the remotest and most inaccessible castle in Ayrshire – but it is only 2km east of Carleton Castle and the Clyde coast at Lendalfoot, and there is a good if unlisted road just north of Knockdaw, following the line of the Water of Lendal. The castle here has shared the fate of many Ayrshire fortifications in becoming part of the outbuildings of its own home farm. It is now a toolshed. The fragmentary walls have been disguised by being built up to a uniform height with brickwork and given a modern roof A barmkin may be traced on one side. It is impossible to date the castle, a possession of the Kennedys, though the surviving literary references indicate that it or a predecessor was in existence at least in the sixteenth century. Apart from that, little is known of this isolated outpost.

> There was a champion I knaw,
> Sprung of the great house of Knockdaw,
> Wha by meikle wit and pains
> Became the knicht o' Girvanmains.[183]

Knockdolian cairn NX 113 848

Knockdolian is the spectacular height (265m OD) dominating Ballantrae and Colmonell. It is one of a series of cairn-crowned hills running south from the Ballantrae region to Finnarts Bay and Loch Ryan. The cairn here appears relatively undamaged and there are a few kerb stones visible.

Knockdolian Castle NX 122 854

Knockdolian Castle is a small ruined tower-house situated in the grounds of the present Knockdolian House. It has four storeys, a parapet and walk on three sides only, and a garret. It has only three corbelled-out corner bartizans. The corbels supporting the walk are continuous on two sides and individually spaced on the third side. The fourth side rises continuously to the gable. This slight departure from the usual pattern in castle-building gives rise to the suspicion that there has been a collapse at some point in the building's history. Davis says that it has clearly been repaired about the middle of the seventeenth century, and that the repairs extend upwards from the fourth floor. Below this point the building may be very much older, perhaps by a century or more.

The site of the castle is east of Knockdolian Hill, between the B7044 and the River Stinchar. At that point it commands the landward mouths of the two passes represented now by the B7044 and the B734, which run on either side of Knockdolian towards the sea. A peculiar feature of this strategic situation is that the road runs above the level of the top of the castle, which stands on a shelf above a steep slope to the river. The site is less than 1km from **Duniewick Fort** on the northward shoulder of Knockdolian.

Knockittis Burn burnt mounds (water heating)

(1)NX 305 845, (2) NX 306 854

These two locations are nearer Black Clauchrie than Clauchrierob, on opposite sides of the same footpath. The Knockittis Burn is another tributary of the Cree, sourced in the Standard Hill. The two burnt mounds, both on the east of the burn, are (1) south of the footpath, kidney-shaped and indented, and (2) north of the footpath, horse-shoe shaped and indented. Both are situated on marshy ground.[184]

Knockjargon Fort NS 235 472

This fort has been built over and around a previously robbed Neolithic hilltop cairn. The remains of fort ramparts built at two and possibly three levels now exist only as terraced scarps broken on the south-east by a broad entrance. Traces of a third rampart are to be seen at the south of the fort. The cairn occupies about a quarter of the interior of the fort.

This fort is on the west of the Busbie Muir reservoir, 3km north of Ardrossan. It is in the neighbourhood of several other archaeological sites, including the cup-and-ring marked stones at **Blackshaw Hill,** and the dun at **Coal Hill**.

Kyle Castle NS 647 192

Beyond the modern satellite village of Logan immediately north-east of Cumnock, an unlisted road heads east alongside the spacious meanders of the Glenmuir Water. On one of these, on the north or Kyle Stewart bank of the watercourse, the slopes of **Dornal Motte** rise near the house of the same name. The road then plunges into a deep and romantic glen, heavily wooded; a left turn across a stone bridge leads to the tiny hamlet of Dalblair – three or four houses only.

The metalled road comes to an end there, but a broad track leads upwards to the east, where a finger of stonework is silhouetted against the sky, rising from a tall eminence on the Kyle Regis side of the confluence of the Guelt and Glenmuir Waters. This is all that is left of Kyle (or Dalblair) Castle. Originally a rectangular keep, it probably had a barmkin extending to the west on the level top of the promontory. To judge by the style of the masonry of the surviving piece of wall, this stone building was erected during the fifteenth or sixteenth century.

Kyles Well, Kilwinning NS 301 431

A pump was latterly fitted to this well which, however, is now hidden by the floor of a yard. It is supposed to have flowed with blood in time of war. A pipe leading from the abbey to the well was discovered in 1826. See p. 26.

Lady Cathcart's House, Ayr NS 336 220

See **Ayr Royal Burgh**

Ladykirk NS 386 266

See **Preceptory of Our Lady Kirk of Kyle**

Ladywell burnt mounds (water heating) NS 203 007

Previously covered by a spoil heap, this site recently (1998) revealed two deposits of burnt-mound material, separated from medieval features by a deep deposit of alluvial clay.[185] Ladywell is only about 1km east of the site at Chapeldonan.

Laggish, White Cairn NX 229 786

Traces of a large cairn are to be found on a small knoll west of the track between Laggish and Dochroyle north of the bridge over the Laggish Burn. At one time it may have been surrounded by a ring of large boulders. Now there is a circle of cairn material overgrown with grass and two boulders in the centre, one of which may be a cist slab. This site is 5km south of Barrhill. There are at least four other 'White Cairns' in the neighbourhood – at **NX 342 791** (west of the eponymous Bargrennan chambered cairn) in Kirkcudbrightshire, at **Corly Craig (NX 178 748)** in Wigtownshire and at **White Cairn of Cairnennock (NS 508 007)** at Loch Doon. There is also a **White Cairn (NX 218 824)** beside a farm of that name less than 1km north-west of Barrhill.

The White Cairn at Laggish is almost inaccessible. The Dochroyle track referred to starts from an unfenced unclassified road 1km south of Barrhill Station and the cairn itself is 1km south-west of Dochroyle.

Laigh Milton Mill Viaduct NS 383 368

This is the oldest railway bridge in Scotland, now disused. It was opened (under the patronage of the Duke of Portland) in 1812 for horse-drawn transport running on an original plateway between Kilmarnock and Troon. Conversion to locomotive transport took place in 1846. When the track was relaid this four-span bridge was bypassed and still survives, though in poor condition. Some of the original plateway may still be there.

Laighpark settlement   NS 400 192

This is a substantial earthwork sited on a steep slope west of Coylton inside a ditch. Although there is no trace of a causeway, it is fairly certainly a prehistoric settlement with a entrance on the east. It is situated at the side of the westernmost of the two side-roads running south from the Joppa suburb of Coylton. Shrubs and trees cover the whole structure.

Laight (Lacht) Castle   NS 450 088

The vestiges of this remote building lie on a promontory high above the Dunaskin Burn, whose gorge runs deep into the south-western flank of Benquhat Hill. Nothing appears but the turf-covered footings of the walls. The structure seems to have been trapezoid in plan, probably a courtyard castle, with a stone building at one end of an enceinte or ring wall whose course can be traced in the flat top of the promontory. There is a defensive ditch crossed by a broad causeway.

Laight Castle on the north-eastern side of the Doon Valley is diagonally opposite **Keirs Castle** on the south-western side: this also occupies a position far up the glen of a burn rushing down from the high hills to join the river at Waterside. Each castle is in a good position to ambush men marching along the frontier between Carrick and Kyle Regis, now the line of the A713. Visitors to Laight will find Dunaskin Glen a convenient approach (east side of Dunaskin Burn), starting at the **Dunaskin Industrial Heritage Museum.**

Lainshaw Castle ('The Langschaw')   NS 410 453

The present Lainshaw House lies west-south-west of and just outside Stewarton. It has been subject to extensive alteration and enlargement over the centuries, but it is clear that the accretions cluster round a still standing early tower, possibly of the seventeenth century. It seems that nothing survives from the sixteenth or earlier centuries. There is, however, a 'Law Mount' at **NS 411 447**, a little less than 1km south of Lainshaw on the other side of the B679, adjacent to two farms with the suggestive names of High and Laigh Castleton. Law Mount could be the original motte, Stewarton Castle, granted in the twelfth century to Godfrey de Ros by Hugo de Morville. This suggestion would have to be confirmed by excavation.

Langdyke Dun   NS 492 429

This is a small dun built on the edge of an escarpment (about 150m OD) overlooking the Craufurdland Water near its source. Very disturbed and overgrown, it may have had a turf and stone wall. It is 3km east of Fenwick, and the A719 runs between that village and the site.

Largs, battle site   NS 207 587

This appears to be the true site of the battle rather than the 1912 coastal monument ('The Pencil') at **NS 206 576** – which is, however, worth looking at.

Largs, Skelmorlie Aisle   *NS 202 594*

The Skelmorlie Aisle is the remaining part of the older parish church of Largs – not the oldest, which has vanished completely. Largs Parish Church is first mentioned in 1263. At that time Largs was a separate lordship owned by the Balliol successors to the de Morvilles, who also owned Cuninghame. After the Wars of Independence and the forfeiture of the Balliols, Largs and Cuninghame both passed to the Stewarts, who granted this church to Paisley Abbey, with which it remained until the Reformation. After 1561 it passed again through various hands to the Montgomeries.

Sir Robert Montgomerie built the Skelmorlie Aisle in 1636 in memory of the accidental death of his wife. It seems to have been the north transept of the original church. The interior is quite astonishing by contrast with the relatively plain seventeenth-century exterior. The monument fills the space, rising above a sunk basement which supports a gallery and a lofty canopy divided in three parts by four double sets of four square columns each fronted by a circular pillar or shaft. On each side two of these double sets – i.e. four tandem supports – bear a horizontal slab or entablature and 'soffit'. The compartments thus formed on either side form the basis from which springs a beautiful small panelled barrel-vault, the central climax of the canopy, under which, no doubt, it was intended to place a reclining effigy of Sir Robert's wife or of Sir Robert himself – but this was never carried out. Another entablature rests on the barrel-vault supported by pilasters, and this structure is 'crowned with foliated and interlaced scroll-work, mingled with cupids, hour-glasses, obelisks, and other ornaments'.[186] The whole monument is fantastically encrusted with decorations of a style that cannot be associated with the prevailing Presbyterian ethos of Scotland at this time (1636–8), though whether Sir Robert employed a foreign designer is an open question. It appears that someone called Stalker was employed in 1638 to paint the overarching ceiling, also barrel-vaulted, of the aisle itself. This ceiling consists of thin timber panels painted with various scenes and figures, including the signs of the zodiac and heraldic emblems.

Key held in **Largs Historical Society Museum** directly adjacent to main gate.

Largs standing stone   NS 205 587

This stone stands on the front at Largs, near the shore line. It is suspected that it is the sole survivor of a number of standing stones in the neighbourhood. It is of course far older than the Battle of Largs, with which it is traditionally associated, and which is thought to have taken place about 0.5km to the east of this site.

Largs, Castle Hill Fort   NS 215 588

A fort sits at the summit of Castle Hill (183m OD) defended by steep slopes on three sides and a gully on the east side. It has a rampart defending a weak point on the south. The entrance is on the north-east.

Castle Hill is a dramatic backdrop to the town of Largs. The fort was built with an eye to the strategic position over the Gogo Water, which runs at the foot of the hill to the north.

Largs and District Historical Society Museum   NS 202 594

This is a small building directly adjacent to the **Skelmorlie Aisle**. (The key to the aisle is held in the museum.) There is a good local collection and useful fact-sheets are available.

Law Castle   NS 210 484

Law is one of a group of four or five late fifteenth-century north Ayrshire castles whose construction and dimensions are very similar. Other members of the group are **Wee Cumbrae, Fairlie** and **Skelmorlie.** Law Castle has four storeys, continuous corbelling supporting the parapet walk, open rounds at the angles, and a garret storey. It has been restored and now stands, a conspicuous white-painted object, on a height above West Kilbride.

Lethanhill   NS 436 104

A company village famed for the rigour of its living conditions, now deserted and ghostly. 2km east of Patna (A713), on rough tracks.

Lightshaw standing stone   NS 716 282

This stone is about 2km east of Muirkirk in a field on the north side of the A70. There appear to be cup-marks on it but their status is disputed.

Lindston: possible henge monument   NS 372 167

This earthwork has been almost completely destroyed by ploughing and bulldozing, but it can still be seen to have been a perfectly circular enclosure surrounded by a broad ditch, which was recently filled with water. There has been a bank, now much reduced, and a causeway crossing the bank and the ditch. Sitting on a broad ridge from which one can see for miles all round, this is likely to have been a henge. Lindston Farm to the south lies close to the intersection of the A713 and the B742 north-east of Dalrymple.

Little Laight Hill (Wigtownshire): Taxing Stone   NX 063 711

This stone is just outside the boundary of Ayrshire on Laight Moor north of Little Laight Farm; it is adjacent to an old gun battery about 0.5km south of the Galloway Burn (March Burn). It was from behind this stone that in 841 a Galloway man is said to have shot Alpin, the freebooter who is alleged to have been the father of Kenneth mac Alpin, the unifier of the Picts and the Scots: hence the alternative name for the area and for the stone, Laight Alpin, 'the grave of Alpin'. The stone is fairly obviously Neolithic and older than 841. It is also likely to have been named in Ayr's Royal Burgh Charter in *c*.1205 as Lacht, for the southern limit for the trading precinct of Ayr: hence the name Taxing Stone (see p. 49).

Little Rigend   NS 541 114

According to Paterson (1847), '[n]ear the source of the Nith, some remains of an old baronial residence exist on the property of Sir John Cathcart of Carleton'.[187] This is probably the totally overgrown structure on the south bank of the Nith visible from Waterhead on the north bank. An investigation in 1994 indicated that it was rectilinear on plan, with the vestiges of two chambers and a possible stair base.[188] This is 8km west of New Cumnock. A direct track running north to the castle may be available from the B741 beyond Craighouse.

Loanfoot (The Law) cairn   NS 592 359

This is yet another example of near total destruction of a cairn, this time for dyke-building material in the 1870s.[189] Its interior has been almost completely gutted to ground level except for the edges and towards the east end. For this reason it is impossible to classify, although it is clearly a long cairn and may have had a horned profile i.e. when viewed from above the eastern end appears wider than the west end and slightly concave.

Loch Bradan Castle   NX 426 970

An island castle like **Loch Doon Castle**. Also like Loch Doon, the water level has been raised in conversion of the loch to a reservoir, and the island

and its castle have been drowned. It seems to have been a relatively small building. The site can be reached by the unlisted road running south from Straiton to the Stinchar Bridge; at the bridge a road or 'forest walk' runs east to Loch Bradan and then north along the west side of an inlet, terminating on the shore just opposite the approximate position of the island; nothing, however, is to be seen above the water.

Loch Doon Castle   NX 4882 9475, NX 4841 9501

Cf. preceding entry. Loch Doon Castle was built on an island at the first of the two references given above. About 1936 the water level in the loch was raised in order to provide a reservoir and the island was drowned. In this case, however, it was decided to rescue the castle and to rebuild it on the western shore of the loch near Craigmalloch. It is a particularly fine early example of a castle of enceinte, consisting originally of a simple defensive wall of eleven unequal sides built of coursed ashlar with an entrance on the north. This structure, built in the thirteenth century, was heavily damaged probably in the course of one of the many sieges it withstood, and when it was repaired a keep was incorporated on the west side. In its new position the castle can be seen to be of particularly fine stonework, incorporating an Early English pointed gateway with a portcullis defence, a postern gate and a fireplace. Before the transplantation the ruined keep, of inferior (possibly sixteenth-century) build, stood next to the fireplace: four storeys high, it was built on to the wall of enceinte. The castle may have been occupied until the early seventeenth century.

The island in Loch Doon on which the castle stood may originally have been a crannog. This theory is supported by the discovery in the early nineteenth century of timbers that may either have been part of a

Fig. 20. Loch Doon Castle in its original position. View from the west.

crannog structure or a number of logboats. The most reliable account of the discoveries assigns four to the year 1831 and two to the year 1823. One of the 1823 discoveries is probably in the Hunterian Museum, Glasgow University. It has a barge-style rounded bow and a vertically cut stern section with a shelf like a duck-bill jutting out behind. A cutting tool (possibly metal) has been used to shape the boat, as has fire, and the ensemble gives the impression of being either unfinished or unseaworthy. A calibrated radio-carbon date has been obtained of 619. This boat has been reconstructed as it might have looked when complete by students of the Scottish Institute of Maritime Studies and the replica is on display in the Scottish Fisheries Museum in Anstruther.

Only one other of these nineteenth-century discoveries has survived, dating from 1831, and it is also in the Hunterian Museum. The port side alone survives. The bow was probably rounded; the stern was formed by a transom, the lower part of which is still in situ.[190]

Loch Doon may be reached on a side road running west from A713 at Mossdale south of Dalmellington.

Loch Doon: flints etc.
NX 482 927, NX 482 928, NX 483 939, NX 484 936 etc

A very large number of sites for Mesolithic flint and other stone implements is to be found on the borders of Loch Doon, including on the western side areas round about the re-erected Loch Doon Castle (Craigmalloch) and Starr Cottage in the south. The presence of these scatters has been interpreted as an indication that the first Mesolithic inhabitants of Scotland were not only sea-coast dwellers but penetrated inland, despite the forbidding forests and hills. It has been suggested that Mesolithic pioneers journeyed north from the Solway coast into the uplands via Clatteringshaws Loch and Loch Doon and then down through the Doon valley to the fertile Ayrshire plains and coast, using the stone implements not only to kill game but also to blaze trails through the forests.[191]

Lochgoin Farmhouse Covenanting Museum   NS 530 469

A museum containing various Covenanting relics, books and papers. Owned during the Covenanting emergency by the Howie family (see **Fenwick)** and subject to repeated raids. Just north of Ayrshire, on a side road off the B764.[192] Intending visitors to Lochgoin Farmhouse should contact Mr James Barr (Loganswell 249).

Loch Hill standing stone   NX 178 822

This stone leans slightly to the east. It is about 0.5km north of a suspected (?chambered) cairn at **Loch Hill NX 173 817.** Both monuments, now almost untraceable in dense forest, were in prominent positions above the head waters of the Water of Tig, about 5km south-east of Colmonell.

Lochlea Crannog and Logboats NS 457 302

This crannog was situated in a loch north-east of Tarbolton. The site, which is now drained and invisible in dry agricultural land, was excavated in 1878. Five logboats were discovered in the vicinity, only one of which has survived, now in the Dick Institute, Kilmarnock.[193]

Lochmodie Castle NS 263 024

In spite of the maps, this castle is difficult to find. The visitor can take the B741, which runs though the west end of Dailly, across the Water of Girvan and up the northward slope of the valley beside the Dalquharran policies towards the railway: just short of this it makes a T-junction with an unlisted road running from Maybole to Girvan. The T-junction is really a crossroads whose northward limb is now only an overgrown track diving into a small valley traversed by the Quarrelhill Burn. This track is a dead end, terminating at the formidable height of the railway embankment. On the left of the path stands – or rather leans – a sorry fragment of a tall stone castle, not so much a gable end as the corner of a structure perhaps 8m high. The topmost stones of the walls do not come up above the level of the railway track, although the tree that sprouts from them is taller. Tumbled and now overgrown fragments of masonry scattered around make for hazardous walking, and the remnant teeters at such an alarming angle that its final collapse surely cannot be far off. The mere construction of the railway embankment, only a few metres away, and the constant rattling and shaking of the trains, must have contributed to the disintegration of the building, probably already well ruined 150 years ago. It may also have suffered subsidence from extensive old mine-workings in the neighbourhood. It is perfectly visible from the railway but completely hidden from the road.

This building, called Lochmodie and now so dilapidated, was possibly the first Dalquharran Castle, and its stones may have been used to build the castle now known as **Old Dalquharran**.

Long Tom standing stone NX 081 718

On Loan Hill just south of the Ayrshire boundary, this stone is situated north-west of the Glen Burn and about 2km east of **Little Laight (The Taxing Stone)**. There is at least one cup-mark on it.

Loudoun Castle NS 506 377

North of the A71 at Galston the A719 runs north at right angles to the major road past Loudoun Academy. Just past the academy there is another crossroads, the left-hand towards Loudoun Kirk, the right-hand to a 'Wagnerian ruin', the burnt-out shell of Loudoun Castle, destroyed in 1940. This was the home of the Loudoun family, one of the most powerful for good and ill in Ayrshire.

Loudoun Castle in its present form was developed at the beginning of the nineteenth century from a possibly fifteenth-century tower-house with seventeenth-century accretions i.e. a 'palace range'. The early complex may be distinguished behind ninteenth-century structures, in particular a tall and still visually impressive fragment of the original tower, four storeys high, with three modern storeys on top of that. The palace range was built at the southern side of the old tower, and both were encased in a huge early nineteenth-century castellated confection, which earned the title of the 'Windsor Castle of Ayrshire'. The older buildings had some resemblance to **Kilbirnie (The Old Place)**, which, like Loudoun, seems to have been built by a branch of the Craufurd family. I cannot say whether any traces of the alleged Kennedy fire-attack in 1527 can still be discerned amid the dismal signs of the final accidental conflagration. Like **Eglinton Castle**, Loudoun Castle owes its ultimate ruin to the Second World War, when Belgian troops were stationed in the grounds here. The treasures of the house had been packed in crates ready to be shipped away when in 1940 the disaster destroyed them as well as everything else.

The ruined castle is in the centre of very extensive grounds, some of which have been taken over for a theme park. To the east of it amid the trees an overgrown motte has been identified as **Old Loudoun Castle (NS 517 377**, at Hindberrybank on the Bowhill Burn near Woodhead). This scarp-edge motte has been severely reduced by quarrying, which has left just a crescentic half of the original structure still *in situ*. The bailey still survives in the shape of a ditch looping outwards from the south and terminating at the northern end of the motte. This motte may be the seat of the original twelfth-century grantee, James fitz Lambinus.

Loudoun Hall, Ayr   NS 336 221

See **Ayr, Royal Burgh**

Loudoun Hill Roman Fort   NS 605 371

This once clearly visible fort has been entirely destroyed by sand-quarrying at Allanton. Well-defined traces of five different levels and periods of occupation were detected. After the fifth period, in the second century AD, the site appears to have been abandoned and deliberately demolished, perhaps at the same time as the Roman withdrawal from the Antonine Wall. Finds, now in the Hunterian Museum in Glasgow University, include a bronze hanging lamp, wagon-wheel tyres and axle fittings.

The Roman fort at Loudoun Hill was sited strategically at what is still a crossroads between a route from the south of Scotland via Nithsdale and a line of communication between eastern and central Scotland and the west. Archaeologists have long suspected that a Roman route ran between Loudoun Hill and the Irvine area, as well as others to Largs and down to the Ayr and Girvan regions, which may have had their own communications with Nithsdale. Today the A71 from Kilmarnock runs east past Allanton and Loudoun Hill just beyond Darvel.

Loudoun Kirk   NS 492 373

The predecessor of the present Loudoun Parish Church in Newmilns. This ruin has a direct communication by road with **Loudoun Castle**, now bisected by the A719. The east gable is still intact, and a large part of one wall, but the rest is almost entirely gone except for the choir, which was converted to a burial vault by the Marquis of Bute in 1898 and is still in good repair. The church formed part of the possessions of **Kilwinning Abbey,** to whom it was probably granted by Hugh de Morville, first Lord of Cuninghame, in the twelfth century. This church was that of Rev. James Nevoy, responsible for the massacre of Dunaverty in 1647.

Loudoun Kirk Covenanter's grave   NS 492 373

Tombstone on an internal wall of the church, of Thomas Fleming, killed 1 June 1679 at the Battle of Drumclog. See preceding entry.

Lugtonridge Hoard   NS 37 49

In 1779 or '80 a hoard of five or six bronze shields set in a ring on edge was discovered about 2m below the surface by peat-diggers at 'Lugtonridge Farm'. One shield has survived the discovery, donated to the Society of Antiquaries of London in 1791. It is 69cm across, and has a central boss surrounded by twenty-nine ribs alternating with rows of small bosses. A hand grip is riveted on behind the central boss. The circumstances of the discovery make it likely that this was a votive hoard buried as an offering to the gods. It has been dated to the Late Bronze Age, probably between 700 and 800 BC. Unfortunately there are today no less than five 'Lugtonridge Farms' south-east of Beith and at none of them has any knowledge of the Lugtonridge hoard been preserved. The shield is currently (2003) on display in the Museum of the Society of Antiquaries of London at Burlington House.

Lynn   NS 281 484

The remnants of an ancient tower stand on the banks of the Caaf Water, south-west of Dalry. Lynn was the home of Bessie Dunlop, a farmer's wife who was condemned and burned for witchcraft in 1576. A successor house was demolished after 1960.

Lyonston (Maybole) standing stone
NS 310 103

The spelling of the name can be either Lyonston or Lyonstone, and the farm on which this stone stands may have taken its name from it. It is rather mushroom-shaped (broader at the top than at the base). It stands on a low rise at the north-eastern boundary of Maybole not far from the A77.

Machrikil
NS 292 011

This is the site of a vanished chapel, whose ruins were finally disposed of by a farmer in 1850. It was very small. Two Christian relics still exist on the site, a stepped cross-base with a rectangular socket, and a five-sided boulder, also with a rectangular socket and a barely visible carved Latin cross. These relics have been tentatively dated to the tenth or eleventh century. Machrikil has been associated with St Machar, but the shape of the name, Machar-i-chill, is unusual for this kind of meaning, and it is more likely to signify 'the chapel in the field' (*machar*, a plain or a field). The site is about 0.5km north-east of the Lindsayston Burn downstream from the ruined **Kilkerran Castle**.[194]

Maidens, Port Murray
NS 207 079

A hoard of five flat axes of the Early Bronze Age was discovered in a rock crevice about 100m from the sea at Maidens, south of **Culzean Castle** in 1883. Three of the axes were Migdale type (Coles type Ba) and two were unclassified (Coles type Bb). A solid bracelet or armlet 59mm in diameter was also found. These may have been a votive hoard. All the finds are in the collections of the National Museums of Scotland (NMS X. DQ 404–9) and are currently in the Archaeology Department Study Collection in Leith.

Mains Hill cairn
NX 095 831

On Mains Hill (OD76) there is an oval cairn 10.1m by 7.7m and 0.9m in height. It is about 1km inland from Ballantrae, and is probably associated with the cairns on the adjacent **Balnowlart Hill**.

Martin Glen cup-markings
NS 228 670

This is a smooth-topped rock at 222m OD, precisely at **NS 2285 6703**, near the confluence of the Skelmorlie Water and the Martin Glen Water. There may be as many as eleven single cup marks, some deeper than others, in two groups. The site is perhaps 400m north-west of the Roman fortlet at **Outerwards**. This area is in the remote uplands of north Ayrshire above Skelmorlie, and may best be reached by following the hillroad (unlisted) 7km north-east from Largs along the Noddsdale Water to **Outerwards**.

Martnaham   NS 395 174

Martnaham is one of the most mysterious places in Kyle Regis. What the name means no one knows. In a parish document of 1700 (a minute of session) the name appears as 'Mertineton', but Martnaham is the more regular form. It looks more Anglian than Gaelic or Cumbrian, and Anglian names are known in the locality, but the 'na' might be Gaelic, and this is not the only name in Ayrshire ending in '-ham' or '-hame' that is not what it seems (e.g. Cuninghame). St Martin of Tours educated St Ninian, but we cannot presume any connection. There is a dearth of documentation about the infeftments in King's Kyle and we have little information about the beginnings (land grants, grants of barony etc.) of many of the lands in the territory, but I think we can assume that Martnaham was early.

At any rate Martnaham Loch is intensely beautiful, surrounded by fields and dense woods. Just to the north of a disused railway line a small thickly wooded promontory juts into the loch from its southern shore. On this peninsula are to be found a causeway and the vestigial traces of a stone building, Martnaham Castle. It has been tentatively dated to the sixteenth century[195] but it would be more cautious not to speculate on a date at all. Salter's plan[196] suggests it was part of a chain of (totally obliterated) fortalices south of the River Ayr including Drongan and Auchencloigh stretching east – possibly indicating either a first line of advance in colonising the king's new territory or a second line of defence internal to the Ayr system.

Mauchline Grange   NS 497 272

The early history of Mauchline is very obscure. Melrose Abbey may have settled a colony of Cistercians here, perhaps at the instance of David I. Walter fitz Alan the first Steward and Lord of Kyle Stewart made a grant of the lands of Mauchline to Melrose before 1177, when the grant was (re)confirmed at the instance of Alan fitz Walter the second Steward, but it seems unlikely that either of these early Stewards founded a monastic cell here; it is more likely that Melrose Abbey itself did that. An extensive tract of land around the head waters of the Water of Ayr was given over to the monks, as well as rights and privileges right down to fishings at the mouth of the river. The wide landward tract was used for grazing sheep and similar purposes; it was extended southward to Cairn Table and the borders of Ayrshire (Kyle Stewart); the peculiar earthwork sometimes called **Dornal Motte** on the north bank of the Glenmuir Water may have had something to do with this. Mauchline town developed round the grange of the estate, which included offices, granaries, barns, a hospice and a chapel, which later became the parish church.

'Mauchline Castle' or 'Abbot Hunter's Tower' as it is sometimes called, right in the centre of Mauchline, is not really a defensive installation, but rather an administrative headquarters. This building, which has been extensively altered over the centuries, is still in reasonable repair, although it has been found necessary to bolt the structure together with iron clamps. The tower has two vaulted cellars in the basement, a ground-floor room and a first-floor hall, as well as an attic. A roof boss in the hall displays the arms of Abbot Andrew Hunter of Melrose (*c.* 1444–71). It is not thought likely that the tower was used to accommodate any monastic community that may have been settled in Mauchline. It is more probable that traces of the monastic buildings were removed during site levelling in the eighteenth century.

Mauchline Covenanters' memorials and gravestone   NS 496 273

Memorial on Loan Green, next to primary school, to five Covenanters hanged 6 May 1685 after raid on Ducat Tower, **Newmilns**. Also tombstone in Mauchline Churchyard to James Smith, died probably of wounds in 1685 (stone inscription says 1684, in error). See **Galston, Hillend Farm** and pp. 100–2 for further information.

Mauchline Church has a Covenanting flag.

Mauchline Moor   NS 497 263

This was the scene of a brief engagement in 1648 between Middleton's forces and early Covenanters who opposed 'The Engagement', a plan to rescue King Charles I from captivity.

Maxwellston Hill Fort   NX 259 989

Maxwellston Hill (314m OD) is the western summit of Hadyard (324m OD). The fort is marked out by two ramparts. They do not cover the steep north-west side, which does not require a defensive rampart.

This fort looks as if it was never quite completed. It is reputed to have been used by Robert the Bruce during his guerrilla campaign against the English in 1307.

Maybole Castle   NS 301 100

According to Lawson and others there used to be no less than twenty-eight fortified houses in Maybole. If so, the place must have been rather like

Fig. 21. Maybole Castle, from the south-west.

some of the hill-towns in Italy of the high Renaissance, where hired bravos skulked at every turning and it was as much as a man's life was worth to stir out of his own door without a large escort armed to the teeth. The only castle now remaining complete in the town is Maybole Castle, fronting the High Street, a beautiful example of an L-plan tower-house of (probably) the early seventeenth century, with four storeys, a garret, large corbelled-out turrets and a magnificent oriel window high above the street. The main block has a vaulted basement and the great hall, as usual, on the first floor. The stair wing projects to the south-west. The interior wood panelling is largely original and the effect is of a cosy town residence. It is now used as an estate office by the Marquis of Ailsa, and low wings were added in the nineteenth century to convert the building into a suitable residence for the estate factor.

Maybole Collegiate Church NS 301 098

In 1371, the year of the accession of King Robert II to the throne, a chapel dedicated to the Blessed Virgin Mary was established near the parish church of Maybole by 'Sir John Kenedy dominus de Dunoure', the real founder of the modern Kennedy dynasty in Ayrshire. Some time afterwards (2 February 1382?) the same man set up a college of secular canons to pray for souls. It was the scene of an act of defiance at Easter 1563, when mass – the celebration of which had been a capital offence since 1561 – was said and sung in the presence of 300 armed Kennedy retainers. The remnants of the building still display a rich arched doorway with three orders and dogtooth ornamentation as well as two double-light windows, and a single narrow window with a piscina.

Maybole Tolbooth NS 300 098

The only other visible example of a survivor of the twenty-seven or twenty-eight fortified houses once embellishing Maybole is the Tolbooth or Town Hall, converted in 1887 from the town house of the Lairds of Blairquhan. The most obviously antique feature of this building is the stair-tower, which

Fig. 22. Maybole Tolbooth, from the north-east.

juts out into the High Street and is surmounted by a pyramid. A clock used to be situated in the tower itself below the belfry and above the continuous corbelling, but it has now been repositioned in the pyramid itself, although the square niche in which it used to lodge is still visible.

Meikle Auchingibbert   NS 592 194

See **Stone Park (Wee Auchingibbert)**

Millmoan Hill cairn   NX 088 743

Between Millmoan and the adjacent Muillbane, on the edge of the 229m contour shelf, there is a much-robbed cairn. Muillbane and Millmoan are two summits of the same hill extending south-eastward from Glen App between the Burn of the Dupin and the Drumahallan Burn.

Minnivey: Scottish Industrial Railway Centre   NS 462 074

This is a transport museum incorporating working steam locomotives preserved after the collapse of the mining industry at Minnivey Colliery and elsewhere. It is 2km north-west of **Dalmellington** close to the A713 and the River Doon.

Monk Castle   NS 291 473

The ruined Monk Castle, north of Kilwinning, is hidden by woods from the railway and from the A737. The present small structure is a T-plan block of the late sixteenth century. There must have been at least one earlier building on the site, i.e. before 1536, when records relating to it start. The whole estate belonged to Kilwinning Abbey, whose abbot used it as a country residence. Later James, Duke of Chatelherault, obtained it and gave it to his son, who had become Commendator of Paisley Abbey; hence, perhaps, the three grotesque sculptures over the principal doorway, two at least of which appear to be mitred.

Monkredding House   NS 323 454

This small and pretty fortified house is on land acquired from Kilwinning Abbey in 1532. The tower is dated 1602 and the extension is dated 1638. The whole mansion, of which the foregoing parts form the west wing, was built by the Cuninghame family (of Clonbeith) in 1698. The house is still occupied.

Monkton, Old Parish Church   NS 358 276

St Cuthbert's Church is now a roofless ruin, of which the earliest part, a magnificent doorway in the south wall, is thirteenth-century in date. It

Fig. 23. Monk Castle. Principal doorway with grotesque carvings above.

has been subject to repeated alterations, including the truncation of the main building at the east end and the addition of an aisle to the north in the seventeenth century, when the interior was also remodelled and lofts (galleries) were added at both ends. The parish was united with Prestwick after the Reformation. This building was abandoned in 1837 and allowed to fall into decay.

Monkwood Mains Dun   NS 337 139

A small circular dun is situated on the summit of Stewart's Craig on the north bank of a near-loop in the River Doon. Facing-stones are to be seen to the north-west of the structure. It is 600m south-east of Monkwood Mains farm at Minishant.

Montfode Castle   NS 226 441

The tiny fragment representing Montfode Castle rises in solitary desolation out of a field – one single round tower perhaps 7m high, with a piece of wall extending in mid-air to the west. No trace of any other masonry is to be seen. The tower has a door frame towards the east. There are slits at various levels in the wall of the tower, and a gun-loop near ground level. It appears to be of the late sixteenth century, probably part of a Z-plan building, and belonged to the Montgomery family. In 1604–8 Timothy Pont said that it was 'a pretty duelling' owned by Hugh Monfodd.

Montfode Castle is about 1km north-west of Ardrossan, east of the railway line on a minor road. **Montfode Mount (NS 226 437)** is about 500m south of the castle on the other side of the railway, even nearer to Ardrossan. This is often taken to be the original motte of Montfode. It is oval, rising from the bank of the Montfode Burn. There are traces of artificial scarping. Air photography has shown up cropmarks of two ditches at some distance from the mount and another round its base. They do not appear on the surface. It has been suggested that they are not vestiges of a bailey and other defences for a Norman motte, but indications of the prehistoric origin of the mound, i.e. that it is an Iron Age fortified settlement or a fort. The question would have to be determined by further excavation.

Montgreenan Castle NS 342 452

Once 'an old strong dungeon' (Pont), Montgreenan Castle is now merely a vestigial collection of overgrown rubble. It was erected above a curve of the Lugton Water at the northernmost point of the modern Montgreenan estate. There may have been a courtyard and a wall with at least one small tower. A fine early nineteenth-century mansion, formerly the residence of Lord Weir but recently a hotel, stands about 1km away in the Montgreenan woods (NS 344 443): side road west of A736 at Torranyard.

Mote Knowe Dun NS 298 001

See **Kilkerran: Mote Knowe**

Muirkirk Covenanter's grave NS 700 278

Tombstone in village churchyard to John Smith, Covenanter, shot February 1685. Muirkirk is on the A70 in the east of Ayrshire.

Nether Auchendrayne Tower NS 337 166

The old tower, which has been added to, is dated 1698. The entire structure, now modernised, has recently been in use as an old people's home. It lies on the left bank of the River Doon, about 2km south of Alloway. Some scholars have thought that the name 'Nether Auchendrayne' should rather be applied to **Brigend Castle,** which is less than 1km to the north, also overlooking the Doon, but this is not confirmed.

Nether Whitehaugh   NS 616 290

There appears to have been a tower-house, now at one corner of an equally ruined farmyard, in this remote steading 7km west of Muirkirk near the head of the Whitehaugh Water. It is merely a pile of rubble. Access may be had from B743 at Garpel.

New Cumnock: Black Bog Castle   NS 617 138

A castle stood on a knoll near the north end of New Cumnock village. It was mentioned in 1580 and again in 1650. Its stones have been entirely removed, although a defensive moat can still be traced. Whether a motte stood on the knoll before the stone-built castle is an open question. The family possessing the property (before 1300) were the Dunbars.

New Cumnock Parish Church   NS 617 137

The Old Church, now a roofless ruin, was erected in 1657 or 1659 (which date appears on the building) after New Cumnock was erected into a separate parish in 1650. The building is rectangular, with a transept to the north, making it T-plan in shape. The windows in the gables are mullioned.

Newark Castle   NS 322 173

The visitor to Ayr can see from the Promenade a fine castellated structure on the north-east slope of the Green Carrick overlooking the town. This is the New Wark of Bargany, built, despite its name, originally in the sixteenth century but added to throughout the centuries in a variety of styles. The first building, founded on a rocky outcrop, was a high, squarish tower of four storeys, a garret and battlements. The ground floor is vaulted and the great hall is on the first floor. Below ground level there is a chamber in the rock known as the Gun Room. This underlies the seventeenth-century extension of the tower, equivalent in height, with access gained from the original spiral staircase in the old part. Another two extensions took place, a good Victorian Scottish Baronial work, in effect a new mansion (unfortunately sweeping away a characteristic outside staircase and satellite structures), and a final, Edwardian addition.

Newark was a Kennedy house, in fact a northern outpost of Carrick looking across the Doon to Ayr, the *caput* of Kyle Regis, but although still occuped it is no longer in the possession of the Kennedy family. It is not open to the public.

Newmilns Castle ('The Ducat Tower')   NS 536 373

In the centre of Newmilns, a small town in the Darvel Valley north of the River Irvine, stands a small but still strong tower, recently rendered wind-

and water-tight by the Strathclyde Building Preservation Trust. It is now called Newmilns Tower or Castle, but in early times it was known as 'The Ducat Tower'. This was not because of any association with the former Venetian currency. The word 'ducat' is the Gaelic *Dhu Chat*, 'dark wood', and in fact 'Blackwood' is a personal and place-name in the neighbourhood to this day.

The tower-house, built probably between 1533 and 1537 for Hugh Campbell of Loudoun, has three storeys below the parapet and a garret storey above. All floors are reached by a single wheel staircase. The corbelling under the parapet is continuous, with open bartizans at each angle. Unusually, there are string courses between the floors, and the building stands on a base with shallow foundations. There is a panel over the doorway but no coat-of-arms or other device within it.

The Loudoun Arms, an elegant eighteenth-century building serving as an inn, has now been demolished, exposing to view the tower, which it used to mask from Main Street.

Fig. 24. Newmilns Castle (The Ducat Tower). View from the south-east.

Newmilns Covenanting memorials and gravestones   NS 535 374

Several Covenanting tombstones and memorials in the parish churchyard, to (1) John Gebbie, shot in Battle of Drumclog 1 June 1679; (2) John Morton, also shot at Drumclog; (3) John Nisbet of Hardhill, hanged in Edinburgh 4 December 1685; (4) late collective memorial to Matthew Paton (executed after Rullion Green 19 December 1666), David Findlay (shot at Newmilns 1666), James Wood (taken at Bothwell Brig and executed at Magus Muir 25 November 1679 in revenge for the assassination of Archbishop Sharp), John Nisbet in Glen, hanged at Kilmarnock 14 April 1683 (See also **Kilmarnock**), and James Nisbet, hanged in Glasgow 11 June 1684.

Memorial on precinct wall of Newmilns Castle to John Law, shot during a rescue of prisoners in 1685. (Part of the inscription is reproduced on a tablet on the church wall.) For more information about all of the above and associated inscriptions at **Mauchline, Galston, Priesthill** and **Hillend,** see sites named and p. 100–2.

Newton-upon-Ayr cross   NS 337 222

There was a market cross in the burgh of Newton upon Ayr at the end of the sixteenth century. The present version, a weather-worn chamfered pillar with a ball finial, was erected in 1778, according to the inscription round the capital. This originally stood in the middle of Main Street opposite the present Newton Steeple (all that remains of the parish church and Town House). It was moved to its present site at the north end of the (Ayr) New Brig before 1847.

Ochiltree Castle   NS 499 232

This castle and its associated village (2km further south on the banks of the Lugar) should not be confused with the well preserved Ochiltree Castle south-west of Linlithgow in West Lothian. The Ayrshire Ochiltree Castle has been completely demolished. There is, however, a large mound on the bank of the Lugar River at this point, perhaps the original motte or even an Iron Age fort or dun.

Old Dailly, Old Parish Church   NX 225 993

The first mention of the church dedicated to St Michael of Dalmaolkeran is in 1236, but the earliest remaining architectural feature of this ruined and roofless building is the built-up south doorway, where the voussoirs of the archway may indicate a fourteenth century date. Most of the other features of the church are sixteenth- or seventeenth-century, including the windows and the internal burial vault for which the north end of the church has been blocked off. The church is a single rectangular chamber now open to the air.

The gables are still erect, each with its own belfry. This church was originally granted to Paisley Abbey but transferred to **Crossraguel** after 1244. It was abandoned in 1696 in favour of the church in the new village of Dailly to the east.

The site, on a circular 'platform' nearly surrounded by gracious trees, is of great beauty.

Old Dailly Covenanting memorials   NX 225 993

Old Dailly churchyard has two memorials, commemorating altogether five martyrs and one historian. (1) John Semple, shot 1685, and Thomas McClorgan, also shot 1685. (2) George Martin, hanged Edinburgh 22 February 1684, and two anonymous Covenanters, one from Killoup and one from Black Clauchrie, possibly shot 1685 (one reputed to be buried in Old Dailly but grave unidentified); and John Stevenson of Camregan, a Covenanter and historian. Old Dailly is on an unlisted road 4km east of Girvan.

Old Kirkcudbright of Innertig   NX 116 839

The church of St Cuthbert on the promontory between the River Stinchar and the Water of Tig at their confluence was the parish church of what is now the Ballantrae area: it was subject to the presbytery of Stranraer, but the tithes of the parsonage were granted by the Earl of Carrick in 1275 to Crossraguel Abbey and the other profits of the church went to the Archbishop of Glasgow. The original church became ruinous and was replaced in 1604 by Thomas Kennedy of Bargany with the church of which the Kennedy Aisle in Ballantrae is the sole remaining part. The remains at Innertig consist mostly of turf-covered footings. The B7044 runs past the confluence on the north side, but access may be gained (with permission) by taking the first unlisted road east from the A77 south of Ballantrae and crossing the Tig at Heronsford 5km east of Ballantrae.

Outerwards Roman Fortlet   NS 231 666

High above Skelmorlie, in one of the more remote corners of the mountainous north of Ayrshire, a Roman fortlet was excavated in 1970. Before excavation it had been seen to consist of an oblong enclosure, with a turf rampart, a berm and an external ditch. The foundations of gateways and timber buildings were discovered. There appear to have been two periods of occupation, both Antonine, and the fort appears to have been deliberately destroyed, perhaps, like the Loudoun Hill fort, at the time of the withdrawal from the Antonine Wall *c.*180. This fortlet may have been an observation post, with extensive views all over the Clyde estuary from Ailsa Craig to

Cowal, and may have been connected with the western end of the wall at Bishopton through another similar fortlet near Greenock, on Lurg Moor (**NS 295 737**). Communications now as then lead from Lurg Moor up past Loch Thom and Rottenburn, then down along the Noddsdale Water past Outerwards and ultimately to the Largs area.

Penderry Hill cairn   NX 064 751

This cairn stands at the summit of Penderry Hill (309m OD). A triangulation pillar has been erected on top of it. Penderry Hill is one of the series of high hills, running from north-east to south-west, that form the steep western wall of Glen App. Nearly every one of these hills has a cairn on top.

Penkill Castle   NX 231 985

As the B734 pushes over the hills from Barr down into the valley of the Water of Girvan, it passes the interesting mansion of Penkill, restored and altered in the nineteenth century after becoming an almost complete ruin. Spencer Boyd, a representative of the original Penkill (and Trochraigue) family, had the building converted from the traditional square tower-house with two pepperpot turrets to a pleasingly inauthentic 'High-Romantic' Victorian design centred on a massive stair-tower with an oversized, battlemented turret-crown. A gable dated 1628, however, is still visible, as are other older features.

Pennyvenie ring-cairn   NS 494 072

This area on the southward-facing slopes of Benbeoch, dotted with disused mine-shafts and 'ingaun ees', was being surveyed in 1997 in connection with a proposed open-cast coal mine when a ring-cairn was discovered and measures taken for its protection. Its date is thought to be late Neolithic or early Bronze Age, i.e. about 2500 BC. The site, which is probably inaccessible now, is a little more than 1km north-east of Dalmellington.

Perceton Parish Church   NS 351 405

Perceton Parish Church is first mentioned in 1468 and was probably allowed to fall into ruin soon after union with Dreghorn parish in 1668. Like other parish churches in the neighbourhood it was a tributary of **Kilwinning Abbey**. Little is known of this parish. The church ruins stand on high ground. The east gable is the tallest survivor. A doorway in the south wall is round-headed. There is a burial vault to the north, perhaps of the seventeenth century. This has a damaged twin-light window with mullions.

Pinmore Viaduct   NX 201 912

This viaduct, another massive yet graceful achievement of the early railway age, crosses the A714 three times in 400m. It was built in 1876 and is still in use to carry the Girvan–Stranraer line.

Pinwherry Castle   NX 197 867

Pinwherry Castle is now so overgrown and obscure that it is hard to make out among the trees that surround it. It is an L-plan five-storey sixteenth-century ruin, with a doorway in the re-entrant angle. The spiral stair in the wing goes up to the first floor, and the higher storeys are reached by a stair in a square corbelled-out turret from the first floor, where, as in most castles of this kind, the great hall is located. The parapet was flush with the wall, and there were two angle turrets, probably with conical roofs. There was a garret storey with tall crow-stepped gables. A barmkin may have existed to the north. It was originally a Kennedy castle.

Pinwherry Castle is situated just at the confluence of the Stinchar and the Duisk Rivers, beside the A714 and the railway.

Polcardoch Cairn   NX 118 842

See **Colmonell**

Portincross, Auld Hill: motte castle   NS 178 491

High above **Portincross Castle**, in the south-western quadrant of the Hunterston Peninsula, stands a steep ridge called Auld Hill. On its top are the ruins of what until recently was assumed to be an Iron Age fort with a secondary dun (*cf.* **Dow Hill, Girvan**). Excavation has now shown the remains to be those of a motte-and-bailey castle of the twelfth and thirteenth centuries. The previous theory was that the dun had been to the south of the site, separated from the Iron Age fort by ditching: the 'dun' has now been shown to be the remains of the motte, which was separated from the bailey by two rock-cut ditches. The original castle on the mound was wooden. Further excavation has demonstrated that the simple timber building was followed by two phases of stone construction, the first a hall-house and the second a larger building perhaps dating from the fourteenth century. Other phases of construction may have been intercalated, and there is also undoubted evidence of an earlier phase than the motte, probably of an Iron Age fort.[197]

Portincross Castle   NS 175 489

Turning west off the A78 at Seamill, the driver follows the B7048 along the south coast of the Hunterston Peninsula to Farland Head and north to a

Fig. 25. Portincross Castle, from the north-east.

very small coastal settlement called Portincross, opposite the south end of the Little Cumbrae. Just north of Portincross is a small but impressive fourteenth-century keep of three storeys and a garret with no angle turrets. An added wing of four storeys is on the same axis as the main block, not at right angles as is usual with L-plan buildings. This arrangement is required by the shape of the site. The castle seems to balance on the waves, so low is its small rocky platform at the very verge of the sea. (*Cf.* **(Little) Cumbrae Castle**.) The hall is as usual on the first floor, and there were apparently two kitchens, one in the first floor and one in the basement, probably for the convenience of royal guests: in particular Robert II and Robert III used the castle as a stop-over on their way from Dundonald Castle to their retreat at Rothesay.

The earliest castle on the site was held by the Rosses of **Tarbet** but after the Wars of Independence at the beginning of the fourteenth century the lands were given to the Boyds of Kilmarnock by Robert the Bruce. It is now partially ruinous and has been uninhabited since 1735, when, after it was deroofed in a storm, the Boyds let it pass to the family of Fullerton of Overton.

Note that the spelling of the name 'Portincross' (as opposed to the alternative 'Portencross') may possibly indicate a Ross thanage ('Port-tinc-Ross').[198]

Preceptory of Our Lady Kirk of Kyle NS 386 266

This may have been the headquarters of a 'quasi-collegiate group of priests' who serviced the chapel here. Today all that is to be seen is one two-storey turret built into the wall of the garden of Ladykirk House. At one side there is a stair-tower, and the main tower has had a small turret with a low spire added. It was reputedly 'founded' in 1446 by John Blair, but it is also reported more reliably that King Robert II, while Lord of Kyle Stewart, married Elizabeth Mure of Rowallan in this chapel in 1347.

Prestwick Burgh of Barony NS 352 262

The village now known as Monkton was the original Prestwick; the administrative centre (a 'demesne burgh') for Kyle Stewart to the south was known as Prestwickburgh. When Walter fitz Alan the first Steward granted the churches and possessions of both Prestwick and Prestwickburgh to Paisley Abbey, Prestwick became known gradually as Monkton and Prestwickburgh was contracted to Prestwick. Prestwick-Monkton's church was dedicated to St Cuthbert and Prestwickburgh-Prestwick's church was dedicated to St Nicholas. (See **Monkton** and **Prestwick Old Parish Churches**.)

This burgh, which lies between Irvine and Ayr, never enjoyed the same success as either. The establishment of Newton-on-Ayr as a burgh on the north bank of the River Ayr (i.e. in Kyle Stewart) was a further attempt by the Steward to rival the royal burgh, but Newton and Prestwick failed perhaps as much because of lack of suitable harbour facilities as because of lack of royal patronage. The position of Prestwick at the convergence of trade routes – from Ayr, from the interior of Kyle Stewart (Dundonald, Symington, Riccarton and the east) and from the north – made it a natural choice for a trading post, but the Pow Burn is not the same as the Waters of Ayr or Irvine. Besides, armed protection was not immediately at hand but at Dundonald some distance to the north, where fitz Alan founded his military *caput* in the twelfth century.

The foundation of the burgh must have taken place after 1136, when fitz Alan came to Scotland at the invitation of David I and before 1173, when he refers in a document to 'my burgh of Prestwick'. Prestwick's acquisition of burghal status may have been more than thirty years before that of Ayr, but the original charter, if there was one, has not survived.

Like those of Ayr and Irvine, the building plan of Prestwick burgh crystallised round a market-place. A church was planted on a small mound to the north-west of the market cross, and the two were connected by a short street, on either side of which burgage plots – often called 'places', never 'tofts' as in other burghs (except in the 1600 charter) – were marked out for settlement by incoming prospective burgesses. The street, which

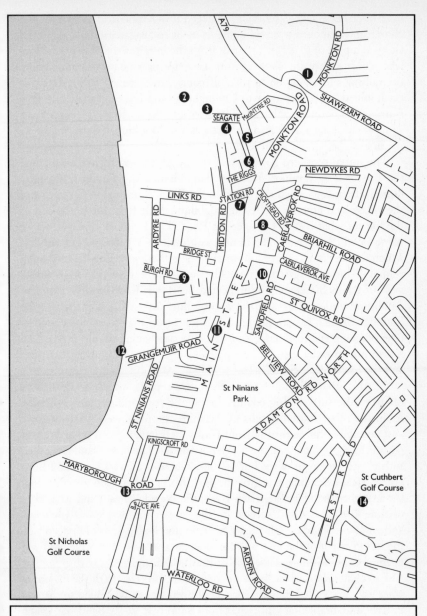

1. Possible site of North-eastern Burgh Port; part of 'indale'
2. Pow Burn
3. Seagate and road to Irvine
4. Prestwick Old Church (St Nicholas)
5. Kirk or King's Street
6. Town House (1844)
7. Prestwick Cross
8. Puddock Sheugh
9. Burgh Road (perhaps south-west limit of burgh)
10. Smiddy Raw (Boyd Street)
11. Approximate site of Sandgate Port
12. Mouth of Puddock Sheugh
13. Kingcase (Bruce's Well; ?St Ninian's hospital/chapel)
14. Part of 'outdale'

Street Map of Prestwick

may have been called the King's Street (now Kirk Street), ran past the church and branched west, changing its name to Seagate, and issuing to the shore at a port or gateway. This exit from the burgh is the only one of four whose position we are relatively sure of – a tiny passage now running under the railway and giving on to the golf-course. In the early burgh days this track joined a main pathway to Cuninghame and Irvine, crossing the Pow Burn, which defined the burgh of Prestwick to the north. Another port was somewhere along a track leading north-east to Monkton, roughly following the line of the present main road.

The initial southern boundary of the burgh may well have been along the line of a very minor streamlet denominated the Puddock Sheugh – literally 'frog ditch' – which started in the Black Burn region to the east of the village and entered the sea at an oblique angle from the north-east at the foot of what is now Grangemuir Road. The Puddock Sheugh, whose name is still known locally, is now confined in a subterranean conduit which for part of its course follows the line of Ladykirk Road, a very small vennel giving on to Main Street. The southern limit of the burgh to the west of Main Street may be indicated by Burgh Road, which comes to an abrupt stop nowadays at the railway line. Just at the point where the Puddock Sheuch crosses the present Main Street may have stood another port blocking the road, later known as the Sandgate, leading to Ayr. The fourth port may have stood on a pathway leading to St Quivox (Sanchar) and the east of Kyle Stewart.

All this gradually filled up with burgage plots, which were ditched off from the surrounding countryside at the rear, and perhaps palisaded. As in the other coastal burghs of Ayrshire, the plots were sandy, meagre and unsuitable for cultivation, and had to be supplemented by arable and pasture land often outwith the burgh boundaries. The nearer land was called 'indale' – to the north of the burgh, round about the Orangefield and Burn Crook area, extending north of the Pow Burn. Other such areas were in the neighbourhood of the Black Burn, the Newdykehead, and what later became known as Caerlaverock. To the east of the burgh was what was known as the 'outdale', also used for cropping and pasture. Land outside the burgh north of the Pow and south as far as the border of Newton was deemed to be 'within the liberties' of Prestwick Burgh.

Later extensions of the 'built-up' area to the south led to the laying out of what was then called Smiddy Raw, now Boyd Street, which led to the east of Kyle, and, branching south-west from Smiddy Raw, the Sandgate, which ran at least as far at the present Grangemuir Road. Both streets would have terminated in gateways.

Beyond the Sandgate, between the present Ayr Road and the sea, lay the possibly very ancient St Ninian's Chapel and hospital at **Kingcase**. The chapel is merely vestigial fragments, the traces of a rectangular building with thick stone walls. The hospital no doubt consisted of wooden huts, of which all trace has vanished, although graves of twenty-four 'lepers' are said to have been uncovered in the course of excavations before 1913. The well is circular (about 20m from the building) and may be reached by a flight of steps going down about 1m below ground level. The hospital is supposed to have been founded by Robert the Bruce (King Robert I, 1306–29) after his cure from leprosy, but indications are that it is very much older, and that Robert may have given money to an existing institution after having been cured by the restorative properties of the well.

The market cross at Prestwick has an early mention in 1473, when it was broken – probably being made of wood – by one Willi Jurdane, who was prosecuted in the burgh court for the offence.[199] The present version, dated 1777, is a chamfered stone pillar with a ball finial. It now stands some 100m south of the original position at the convergence of Main Street, Station Road, Monkton Road, Alexandra Avenue and Crofthead Road. The opening of Kirk Street is just round the corner to the north, neighbouring the 1844 Town House.

Prestwick never became a trading centre, instead developing as an agricultural village. Even less than Irvine, it did not or was not able to exploit industrial resources in its hinterland fully. However, for many centuries it retained its status as head burgh and administrative centre of Kyle Stewart. Latterly, with the coming of steam transport, Prestwick became a favoured spot for retirement, golf and tourism. It is now merely a pretty section of the Ayr conurbation. This stretches from Doonfoot (and now Greenan) in the south to Barassie in the north, interrupted only by the vast tract of Prestwick Airport, once reputedly the most productive corn land in Ayrshire, extending between the Pow Burn and Monkton.

Prestwick Old Parish Church   NS 350 266

Situated high on a knoll to the north of Prestwick town, this church, now a gable-ended roofless ruin, was dedicated to St Nicholas, and it was granted, together with St Cuthbert's Church at **Monkton,** to Paisley Abbey before 1172 by Walter fitz Alan, the first Steward. This building, however, is probably no earlier than the thirteenth century, as suggested by two moulded capitals which have been built into an early alteration, the blocking of two windows. After the Reformation the parish was united with Monkton. This building continued in use until 1779.

Prestwick Airport   centred on NS 360 270

This large parcel of coastal territory between Prestwick Town and Monkton was, during the war years (1939–45) and for some time afterwards, a most important air facility, being a fog-free all-weather European terminal for transatlantic war flights. Thousands of personnel and transport and military aircraft arrived in Prestwick or were shuttled through to war theatres and bases from the United States and Canada. The constant drone of the air traffic reassured Ayrshire people of the strength and determination of the Allied military build-up before and during the European invasion. However, after the war Prestwick's history was chequered and it nearly succumbed to intense local competition, despite its technical advantages. It is currently (2003) run privately and its future appears to be fairly secure as it caters for charter flights.

Priesthill Covenanter's grave   NS 730 314

Isolated tomb of John Brown, the Christian Carrier, shot 1 May 1685 by John Graham of Claverhouse. The tomb is about 2km east of Priesthill Farm across open moorland just within the Ayrshire border. The farm can be reached by a track from the A73 north of Muirkirk.

Rig Hill, near Nith Lodge: burial site   NS 530 097

This site is probably no longer in existence, destroyed through deep ploughing and afforestation. It may have been situated just north of the highest point of Rig Hill (OD 347) at **NS 5307 0980**. It is known that there was an elliptical enclosure bounded by fifteen standing stones at or near this location. When the site was excavated in 1937, eight cremation burial pits were found, two with pygmy vessels and one, which had a collared cinerary urn inverted over it, was associated with a Scotsburn-group battle-axe. A kerb of packed boulders surrounded the enclosure. The site was later recognised as an enclosed cremation cemetery. The battle-axe, of the Intermediate-Developed variant, is now held in the collections of the National Museums of Scotland (NMS X.EP 57), currently in the Archaeological Department Study Collection, Leith. The site is now unrecognisable, and it cannot be identified in air photographs (flown in 1946).[200]

There are two Rig Hills in the neighbourhood: this one is on the west side of the B741, about 0.75km north of Nith Lodge, which is itself 5km north-west of Dalmellington.

Robertland Castle   NS 442 469

This is a Cuninghame property surviving only as a few stones not far from the existing Robertland House, which lies at the end of a driveway from the B769 north-east of Stewarton. In the gardens of the present mansion there is a stone dated 1590. David Cuninghame of Robertland was yet another participant in the murder of the Earl of Eglinton in 1586. David appears to have escaped the vengeance of the Montgomeries, but his castle was apparently burnt down by them that year.

Rowallan Castle   **NS 434 424, NS 432 426**

Unfortunately, Old Rowallan Castle, an outstanding building, is not open to the public at the moment (2003) and there is no information about a possible reopening.

There are two castles in these grounds, the earlier abandoned in the twentieth century when the second mansion was built. The first castle is highly interesting from the historical and architectural point of view. Its eastern façade has a central focus consisting of two large drum towers flanking an entrance doorway at the head of a steep flight of stairs. Visitors see why the stairs are so steep when they have walked through the entrance passageway to the courtyard beyond: it is at a higher level than the ground outside, because the castle has grown in a U-formation around the sides of a knoll, of which the courtyard is the level top. The southern and eastern buildings forming the U are lower by about one storey on the courtyard side than they are on the outside of the castle. On the western

Fig. 26. Rowallan Castle. Interior of private room.

side there is only a curtain wall, and on the northern side the remnants of a seventeenth-century building adjoin the oldest part of the complex, a ruined keep at the north-east corner.

The keep has recently (1999) been the subject of archaeological investigation following the clearance of a great deal of rubble that had fallen inward over the centuries. It was discovered that the mound on which the earliest stone building was constructed was itself partly artificial and partly natural, suggesting that it may have been an Iron Age fort or fortified settlement and/or a motte used by the first Norman settlers. The indications that this was at least a motte site are strengthened by the discovery of timber remains and post-holes below the level of the first stone buildings. Further discoveries included a burial site with cremated human remains dating back to the Bronze or Neolithic Age, within the south-east corner of the tower area.

*Above these remains there came a series of stone buildings, the first a hall house of massive stone build, dating to the mid twelfth century, i.e. to the time of the Norman take-over of the Cuninghame district of the old Strathclyde kingdom. Its existence is signalled by the presence of a characteristic scarcement or ledge (here at exterior ground level), above which the building is set back. Later a tower was built, founded on the remains of the hall house and dating probably from the time of the accession of the first Stewart monarch, Robert II, in 1371. He had previously been the Steward of Scotland based at **Dundonald** in Kyle Stewart, and had married Elizabeth Mure of Rowallan in 1347 in the **Preceptory of Our Lady Kirk of Kyle** near Prestwick. The Auld Toure at Rowallan, passing through various stages, probably had three storeys, of which only the undercroft (basement) and first-floor hall are traceable. From the sixteenth to the seventeenth century various improvements and enlargements of this building were undertaken, including the provision of a barrel vault. From the seventeenth century, use of the tower decreased with the developments of other parts of the complex, and after the eighteenth century it went into terminal decline and collapsed completely.*

Meanwhile, in 1562 or 1567, a building and improving owner had constructed the eastern and southern sides of the square, including a semi-subterranean kitchen suite whose windows, narrow loops with oylets, appear at ground-level on the south external face of the castle. The courtyard has a main entrance in the south range with stairs leading down to the kitchens and up to the main entertainment areas, of which the most important room must have been the one situated immediately over the entrance passage, with entry into the two drum towers. The building was a lavishly constructed palace, the most powerful elevation at the east front with the two towers and the entrance stairway. For several years now it has been under the guardianship of Historic Scotland, and is being gradually restored with a view to opening it to the public.

At the end of the nineteenth century the owners of the castle suddenly decided to abandon it and employed the architect Robert Lorimer to design an entirely new mansion about 400m to the north. In itself, this is a very impressive house, though not as large as the original plan.

Rowallan Castle, which stands on the Carmel Water about 3km north-east of Kilmaurs, may be reached on an unlisted road turning north from the B751 just before Meikle Mosside.

St Inan's Well (I)   NS 371 554

This holy well, a spring at the base of Lochlands Hill (adjacent to Cuff Hill), is now stone-lined and covered with flagstones. The water is piped to the roadside. Nearby is 'St Inan's Chair', a cleft in the hillside that may have been landscaped artificially. See also **Cuff Hill chambered cairn.**

St Inan's Well (II)   NS 322 385

See **St Mary's Well, Irvine**

St John's Tower, Ayr   NS 333 220

See **Ayr Royal Burgh (Kirk of St John)**

St Mary's Well, Dunlop   NS 407 503

About 1km to the north-west of Dunlop village, near Thougritstane farm, there is a spring from which baptismal water for Dunlop Kirk was recently still being drawn. It was associated with a vanished chapel dedicated to the Blessed Virgin Mary.

St Mary's Well, Irvine   NS 322 385

On the east bank of the River Irvine, about 100m from the **Old Parish Church, Irvine**; a well-head set into a wall overlooking the river and now sealed in concrete. There was probably a St Mary's Chapel near here. An inscription on a stone plaque reads 'St Inan's Well AD 839–1921'. The attribution to St Mary may possibly be the more recent.

St Ninian's Chapel   NS 346 247

See **Kingcase (Prestwick)**

St Quivox Parish Church   NS 375 240

Another name for this parish is West Sanquhar (also Senechar or Sanchar). The church was dedicated to Mo Choemoc, whose name also appears as St Kevoce, and who is reputed to have died in 636. It was a rectory in 1212. In 1229 Walter II fitz Alan, the third Steward, granted it to the Dalmilling convent, and when this venture collapsed in 1238, regranted it to Paisley Abbey, with whom it remained until the Reformation. There may well be medieval work incorporated in the present building, much of which, however, appears to be of the seventeenth century. It is gable ended and rectangular on plan, 18.85m by 5.9m within walls 1m thick. The date 1508 appears on the building. The Oswald burial aisle was erected in 1767.

Sallochan Cairn
NX 121 844

See **Colmonell**

Saltcoats: North Ayrshire Museum, Kirkgate
NS 245 415

This museum, in the former (eighteenth-century) parish church, has a good local collection including many prehistoric finds.

Saugh Hill: cairns and barrow
(1) NX 212 973, (2) NX 207 971, (3) NX 212 971

Saugh Hill is 2km east of Girvan. (1) This is one of a series of hill-top cairns in and south of the Girvan area. Saugh Hill is 293m OD and a triangulation pillar stands on top of the robbed cairn. (2) The second cairn is lower down, on the western spur of the hill 0.5km south-west of the first cairn. It is no more than a rim of cairn material, with a central mound. (3) This mound is likely to be a barrow, constructed more of earth than of stones. It is situated on the crest of the hill about 300m south of the summit cairn.

Seamill Fort, West Kilbride
NS 203 471

This coastal fort is now almost indistinguishable from the garden into which it has been moulded. Originally it occupied the tongue of land extending from the south bank of the Kilbride Burn at the mouth of its ravine. There was a mound with an oval summit round which were ramparts, with a further large rampart cutting off the eastern approach along the narrow neck of land. The whole structure was massively strong. The ramparts are still in situ on the north-east and south-east sides, and there is a scarp on the west. The whole of the interior is now covered by the lawn of a private garden and has been heavily landscaped.

Artefacts unearthed during the initial nineteenth-century excavations include objects and implements of stone, bone and horn, a hammer-stone, a stone ball, and a thick bronze ring.

The A78 now runs to the west of the fort, which lies between Seamill and West Kilbride.

Skeldon Castle NS 377 134

Skeldon Castle, the remains of which have been built into a cottage near the present Skeldon House, on a loop bend on the north bank of the River Doon, was a possession of the Craufurd family from the earliest times, but no grant of barony or anything of that sort has survived.

Skelmorlie Castle NS 195 658

The present castle, the northernmost in Ayrshire, overlooking the Water where it enters Wemyss Bay, seems to have been first built in stone no later than 1502. The existing stone tower-house was altered about 1600, when corbelling and parapets were removed and angle turrets, later roofed in, were provided. The first floor contains both great hall and kitchen which, however, is really no more than a recess at one end of the hall beneath an impressive chimney-stack. (*Cf.* **Law**, **Cumbrae** and **Fairlie**, with which this castle forms a group.) The most substantial early addition is a still surviving seventeenth-century range built for Sir Robert Montgomerie. In the nineteenth century further additions were made, some of which were demolished in 1959 after a serious fire, which also damaged the tower itself; this, however, was restored, and the castle is still occupied.

The original Skelmorlie motte may be sited at **NS 213 660**, beside the Skelmorlie Water.[201] It is not very identifiable, but occupies a promontory on falling ground between the Skelmorlie Water and a tributary burn. It has a defensive rampart stretching between a river gorge and a steep scarp.

Skelmorlie Aisle NS 202 594

See **Largs, Skelmorlie Aisle**

Smyrton Hill cairn NX 112 797

Smyrton Hill is one of the north-east to south-west range of big hills that in its lower reach forms a west wall for Glen App. This is near the source of the Water of App, looking north-west to Glenapp Castle and beyond to Ballantrae. There does not seem to be a summit cairn here, but round the foot of the precipitous north-west slopes there is a collection of small cairns, at least eight in number.

Sorn Castle NS 548 269

This castle sits on the lip of a high cliff at the junction of two streams, the River Ayr and the Cleuch Burn; *cleuch*, here as elsewhere, means 'ravine'.

The oldest portion of this still-inhabited castle is the south-western quarter, a square tower of the mid fifteenth century, of three storeys and a garret. An additional block to the north-east was built on to the tower in about 1500, with the purpose of providing a great hall on the first floor. The parapet, distinctive corbels and bartizans of this extension (added also to the original tower) are very characteristic of that period and remind us of Fairlie and other north Ayrshire castles. The castle remained unaltered for 300 years, but in the late eighteenth century a new north-eastward extension was discreetly modelled upon Adam's style at Culzean, with fake turrets and arched corbelling. Further alterations in 1864 brought a not unpleasing Victorian Scottish Baronial flavour to the architecture. H.E. Clifford's twentieth-century porte-cochère is, however, out of proportion.

Sorn has the usual complicated family history, passing in 1406 from the Keiths of Galston to the Hamiltons of Cadzow, in 1585 to the Setons of Winton and 1680 to the Earl of Loudoun. An eighteenth-century Countess of Loudoun, a celebrated beauty and wit in her youth, lived at Sorn until she was nearly 100 years old and carried out extensive estate works including tree-planting and reclamation.

Access to Sorn Castle is from B743 west of Sorn village.

Sorn Covenanting memorials   NS 550 266

Two memorial inscriptions on east wall of parish church to George Wood, the last and youngest (sixteen years old) victim of government persecution of Covenanters, shot during a dragnet operation in 1688 following the arrest of James Renwick. See p. 102. Sorn is on the B743 east of Mauchline.

Sorn, Merkland motte (Castle Hill)   NS 588 263

The promontory called Castle Hill carries an artificially scarped motte, circular and flat-topped, high above the River Ayr. The slopes descending to it are precipitous. A narrow dangerous causeway to the north-east forms an entrance. A smaller mound lies south of the main motte and is divided from it by a ditch. To the west lies a square bailey formed by a bank higher on the outside than the internal ground level. The nearest road is the B743 from Sorn to Muirkirk.

Sorn Old Bridge   NS 549 267

This pretty, twin-arched, hump-backed bridge stands at the west end of Sorn Village opposite Sorn Parish Church (on the other side of the B743). It spans the River Ayr just at a bend in its course. Built c.1710, it has two triangular cutwaters, one on each side, between the arches, which are nearly semi-circular.

Sourlie: animal remains   NS 343 414

In the general locality of this place, north-east of Irvine, remains of the prehistoric woolly rhinoceros have been found. The A736 runs past the site, between High Armsheugh and Lawthorn, not far from Perceton.

South Burnt Hill cairn   NS 256 650

During a survey for a windfarm in 1994 researchers discovered the small top part of what may be a larger cairn poking up from beneath the peat cover near the summit of South Burnt Hill (454m OD). This hill is in the remote upper part of north Ayrshire near the Renfrewshire border (Inverclyde). It is adjacent to the Duchal Moor.

Southannan Mains (Underbank): cup-marked rock   NS 212 535

In gorse behind Southannan Mains farmhouse are to be found three small rocky outcrops with respectively one, six and nine single cup marks. This is only 0.5km south of the cup-and-ring-marked rock and standing stone at **Diamond Hill (NS 213 539** and **215 539** respectively).

Stair Bridge   NS 437 234

Stair Bridge was built in 1745. It has three arches spanning the River Ayr. It is very narrow, and little bays in the parapet have been provided to allow the foot passenger to get out of the way of the gentlemen's coaches – and modern automobiles – as they rattle across. The approaches to the bridge on the B730 are very steep and winding on either side. At one side is the Stair coaching inn.

Stair House   NS 440 238

Some time in the sixteenth century an L-plan tower-house – not necessarily the first fortalice on the site – was built within the crook of a wide meander of the Water of Ayr. It was three storeys high, with a round tower on the external angle of the L and a square tower containing the ground-floor doorway in the re-entrant angle. About a century later extensions were built, one to the east and one to the south, each with a round tower at its end, the southern one only two storeys high and its tower correspondingly low. In spite of these accretions, the house is small and quaint, with sneck-harling covering the exterior. Some good examples of probably eighteenth-century panelling survive in the interior, and there are several interesting antique fireplaces, one from the seventeenth century.

The house, which is privately occupied, though not by the Stair family, was carefully and tastefully restored in the 1930s. The grouping of

Fig. 27. Stair House, from the south-west.

this typically complex building is very Scottish in profile, rather douce by comparison with more grandiloquent structures such as **Killochan** or **Rowallan**, but none the worse for that. It is one of the minor jewels of Scottish castle-building. The house is not open to the public but it is possible to approach the building directly along an unlisted road running north from the Stair Inn, which is adjacent to the **Stair Bridge** (1745) and to an old but still operative hone stone works just beyond.

Starling Knowe burnt mound (water heating)   NX 054 722

Starling Knowe is almost at the southern extremity of Ayrshire, not far from the mouth of the Water of App where it issues into Finnarts Bay and Loch Ryan. The burnt mound is situated comparatively high on a terrace on a cliff near a stream. It is crescent-shaped, 7.5m in diameter and 0.7m high. It has almost no turf cover, and the burnt stones are visible.[202]

Stonepark (Wee Auchingibbert) Covenanter's grave   NS 592 194

Tombstone of John MacGeachan, shot by dragoons in 1688 after rescue of Rev. David Houston, who was brain-injured during the operation. Stonepark is on private ground near Wee Auchengibbert.

Straiton Parish Church   NS 380 049

This is one of the oldest church buildings (in part) still in continuous use in Ayrshire. Although the church was rebuilt in 1758, the south aisle, in part dating from the fourteenth century, was retained. This transept had been built in the sixteenth century to accommodate a chantry founded in 1350 and was divided into a laird's burial vault and loft. The south gable has a sixteenth-century four-light window with cusped roundels and a gable above of four wide steps. Like other churches in Carrick, Straiton was initially granted by Duncan, Earl of Carrick to Paisley Abbey but, after a dispute about the independence of Crossraguel Abbey had been settled in 1244, it was transferred to the latter institution.

Straiton is south-east of Maybole at the junction between the B7045 and the B741.

Straiton Covenanter's gravestones   NS 380 049

Two tombstones in parish churchyard for Thomas McHaffie, shot 1686.

Struil Well   NX 251 929

See **Kirkdominae**

Sundrum Castle   NS 410 212

After the accession of King Robert II in 1371 Sir Duncan Wallace was granted the barony of Sundrum, having married Eleanor Bruce, Countess of Carrick. It was at this time, probably 1373, that Sundrum Castle was built or acquired and improved. A fourteenth-century tower still survives as the core of the existing mansion. It was rectangular, with a scarcement at the base of the house. There were at least three main storeys, all vaulted (including the basement), two probably divided for entresol floors. The great hall was on the first floor, where the main entrance was, reached by an outside staircase; a straight stair went down inside to the basement. A spiral staircase, of which there are only traces, rose right to the parapet level. This tower-house, minus its battlements and upper works, is incorporated in the east end of the massive modern building (begun around 1792). After the Wallaces, the castle was possessed by the Cathcarts and more recently (from the middle of the eighteenth century) by the Hamiltons.

The castle is built on a high cliff overlooking the Water of Coyle and its waterfall ('The Ness'), about 2km above the confluence with the River Ayr. The waterfall was used to provide the house with one of the earliest systems of electric lighting in Ayrshire. Recently the house was run as a hotel. A long drive runs north-east from the A70 at Corbieston.

About 0.5km north-east of the castle, at **NS 415 214**, there is a possible motte with a circular top situated high above the Water of Coyle on a steep scarp. Traces of ditching can be made out at the base.

Symington, Helenton Motte NS 393 311

Helenton Motte is now divided from Symington by the A77 Monkton–Kilmarnock road, to the east of which it stands. It is situated above the Pow Burn. The summit is nearly square. It is of varying height, probably because of mutilation. Ditch defences at the base are sparse and doubtful. On its top is a low mound, which may conceal the vestiges of a previously reported ruined building of some sort.

Symington Parish Church NS 384 314

This is another very old church building still in current use. (*Cf.* entry for **Straiton**.) Simon Loccard, after whom the village is named, held the territory of Walter fitz Alan the first Steward in 1165. A parson of Symington named Jordan is recorded in 1165.

The church was granted to the monastery/hospital at Fail, which was founded in 1252. It was extensively restored in 1919–20. The original building is twelfth- to thirteenth-century in date, gable-ended and thick-walled. The roof is raftered with open trusses. Three windows with semi-circular heads are framed in the gable by heavy hoodmoulds with dog-tooth ornaments. In the sill of a south-facing window sits the base-slab of an aumbry incorporating a piscina.

Tarbet NS 215 470

There are not even vestigial remains of the seat of the once mighty family of Ross of Tarbet, who controlled, among other fortresses, Portincross and Fairlie. They made the mistake of being on the wrong side in the Wars of Independence, and King Robert the Bruce redistributed their possessions among other families. The name of the castle, Tarbet, is confusingly spelt differently from the name of the hill on which it is situated, Tarbert Hill, just south of West Kilbride and Law Castle. The putative site is perhaps 200m from Meadowhead Farmhouse.

Tarbolton Bachelors' Club NS 431 271

Originally a club founded by Robert Burns the poet with some friends. Now a museum.

Tarbolton Motte NS 432 273

This probably twelfth-century motte-and-bailey castle may incorporate an additional ringwork. The motte occupies the middle of a promontory to the north of Tarbolton village, at the side of the B744. The steep sides of the promontory give the motte the appearance of being taller than it actually is.

At ground level the structure is circular, but the top surface is sub-circular. A ditch probably surrounded the base. The main bailey, which has been steeply scarped, stretches to the east of the motte along the top of the promontory. What may be a secondary bailey, or possibly an independent ringwork, less well defined, lies west of the motte.

Tarbolton Parish Church   NS 430 272

The present church building, on a mound in the centre if the village, is a typical eighteenth-century preaching box, not dissimilar to **Irvine Parish Church**. In 1338 John de Graham of Tarbolton granted the patronage of Tarbolton Church to Failford, but it appears to have gone with the manor of Tarbolton to the Stewarts of Darnley in 1361–2. In 1429 it was erected into a prebend of Glasgow, with which it remained until the Reformation.

Tarbolton is off the A758 between Ayr and Mauchline.

Tarbolton Covenanter's gravestone   NS 430 272

Tombstone in parish churchyard to William Shillilaw, shot probably July 1685.

The Taxing Stone   NX 062 709

See **Little Laight Hill**

Terringzean (Taringzean) Castle   NS 555 204

This fragment of a castle is probably among the earliest antiquities in the immediate Cumnock area. It stands on a steep bank on the south side of the Lugar within the grounds of Dumfries House just to the west of Holmhead. A later fortification appears to have been built over a demolished hall block. The surviving ruins, which include a tower, appear to indicate a massive walled enclosure, i.e. a 'castle of enceinte' like **Loch Doon Castle**. The earliest date associated with the main building is *c*.1380, i.e. after the accession of the first Stewart king, Robert II. Archaeological investigation might confirm a thirteenth-century date for the hall block, which might indicate an even earlier motte.

Terringzean Castle is found in the former pleasure-grounds of Dumfries House.

Thomaston Castle   NS 239 095

Although Thomaston was said to have been built for Thomas, Robert Bruce's nephew, recent probing has confirmed that the existing building at least was erected no earlier than 1500, which would agree with the reported

Fig. 28. Thomaston Castle. View from the south-west.

acquisition of the property by Thomas Correy in 1507. It is L-shaped with a long main block and a short wing. The garret storey has vanished, but there are three storeys beneath the parapet walk, which is supported by three lines of continuous corbelling. Open angle turrets were at all the corners. A square stair-tower rises against the re-entrant angle, but the entrance door is in the main block, facing out into the vanished courtyard: the only way into the castle itself was via an archway in the shorter of the two wings, which led into the courtyard.

Thomaston is now a farmyard ruin adjacent to the A719 south of **Culzean Castle.**

Tongue Cairn NX 154 862

See **Colmonell**

Trabboch Castle NS 458 221

This is a phantom castle – very difficult to find, consisting of two vestigial walls above a stream near Trabboch Farm. It seems to form part of a defensive chain running in an irregular diagonal across Kyle Regis and including **Stair, Auchencloigh** and perhaps **Drongan** and **Drumsuie**. All of these except Stair have been almost totally obliterated. The vestiges of Trabboch Castle may stand upon a motte.

Latterly Trabboch Village **(NS 438 219)** was a miner's row, now deserted.

Turnberry Castle   NS 196 072

This was the *caput* of Carrick, used as headquarters both by Robert the Bruce and by his father, who acquired it in 1271. A complete ruin now, it was an early castle of enceinte, i.e. having a formidable circuit of curtain walls like **Loch Doon Castle**. In this case the castle has been erected right on the seashore, incorporating wild and precipitous crags. Two inlets of the sea are bridged over by the wall, and provide a little haven for supply boats with direct access to the castle. There appears to have been a keep with some vaulting within the circuit of the walls, but only fragments remain. Robert the Bruce apparently demolished it himself after 1307 in order to deny its use to the English.

Turnberry Castle may be reached from Maidens village about 1km to the north-east. A lighthouse has been erected on the ruins.

Waistland Covenanting memorial   NS 664 129

Memorial to George Corson and John Hair, shot 1685. These were probably members of the party being pursued from Dalmellington, other members of which were shot at **Carsgailoch** and **Cumnock**. Waistland is about 3km east of Afton Bridgend (New Cumnock), on rising farmland bordering the A76.

Wallace's Stone   NS 332 165

This recumbent stone on Blairston Farm (near **Nether Auchendrane** above the west bank of the River Doon) is probably a fallen standing stone. The incised cross on one face has expanded terminals and a tapering shaft; its form suggests a tenth- to twelfth-century date i.e. at least one century earlier than the time of William Wallace.

Wallace Tower, Ayr: folly   NS 338 217

This costly confection, constructed in 1834 on a site now very awkward for traffic using Ayr High Street, has no connection with William Wallace, although it is adorned with a statue of that hero. It is built at the corner of Mill Street and High Street, where stood formerly one (? the older) of the two tolbooths of Ayr, which can be seen in Slezer's print of 1692. That tower can hardly have stood since the thirteenth century, when Wallace's still-living body was thrown onto a dunghill from some kind of building near there and resuscitated from some dreadful illness by his old nurse – according to Blind Harry. The present tower is occasionally used for meetings and functions of one sort or another, and is not an unhandsome structure.

Wardlaw Hill I: cairn   NS 687 225

This summit cairn on Wardlaw Hill (497m OD) is 3km to the west of
the pair at the top of **Cairn Table.** These are two of the great heights of
eastern Ayrshire, dominating the Muirkirk area. The Wardlaw Hill cairn
is now merely a ring of cairn material, with a mound within it, built in an
endeavour to 'reconstitute' the cairn. The same reason probably accounts
for the modern positioning of orthostats around the site. Earlier the cairn
had been pillaged for a memorial nearby to a Colonel Baird. One Celtic
bronze finger-ring was recovered from the edge of the cairn. It is now in
the collections of the National Museums of Scotland (NMS X.FA 86);
currently in the Archaeology Department Study Collection in Leith.

Wardlaw Hill Fort (Wardlaw II)   NS 359 327

This hill must be distinguished from **Wardlaw Hill I** (previous entry).
Wardlaw Hill II is the highest (145m OD) of the Claven or Clevance Hills
above Dundonald, and it carries the remains of a fort rather smaller than the
one on **Harpercroft** about 0.5km to the south. It is circular. Half-obliterated
traces of ramparts and ditches are to be seen on the north-west and south-
west, but the eastern defences are gone. The mound in the middle is the
remnant of an old Ordnance Survey triangulation station. The connecting
road between Loans and Dundonald runs past the foot of the hill.

Waterside   NS 438 085

See **Dunaskin Industrial Heritage Museum**

Wee Auchingibbert   NS 592 194

See **Stonepark**

Wellwood Covenanter's gravestone   NS 674 256

Isolated tombstone to William Adam, shot March 1685 near the Proscribe
Burn. The stone is on private ground. Upper Wellwood farm is on a
farm road running south and west from the A70 just beyond the western
boundary of Muirkirk.

Wetherhill cairn   NS 722 303

This is possibly the easternmost cairn in Ayrshire, overlooking the tiny
community of Glenbuck about 4km east of Muirkirk. The cairn is situated
among high rolling uplands at the western end of Wetherhill not far from

Priesthill and John Brown's grave. It is circular. When excavated, it revealed fragments of charcoal and burnt bone as well as a food vessel and fragments of a cinerary urn.

White Cairn   NX 218 824

This cairn lies on the other side of the railway from the farmhouse to which it has given its name. It has been much robbed. The site is about 1.5km west of Barrhill, not to be confused with the **Laggish White Cairn** at **NX 229 786**.

Whitefield burnt mound (water heating)   NS 704 306

This mound sits on the north bank of a tributary of the Greenock Water at Brown Hill. The A723 runs close by. The mound is oval in shape, with a possible indent facing a dried-up stream channel. The material is evidently fire-cracked stone, packed tightly in black earth.[203]

White Laise Cairn   NS 467 007

This mutilated cairn is on the south-facing slopes of the Glessel Hills at the 290m contour overlooking Loch Doon, north of Beoch farmhouse. It is one of a series of high cairns in the Dalmellington–Loch Doon area.

Whitehill   NS 266 564

At the north-east point of Camphill Reservoir, at precisely **NS 2662 5641**, near Whitehill farmhouse, a cup-marked boulder has been identified.[204] The A760 runs just beside the site.

APPENDIX I
THE KINGDOM OF STRATHCLYDE

One of the most lasting achievements of the Dark Age civilisation of Europe is the steady development of a concept of kingship which has endured – just – to the present day. At first, however, kings were very different creatures from the steadily dwindling number of holders of royal authority whom we still have in the twenty-first century. Warlords would be a more accurate name.

In the beginning in Scotland leaders of warbands established themselves at strongpoints – for instance, Dunadd, Dunollie, Dunragit, Traprain Law, Edinburgh, Stirling, Bamburgh – and Dumbarton, 'the Dun of the Britons', which was the *caput*, the military head, of Strathclyde. The leaders, or kings, ruled small territories throughout the two islands of Britain and Ireland. Gradually these small territories grew to larger units and sometimes articulated themselves into subordinate and superordinate 'provinces', depending very much upon the personality and the luck of the individual leader, and often after repeated attempts at conquest or annexation by marriage. Thus Kenneth mac Alpin finally brought the Picts and the Scots of Dalriada together in one realm called Alba in *c.*850; Lothian and Strathclyde were more or less securely added to Alba after the Battle of Carham, although the absorption process extended on either side of 1018; then, after 1160, Galloway was painfully added to the union which eventually began to be called 'Scotland'; and finally, much later, the Western and the Northern Isles were brought into the fold not only by battle but also by the modern route of financial subterfuge.

Most of the material upon which our knowledge of Strathclyde and its neighbours is based is genealogical. What we know or can guess of the family relationships – from the early Kings of Strathclyde to Kenneth mac Alpin and beyond him to David I and Robert the Bruce – provides the armature of the following speculation.

In Strathclyde, a credible list of kings has survived, proof at least of steady, coherent political and cultural development over a period of about six centuries. Reading historical texts, the scantiness of the evidence for this period may sometimes mislead students into dismissing Strathclyde as a merely transitory episode of no importance. However, one has to register the fact that between about 450 and 1018 – a respectable life-span for any state – it was a vibrant British ethnic presence in the region of the River and Firth of Clyde and that people subsisted, farmed, traded, made love and war, were born, married and died within the security of that realm. This British presence was no weakling state but held the balance repeatedly while other, younger cultures rose and fell around it in the fierce struggle towards Alban and Scottish unity.

The first notice of Strathclyde that we can be reasonably sure of is an indignant letter from none other than St Patrick in Ireland, protesting about the slave-raiding activities of the *milites Corotici*, 'the soldiers of Coroticus', a fifth-century ruler who has been identified with Ceredig, the King of Ail [Cluaide], 'the rock of the clyde', Dumbarton.[205] This letter shows Dumbarton to have been the centre of a particularly predatory war-band who, nevertheless, had some pretensions to Christianity which St Patrick mentions in a probably vain endeavour to shame them. In this respect we may recollect the similar veneer of Christianity of the (somewhat later) Aneirin and Taliesin.

Ceredig is referred to in ancient pedigrees as the grandfather of Dyfnwal Hen, who may have been living at the same time as 'King Cole', Coel Hen, perhaps the founder of the southernmost segment of Strathclyde, the province of Kyle. If this time-relationship is cautiously accepted, it would show that for at least two generations after the time of Ceredig Strathclyde was an expanding state, probing south from Dumbarton.[206] Coel's descendants, the Coelingas (as the Anglo-Saxons called them), were involved in the battle of Catraeth (Catterick in Yorkshire) in *c.*600 against the increasing power of the Anglians, who there defeated and later wiped out the Goddodin – the representatives of the Votadini of Roman times. The Anglians were also an imperialist people, flexing their muscles for a drive to the north, to Lothian and the Forth. But Strathclyde and presumably Kyle remained intact, although Galloway came under Anglian domination in that century.

It is not until some time after the reign of Ceredig that the Kings of Strathclyde emerge into the light of verifiable history, with Tudwal or Titagual, who reigned some time in the middle of the sixth century, perhaps a late contemporary of St Ninian, as related in the *Miracula Nyniae Episcopi*.[207] Tudwal's son, Rhydderch Hael, is known to have been a contemporary of St Columba because Adamnan, Columba's biographer, refers to him as such; he appears to have died *c.*614. There is evidence of diplomatic activity involving Columba and Rhydderch and demonstrating rivalry at that stage between the Dalriadan Cenel Gabhrain and Strathclyde; this ended in a treacherous attack and the storming and sacking of Al Cluit, Dumbarton Rock, by Aedan mac Gabhrain.

Rhydderch is also credibly reported to have been a patron and almost exact contemporary of Kentigern or St Mungo, Glasgow's saint, who died *c.*612 near where Rhydderch died 'at his royal estate of "Pertnech" [Partick]' a year later.[208]

Strathclyde kings and Pictish mothers-in-law

In our time we have become accustomed to the idea that an eldest son should inherit from his father; any modifications to this rule are nevertheless rooted in the concept of primogeniture. This custom is particularly noticeable in the case of the surviving monarchies of present-day Europe. But if we look at the king-lists of ancient Scotland, we become aware of some striking differences from the modern practice. The first of these appears in the problem of the Pictish succession.

The Venerable Bede tells the following story:

> So the Picts crossed into Britain, and began to settle in the north of the island, since the Britons were in possession of the south. Having no women with them, these Picts asked wives of the Scots, who consented on condition that, when any dispute arose, they should choose a king from the female royal line rather than the male. This custom continues among the Picts to this day.[209]

This tale contains obviously fabulous elements, but when these are stripped away we are left with a clear statement by Bede, a meticulous and honest witness, that the Picts, at least under certain circumstances, observed matrilineal rather than patrilineal succession in his day (not later than 735). Mother to son succession of lordship of any sort, including royal succession, would be a highly unusual arrangement in Europe, and might give support to the theories of a non-Indo-European sub-stratum among the Picts, a people enigmatic because of their non-literacy. In spite of Bede's positive statement, many scholars have disbelieved it, and the Pictish succession is one of the moot points of Scottish history. However, when the surviving Pictish king-lists are inspected, one feature stands out: none of the kings listed appears to have succeeded his father (with one or two doubtful exceptions).

Matrilineal succession combined with marriages between dynasties could lead to the inheritance of dual kingship i.e. the same man becoming king of two peoples (with versions of his name appearing in two different languages). Nwython, the grandson of Dumnagual Hen, who died in *c.*620 and was King of Strathclyde, may be the same man as Nechton, King of Pictish Fortriu, whose death is recorded as falling in 621. Nwython could have inherited the kingship of Strathclyde from his father Gwyddno, and, as Nechton, the kingship of Fortriu from his mother, the daughter of a previous Pictish king called 'Uerb' – or, as has been suggested, from his aunt or grandmother, since Uerb may be a feminine name in Pictish.[210]

King Ywain of Strathclyde, the son of Beli and grandson of Nwython, won a famous victory at Strathcarron in 642 over the Dalriadan Scots and their king, Domnall Brecc. Again, according to one authority, Ywain had a son called Brude – and Brude was the highly successful Pictish King of Fortriu who defeated and slew the Anglian king Ecgfrith (Brude's cousin) in 685 at the great Battle of Nechtansmere, and permanently halted the Anglo-Saxon advance beyond the Firth of Forth. But, in another manuscript, Brude is called the son of Beli, which could imply that Ywain and Beli were half-brothers – their mother being a Pictish princess who would carry the royal descent to Brude, if the theory of matrilinear succession is accepted.[211]

These and similar cases could have led to a dominant position for Strathclyde among the warring states of early Scotland.

It was during the seventh century that the summit of success was reached by Strathclyde. Later, shifts in diplomacy and alliances shifted the balance against the kingdom. The Picts and the Angles acting in concert attacked the Britons. In 750 Tewdwr (Theodore), King of Strathclyde, defeated and killed Talorgen, King of Picts, at the Battle of 'Mygedawc' (Mugdock), but also in 750 Tewdwr was worsted by the Anglian king Eadhberht, who invaded and occupied Kyle (as well, perhaps, as northern Carrick and at least part of Cuninghame).

Tewdwr died in 752; in 756 his son Dyfnwal was besieged at Dumbarton Rock by a combined Pictish and Anglian army and had to submit, but later in the same year the army of King Eadhberht was treacherously attacked and destroyed by his erstwhile ally the Pict Angus ('Onuist'). After this episode Strathclyde seems to have kept a low profile for more than a century, and may have been under foreign control. Then, finally, in 870, came the great siege of Dumbarton by Olaf and Ivar, the 'Irish Vikings' from Dublin; Al-Cluit was sacked and destroyed, the defenders were enslaved and King Arthgal was captured. Arthgal was later put to death on the advice of King Constantine, son of Kenneth Mac Alpin, the unifier of the Picts and the Scots.

Strathclyde and Alba

Strathclyde appears to have survived as a territorial unit after the destruction of Dumbarton, but opinions differ as to the amount of political independence it enjoyed. MacQuarrie reckons that the dynasty of kings continued in independence down to Ywain the Bald, whose death is recorded in 1018 or thereabouts, possibly at the Battle of Carham, when he fought at the side of Malcolm II, King of Scots, who reclaimed Lothian for Scotland. Certainly the names of the Strathclyde dynasty down to 1018 (Ywain, Dyfnwal, Rhydderch) are traditionally British, which may suggest political independence. But since the (final) unification of the Picts and the Scots in *c.*850 the kingdom of Alba under the line of Kenneth mac Alpin had become dominant in Scotland.

Although, as a result of Viking pressure in the west, the centre of the old Gaelic kingdom had shifted from Dunadd and Dunollie in Argyll to Fortriu, the amalgam of Gaeldom and Pictland produced a strong state, and it became stronger with the virtual addition of Strathclyde. The process is obscured in the old records by constant feuding and faction-fighting within the Gaelic dynasty, but it is clear that Strathclyde came under Alban control from about 878 – a process at least assisted by the fact that Eochaid 'son of Rhun, king of the Britons' was the grandson not only of the slain King Arthgall but also (on his mother's side) of Kenneth mac Alpin himself.[212]

When Kenneth mac Alpin's second son, Aed, was murdered by his cousin Giric in 878, Eochaid of Strathclyde and Giric shared the Alban kingship and, as often happens in such situations, the stronger nation moved into a relation of dominance even though Eochaid had co-sovereignty. Then, when in 889 King Donald II, another grandson of Kenneth mac Alpin, expelled Giric and Eochaid, Strathclyde remained under Alban control and the leaders of the original Strathclyde aristocracy betook themselves and their entourages south to the hospitality of King Anarawd of Gwynedd – thereby preserving in Wales the *Gododdin* and other monuments of northern British culture.[213]

Turmoil in the south then made the territory of Strathclyde into a bone of contention between at least six powers: the Danes of York, the Anglians of Northumbria, the Irish-Norwegians of the kingdom of Dublin, the Vikings of the Hebrides, the Scoto-Pictish Alban state ('Scotia'), and the burgeoning power of the English kingdom of Wessex. The fundamental problem was that Strathclyde was an obvious 'land-bridge' between the Scandinavian kingdoms of York and Dublin – whether these were in conflict or alliance. After the great siege of Al-Cluit in 870, the Norsemen fought their way backwards and forwards through Strathclyde and northern England in their (ultimately unsuccessful) campaigns to secure a unified dynasty and empire based on York and Dublin. Occasionally peace was arranged, as in 920, when a King of Strathclyde is mentioned as participating in a treaty which the Wessex Anglo-Saxons represented as a submission by all the northern kings to their ruler Edward the Elder, but this was more probably a mere holding agreement.

In later times the name 'Cumbria' appears as an alternative to 'Strathclyde', and it seems that the original kingdom may have extended itself beyond even Dumfries to Carlisle and the lands surrounding that settlement. Struggles continued, including a massive defeat of Constantine II of Alba and Ywain or Owen of Strathclyde by King Athelstan of Wessex in 937 at an unidentified site called Brunanburh. In 945 King Edmund of Wessex invaded Cumbria, including Strathclyde, and after harrying it commended it to King Malcolm I of Alba – an act which has been interpreted as a combined warning and plea not to let the territory be used by the Norsemen in their communications between York and Dublin.[214] After 889, then, Strathclyde did not vanish but became a factor in internal power politics in the kingdom of Alba.

Here another inheritance anomaly comes to our notice, this time in Alba itself. If we look at the family trees of the ancient monarchs of Alba (Scotland north of the Forth–Clyde isthmus) between the times of Kenneth mac Alpin (840–858)and those of Malcolm Canmore (1057–93) we perceive that no king succeeded his father, yet (with one or two exceptions), no king was not a king's son. There appears to have been an alternation or oscillation between different branches or 'segments' of the mac Alpin family. For instance, Constantine I (862–77) was succeeded not by his son Donald but by his brother Aed, who reigned only from 877 to 878, when he was killed by Giric, the son of Constantine I's uncle, Donald I (858–862). Giric then reigned with Eochaid (as mentioned above) until they were both 'expelled' in 889. Constantine's son then became king as Donald II (889–900). This rule of alternation appears to have been strictly observed even if the king was assassinated by his successor, as in the case of King Dubh (*d.* 966).

It may even have been the case that the king nominated his successor from the other branch of the family. This brings us on to the related practice of 'tanistry'. In this practice the king nominates a successor who is not necessarily his eldest or any son, but who may look after the son until he comes of age, in fosterage: this man, the tanist (or *tutor*), often becomes visibly and publicly the second in command and heir apparent. The fourteenth-century historian Fordun suggested that Strathclyde, or Cumbria, as a sub-kingdom, was used as an 'appanage', a realm in which the heir-in-waiting, the nominated 'tanist', could train for the responsibilities of the major kingdom. Whether Fordun's idea is accurate or not, it seems to have been thus that David I obtained the inheritance of Strathclyde before he became King of Scotland in 1124. Rather than retain the territory as an appanage for his successor, David chose to break the custom and amalgamate Strathclyde altogether into his new kingdom, dividing it up into 'lots for feuing' such as Cuninghame and Kyle.

APPENDIX II
SOME SITES/BUILDINGS LOST OR DESTROYED

Ardmillan Castle   NX 169 945

Destroyed by fire 1972. Ruins subsequently demolished.

Barbieston Castle, Dalrymple   NS 367 141

Vanished without trace.

Busbie Castle   NS 397 390

Demolished 1952. Site cleared 1977.

Drumsoy or Drumsuie   NS 442 178

Site now completely unidentifiable. A Craufurd castle.

Hessilhead (or Hazlehead)   NS 379 533

Demolished by explosives after the Second World War and site cleared.

Montgomerie House (Coilsfield)   NS 440 262

Destroyed by fire in 1969 and demolished thereafter. Near Tarbolton.

Pinmore   NX 206 903

Pinmore Castle finally demolished in 1981, together with its modern
successor.

St Leonard's Chapel and Hospice, Ayr   NS 335 196

Entirely vanished – probably near Chapel Park Road.

Tannahill, Meikle Mosside   NS 438 419

Site of a possible prehistoric iron-smelter, not now visible.

LIST OF AUTHORITIES CONSULTED

AANHS Ayrshire Archaeological and Natural History Society

DES Discovery and Excavation in Scotland

PPS Proceedings of the Prehistorical Society

PSAS Proceedings of the Society of Antiquaries of Scotland

SAF Scottish Archaeological Forum

SAR Scottish Archaeological Review

SAS Scottish Archaeological Society

SS Scottish Studies

RCAHMS Royal Commission on the Ancient and Historical Monuments of Scotland

TCWAAS Transactions of the Cumberland and Westmorland Antiquarian and Archaeological Society

TDGNHAS Transactions of the Dumfriesshire and Galloway Natural History and Antiquarian Society

T.L. Affleck, 'Excavation at Starr, Loch Doon 1985' *SAS Bulletin 22*

Aneirin, *The Gododdin* tr. Steve Short (Lampeter 1994)

P.J. Ashmore, *Neolithic and Bronze Age Scotland* (London 1996)

John Barbour, *The Bruce*, tr. and notes A.A.M. Duncan (Edinburgh 1997)

G.W.S. Barrow, *Kingship and Unity: Scotland 1000–1306* (Edinburgh 1989)

G.W.S. Barrow, 'Robert Bruce and Ayrshire', *AANHS* 1980

G.W.S. Barrow, *Robert Bruce & the Community of The Realm of Scotland* (Edinburgh 1988)

Robert Beattie, *Kilmaurs Past and Present* (Kilmaurs Historical Society nd)

Bede, *A History of the English Church and People*, tr. Leo Sherley-Price (London 1955)

Harry Broad, 'Rails to Ayr' *AANHS* 1981

Stephen Boardman, *The Stewart Dynasty in Scotland: the Early Stewart Kings: Robert II and Robert III 1371–1406 I* (East Linton 1996)

Daphne Brooke, 'The Northumbrian settlements in Galloway and Carrick: an historical assessment', *PSAS* 121 (1991)

Daphne Brooke, *Wild Men and Holy Places: St Ninian, Whithorn and the Medieval Realm of Galloway* (Edinburgh 1994)

Michael Brown, *The Stewart Dynasty in Scotland: James I* (Edinburgh 1994)

David Buchan, 'The Legend of the Lughnasa Musician in Lowland Britain', *SS* Vol. 23, 1979

C. Burgess, 'The Bronze Age', in C Renfrew, *British Prehistory: A New Outline* (London 1974)

Robert Burns, 'Tam o' Shanter', in Roderick Watson ed., *The Poetry of Scotland: Gaelic, Scots and English* (Edinburgh 1995)

Debbie Camp, 'Coif Castle by Maidens', in Michael C Davis, *The Castles and Mansions of Ayrshire* (Ardrishaig, Argyll 1991) pp. 208–9

Thorbjørn Campbell, *Standing Witnesses: an Illustrated Guide to the Scottish Covenanters* (Edinburgh 1996)

Ernst Cassirer, *Die Philosophie der Symbolischen Formen*, II, *Mythische Denken*, Engl. tr. (*Mythical Thought*) Ralph Manheim (Yale 1955)

H.M. Chadwick, *Early Scotland: the Picts, the Scots and the Welsh of southern Scotland* (Cambridge 1949)

George Chalmers, *Caledonia: or a historical and topographical account of North Britain* Vols I-VIII (Paisley 1807–24)

Rob Close, *Ayrshire and Arran: an Illustrated Architectural Guide* (Royal Incorporation of Architects in Scotland 1992)

Martin Coventry, *The Castles of Scotland* (Edinburgh 1995)

Ian B. Cowan (*ed.* James Kirk) *The Medieval Church in Scotland*

Ian B. Cowan, *Ayrshire Abbeys*, Ayrshire Collections 12 *AANHS* nd

P.W. Cox 'Girvan Mains (Girvan Parish): Roman temporary camps' *DES* 1993

Barbara A. Crone, 'Buiston Crannog' (Kilmaurs Parish) *DES 1989*; 'Excavation at Buiston crannog, Ayrshire, Scotland' *Newswarp* (Wetland Archaeology Research Project) Exeter 1990; 'Crannogs and Chronologies' *PSAS* 123 (1993); 'Buiston Crannog', *Curr. Archaeol.*, Vol. 11, 7 no 127 (Dec.1991);

Michael C. Davis, *The Castles and Mansions of Ayrshire* (Ardrishaig 1991)

William Dodd, 'Ayr: a Study of Urban Growth' *AANHS* 1972

Gordon Donaldson, *Scotland: James V-James VII* (Edinburgh 1978)

David Dorward, *Scotland's Place-names* (Edinburgh 1995)

A.A.M. Duncan, *Scotland: The Making of the Kingdom* (Edinburgh 1996)

Annie I. Dunlop, ed., *The Royal Burgh of Ayr: Seven Hundred and Fifty Years of History* (Edinburgh 1953)

Kevin J. Edwards, Michael Ansell and Bridget A Carter, 'New Mesolithic Sites in South-West Scotland and their Importance as Indicators of Inland Penetration', *TGDNHAS* Third Series Vol LVIII 1983

G.J. Ewart, 'Auldhill, Portencross (W Kilbride parish), motte and bailey castle, stone ramparts, hearths, pottery', *DES* 1987; 'Auldhill, Portencross (W Kilbride Parish), enclosures, foundations, medieval pottery, prehistoric artefacts', *DES* 1988; 'Auldhill, Portencross (West Kilbride Parish), castle', *DES* 1989

Richard Feachem, *A Guide to Prehistoric Scotland* (London 1963)

Sir James Fergusson of Kilkerran, *The Kennedys* (Edinburgh 1958)

Thomas Findlay, *Garan 1631 to Muirkirk 1950* (unpublished, South Ayrshire District Council Libraries Headquarters (Carnegie Library): local collection)

John Foster, *Ayrshire* (Cambridge 1910)

Sally M. Foster, *Picts, Gaels and Scots: Early Historic Scotland* (London 1996)

Sally M. Foster and J Marshall, 'Starling Knowe (Ballantrae Parish): burnt mound' *DES* 1992

Alexander Grant, 'Thanes and Thanages, from the Eleventh to the Fourteenth Centuries' in Grant and Stringer eds. *Medieval Scotland: Crown, Lordship and Community* (Edinburgh 1993–8)

Alastair Hendry, *The Barony of Alloway 1324–1754 AANHS* nd

T.A. Hendry, 'Gourock Burn (Glenhead) double fort', *DES* 1968, and 'Gourock Burn double fort', *DES* 1972

Audrey Shore Henshall, *The Chambered Tombs of Scotland* Vol. II (Edinburgh 1972)

Isobel Hughes, 'Megaliths: Space, Time and the Landscape', *SAR* 5 (parts 1 and 2)

K.H. Jackson, *Language and History in Early Britain* (Edinburgh 1953)

J.B. Johnston, *Place-Names of Scotland* (3rd edn., London 1934)

Lawrence Keppie, *Scotland's Roman Remains* (Edinburgh 1998)

Charles Kightly, *Folk Heroes of Britain* (London 1982)

D.P. Kirby, 'Strathclyde and Cumbria: a survey of historical development to 1092', *TCWAAS* LXII (1962)

Robert A. Lambert ed., *Species History in Scotland* (Edinburgh 1998)

W.J. Lindsay, 'Digging Up Auld Ayr: An Excavation at 102–104 High Street', *AANHS Ayrshire Collections* Vol. 14 No. 5 1985

J. Philip McAleer, 'Towards an architectural history of Kilwinning Abbey', *PSAS* 125 (1995)

Proinsias Mac Cana, *Celtic Mythology* (Feltham, Middlesex 1983)

H., M. and D. MacFadzean, 'Glenmuirshaw (Auchinleck p), agate implements, waste flakes, chipping floor', *DES* 1984

David MacGibbon and Thomas Ross, *The Castellated and Domestic Architecture of Scotland from the Twelfth to the Eighteenth Century* Vols I-V (Edinburgh 1990: reprint of the 1887 Edinburgh edition)

Christine McGladdery, *The Stewart Dynasty in Scotland: James II* (Edinburgh 1990)

Archibald Mackenzie, *An Ancient Church: the Pre-Reformation Church of St John the Baptist at Ayr* (Ayr 1935)

H. McKerrell, 'On the origin of British faience beads and some aspects of the Wessex-Mycenae relationship', *PPS* 38 (1972)

James Murray MacKinlay, *Influence of the Pre-Reformation Church on Scottish Place-Names* (Edinburgh and London 1904)

Alan MacQuarrie, 'The Kings of Strathclyde, *c.*400–1018' in Grant and Stringer eds., *Medieval Scotland: Crown, Lordship and Community* (Edinburgh 1998)

Hector L. MacQueen, 'The Kin of Kennedy, "Kenkynnol" and the Common Law' in Grant and Stringer eds., *Medieval Scotland: Crown, Lordship and Community* (Edinburgh 1998)

James Mair, 'Cessnock: an Ayrshire Estate in the Age of Improvement,' *AANHS* 1996

James A. Morris, *The Brig of Ayr and something of its Story* (Ayr 1911)

Alex Morrison, 'The Bronze Age in Ayrshire', *Ayrshire Collections Vol. 12, AANHS* 1979

Alex Morrison and Clive Bonsall, 'The Early Post-Glacial Settlement of Scotland: a Review' in *The Mesolithic in Europe: Papers presented at the Third International Symposium*, Edinburgh (1989)

R.J.C Mowat, *The Logboats of Scotland and notes on related artefact types* (Oxford 1996)

Ranald Nicholson, *Scotland: The Later Middle Ages* (Edinburgh 1978)

W.F.H. Nicolaisen, *Scottish Place-Names* (London 1986)

James Paterson, *History of the County of Ayr with a Genealogical Account of the Families of Ayrshire* Vol I (Ayr 1848); Vol II (Edinburgh 1852)

James Paterson, *History of the Counties of Ayr and Wigton* (3 volumes: Edinburgh 1856–66) NB Most unreliably printed and bound.

Edward M. Patterson, 'Ancient Fish Traps on the North Ayrshire Coast: Ardrossan to Hunterston' in *Ayrshire Monographs, Ayrshire Collections* Vol. 12, *AANHS* 1989

R. Pitcairn ed., *Historie of the Kennedyis* (Edinburgh 1830)

George S. Pryde, 'Charter of Foundation', in *The Royal Burgh of Ayr*, ed. Annie I Dunlop, Edinburgh 1953

John L. Roberts, *Lost Kingdoms: Celtic Scotland and the Middle Ages* (Edinburgh 1997)

A.S. Robertson, 'Roman finds from non-Roman sites in Scotland', *Britannia* I (1970)

A.S. Robertson, 'Agricola's campaigns in Scotland and their aftermath', *SAF* 7 (1975)

Royal Commission on the Ancient and Historical Monuments of Scotland, *Canmore Database,* all Ayrshire entries

RCAHMS, 'Blackclauchrie (Barr parish): cairns, cairn fields, rig and furrow, field systems and burnt mounds' *DES* 1991

RCAHMS: *Eastern Dumfriesshire: an archaeological landscape* (Edinburgh 1997)

Mike Salter, *The Castles of South-West Scotland* (Malvern 1993)

Mike Salter, *The Old Parish Churches of Scotland* (Malvern 1994)

Peter Salway, *Roman Britain* (Oxford 1981)

Margaret H.B. Sanderson, 'Robert Adam in Ayrshire', *Ayrshire Monographs no. II, AANHS* 1993

J.G. Scott., 'The hall and motte at Courthill, Dalry, Ayrshire', *PSAS* 119, 1989

William F. Skene, *Celtic Scotland: a History of Ancient Alban* (Edinburgh 1890)

D. Sloan, 'Troon (Dundonald p) flint scraper', *DES* 1985

Alfred P. Smyth, *Warlords and Holy Men* (Edinburgh 1984)

K. Speller 'Girvan Mains Farm (Girvan Parish), Roman temporary camp' *DES* 1996

K. Speller, I Banks, P Duffy and G MacGregor, 'Ladywell Farm, Girvan (Girvan parish), burnt mound; prehistoric and medieval features', *DES* 1997

Sir Frank Stenton et al., *The Bayeux Tapestry: a Comprehensive Survey* (London 1965)

John Strawhorn, *Ayrshire: The Story of a County* (*AANHS* 1975)

John Strawhorn, *The History of Ayr: Royal Burgh and County Town* (Edinburgh 1989)

John Strawhorn, *The History of Irvine: Royal Burgh and New Town* (Edinburgh 1985)

John Strawhorn, *The History of Prestwick* (Edinburgh 1994)

John Strawhorn and Ken Andrew, *Discovering Ayrshire* (Edinburgh 1988)

Keith J. Stringer, 'Periphery and Core in Thirteenth-Century Scotland: Alan son of Roland, Lord of Galloway and Constable of Scotland' in Grant and Stringer eds., *Medieval Scotland: Crown, Lordship and Community* (Edinburgh 1998)

Cornelii Taciti *de Vita Agricolae* eds Furneaux and Anderson (Oxford 1922)

E.J. Talbot, 'Early Scottish castles of earth and timber – recent field-work and excavation' *SAF* 6 (1974)

Taliesin, *Poems: Introduction and English translation by* Meirion Pennar (Lampeter 1988*)*

Edwin Sprott Towill, *The Saints of Scotland* (Edinburgh 1978)

Nigel Tranter, *The Fortified House in Scotland,* Vol III *South-West Scotland* (Edinburgh 1962)

Hermann K. Usener, *Götternamen: Versuch einer Lehre von der religiösen Begriffsbildung* (Bonn 1896)

Robert Waite, 'An Excavation in the Citadel, Ayr', *AANHS Collections* Vol. 12, 1989

W.J. Watson, *The Celtic Place-names of Scotland* (Edinburgh 1993 reprint of 1926 ed.)

Peter C. Woodman, 'A review of the Scottish Mesolithic: a plea for normality!' *PSAS* 119 (1989)

Jenny Wormald, *Court, Kirk and Community: Scotland 1470–1625* (Edinburgh 1991)

ENDNOTES

1 D. Sloan, 'Troon (Dundonald p) flint scraper', *DES* (1985)

2 Alex Morrison and Clive Bonsall, 'The Early Post-Glacial Settlement of Scotland: a Review' in *The Mesolithic in Europe: Papers presented at the Third International Symposium*, Edinburgh (1989), 140–1

3 Peter C. Woodman, 'A review of the Scottish Mesolithic: a plea for normality!', *PSAS*, 119 (1989), 8–15

4 Kevin J. Edwards, Michael Ansell and Bridget A. Carter, 'New Mesolithic Sites in South-West Scotland and their Importance as Indicators of Inland Penetration', *TDGNHAS*, Third Series, Vol. LVIII (1983) 9–10. At all the named locations stone implements have been found, cf. T.L. Affleck, 'Excavation at Starr, Loch Doon 1985', *SAS*, 22, 10–21.

5 Isobel Hughes, 'Megaliths: Space, Time and the Landscape', *SAR*, Vol. 5 (parts 1 and 2), 41

6 See Audrey Shore Henshall, *The Chambered Tombs of Scotland* (Edinburgh, 1972), Vol. 2, 2–14 (Bargrennan Group); 15–110 (Clyde Group)

7 P.J. Ashmore, *Neolithic and Bronze Age Scotland* (London, 1996), 34

8 See Edward M. Patterson, 'Ancient Fishtraps on the North Ayrshire Coast: Ardrossan to Hunterston', *Ayrshire Monographs, Ayrshire Collections*, Vol. 12 (*AANHS* 1989), 29–40

9 See Alex Morrison, 'The Bronze Age in Ayrshire', *AANHS Publications, 1979*, 128–30

10 *Cf.* C. Burgess, 'The Bronze Age', in C. Renfrew, *British Prehistory: A New Outline* (London, 1974), 196.

11 *Cf.* H. McKerrell, 'On the origin of British faience beads and some aspects of the Wessex-Mycenae relationship', *PPS*, 38 (1972), 286–301

12 Morrison *op. cit.*, 128

13 *Cf.* P. J. Ashmore *op. cit.*, 55

14 Varieties of Celtic speech specific to Great Britain and Ireland and giving rise to Welsh and Gaelic respectively

15 See T.A. Hendry, 'Gourock Burn (Glenhead) double fort', *DES* (1968), and 'Gourock Burn double fort', *DES* (1972). Also A.S. Robertson, 'Roman finds from non-Roman sites in Scotland', *Britannia*, I (1970), Table 1, and 'Agricola's campaigns in Scotland and their aftermath', *SAF*, 7 (1975), 6.

16 R.J.C. Mowat, *The Logboats of Scotland* (Oxford, 1996), 45–7

17 J.B. Johnston, *Place-Names of Scotland* (3rd ed., London, 1934), 95

18 W.F.H. Nicolaisen, *Scottish Place-Names* (London, 1986), 187.

19 Proinsias Mac Cana, *Celtic Mythology* (revised ed., Feltham, Middlesex, 1983), 86; *cf.* W.J. Watson, *The History of the Celtic Place-names of Scotland* (Edinburgh and London, 1926; Edinburgh, 1993), 342

20 Taliesin, *Poems, tr.* Meirion Pennar (Felinfach, Lampeter, Dyfed, 1988), 108–11; *cf.* Watson, *loc. cit.*

21 Aneirin, *The Goddodin,* tr. Steve Short (Felinfach, Lampeter, Dyfed, 1994), 43

22 *Cf.* Daphne Brooke, *Wild Men and Holy Places* (Edinburgh, 1994), 79

23 Mac Cana *op.cit.*, 109

24 Dinvin is now classed as a motte, but I suspect that the site goes back before the time of the mottes, the Norman incursion into Ayrshire in the twelfth century.

25 Mac Cana *op. cit.*

26 W.J. Watson, *op.cit.*, 199; corresponding to *Lugudunon,* 'fort of Lugus'. *Cf.* Loudun in France

27 Mac Cana *op. cit.*, 86–9

28 J.M. MacKinlay, *Influence of the Pre-Reformation Church on Scottish Place-Names* (Edinburgh, 1904), 111–2

29 Mac Cana *op. cit.*, 88

30 *Cf. Minishant,* apparently 'sacred grove' (just north of Maybole), and, in the neighbourhood, St Helen's Well – both close to the Doon, Devona's river. Cf. also 'Vindogara' [supra] – and 'Garan' – the old name of Muirkirk

31 *Cf.* Mac Cana, *op. cit.*, 66 and 86.

32 See Paterson, *History of the County of Ayr &c* (Edinburgh, 1852), Vol. II, 225

33 *Cf.* David Buchan, 'The Legend of the Lughnasa Musician in Lowland Britain', *Scottish Studies,* Vol. 23 (1979)

34 Hermann K. Usener, *Götternamen: Versuch einer Lehre von der religiösen Begriffsbildung* (Bonn, 1896), 391 ff; cf. Ernst Cassirer, *Die Philosophie der Symbolischen Formen,* II, *Mythische Denken, tr.* Ralph Manheim, *Mythical Thought,* (Yale, 1955), 22 ff., 169 and *passim*

35 See H.M. Chadwick, *Early Scotland: the Picts, the Scots and the Welsh of southern Scotland* (Cambridge, 1949), 143–6. Cf. Charles Kightly, *Folk Heroes of Britain* (London, 1982), 55–93

36 'rough': the difficulties of exactitude in Dark Age chronology are well illustrated in Alan MacQuarrie, 'The Kings of Strathclyde' in *Medieval Scotland: Crown, Lordship and Community,* eds. A. Grant and K.J. Stringer (Edinburgh, 1998), 3

37 *Cf.* Taliesin, *Gwaith Argoed Llwyfain* (The Battle of Argoed Llwyfain): '*Owein dwyrein ffossawt. nyt dodynt nyt ydynt nyt ynt parawt. Acheneu vab coel bydei kymwyawc lew. kyn astalei owystyl nebawt.* 'And answered Owain, /the scourge of the east, /-They [the hostages] haven't come, /They don't exist, /they aren't ready, - /And the whelp of Coel /would be a pathetic warrior /before he would pay anybody a hostage.' (*tr.* Meirion Pennar) (Felinfach, Lampeter, Dyfed, 1988), 73–5. Cf. also D.P. Kirby, 'Strathclyde and Cumbria: a survey of historical development to 1092', *Transactions of the Cumberland and Westmorland Antiquarian & Archaeological Society,* Vol. LXII (1962), 80.

38 The name *Coel* is closely associated with the Welsh *Howell, Powell* [ap-Howell]

39 Daphne Brooke, *op. cit.*, 10

40 *Cf.* Alfred P. Smyth, *Warlords and Holy Men: Scotland* AD *80–1000* (Edinburgh, 1984), 27–8

41 Bede, *A History of the English Church and People*, tr. Leo Sherley-Price (London, 1955), 143

42 J.B. Johnston, *Place-names of Scotland* (London, 1934), 323

43 Brooke, *op. cit.*, 16–17 and *passim.*

44 A.A.M. Duncan, *The Making of the Kingdom* (Edinburgh, 1977), 37–8

45 Brooke, *op. cit.*, 30

46 Brooke, *op. cit.*, 24

47 *Cf.* D. P. Kirby, 'Strathclyde and Cumbria: a survey of historical development to 1092', *TCWAAS*, LXII (1962), 82

48 Daphne Brooke, 'The Northumbrian settlements in Galloway and Carrick: an historical assessment', *PSAS*, 121 (1991), 310

49 These Cymric areas may be indicated, for instance, by the occurrence in the upper Girvan valley of names like *Threave* (NS 338 067), *Tranew* (NS 352 071), *Troquhain* (NS 374 092) and *Traboyack* (NS 385 048), all of which contain in various guises the Cymric element *-tref*, a dwelling. *Cf.* W. F. H. Nicolaisen, *Scottish Place Names* (London, 1989), 166–8.

50 Brooke, *op. cit.*, 311 and 318

51 *Cf.* Kirby, *op. cit.*, 84

52 J.B. Johnston, *Place-Names of Scotland* (London 1934), 296

53 W.F.H. Nicolaisen, *op. cit.*, 77

54 It may be that a roughly contemporary colony was made from the same area of Ireland, settling just across the water from Ulster in the Rhinns of Galloway – at the same time, perhaps, as the Ninianic settlement at Whithorn. The main evidence for the existence of this Irish colony is the unusually dense concentration in that region of occurrences of the word *sliabh*, meaning in Irish Gaelic 'mountain' or 'moor', which otherwise occurs only sparsely, in areas under the control of the Scottish Dalriada or associated Irish immigrants. Cf. Nicolaisen, *op.cit.*, 39–46. But, as indicated in the text, the possibility remains that the Goidelic Celts had been in possession of British territory long before 450. Both in Ireland and in north-west Britain the existence is now suspected of a Goidelic civilization speaking *Gaelic* (different from *Brythonic Cymric*) from very early times. The invasion theory has as uncertain an application to Goidelic Celts as to earlier peoples.

55 The formation with *-mo* is to be seen in e.g. Lamlash [Arran], *[Ei]-lean-M'Laise*, where the saint is *mo-Laise, mo Laisren*, whose cave exists on the island known as Holy Island in the present Lamlash Bay. See Watson *op. cit.*, 305–6. See also Edwin Sprott Towill, *The Saints of Scotland*, (Edinburgh, 1978), 106–7, for problems involved in identifying the saint involved in 'Kilmarnock'.

56 Watson *op. cit.*, 188

57 Watson *op. cit.*, 187

58 Watson *op. cit.*, 188

59 I owe the information on *Machar-i-Kill* to Mr David Hunter of Dailly, whose investigation turned up the base of a cross identified as of the tenth century and other artefacts

60 Watson *op. cit.*, 187

61 This site name has, however, variants including 'Kildomine' and 'Kildamnie'.

62 *Cf.* MacKinlay *op. cit.*, 110 (on Kilrenny in Fife). Cf. also Kilranny Hill and Bridge south of Girvan in Carrick.

63 I am indebted for this section to Mr Nicolaisen's analysis of Gaelic and other names, especially pp. 121–48 of his *Scottish Place Names*.

64 Nicolaisen, *op. cit.*, 127

65 A.A.M. Duncan, *op. cit.*, 119

66 This raid itself was the consequence of a failed diplomatic mission scuppered by the refusal of King William II Rufus to meet Malcolm in 1093

67 Principally Donald III Ban Malcolm's brother, Duncan II Malcolm's eldest son by his first wife, and Edgar's two elder brothers Edmund and (perhaps) Æthelred

68 *Cf.* A.A.M. Duncan, *op.cit.*, 135

69 *Cf.* Brooke, *Wild Men and Holy Places*, 108–9

70 See Sir Frank Stenton *et al.*, *The Bayeux Tapestry: a Comprehensive Survey* (London, 1965), colour plates I and IV and plate 51 and detail

71 See Brooke *op. cit.*, 129

72 See John Strawhorn, *Ayrshire: the Story of a County* (Ayr, 1975), 23. *Cf.* also map on p. 20

73 *Cf.* James Paterson, *op. cit.*, Vol. I, 50: 'October 30 [1510] ... "William Craufurde, son of William Craufurde of Lefnorys" is "admitted to compound for art and part of the treasonable taking of the King's Castle of Lochdoun from Sir David Kennedy, Knt. (Captain thereof) ..."' 'Lefnorys' is in Cumnock in King's Kyle

74 See Brooke, *op. cit.*, 59–60

75 See George S. Pryde, 'Charter of Foundation', in *The Royal Burgh of Ayr*, ed. Annie I. Dunlop (Edinburgh, 1953), 13

76 See Brooke *ibid.*

77 It is also possible that the customs post was the now vanished Black Bog Castle at the northern end of what is now New Cumnock

78 *Cf.* Ian B. Cowan (*ed.* James Kirk), *The Medieval Church in Scotland*, in particular, 27–29

79 Ian B. Cowan, *Ayrshire Abbeys*, Ayrshire Collections, Vol. 12, *AANHS*, nd, 268

80 This was an institution whose monks were drawn from the monastery at Tiron in France (founded in 1109). Cluniac monks came originally from Cluny and Cistercians from Citeaux.

81 Kilwinning parish itself was with the abbey from the beginning; Ardrossan, Loudoun and Beith were acquired during the thirteenth century; in the fourteenth century Dunlop, Irvine, Kilbirnie and Kilmarnock were added to the fold; Dreghorn, Perceton, Stewarton, Stevenston and Dalry were annexed by the fifteenth century, and in the sixteenth Kilbride came in, just before the Reformation. *Cf.* Cowan, *op.cit.*, 270

82 Quoted in James Paterson, *op. cit.*, Vol. II, 485

83 Paterson, *loc. cit.*

84 See Archibald Mackenzie, *An Ancient Church: the Pre-Reformation Church of St John the Baptist at Ayr* (Ayr, 1935), 9

85 Crossraguel was staffed by Cluniac monks from Paisley in spite of the dispute between Duncan fitz Gilbert and Paisley Abbey

86 Hugo de Morville *d.* 1163; Richard de Morville 1163–1189; William de Morville (last of the line) 1189–1196

87 John Strawhorn, *The History of Irvine: Royal Burgh and New Town* (Edinburgh, 1985), 6

88 See Strawhorn, *The History of Prestwick* (Edinburgh, 1994), 6

89 See above, p. 24

90 *Cf.* G.W.S. Barrow, *Kingship and Unity* (Edinburgh, 1981), 5–7

91 Alexander Grant, 'Thanes and Thanages, from the Eleventh to the Fourteenth Centuries', in *Medieval Scotland: Crown, Lordship and Community*, ed. Grant and Stringer (Edinburgh, 1993–8), 43–5; there is a very clear map on p. 44. Note, however, the presence of *Distinkhorn Hill* in Galston parish (see above, p. 49) and *Tinkhorn* further south in Sorn, both of which announce the presence of a thane *(-tink)*, though at what period I cannot say. *Cf.* also entry for **Portincross** in Gazetteer.

92 Duncan, *op. cit.*, 163

93 Strawhorn (*The History of Ayr, Royal Burgh and County Town* (Edinburgh, 1989), 7) thinks the appointment took place 10 years later, in 1207. A sheriff of Ayr and Carrick only may have held office as early as 1195. See Duncan, *op. cit.*, 204

94 During the Ayr sheriffdom of William Cumyn of Kilbryde, what appears to be a reassertion or even a first assertion of the functions of a shire in the Anglo-Saxon sense is to be found among the early charters of William the Lion in 1265: ' "the Earl of Buchan, who had Carrick in farm from the Crown" was directed to provide for "the consumpt of the Lord King", that he "may hold a better Court, 12 chalders wheat, 40 cows, 40 chalders barley or malt, 20 chalders oats; so that the Lord King might have all these aforesaid ready for his service in whatever year in October at St Martin's, if it can be done, that it shall be provided fifteen days before the festival of the blessed Sanct Martin." ' Chamberlain Rolls for 1265 quoted in Paterson, *op. cit.*, Vol. I, 159.

95 See Duncan, *op. cit.*, 201–2

96 Alan had a bastard son, also called Thomas, who was styled 'of Galloway' and lived to a great but desolate old age

97 See Keith J. Stringer, 'Periphery and Core: Alan of Galloway' in Grant and Stringer, *Medieval Scotland: Crown, Lordship and Community* (Edinburgh, 1993–8), 100–2

98 I am indebted to Dr Richard Oram for this information and that in the previous note

99 This is a very odd story. One suspects that if there is any truth in it, the whole encounter was prearranged between the two families to overcome the opposition of King Alexander III.

100 Paterson (*op. cit.*, Vol. I, 419) reckons that this took place in 1297. In another place he suggests the less likely date of 1296.

101 Quoted from Hasting's report (document C.47/22/8 [Public Records Office]) in G.W.S. Barrow, *Robert Bruce and the Community of The Realm of Scotland*, (Third Edition) (Edinburgh, 1988), 107

102 John Barbour, *The Bruce*, tr. and notes A.A.M. Duncan (Edinburgh, 1997), 91 (Book 2, l.205)

103 Barrow, *op.cit.*, 91–2

104 Barbour, *op. cit.*, 271 (Book 7 p. 250–6)

105 Barrow, *op.cit.*, 204–9

106 Barrow, *op. cit.*, 288

107 Nicholson, *Scotland: the Later Middle Ages*, 125

108 *Historie of the Kennedyis*, ed. Pitcairn (Edinburgh, 1830), 1

109 *Cf.* MacQueen *op. cit.*, 282, and Sir James Fergusson of Kilkerran, *The Kennedys* (Edinburgh, 1958)

110 For a possible explanation of this transfer of responsibilities, see Hector L. MacQueen, 'The Kin of Kennedy' in *Medieval Scotland: Crown, Lordship and Community* (Grant and Stringer eds.) (Edinburgh, 1998) 273–96

111 Paterson, *op. cit.*, Vol. I, 433

112 Paterson, *ibid.*, 437

113 G.W.S. Barrow, *op. cit.*, 289

114 J. Paterson, *op. cit.*, Vol. II, 405–7

115 *Cf.* John Strawhorn, *Prestwick*, 28–37 and *passim.*

116 APS (Acts of the Parliament of Scotland), ii, 346: quoted in Gordon Donaldson, *Scotland: James V–James VII* (Edinburgh, 1978), 9

117 This is according to my own conjectured chronology: for another, possibly better, arrangement of the events, see John Strawhorn, *Irvine*, 38–40

118 See John Strawhorn, *Prestwick*, 28–9

119 See Paterson, *op. cit.*, Vol. II, 320

120 MS history of the Eglinton family, quoted in Paterson, *op. cit.*, Vol. I, 88

121 *ibid.*

122 Donaldson, *op. cit.*, 93

123 Paterson, *op. cit.*, Vol. II, 122

124 Paterson, *op. cit.*, Vol. I, 285–6. *Cf.* 108–11 and 280–4.

125 It is related of Welch that, on hearing a hubbub in the streets beside his house, he used to don a steel cap, run outside and belabour the combatants with the flat of his sword until they fled in different directions. *Cf.* Paterson, *op. cit.*, Vol. I, 193.

126 'Whiggamore' was a word used to denote an extreme anti-royalist Presbyterian or Covenanter from the West. The name was shortened to 'Whig', which came to mean a member of the British parliamentary party later known as 'Liberal'.

127 Strawhorn, *The History of Ayr*, 72

128 John Strawhorn, *Ayrshire*, 215

129 Robert Burns, 'Tam o' Shanter', in Roderick Watson ed., *The Poetry of Scotland: Gaelic, Scots and English* (Edinburgh, 1995), 388

130 E.J. Talbot, 'Early Scottish castles of earth and timber – recent field-work and excavation' *SAF*, 6 (1974), 56

131 Note that the name 'Ardrossan' could mean something like 'the heights or promontory of Ross'. The Ross family were associated with the area before the Wars of Independence. Also cf. 'Horse Island', an islet off the Ardrossan coast (possible relation to a former 'Hross', on the analogy of German *Ross*, 'horse').

132 See Audrey Shore Henshall, *The Chambered Tombs of Scotland* (Edinburgh, 1972), Vol. 2, 396–7

133 Paterson, *op. cit.*, Vol. II, 204

134 Martin Coventry, *The Castles of Scotland* (Edinburgh, 1995), 56

135 Quoted in Paterson, *op. cit.*, II, 352

136 *Cf.* Thomas Findlay, *Garan 1631 to Muirkirk 1950* (unpublished, South Ayrshire District Council Libraries Headquarters (Carnegie Library): local collection), 6

137 See W.J. Lindsay, 'Digging Up Auld Ayr: An Excavation at 102–104 High Street, *AANHS Ayrshire Collections*, Vol. 14, No. 5 (1985), 206 and *passim*

138 *Cf.* James A. Morris, *The Brig of Ayr and something of its Story* (Ayr, 1911), 39–41

139 *Cf.* Robert Waite, 'An Excavation in the Citadel, Ayr', *AANHS Collections*, Vol. 12 (1989)

140 See William Dodd, 'Ayr: a Study of Urban Growth' *AANHS* (1972); and John Strawhorn, *The History of Ayr: Royal Burgh and County Town* (Edinburgh, 1989), esp. 9–25

141 Data relating to the Ballantrae Bridge complex all derive from RCAHMS *Canmore* database NMRS nos. NX08SE 1, 3, 8, 17, 31, 32, 33, 35 and 36

142 RCAHMS: *Eastern Dumfriesshire: an archaeological landscape* (Edinburgh, 1997), 116, fig. 111

143 See Henshall, *op. cit.*, Vol. 2, 398

144 E.J. Talbot *op. cit.*, 50

145 See W. F. H. Nicolaisen, *op. cit.*, 166

146 Ordnance Survey Report quoted in RCAHMS 'Canmore' data base entry for Bellsbank 'Bubbly Cairn'

147 Many of the finds are now held in the collections of the National Museums of Scotland (NMS X.HV1–201); some are on display in the Museum of Scotland, Chambers Street, Edinburgh, and other are held in the Archaeology Department Study Collection, Leith.

148 B.A. Crone, 'Buiston Crannog (Kilmaurs Parish)' *DES*, 1989, 59–60; 'Buiston (Kilmaurs Parish) Crannog' *DES*, 1990, 36; 'Excavation at Buiston Crannog, Ayrshire, Scotland' *Newswarp: the newsletter of the Wetland Archaeology Research Project* (Exeter, Oct 1990), 17–9; 'Crannogs and Chronologies' *PSAS*, 123 (1993)

   Cf. also R.J.C. Mowat, *The Logboats of Scotland with notes on related artefact types* (Oxford, 1996), 13–15

149 The armlet is held in the collections of the National Museums of Scotland (NMS X.FA90–91) and is currently in the Archaeology Department Study Collection in Leith

150 See Henshall, *op. cit.*, Vol. 2, 399–400

151 K. Speller, I. Banks, P. Duffy and G. MacGregor, 'Ladywell Farm, Girvan (Girvan parish), burnt mound; prehistoric and medieval features', *DES*, 1997, 73–4

152 As quoted in RCAHMS 'Canmore' database, entry NX38NW 8.01: 'Blackclauchrie (Barr parish): cairns, cairn fields, rig and furrow, field systems and burnt mounds' *DES*, 1991, 61

153 Stuart Cruden, *The Scottish Castle* (Edinburgh, 1981), 94

154 See Henshall, *op. cit.*, Vol. 2, 400–3

155 Brooke, *op. cit.*, 53–4. See p. 55.

156 Debbie Camp, 'Coif Castle by Maidens', in Michael C. Davis, *The Castles and Mansions of Ayrshire* (Ardrishaig, Argyll, 1991), 208–9

157 Paterson, *op cit.*, Vol. II, 369

158 See Brooke, *op. cit.*, 129. See also p. 48.

159 *Cf.* J.G. Scott 'The hall and motte at Courthill, Dalry, Ayrshire', *PSAS*, 119, 1989

160 Quoted from the entry for Dornal Moat in the RCAHMS 'Canmore' database.

161 AOC (Scotland) Ltd as quoted in entry in RCAHMS 'Canmore' database for Drumdowns (Altimeg) (NMRS no. NX17NW 7)

162 RCAHMS: *Eastern Dumfriesshire: an archaeological landscape* (Edinburgh, 1997), 116, fig. 111 (as quoted in RCAHMS 'Canmore' database entry for Finnarts Hill NX07SE 6)

163 OS Name Book 1856 quoted in entry for Finnarts Hill in *RCAHMS* 'Canmore' database NX07SE 6

164 See entries for Enoch (Girvan) in RCAHMS 'Canmore' database NMRS nos. NX29NW 18, 19 and 22

165 See RCAHMS 'Canmore' database NMRS no. NX29NW 20

166 See entries for Girvan Mains in RCAHMS 'Canmore' database NMRS nos. NX19NE 24, 43, and 47; also P. W. Cox 'Girvan Mains (Girvan Parish): Roman temporary camps' *DES*, 1993, 86; and K. Speller 'Girvan Mains Farm (Girvan Parish), Roman temporary camp' *DES*, 1996, 97

167 H.M. and D. MacFadzean, 'Glenmuirshaw (Auchinleck p), agate implements, waste flakes, chipping floor', *DES*, 1984

168 Daphne Brooke, *Wild Men and Holy Places* (Edinburgh, 1994), 109. But *cf.* the entry above for **Dalmellington** and pp. 44–5

169 See Henshall, *op. cit.*, Vol. 2, 396–7

170 See entries for High Altercannoch in RCAHMS 'Canmore' database NMRS nos. NX28SW 3, 4, 5, 8,12, 13, 14 and 27.

171 See entry NS33NE53 for Holms, 2 February 2000, in RCAHMS 'Canmore' database

172 Paterson, *op. cit.*, Vol. II, 469

173 R.J.C. Mowat, *op. cit.*, 45–7

174 Nigel Tranter, *The Fortified House in Scotland*, Vol. III, *South-West Scotland*, 43

175 Paterson, *op. cit.*, Vol. II, 165

176 See entries for Kilwhannel High Plantation in RCAHMS 'Canmore' database NMRS nos. 14 and 15

177 J. Philip McAleer, 'Towards an architectural history of Kilwinning Abbey', *Proc Soc Antiq Scot*, *125* (1995), 816–824

178 *Ibid.*, 824–835

179 *Ibid.*, 841–853

180 *Ibid.*, 853–862

181 Sir Claud Hagart-Alexander of Ballochmyle, Bt., Kingencleugh House

182 Mike Salter, *The Castles of South-West Scotland* (Malvern, 1993), 45

183 Paterson, *op. cit.*, Vol. I, 303

184 As quoted in RCAHMS 'Canmore' database, NMRS entries NX38NW 6 and 11.01: 'Blackclauchrie (Barr parish): cairns, cairn fields, rig and furrow, field systems and burnt mounds' *DES*, 1991, 61

185 K. Speller, I. Banks, P. Duffy and G. MacGregor, 'Ladywell Farm, Girvan (Girvan parish), burnt mound; prehistoric and medieval features', *DES*, 1997, 73

186 David MacGibbon and Thomas Ross, *The Castellated and Domestic Architecture of Scotland from the Twelfth to the Eighteenth Century* (Edinburgh, 1886 and 1990), Vol. V, 198

187 Paterson, *op. cit.*, Vol. I, 353

188 See RCAHMS 'Canmore' database, entry no. NS51SW 2 for Little Rigend

189 See Henshall, *op. cit.*, Vol. 2, 403–4

190 Information in RCAHMS 'Canmore' database entry NX49SE 11 for Loch Doon. See also Mowat, *op. cit.*, 55–8.

191 K.J. Edwards, M. Ansell and B.A. Carter, 'New Mesolithic sites in south-

west Scotland and their importance as indicators of inland penetration' *TDGNHAS*, 1983. Also RCAHMS entries for Loch Doon in 'Canmore' database in NX49SE and NE.

192 Paterson, *History of the Counties of Ayr and Wigton* (Edinburgh, 1856–66) Vol. I, Kyle pt. II, 393

193 See Mowat, *op. cit.*, 69

194 Mr David Hunter of New Dailly very kindly informed me about his investigations at Machar-i-Kill.

195 Coventry, *op. cit.*, 219

196 Salter, *op. cit.*, 59

197 G.J. Ewart, 'Auldhill, Portencross (W. Kilbride Parish), motte and bailey castle, stone rampart, hearths, pottery', *DES*, 1987; 'Auldhill, Portencross (W Kilbride Parish), enclosures, foundations, medieval pottery, prehistoric artefacts', *DES*, 1988; 'Auldhill Portencross (West Kilbride Parish), castle', *DES*, 1989

198 See above n. 91

199 Strawhorn, *Prestwick*, 16

200 See RCAHMS entry for Rig Hill in 'Canmore' database NMRS no. NS50NW 3

201 J.G. Scott, 'The hall and motte at Courthill, Dalry, Ayrshire', *PSAS* 119, 1989, 272

202 Sally Foster and J. Marshall, 'Starling Knowe (Ballantrae Parish): burnt mound' *DES*, 1992

203 RCAHMS 'Canmore' database entry no. NS73SW 6 for Whitefield

204 West of Scotland Archaeology Service, 'Sites identified and recorded in North Ayrshire during fieldwork carried out by WoSAS' *DES*, 1997, 56

205 Alan MacQuarrie, 'The Kings of Strathclyde', in (eds) Alexander Grant and Keith Stringer, *Medieval Scotland: Crown, Lordship and Community* (Edinburgh, 1998), 3

206 *Cf.* Kirby, *op. cit.*, 80

207 Cited in MacQuarrie, *op. cit.*, 7

208 Jocelin, *Vita Kentigerni*; cited in MacQuarrie, *op. cit.*, 8

209 Bede, *op. cit.*, 39

210 MacQuarrie, *op. cit.*, 8–9

211 *Cf.* MacQuarrie, *op.cit.*, 9

212 This is according to A. P. Smyth (*op. cit.*, 215). In the view of A. A. M. Duncan, Eochaid, although the son of Rhun of Strathclyde, 'surely represents Pictish rights of succession'. (*The Making of the Kingdom*, 91)

213 *Cf.* Smyth, *op. cit.*, 215–8

214 Smyth, *op. cit.*, 205–6